THE AENEID

THE
AENEID
VIRGIL

TRANSLATED BY

ROBERT FITZGERALD

VINTAGE BOOKS
A DIVISION OF RANDOM HOUSE
NEW YORK

Second Vintage Books Edition, August 1985
Copyright © 1980, 1982, 1983 by Robert Fitzgerald
All rights reserved under International and Pan-American
Copyright Conventions. Published in the United States by
Random House, Inc., New York, and simultaneously in Canada by
Random House of Canada Limited, Toronto. Originally published
in hardcover by Random House, Inc., in 1983 and in paperback by
Vintage Books, a division of Random House, Inc., in 1984.

Portions of this work previously appeared in the following
publications: *Conjunctions, Grand Street, The Kenyon Review,
New Boston Review, The New York Review of Books, Poetry,
Vanity Fair,* and *Yale Review*.

Library of Congress Cataloging in Publication Data
Virgil.
The Aeneid.
Translation of: Aeneis.
Reprint. Originally published: New York:
Random House, © 1983.
Aeneas—Poetry.
Fitzgerald, Robert, 1910-1985.
II. Title.
[PA6807.A5F53 1985]   873'.01   85-7154
ISBN 0-394-74111-0

Manufactured in the United States of America.

456789

For Penny

Aeternum dictis da diva leporem.
DE RERUM NATURA

CONTENTS

BOOK

I

A FATEFUL HAVEN

I sing of warfare and a man at war.
From the sea-coast of Troy in early days
He came to Italy by destiny,
To our Lavinian western shore,
5   A fugitive, this captain, buffeted
Cruelly on land as on the sea
By blows from powers of the air—behind them
Baleful Juno in her sleepless rage.
And cruel losses were his lot in war,
10   Till he could found a city and bring home
His gods to Latium, land of the Latin race,
The Alban lords, and the high walls of Rome.
Tell me the causes now, O Muse, how galled
In her divine pride, and how sore at heart
15   From her old wound, the queen of gods compelled him—
A man apart, devoted to his mission—
To undergo so many perilous days
And enter on so many trials. Can anger
Black as this prey on the minds of heaven?
20   Tyrian settlers in that ancient time
Held Carthage, on the far shore of the sea,
Set against Italy and Tiber's mouth,
A rich new town, warlike and trained for war.
And Juno, we are told, cared more for Carthage
25   Than for any walled city of the earth,
More than for Samos, even. There her armor

And chariot were kept, and, fate permitting,
Carthage would be the ruler of the world.
So she intended, and so nursed that power.
30 But she had heard long since
That generations born of Trojan blood
Would one day overthrow her Tyrian walls,
And from that blood a race would come in time
With ample kingdoms, arrogant in war,
35 For Libya's ruin: so the Parcae spun.
In fear of this, and holding in memory
The old war she had carried on at Troy
For Argos' sake (the origins of that anger,
That suffering, still rankled: deep within her,
40 Hidden away, the judgment Paris gave,
Snubbing her loveliness; the race she hated;
The honors given ravished Ganymede),
Saturnian Juno, burning for it all,
Buffeted on the waste of sea those Trojans
45 Left by the Greeks and pitiless Achilles,
Keeping them far from Latium. For years
They wandered as their destiny drove them on
From one sea to the next: so hard and huge
A task it was to found the Roman people.

50 They were all under sail in open water
With Sicily just out of sight astern,
Lighthearted as they plowed the whitecapped sea
With stems of cutting bronze. But never free
Of her eternal inward wound, the goddess
55 Said to herself:

    "Give up what I began?
Am I defeated? Am I impotent
To keep the king of Teucrians from Italy?
The Fates forbid me, am I to suppose?
60 Could Pallas then consume the Argive fleet

With fire, and drown the crews,
Because of one man's one mad act—the crime
Of Ajax, son of Oïleus? She—yes, she!—
Hurled out of cloudland lancing fire of Jove,
65 Scattered the ships, roughed up the sea with gales,
Then caught the man, bolt-struck, exhaling flames,
In a whirlwind and impaled him on a rock.
But I who walk as queen of all the gods,
Sister and wife of Jove, I must contend
70 For years against one people! Who adores
The power of Juno after this, or lays
An offering with prayer upon her altar?"

Smouldering, putting these questions to herself,
The goddess made her way to stormcloud country,
75 Aeolia, the weather-breeding isle.
Here in a vast cavern King Aeolus
Rules the contending winds and moaning gales
As warden of their prison. Round the walls
They chafe and bluster underground. The din
80 Makes a great mountain murmur overhead.
High on a citadel enthroned,
Scepter in hand, he mollifies their fury,
Else they might flay the sea and sweep away
Land masses and deep sky through empty air.
85 In fear of this, Jupiter hid them away
In caverns of black night. He set above them
Granite of high mountains—and a king
Empowered at command to rein them in
Or let them go. To this king Juno now
90 Made her petition:
                    "Aeolus, the father
Of gods and men decreed and fixed your power
To calm the waves or make them rise in wind.
The race I hate is crossing the Tuscan sea,
95 Transporting Ilium with her household gods—
Beaten as they are—to Italy.
                        Put new fury
Into your winds, and make the long ships founder!

Lines 40–69

Drive them off course! Throw bodies in the sea!
100 I have fourteen exquisite nymphs, of whom
The loveliest by far, Deïopëa,
Shall be your own. I'll join you two in marriage,
So she will spend all future years with you,
As you so well deserve,
105 And make you father of her lovely children."

Said Aeolus:
                    "To settle on what you wish
Is all you need to do, your majesty.
I must perform it. You have given me
110 What realm I have. By your good offices
I rule with Jove's consent, and I recline
Among the gods at feasts, for you appoint me
Lord of wind and cloud."
                                        Spearhaft reversed,
115 He gave the hollow mountainside a stroke,
And, where a portal opened, winds in ranks,
As though drawn up for battle, hurtled through,
To blow across the earth in hurricane.
Over the sea, tossed up from the sea-floor,
120 Eastwind and Southwind, then the wild Southwest
With squall on squall came scudding down,
Rolling high combers shoreward.
                                            Now one heard
The cries of men and screech of ropes in rigging
125 Suddenly, as the stormcloud whipped away
Clear sky and daylight from the Teucrians' eyes,
And gloom of night leaned on the open sea.
It thundered from all quarters, as it lightened
Flash on flash through heaven. Every sign
130 Portended a quick death for mariners.
Aeneas on the instant felt his knees
Go numb and slack, and stretched both hands to heaven,
Groaning out:
                    "Triply lucky, all you men
135 To whom death came before your fathers' eyes
Below the wall at Troy! Bravest Danaan,

Diomedes, why could I not go down
When you had wounded me, and lose my life
On Ilium's battlefield? Our Hector lies there,
140   Torn by Achilles' weapon; there Sarpedon,
Our giant fighter, lies; and there the river
Simoïs washes down so many shields
And helmets, with strong bodies taken under!"

As he flung out these words, a howling gust
145   From due north took the sail aback and lifted
Wavetops to heaven; oars were snapped in two;
The prow sheered round and left them broadside on
To breaking seas; over her flank and deck
A mountain of grey water crashed in tons.
150   Men hung on crests; to some a yawning trough
Uncovered bottom, boiling waves and sand.
The Southwind caught three ships and whirled them down
On reefs, hidden midsea, called by Italians
"The Altars"—razorbacks just under water.
155   The Eastwind drove three others from deep water
Into great shoals and banks, embedding them
And ringing them with sand, a desperate sight.
Before Aeneas' eyes a toppling billow
Struck the Lycians' ship, Orontës' ship,
160   Across the stern, pitching the steersman down
And overboard. Three times the eddying sea
Carried the ship around in the same place
Until the rapid whirlpool gulped it down.
A few men swimming surfaced in the welter.
165   So did shields, planks, precious things of Troy.
Ilioneus' good ship, brave Achatës' ship,
The ship that carried Abas, and the one
Aletës sailed in, hale in his great age,
Were all undone by the wild gale: their seams
170   Parted and let the enemy pour in.
During all this, Neptune became aware
Of hurly-burly and tempest overhead,
Bringing commotion to the still sea-depth
And rousing him. He lifted his calm brow

175 Above the surface, viewing the great sea,
And saw Aeneas' squadron far and wide
Dispersed over the water, saw the Trojans
Overwhelmed, the ruining clouds of heaven,
And saw his angry sister's hand in all.

180 He called to him Eastwind and South and said:

"Are you so sure your line is privileged?
How could you dare to throw heaven and earth
Into confusion, by no will of mine,
And make such trouble? You will get from me—

185 But first to calm the rough sea; after this,
You'll pay a stricter penalty for your sins.
Off with you! Give this message to your king:
Power over the sea and the cruel trident
Were never his by destiny, but mine.

190 He owns the monstrous rocks, your home, Eastwind.
Let Aeolus ruffle in that hall alone
And lord it over winds shut in their prison."

Before the words were out, he quieted
The surging water, drove the clouds away,

195 And brought the sunlight back. Cymothoë
And Triton, side by side, worked to dislodge
The grounded ships; then Neptune with his trident
Heaved them away, opened the miles of shoals,
Tempered the sea, and in his car departed

200 Gliding over the wave-tops on light wheels.

When rioting breaks out in a great city,
And the rampaging rabble goes so far
That stones fly, and incendiary brands—
For anger can supply that kind of weapon—

205 If it so happens they look round and see
Some dedicated public man, a veteran
Whose record gives him weight, they quiet down,
Willing to stop and listen.
Then he prevails in speech over their fury

210 By his authority, and placates them.

Lines 127–153

Just so, the whole uproar of the great sea
Fell silent, as the Father of it all,
Scanning horizons under the open sky,
Swung his team around and gave free rein
215   In flight to his eager chariot.

                        Tired out,
Aeneas' people made for the nearest land,
Turning their prows toward Libya. There's a spot
Where at the mouth of a long bay an island
220   Makes a harbor, forming a breakwater
Where every swell divides as it comes in
And runs far into curving recesses.
There are high cliffs on this side and on that,
And twin peaks towering heavenward impend
225   On reaches of still water. Over these,
Against a forest backdrop shimmering,
A dark and shaggy grove casts a deep shade,
While in the cliffside opposite, below
The overhanging peaks, there is a cave
230   With fresh water and seats in the living rock,
The home of nymphs. Here never an anchor chain,
Never an anchor's biting fluke need hold
A tired ship.

                  Aeneas put in here,
235   With only seven ships from his full number,
And longing for the firm earth underfoot
The Trojans disembarked, to take possession
Of the desired sand-beach. Down they lay,
To rest their brinesoaked bodies on the shore.
240   Achatës promptly struck a spark from flint
And caught it in dry leaves; he added tinder
Round about and waved it for a flame-burst.
Then they brought out the grain of Ceres, tainted
By sea water, and Ceres' implements,
245   And, weary of their troubles, made all ready
To dry and grind with millstones what they had.

Meanwhile, Aeneas climbed one of the peaks
For a long seaward view, hoping to sight

Gale-worn Antheus and the Phrygian biremes,
250 Capys, or high poops bearing Caïcus' arms.
He found no ship in sight, but on the shore
Three wandering stags. Behind them whole herds followed,
Grazing in a long line down the valleys.
Planting his feet, he took in hand the bow
255 And arrows carried by his aide, Achatës,
Then, aiming for the leaders with heads high
And branching antlers, brought them first to earth.
Next he routed the whole herd,
Driving them with his shafts through leafy places,
260 Shooting and shooting till he won the hunt
By laying seven carcasses on the ground,
A number equal to his ships. Then back
To port he went, and parcelled out the game
To his ships' companies. There he divided
265 The wine courtly Acestës had poured out
And given them on the Sicilian shore—
Full jugs of it—when they were about to sail.
By this and by a simple speech Aeneas
Comforted his people:
270   "Friends and companions,
Have we not known hard hours before this?
My men, who have endured still greater dangers,
God will grant us an end to these as well.
You sailed by Scylla's rage, her booming crags,
275 You saw the Cyclops' boulders. Now call back
Your courage, and have done with fear and sorrow.
Some day, perhaps, remembering even this
Will be a pleasure. Through diversities
Of luck, and through so many challenges,
280 We hold our course for Latium, where the Fates
Hold out a settlement and rest for us.
Troy's kingdom there shall rise again. Be patient:
Save yourselves for more auspicious days."

So ran the speech. Burdened and sick at heart,
285 He feigned hope in his look, and inwardly
Contained his anguish. Now the Trojan crews

Made ready for their windfall and their feast.
They skinned the deer, bared ribs and viscera,
Then one lot sliced the flesh and skewered it
290   On spits, all quivering, while others filled
Bronze cooking pots and tended the beach fires.
All got their strength back from the meal, reclining
On the wild grass, gorging on venison
And mellowed wine. When hunger had been banished,
295   And tables put away, they talked at length
In hope and fear about their missing friends:
Could one believe they might be still alive,
Or had they suffered their last hour,
Never again to hear a voice that called them?
300   Aeneas, more than any, secretly
Mourned for them all—for that fierce man, Orontës,
Then for Amycus, then for the bitter fate
Of Lycus, for brave Gyas, brave Cloanthus.

I t was the day's end when from highest air
305   Jupiter looked down on the broad sea
Flecked with wings of sails, and the land masses,
Coasts, and nations of the earth. He stood
On heaven's height and turned his gaze toward Libya,
And, as he took the troubles there to heart,
310   Venus appealed to him, all pale and wan,
With tears in her shining eyes:

>   "My lord who rule
> The lives of men and gods now and forever,
> And bring them all to heel with your bright bolt,
315   What in the world could my Aeneas do,
What could the Trojans do, so to offend you
That after suffering all those deaths they find
The whole world closed to them, because of Italy?
Surely from these the Romans are to come
320   In the course of years, renewing Teucer's line,
To rule the sea and all the lands about it,

According to your promise. What new thought
Has turned you from them, Father? I consoled myself
For Troy's fall, that grim ruin, weighing out
325   One fate against another in the scales,
But now, when they have borne so many blows,
The same misfortune follows them. Great king,
What finish to their troubles will you give?
After Antenor slipped through the Achaeans
330   He could explore Illyrian coves and reach
In safety the Liburnians' inland kingdoms
And source of the Timavus. Through nine openings
With a great rumble in the mountain wall
It bursts from the ground there and floods the fields
335   In a rushing sea. And yet he chose that place
For Padua and new homes for Teucrians,
Gave them a name, set up the arms of Troy,
And now rests in his peace. As for ourselves,
Your own children, whom you make heirs of heaven,
340   Our ships being lost (this is unspeakable!),
We are forsaken through one enemy's rage
And kept remote from Italy. Is this
The palm for loyalty? This our power restored?"

He smiled at her, the father of gods and men,
345   With that serenity that calms the weather,
And lightly kissed his daughter. Then he said:

"No need to be afraid, Cytherëa.
Your children's destiny has not been changed.
As promised, you shall see Lavinium's walls
350   And take up, then, amid the stars of heaven
Great-souled Aeneas. No new thought has turned me.
No, he, your son—now let me speak of him,
In view of your consuming care, at length,
Unfolding secret fated things to come—
355   In Italy he will fight a massive war,
Beat down fierce armies, then for the people there
Establish city walls and a way of life.

Lines 237–264

When the Rutulians are subdued he'll pass
Three summers of command in Latium,
360 Three years of winter quarters. But the boy,
Ascanius, to whom the name of Iulus
Now is added—Ilus while Ilium stood—
Will hold the power for all of thirty years,
Great rings of wheeling months. He will transfer
365 His capital from Lavinium and make
A fortress, Alba Longa. Three full centuries
That kingdom will be ruled by Hector's race,
Until the queen and priestess, Ilia,
Pregnant by Mars, will bear twin sons to him.
370 Afterward, happy in the tawny pelt
His nurse, the she-wolf, wears, young Romulus
Will take the leadership, build walls of Mars,
And call by his own name his people Romans.
For these I set no limits, world or time,
375 But make the gift of empire without end.
Juno, indeed, whose bitterness now fills
With fear and torment sea and earth and sky,
Will mend her ways, and favor them as I do,
Lords of the world, the toga-bearing Romans.
380 Such is our pleasure. As the years fall away,
An age comes when Assaracus' royal house
Will bring to servitude Thessalian Phthia,
Renowned Mycenae, too; and subjugate
Defeated Argos. From that comely line
385 The Trojan Caesar comes, to circumscribe
Empire with Ocean, fame with heaven's stars.
Julius his name, from Iulus handed down:
All tranquil shall you take him heavenward
In time, laden with plunder of the East,
390 And he with you shall be invoked in prayer.
Wars at an end, harsh centuries then will soften,
Ancient Fides and Vesta, Quirinus
With Brother Remus, will be lawgivers,
And grim with iron frames, the Gates of War
395 Will then be shut: inside, unholy Furor,

Lines 265–294

Squatting on cruel weapons, hands enchained
Behind him by a hundred links of bronze,
Will grind his teeth and howl with bloodied mouth."

That said, he sent the son of Maia down
400   From his high place to make the land of Carthage,
The new-built town, receptive to the Trojans,
Not to allow Queen Dido, all unknowing
As to the fated future, to exclude them.
Through the vast air with stroking wings he flew
405   And came down quickly on the Libyan coast,
Performing Jove's command, so that at once
Phoenicians put aside belligerence
As the god willed. Especially the queen
Took on a peaceful mood, an open mind
410   Toward Teucrians.

But the dedicated man,
Aeneas, thoughtful through the restless night,
Made up his mind, as kindly daylight came,
To go out and explore the strange new places,
415   To learn what coast the wind had brought him to
And who were living there, men or wild creatures—
For wilderness was all he saw—and bring
Report back to his company. The ships
He hid beneath a hollowed rocky cliff
420   And groves that made a vault, trees all around
And deep shade quivering. He took his way
With only one man at his side, Achatës,
Hefting two hunting spears with broad steel points.
Then suddenly, in front of him,
425   His mother crossed his path in mid-forest,
Wearing a girl's shape and a girl's gear—
A Spartan girl, or like that one of Thrace,
Harpalycë, who tires horses out,
Outrunning the swift Hebrus. She had hung

430 About her shoulders the light, handy bow
A huntress carries, and had given her hair
To the disheveling wind; her knees were bare,
Her flowing gown knotted and kirtled up.

She spoke first:

435   "Ho, young fellows, have you seen—
Can you say where—one of my sisters here,
In a spotted lynx-hide, belted with a quiver,
Scouting the wood, or shouting on the track
Behind a foam-flecked boar?"

440   To Venus then
The son of Venus answered:

                                     "No, I've heard
Or seen none of your sisters—only, how
Shall I address you, girl? Your look's not mortal,
445 Neither has your accent a mortal ring.
O Goddess, beyond doubt! Apollo's sister?
One of the family of nymphs? Be kind,
Whoever you may be, relieve our trouble,
Tell us under what heaven we've come at last,
450 On what shore of the world are we cast up,
Wanderers that we are, strange to this country,
Driven here by wind and heavy sea.
By my right hand many an offering
Will be cut down for you before your altars."

455 Venus replied:

                       "Be sure I am not fit
For any such devotion. Tyrian girls
Are given to wearing quivers and hunting boots
Of crimson, laced on the leg up to the knee.
460 This is the Punic kingdom that you see,
The folk are Tyrian, the town Agenor's.
But neighboring lands belong to Libya,
A nation hard to fight against in war.
The ruler here is Dido, of Tyre city,
465 In flight here from her brother—a long tale
Of wrong endured, mysterious and long.

Lines 318–342

But let me tell the main events in order.
Her husband was Sychaeus, of all Phoenicians
Richest in land, and greatly loved by her,
470 Ill-fated woman. Her father had given her,
A virgin still, in marriage, her first rite.
Her brother, though, held power in Tyre—Pygmalion,
A monster of wickedness beyond all others.
Between the two men furious hate arose,
475 And sacrilegiously before the altars,
Driven by a blind lust for gold, Pygmalion
Took Sychaeus by surprise and killed him
With a dagger blow in secret, undeterred
By any thought of Dido's love. He hid
480 What he had done for a long time, cozening her,
Deluding the sick woman with false hope.
But the true form of her unburied husband
Came in a dream: lifting his pallid face
Before her strangely, he made visible
485 The cruel altars and his body pierced,
Uncovering all the dark crime of the house.

He urged her then to make haste and take flight,
Leaving her fatherland, and to assist the journey
Revealed a buried treasure of old time,
490 Unknown to any, a weight of gold and silver.
Impelled by this, Dido laid her plans
To get away and to equip her company.
All who hated the tyrant, all in fear
As bitter as her own, now came together,
495 And ships in port, already fitted out,
They commandeered, to fill with gold: the riches
Pygmalion had itched for went to sea,
And captaining the venture was a woman.
They sailed to this place where today you'll see
500 Stone walls going higher and the citadel
Of Carthage, the new town. They bought the land,
Called Drumskin from the bargain made, a tract
They could enclose with one bull's hide.

But now,
505 What of yourselves? From what coast do you come?
Where are you bound?"

Then to the questioner
He answered sighing, bringing out the words
From deep within him:

510 "Goddess, if I should tell
Our story from the start, if you had leisure
To hear our annals of adversity,
Before I finished, the fair evening star
Would come to close Olympus and the day.

515 From old Troy—if the name of Troy has fallen
Perhaps upon your ears—we sailed the seas,
And yesterday were driven by a storm,
Of its own whim, upon this Libyan coast.
I am Aeneas, duty-bound, and known

520 Above high air of heaven by my fame,
Carrying with me in my ships our gods
Of hearth and home, saved from the enemy.
I look for Italy to be my fatherland,
And my descent is from all-highest Jove.

525 With twenty ships I mounted the Phrygian sea,
As my immortal mother showed the way.
I followed the given fates. Now barely seven
Ships are left, battered by wind and sea,
And I myself, unknown and unprovisioned,

530 Cross the Libyan wilderness, an exile
Driven from Europe and from Asia—"

But Venus chose to hear no more complaints
And broke in, midway through his bitterness:

"Whoever you are, I doubt Heaven is unfriendly
To you, as you still breathe life-giving air
535 On your approach to the Tyrian town. Go on:
Betake yourself this way to the queen's gate.
Your friends are back. This is my news for you:
Your ships were saved and brought to shore again

540   By winds shifting north, or else my parents
     Taught me augury to no purpose. Look:
     See the twelve swans in line rejoicing there!
     Jove's eagle, like a bolt out of the blue,
     Had flurried them in open heaven, but now
545   They seem to be alighting one by one
     Or looking down on those already grounded.
     As they disport themselves, with flapping wings,
     After their chanting flight about the sky,
     Just so your ships and your ships' companies
550   Are either in port or entering under sail.
     Go on then, where the path leads, go ahead!"

     On this she turned away. Rose-pink and fair
     Her nape shone, her ambrosial hair exhaled
     Divine perfume, her gown rippled full length,
555   And by her stride she showed herself a goddess.
     Knowing her for his mother, he called out
     To the figure fleeting away:
                 "You! cruel, too!
     Why tease your son so often with disguises?
560   Why may we not join hands and speak and hear
     The simple truth?"
                So he called after her,
     And went on toward the town. But Venus muffled
     The two wayfarers in grey mist, a cloak
565   Of dense cloud poured around them, so that no one
     Had the power to see or to accost them,
     Make them halt, or ask them what they came for.
     Away to Paphos through high air she went
     In joy to see her home again, her shrine
570   And hundred altars where Sabaean incense
     Fumed and garlands freshened the air.
                    Meanwhile
     The two men pressed on where the pathway led,
     Soon climbing a long ridge that gave a view
575   Down over the city and facing towers.
     Aeneas found, where lately huts had been,
     Marvelous buildings, gateways, cobbled ways,

And din of wagons. There the Tyrians
Were hard at work: laying courses for walls,
580 Rolling up stones to build the citadel,
While others picked out building sites and plowed
A boundary furrow. Laws were being enacted,
Magistrates and a sacred senate chosen.
Here men were dredging harbors, there they laid
585 The deep foundation of a theatre,
And quarried massive pillars to enhance
The future stage—as bees in early summer
In sunlight in the flowering fields
Hum at their work, and bring along the young
590 Full-grown to beehood; as they cram their combs
With honey, brimming all the cells with nectar,
Or take newcomers' plunder, or like troops
Alerted, drive away the lazy drones,
And labor thrives and sweet thyme scents the honey.
595 Aeneas said: "How fortunate these are
Whose city walls are rising here and now!"

He looked up at the roofs, for he had entered,
Swathed in cloud—strange to relate—among them,
Mingling with men, yet visible to none.
600 In mid-town stood a grove that cast sweet shade
Where the Phoenicians, shaken by wind and sea,
Had first dug up that symbol Juno showed them,
A proud warhorse's head: this meant for Carthage
Prowess in war and ease of life through ages.
605 Here being built by the Sidonian queen
Was a great temple planned in Juno's honor,
Rich in offerings and the godhead there.
Steps led up to a sill of bronze, with brazen
Lintel, and bronze doors on groaning pins.
610 Here in this grove new things that met his eyes
Calmed Aeneas' fear for the first time.
Here for the first time he took heart to hope
For safety, and to trust his destiny more
Even in affliction. It was while he walked
615 From one to another wall of the great temple

Lines 422–453

And waited for the queen, staring amazed
At Carthaginian promise, at the handiwork
Of artificers and the toil they spent upon it:
He found before his eyes the Trojan battles
620   In the old war, now known throughout the world—
The great Atridae, Priam, and Achilles,
Fierce in his rage at both sides. Here Aeneas
Halted, and tears came.
                              "What spot on earth,"
625   He said, "what region of the earth, Achatës,
Is not full of the story of our sorrow?
Look, here is Priam. Even so far away
Great valor has due honor; they weep here
For how the world goes, and our life that passes
630   Touches their hearts. Throw off your fear. This fame
Insures some kind of refuge."
                              He broke off
To feast his eyes and mind on a mere image,
Sighing often, cheeks grown wet with tears,
635   To see again how, fighting around Troy,
The Greeks broke here, and ran before the Trojans,
And there the Phrygians ran, as plumed Achilles
Harried them in his warcar. Nearby, then,
He recognized the snowy canvas tents
640   Of Rhesus, and more tears came: these, betrayed
In first sleep, Diomedes devastated,
Swording many, till he reeked with blood,
Then turned the mettlesome horses toward the beachhead
Before they tasted Trojan grass or drank
645   At Xanthus ford.
                              And on another panel
Troilus, without his armor, luckless boy,
No match for his antagonist, Achilles,
Appeared pulled onward by his team: he clung
650   To his warcar, though fallen backward, hanging
On to the reins still, head dragged on the ground,
His javelin scribbling S's in the dust.
Meanwhile to hostile Pallas' shrine
The Trojan women walked with hair unbound,

655　Bearing the robe of offering, in sorrow,
　　　Entreating her, beating their breasts. But she,
　　　Her face averted, would not raise her eyes.
　　　And there was Hector, dragged around Troy walls
　　　Three times, and there for gold Achilles sold him,
660　Bloodless and lifeless. Now indeed Aeneas
　　　Heaved a mighty sigh from deep within him,
　　　Seeing the spoils, the chariot, and the corpse
　　　Of his great friend, and Priam, all unarmed,
　　　Stretching his hands out.
665　　　　　　　　　　　　　　He himself he saw
　　　In combat with the first of the Achaeans,
　　　And saw the ranks of Dawn, black Memnon's arms;
　　　Then, leading the battalion of Amazons
　　　With half-moon shields, he saw Penthesilëa
670　Fiery amid her host, buckling a golden
　　　Girdle beneath her bare and arrogant breast,
　　　A girl who dared fight men, a warrior queen.
　　　Now, while these wonders were being surveyed
　　　By Aeneas of Dardania, while he stood
675　Enthralled, devouring all in one long gaze,
　　　The queen paced toward the temple in her beauty,
　　　Dido, with a throng of men behind.

　　　As on Eurotas bank or Cynthus ridge
　　　Diana trains her dancers, and behind her
680　On every hand the mountain nymphs appear,
　　　A myriad converging; with her quiver
　　　Slung on her shoulders, in her stride she seems
　　　The tallest, taller by a head than any,
　　　And joy pervades Latona's quiet heart:
685　So Dido seemed, in such delight she moved
　　　Amid her people, cheering on the toil
　　　Of a kingdom in the making. At the door
　　　Of the goddess' shrine, under the temple dome,
　　　All hedged about with guards on her high throne,
690　She took her seat. Then she began to give them
　　　Judgments and rulings, to apportion work
　　　With fairness, or assign some tasks by lot,

Lines 480–508

When suddenly Aeneas saw approaching,
Accompanied by a crowd, Antheus and Sergestus
695   And brave Cloanthus, with a few companions,
Whom the black hurricane had driven far
Over the sea and brought to other coasts.
He was astounded, and Achatës too
Felt thrilled by joy and fear: both of them longed
700   To take their friends' hands, but uncertainty
Hampered them. So, in their cloudy mantle,
They hid their eagerness, waiting to learn
What luck these men had had, where on the coast
They left their ships, and why they came. It seemed
705   Spokesmen for all the ships were now arriving,
Entering the hall, calling for leave to speak.
When all were in, and full permission given
To make their plea before the queen, their eldest,
Ilioneus, with composure said:
710   "Your majesty,
Granted by great Jupiter freedom to found
Your new town here and govern fighting tribes
With justice—we poor Trojans, worn by winds
On every sea, entreat you: keep away
715   Calamity of fire from our ships!
Let a godfearing people live, and look
More closely at our troubles. Not to ravage
Libyan hearths or turn with plunder seaward
Have we come; that force and that audacity
720   Are not for beaten men.
                                       There is a country
Called by the Greeks Hesperia, very old,
Potent in warfare and in wealth of earth;
Oenotrians farmed it; younger settlers now,
725   The tale goes, call it by their chief's name, Italy.
We laid our course for this.
But stormy Orion and a high sea rising
Deflected us on shoals and drove us far,
With winds against us, into whelming waters,
730   Unchanneled reefs. We kept afloat, we few,
To reach your coast. What race of men is this?

What primitive state could sanction this behavior?
Even on beaches we are denied a landing,
Harried by outcry and attack, forbidden
735 To set foot on the outskirts of your country.
If you care nothing for humanity
And merely mortal arms, respect the gods
Who are mindful of good actions and of evil!

We had a king, Aeneas—none more just,
740 More zealous, greater in warfare and in arms.
If fate preserves him, if he does not yet
Lie spent amid the insensible shades but still
Takes nourishment of air, we need fear nothing;
Neither need you repent of being first
745 In courtesy, to outdo us. Sicily too
Has towns and plowlands and a famous king
Of Trojan blood, Acestës. May we be
Permitted here to beach our damaged ships,
Hew timbers in your forest, cut new oars,
750 And either sail again for Latium, happily,
If we recover shipmates and our king,
Or else, if that security is lost,
If Libyan waters hold you, Lord Aeneas,
Best of Trojans, hope of Iulus gone,
755 We may at least cross over to Sicily
From which we came, to homesteads ready there,
And take Acestës for our king."
                       Ilioneus
Finished, and all the sons of Dardanus
760 Murmured assent. Dido with eyes downcast
Replied in a brief speech:
                      "Cast off your fear,
You Teucrians, put anxiety aside.
Severe conditions and the kingdom's youth
765 Constrain me to these measures, to protect
Our long frontiers with guards.
                          Who has not heard
Of the people of Aeneas, of Troy city,
Her valors and her heroes, and the fires

770 Of the great war? We are not so oblivious,
We Phoenicians. The sun yokes his team
Within our range at Carthage. Whether you choose
Hesperia Magna and the land of Saturn
Or Eryx in the west and King Acestës,
775 I shall dispatch you safely with an escort,
Provisioned from my stores. Or would you care
To join us in this realm on equal terms?
The city I build is yours; haul up your ships;
Trojan and Tyrian will be all one to me.
780 If only he were here, your king himself,
Caught by the same easterly, Aeneas!
Indeed, let me send out trustworthy men
Along the coast, with orders to comb it all
From one end of Libya to the other,
785 In case the sea cast the man up and now
He wanders lost, in town or wilderness."

Elated at Dido's words, both staunch Achatës
And father Aeneas had by this time longed
To break out of the cloud. Achatës spoke
790 With urgency:
        "My lord, born to the goddess,
What do you feel, what is your judgment now?
You see all safe, our ships and friends recovered.
One is lost; we saw that one go down
795 Ourselves, amid the waves. Everything else
Bears out your mother's own account of it."

He barely finished when the cloud around them
Parted suddenly and thinned away
Into transparent air. Princely Aeneas
800 Stood and shone in the bright light, head and shoulders
Noble as a god's. For she who bore him
Breathed upon him beauty of hair and bloom
Of youth and kindled brilliance in his eyes,
As an artist's hand gives style to ivory,
805 Or sets pure silver, or white stone of Paros,
In framing yellow gold. Then to the queen

Lines 566–594

He spoke as suddenly as, to them all,
He had just appeared:

     "Before your eyes I stand,
810 Aeneas the Trojan, that same one you look for,
Saved from the sea off Libya.

       You alone,
Moved by the untold ordeals of old Troy,
Seeing us few whom the Greeks left alive,
815 Worn out by faring ill on land and sea,
Needy of everything—you'd give these few
A home and city, allied with yourselves.
Fit thanks for this are not within our power,
Not to be had from Trojans anywhere
820 Dispersed in the great world.

       May the gods—
And surely there are powers that care for goodness,
Surely somewhere justice counts—may they
And your own consciousness of acting well
825 Reward you as they should. What age so happy
Brought you to birth? How splendid were your parents
To have conceived a being like yourself!
So long as brooks flow seaward, and the shadows
Play over mountain slopes, and highest heaven
830 Feeds the stars, your name and your distinction
Go with me, whatever lands may call me."

With this he gave his right hand to his friend
Ilioneus, greeting Serestus with his left,
Then took the hands of those brave men, Cloanthus,
835 Gyas, and the rest.

     Sidonian Dido
Stood in astonishment, first at the sight
Of such a captain, then at his misfortune,
Presently saying:

840   "Born of an immortal
Mother though you are, what adverse destiny
Dogs you through these many kinds of danger?
What rough power brings you from sea to land
In savage places? Are you truly he,

Lines 594–617

845 Aeneas, whom kind Venus bore
To the Dardanian, the young Anchisës,
Near to the stream of Phrygian Simoïs?
I remember the Greek, Teucer, came to Sidon,
Exiled, and in search of a new kingdom.

850 Belus, my father, helped him. In those days
Belus campaigned with fire and sword on Cyprus
And won that island's wealth. Since then, the fall
Of Troy, your name, and the Pelasgian kings
Have been familiar to me. Teucer, your enemy,

855 Spoke often with admiration of the Teucrians
And traced his own descent from Teucrian stock.
Come, then, soldiers, be our guests. My life
Was one of hardship and forced wandering
Like your own, till in this land at length

860 Fortune would have me rest. Through pain I've learned
To comfort suffering men."
                                    She led Aeneas
Into the royal house, but not before
Declaring a festal day in the gods' temples.

865 As for the ships' companies, she sent
Twenty bulls to the shore, a hundred swine,
Huge ones, with bristling backs, and fatted lambs,
A hundred of them, and their mother ewes—
All gifts for happy feasting on that day.

870 Now the queen's household made her great hall glow
As they prepared a banquet in the kitchens.
Embroidered table cloths, proud crimson-dyed,
Were spread, and set with massive silver plate,
Or gold, engraved with brave deeds of her fathers,

875 A sequence carried down through many captains
In a long line from the founding of the race.
Meanwhile paternal love would not allow
Aeneas' mind to rest. He sent Achatës
On a quick mission to the ships, to tell

880 Ascanius and bring him to the city—
Fond father, as always thoughtful of his son—
And told Achatës to fetch gifts as well,

Relics of Ilium: a robe stiff with figures
Worked in gold, and a veil woven round
885 With yellow acanthus flowers—both adornments
Worn by Argive Helen when she sailed
For Pergamum and her forbidden marriage,
Marvelous keepsakes of her mother, Leda.
Along with these, a scepter Ilionë,
890 Eldest of Priam's daughters, once had used,
A collar hung with pearls, and a coronet
Doubled in gems and gold,
                                        Given these orders,
Achatës lost no time seeking the ships.

895   Our Lady of Cythera, however, pondered
New interventions, a new strategy:
That her young godling son, Desire, should take
The face and figure of Ascanius,
Then come and use his gifts to make the queen
900 Infatuated, inflaming her with lust
To the marrow of her bones. Venus no doubt
Lacked faith in the ambiguous royal house
And Tyrians' double dealing; then, the spite
Of Juno vexed her. Her anxieties
905 Recurred as night came on. So she addressed him,
Amor, god of caressing wings:
                                        "My son,
My strength, my greatest power, my one and only,
Making light of our High Father's bolt,
910 His giant-killer! I must turn to you
And beg the force of your divinity.
You know how Brother Aeneas has been tossed
From one coast to another on the high seas
By bitter Juno's hatred; you know this
915 And in my grieving for him grieve as well.
Now the Phoenician woman, Dido, has him,
Making him linger with her blandishments,

And what may come of this Junonian welcome
Worries me seriously. Juno will act
920 At such a crisis of affairs. Accordingly,
What I propose is to ensnare the queen
By guile beforehand, pin her down in passion,
So she cannot be changed by any power
But will be kept on my side by profound
925 Love of Aeneas. Take heed of our thought
How you may do this. The boy prince, my greatest
Care in the world, must go now to the city,
Summoned by his father, taking gifts
Saved from the great sea and the fires of Troy.
930 I'll drug him in his sleep, then hide him well
High up in Cythera, or on Cyprus, over
Idalium in my shrine. There is no way
For him to learn this trick or interfere.
You counterfeit his figure for one night,
935 No more, and make the boy's known face your mask,
So that when Dido takes you on her lap
Amid the banquetting and wine, in joy,
When she embraces you and kisses you,
You'll breathe invisible fire into her
940 And dupe her with your sorcery."
                                    Amor
Agreed with his fond mother's plan of action,
Put off his wings and gaily walked as Iulus.
Venus in turn sent through Ascanius' body
945 Rills of slumber, caught him to her breast,
And bore him to Idalia's aerial groves
Where beds of marjoram
Embraced him in soft bloom and breathing shade.
Soon then the godling, doing as she wished,
950 Happily following where Achatës led,
Carried the royal gifts to the Tyrians.
He found the queen amid magnificence
Of tapestries, where she had placed herself
In the very center, on a golden couch.
955 Then Father Aeneas and the Trojan company
Came in to take their ease on crimson cloth.

Lines 671–700

Houseboys filled their finger bowls and brought them
Bread in baskets, napkins nubbled smooth.
In the great kitchen there were fifty maids
960 To set the dishes out in a long line
And tend the fires that shone for the hearth gods.
A hundred others, and as many boys
Of the same age, loaded the boards with meat
And placed the wine cups. Tyrians as well
965 Came crowding through the radiant doors, all bidden
To take their ease on figured cushioning.
There they admired Aeneas' gifts, admired
Iulus with his godling's face aglow
And simulated speech; then the great robe,
970 The veil that yellow acanthus flowers edged.
And more than anyone, the Phoenician queen,
Luckless, already given over to ruin,
Marveled and could not have enough: she burned
With pleasure in the boy and in the gifts.
975 After hugging Aeneas round the neck
And clinging to him, answering the love
Of the deluded father, he sought the queen;
And she with all her eyes and heart embraced him,
Fondling him at times upon her breast,
980 Oblivious of how great a god sat there
To her undoing. Mindful of his mother,
He had begun to make Sychaeus fade
From Dido's memory bit by bit, and tried
To waken with new love, a living love,
985 Her long settled mind and dormant heart.

After the first pause in the feast, and after
Trenchers were taken off, they put out wine bowls,
Grand and garlanded. A festive din
Now rose and echoed through the palace halls.
990 Lighted lamps hung from the coffered ceiling
Rich with gold leaf, and torches with high flames
Prevailed over the night. And now the queen
Called for a vessel heavy with gems and gold
That Belus and his line had always used.

995   She filled it, dipping wine, and her long hall
      Fell silent.

                    "Jupiter," she prayed,
      "You make the laws for host and guest, they say.
      Grant that this day be one of joy for Tyrians
1000 And men of Troy; grant that it be remembered
      By our descendants. Now be with us, Bacchus,
      Giver of happiness, and kindly Juno,
      And all you Tyrians attend
      In friendliness this meeting that unites us."

1005 At this she tilted a libation out
      And put the vessel lightly to her lips,
      Then, with a jest, gave it to Bitias,
      Who nearly immersed himself in brimming gold
      As he drank down the foaming wine. The bowl
1010 Passed then to other lords. And Lord Iopas,
      With flowing hair, whom giant Atlas taught,
      Made the room echo to his golden lyre.
      He sang the straying moon and toiling sun,
      The origin of mankind and the beasts,
1015 Of rain and fire; the rainy Hyadës,
      Arcturus, the Great Bear and Little Bear;
      The reason winter suns are in such haste
      To dip in Ocean, or what holds the nights
      Endless in winter. Tyrians at this
1020 Redoubled their applause; the Trojans followed.
      And Dido, fated queen, drew out the night
      With talk of various matters, while she drank
      Long draughts of love. Often she asked of Priam,
      Often of Hector; now of the armor Memnon,
1025 The son of Dawn, had worn; now of the team
      Diomedes drove; now of the huge Achilles.

      "Come, rather," then she said, "dear guest, and tell us
      From the beginning the Greek stratagems,
      The ruin of your town and your sea-faring,
1030 As now the seventh summer brings you here
      From wandering all the lands and all the seas."

Lines 730–756

BOOK

II

HOW THEY TOOK THE CITY

The room fell silent, and all eyes were on him,
As Father Aeneas from his high couch began:

"Sorrow too deep to tell, your majesty,
You order me to feel and tell once more:
5   How the Danaans leveled in the dust
The splendor of our mourned-forever kingdom—
Heartbreaking things I saw with my own eyes
And was myself a part of. Who could tell them,
Even a Myrmidon or Dolopian
10 Or ruffian of Ulysses, without tears?
Now, too, the night is well along, with dewfall
Out of heaven, and setting stars weigh down
Our heads toward sleep. But if so great desire
Moves you to hear the tale of our disasters,
15 Briefly recalled, the final throes of Troy,
However I may shudder at the memory
And shrink again in grief, let me begin.

Knowing their strength broken in warfare, turned
Back by the fates, and years—so many years—
20 Already slipped away, the Danaan captains
By the divine handicraft of Pallas built
A horse of timber, tall as a hill,
And sheathed its ribs with planking of cut pine.
This they gave out to be an offering

25 For a safe return by sea, and the word went round.
    But on the sly they shut inside a company
    Chosen from their picked soldiery by lot,
    Crowding the vaulted caverns in the dark—
    The horse's belly—with men fully armed.

30 Offshore there's a long island, Tenedos,
    Famous and rich while Priam's kingdom lasted,
    A treacherous anchorage now, and nothing more.
    They crossed to this and hid their ships behind it
    On the bare shore beyond. We thought they'd gone,
35 Sailing home to Mycenae before the wind,
    So Teucer's town is freed of her long anguish,
    Gates thrown wide! And out we go in joy
    To see the Dorian campsites, all deserted,
    The beach they left behind. Here the Dolopians
40 Pitched their tents, here cruel Achilles lodged,
    There lay the ships, and there, formed up in ranks,
    They came inland to fight us. Of our men
    One group stood marveling, gaping up to see
    The dire gift of the cold unbedded goddess,
45 The sheer mass of the horse.
                              Thymoetes shouts
    It should be hauled inside the walls and moored
    High on the citadel—whether by treason
    Or just because Troy's fate went that way now.
50 Capys opposed him; so did the wiser heads:
    'Into the sea with it,' they said, 'or burn it,
    Build up a bonfire under it,
    This trick of the Greeks, a gift no one can trust,
    Or cut it open search the hollow belly!'

55 Contrary notions pulled the crowd apart.
    Next thing we knew, in front of everyone,
    Laocoön with a great company
    Came furiously running from the Height,
    And still far off cried out: 'O my poor people,
60 Men of Troy, what madness has come over you?
    Can you believe the enemy truly gone?

A gift from the Danaans, and no ruse?
Is that Ulysses' way, as you have known him?
Achaeans must be hiding in this timber,
65   Or it was built to butt against our walls,
Peer over them into our houses, pelt
The city from the sky. Some crookedness
Is in this thing. Have no faith in the horse!
Whatever it is, even when Greeks bring gifts
70   I fear them, gifts and all.'
                                        He broke off then
And rifled his big spear with all his might
Against the horse's flank, the curve of belly.
It stuck there trembling, and the rounded hull
75   Reverberated groaning at the blow.
If the gods' will had not been sinister,
If our own minds had not been crazed,
He would have made us foul that Argive den
With bloody steel, and Troy would stand today—
80   O citadel of Priam, towering still!

But now look: hillmen, shepherds of Dardania,
Raising a shout, dragged in before the king
An unknown fellow with hands tied behind—
This all as he himself had planned,
85   Volunteering, letting them come across him,
So he could open Troy to the Achaeans.
Sure of himself this man was, braced for it
Either way, to work his trick or die.
From every quarter Trojans run to see him,
90   Ring the prisoner round, and make a game
Of jeering at him. Be instructed now
In Greek deceptive arts: one barefaced deed
Can tell you of them all.
As the man stood there, shaken and defenceless,
95   Looking around at ranks of Phrygians,
'Oh god,' he said, 'what land on earth, what seas

Can take me in? What's left me in the end,
Outcast that I am from the Danaans,
Now the Dardanians will have my blood?'

100 The whimpering speech brought us up short; we felt
A twinge for him. Let him speak up, we said,
Tell us where he was born, what news he brought,
What he could hope for as a prisoner.
Taking his time, slow to discard his fright,
105 He said:
               'I'll tell you the whole truth, my lord,
No matter what may come of it. Argive
I am by birth, and will not say I'm not.
That first of all: Fortune has made a derelict
110 Of Sinon, but the bitch
Won't make an empty liar of him, too.
Report of Palamedes may have reached you,
Scion of Belus' line, a famous man
Who gave commands against the war. For this,
115 On a trumped-up charge, on perjured testimony,
The Greeks put him to death—but now they mourn him,
Now he has lost the light. Being kin to him,
In my first years I joined him as companion,
Sent by my poor old father on this campaign,
120 And while he held high rank and influence
In royal councils, we did well, with honor.
Then by the guile and envy of Ulysses—
Nothing unheard of there!—he left this world,
And I lived on, but under a cloud, in sorrow,
125 Raging for my blameless friend's downfall.
Demented, too, I could not hold my peace
But said if I had luck, if I won through
Again to Argos, I'd avenge him there.
And I roused hatred with my talk; I fell
130 Afoul now of that man. From that time on,
Day in, day out, Ulysses
Found new ways to bait and terrify me,
Putting out shady rumors among the troops,
Looking for weapons he could use against me.

135 He could not rest till Calchas served his turn—
But why go on? The tale's unwelcome, useless,
If Achaeans are all one,
And it's enough I'm called Achaean, then
Exact the punishment, long overdue;
140 The Ithacan desires it; the Atridae
Would pay well for it.'

                            Burning with curiosity,
We questioned him, called on him to explain—
Unable to conceive such a performance,
145 The art of the Pelasgian. He went on,
Atremble, as though he feared us:

                             'Many times
The Danaans wished to organize retreat,
To leave Troy and the long war, tired out.
150 If only they had done it! Heavy weather
At sea closed down on them, or a fresh gale
From the Southwest would keep them from embarking,
Most of all after this figure here,
This horse they put together with maple beams,
155 Reached its full height. Then wind and thunderstorms
Rumbled in heaven. So in our quandary
We sent Eurypylus to Phoebus' oracle,
And he brought back this grim reply:

'Blood and a virgin slain
160 You gave to appease the winds, for your first voyage
Troyward, O Danaans. Blood again
And Argive blood, one life, wins your return.'

When this got round among the soldiers, gloom
Came over them, and a cold chill that ran
165 To the very marrow. Who had death in store?
Whom did Apollo call for? Now the man
Of Ithaca haled Calchas out among us
In tumult, calling on the seer to tell
The true will of the gods. Ah, there were many
170 Able to divine the crookedness
And cruelty afoot for me, but they

Looked on in silence. For ten days the seer
Kept still, kept under cover, would not speak
Of anyone, or name a man for death,
175 Till driven to it at last by Ulysses' cries—
By prearrangement—he broke silence, barely
Enough to designate me for the altar.
Every last man agreed. The torments each
Had feared for himself, now shifted to another,
180 All could endure. And the infamous day came,
The ritual, the salted meal, the fillets . . .
I broke free, I confess it, broke my chains,
Hid myself all night in a muddy marsh,
Concealed by reeds, waiting for them to sail
185 If they were going to.
                                   Now no hope is left me
Of seeing my home country ever again,
My sweet children, my father, missed for years.
Perhaps the army will demand they pay
190 For my escape, my crime here, and their death,
Poor things, will be my punishment. Ah, sir,
I beg you by the gods above, the powers
In whom truth lives, and by what faith remains
Uncontaminated to men, take pity
195 On pain so great and so unmerited!'

For tears we gave him life, and pity, too.
Priam himself ordered the gyves removed
And the tight chain between. In kindness then
He said to him:
200   'Whoever you may be,
The Greeks are gone; forget them from now on;
You shall be ours. And answer me these questions:
Who put this huge thing up, this horse?
Who designed it? What do they want with it?
205 Is it religious or a means of war?'

These were his questions. Then the captive, trained
In trickery, in the stagecraft of Achaea,
Lifted his hands unfettered to the stars.

'Eternal fires of heaven,' he began,
210   'Powers inviolable, I swear by thee,
As by the altars and blaspheming swords
I got away from, and the gods' white bands
I wore as one chosen for sacrifice,
This is justice, I am justified
215   In dropping all allegiance to the Greeks—
As I had cause to hate them; I may bring
Into the open what they would keep dark.
No laws of my own country bind me now.
Only be sure you keep your promises
220   And keep faith, Troy, as you are kept from harm
If what I say proves true, if what I give
Is great and valuable.

                              The whole hope
Of the Danaans, and their confidence
225   In the war they started, rested all along
In help from Pallas. Then the night came
When Diomedes and that criminal,
Ulysses, dared to raid her holy shrine.
They killed the guards on the high citadel
230   And ripped away the statue, the Palladium,
Desecrating with bloody hands the virginal
Chaplets of the goddess. After that,
Danaan hopes waned and were undermined,
Ebbing away, their strength in battle broken,
235   The goddess now against them. This she made
Evident to them all with signs and portents.
Just as they set her statue up in camp,
The eyes, cast upward, glowed with crackling flames,
And salty sweat ran down the body. Then—
240   I say it in awe—three times, up from the ground,
The apparition of the goddess rose
In a lightning flash, with shield and spear atremble.
Calchas divined at once that the sea crossing
Must be attempted in retreat—that Pergamum
245   Cannot be torn apart by Argive swords
Unless at Argos first they beg new omens,
Carrying homeward the divine power

Lines 154–178

Brought overseas in ships. Now they are gone
Before the wind to the fatherland, Mycenae,
250 Gone to enlist new troops and gods. They'll cross
The water again and be here, unforeseen.
So Calchas read the portents. Warned by him,
They set this figure up in reparation
For the Palladium stolen, to appease
255 The offended power and expiate the crime.
Enormous, though, he made them build the thing
With timber braces, towering to the sky,
Too big for the gates, not to be hauled inside
And give the people back their ancient guardian.
260 If any hand here violates this gift
To great Minerva, then extinction waits,
Not for one only—would god it were so—
But for the realm of Priam and all Phrygians.
If this proud offering, drawn by your hands,
265 Should mount into your city, then so far
As the walls of Pelops' town the tide of Asia
Surges in war: that doom awaits our children.'

This fraud of Sinon, his accomplished lying,
Won us over; a tall tale and fake tears
270 Had captured us, whom neither Diomedes
Nor Larisaean Achilles overpowered,
Nor ten long years, nor all their thousand ships.

And now another sign, more fearful still,
Broke on our blind miserable people,
27 Filling us all with dread. Laocoön,
Acting as Neptune's priest that day by lot,
Was on the point of putting to the knife
A massive bull before the appointed altar,
When ah—look there!
280 From Tenedos, on the calm sea, twin snakes—
I shiver to recall it—endlessly

Lines 179–204

Coiling, uncoiling, swam abreast for shore,
Their underbellies showing as their crests
Reared red as blood above the swell; behind
285   They glided with great undulating backs.
Now came the sound of thrashed seawater foaming;
Now they were on dry land, and we could see
Their burning eyes, fiery and suffused with blood,
Their tongues a-flicker out of hissing maws.
290   We scattered, pale with fright. But straight ahead
They slid until they reached Laocoön.
Each snake enveloped one of his two boys,
Twining about and feeding on the body.
Next they ensnared the man as he ran up
295   With weapons: coils like cables looped and bound him
Twice round the middle; twice about his throat
They whipped their back-scales, and their heads towered,
While with both hands he fought to break the knots,
Drenched in slime, his head-bands black with venom,
300   Sending to heaven his appalling cries
Like a slashed bull escaping from an altar,
The fumbled axe shrugged off. The pair of snakes
Now flowed away and made for the highest shrines,
The citadel of pitiless Minerva,
305   Where coiling they took cover at her feet
Under the rondure of her shield. New terrors
Ran in the shaken crowd: the word went round
Laocoön had paid, and rightfully,
For profanation of the sacred hulk
310   With his offending spear hurled at its flank.

'The offering must be hauled to its true home,'
They clamored. 'Votive prayers to the goddess
Must be said there!'
               So we breached the walls
And laid the city open. Everyone
315   Pitched in to get the figure underpinned
With rollers, hempen lines around the neck.
Deadly, pregnant with enemies, the horse
Crawled upward to the breach. And boys and girls

320 Sang hymns around the towrope as for joy
They touched it. Rolling on, it cast a shadow
Over the city's heart. O Fatherland,
O Ilium, home of gods! Defensive wall
Renowned in war for Dardanus's people:
325 There on the very threshold of the breach
It jarred to a halt four times, four times the arms
In the belly thrown together made a sound—
Yet on we strove unmindful, deaf and blind,
To place the monster on our blessed height.
330 Then, even then, Cassandra's lips unsealed
The doom to come: lips by a god's command
Never believed or heeded by the Trojans.
So pitiably we, for whom that day
Would be the last, made all our temples green
335 With leafy festal boughs throughout the city.

As heaven turned, Night from the Ocean stream
Came on, profound in gloom on earth and sky
And Myrmidons in hiding. In their homes
The Teucrians lay silent, wearied out,
340 And sleep enfolded them. The Argive fleet,
Drawn up in line abreast, left Tenedos
Through the aloof moon's friendly stillnesses
And made for the familiar shore. Flame signals
Shone from the command ship. Sinon, favored
345 By what the gods unjustly had decreed,
Stole out to tap the pine walls and set free
The Danaans in the belly. Opened wide,
The horse emitted men; gladly they dropped
Out of the cavern, captains first, Thessandrus,
350 Sthenelus and the man of iron, Ulysses;
Hand over hand upon the rope, Acamas, Thoas,
Neoptolemus and Prince Machaon,
Menelaus and then the master builder,
Epeos, who designed the horse decoy.
355 Into the darkened city, buried deep
In sleep and wine, they made their way,
Cut the few sentries down,

Let in their fellow soldiers at the gate,
And joined their combat companies as planned.

360 That time of night it was when the first sleep,
Gift of the gods, begins for ill mankind,
Arriving gradually, delicious rest.
In sleep, in dream, Hector appeared to me,
Gaunt with sorrow, streaming tears, all torn—
365 As by the violent car on his death day—
And black with bloody dust,
His puffed-out feet cut by the rawhide thongs.
Ah god, the look of him! How changed
From that proud Hector who returned to Troy
370 Wearing Achilles' armor, or that one
Who pitched the torches on Danaan ships;
His beard all filth, his hair matted with blood,
Showing the wounds, the many wounds, received
Outside his father's city walls. I seemed
375 Myself to weep and call upon the man
In grieving speech, brought from the depth of me:

'Light of Dardania, best hope of Troy,
What kept you from us for so long, and where?
From what far place, O Hector, have you come,
380 Long, long awaited? After so many deaths
Of friends and brothers, after a world of pain
For all our folk and all our town, at last,
Boneweary, we behold you! What has happened
To ravage your serene face? Why these wounds?'

385 He wasted no reply on my poor questions
But heaved a great sigh from his chest and said:
'Ai! Give up and go, child of the goddess,
Save yourself, out of these flames. The enemy
Holds the city walls, and from her height
390 Troy falls in ruin. Fatherland and Priam
Have their due; if by one hand our towers
Could be defended, by this hand, my own,
They would have been. Her holy things, her gods

Of hearth and household Troy commends to you.
395   Accept them as companions of your days;
Go find for them the great walls that one day
You'll dedicate, when you have roamed the sea.'

As he said this, he brought out from the sanctuary
Chaplets and Vesta, Lady of the Hearth,
400   With her eternal fire.
                While I dreamed,
The turmoil rose, with anguish, in the city.
More and more, although Anchises' house
Lay in seclusion, muffled among trees,
405   The din at the grim onset grew; and now
I shook off sleep, I climbed to the roof top
To cup my ears and listen. And the sound
Was like the sound a grassfire makes in grain,
Whipped by a Southwind, or a torrent foaming
410   Out of a mountainside to strew in ruin
Fields, happy crops, the yield of plowing teams,
Or woodlands borne off in the flood; in wonder
The shepherd listens on a rocky peak.
I knew then what our trust had won for us,
415   Knew the Danaan fraud: Deïphobus'
Great house in flames, already caving in
Under the overpowering god of fire;
Ucalegon's already caught nearby;
The glare lighting the straits beyond Sigeum;
420   The cries of men, the wild calls of the trumpets.

To arm was my first maddened impulse—not
That anyone had a fighting chance in arms;
Only I burned to gather up some force
For combat, and to man some high redoubt.
425   So fury drove me, and it came to me
That meeting death was beautiful in arms.
Then here, eluding the Achaean spears,
Came Panthus, Othrys' son, priest of Apollo,

Carrying holy things, our conquered gods,
430   And pulling a small grandchild along: he ran
Despairing to my doorway.

                    'Where's the crux,
Panthus,' I said. 'What strongpoint shall we hold?'

Before I could say more, he groaned and answered:
435   'The last day for Dardania has come,
The hour not to be fought off any longer.
Trojans we have been; Ilium has been;
The glory of the Teucrians is no more;
Black Jupiter has passed it on to Argos.
440   Greeks are the masters in our burning city.
Tall as a cliff, set in the heart of town,
Their horse pours out armed men. The conqueror,
Gloating Sinon, brews new conflagrations.
Troops hold the gates—as many thousand men
445   As ever came from great Mycenae; others
Block the lanes with crossed spears; glittering
In a combat line, swordblades are drawn for slaughter.
Even the first guards at the gates can barely
Offer battle, or blindly make a stand.'

450   Impelled by these words, by the powers of heaven,
Into the flames I go, into the fight,
Where the harsh Fury, and the din and shouting,
Skyward rising, calls. Crossing my path
In moonlight, five fell in with me, companions:
455   Ripheus, and Epytus, a great soldier,
Hypanis, Dymas, cleaving to my side
With young Coroebus, Mygdon's son. It happened
That in those very days this man had come
To Troy, aflame with passion for Cassandra,
460   Bringing to Priam and the Phrygians
A son-in-law's right hand. Unlucky one,
To have been deaf to what his bride foretold!
Now when I saw them grouped, on edge for battle,
I took it all in and said briefly,

Lines 320–348

'Soldiers,

465 Brave as you are to no end, if you crave
To face the last fight with me, and no doubt of it,
How matters stand for us each one can see.
The gods by whom this kingdom stood are gone,
Gone from the shrines and altars. You defend

470 A city lost in flames. Come, let us die,
We'll make a rush into the thick of it.
The conquered have one safety: hope for none.'

The desperate odds doubled their fighting spirit:

475 From that time on, like predatory wolves
In fog and darkness, when a savage hunger
Drives them blindly on, and cubs in lairs
Lie waiting with dry famished jaws—just so
Through arrow flights and enemies we ran

480 Toward our sure death, straight for the city's heart,
Cavernous black night over and around us.
Who can describe the havoc of that night
Or tell the deaths, or tally wounds with tears?
The ancient city falls, after dominion

485 Many long years. In windrows on the streets,
In homes, on solemn porches of the gods,
Dead bodies lie. And not alone the Trojans
Pay the price with their heart's blood; at times
Manhood returns to fire even the conquered

490 And Danaan conquerors fall. Grief everywhere,
Everywhere terror, and all shapes of death.

Androgeos was the first to cross our path
Leading a crowd of Greeks; he took for granted
That we were friends, and hailed us cheerfully:

495 'Men, get a move on! Are you made of lead
To be so late and slow? The rest are busy
Carrying plunder from the fires and towers.
Are you just landed from the ships?'

His words

500 Were barely out, and no reply forthcoming

Credible to him, when he knew himself
Fallen among enemies. Thunderstruck,
He halted, foot and voice, and then recoiled
Like one who steps down on a lurking snake
505 In a briar patch and jerks back, terrified,
As the angry thing rears up, all puffed and blue.
So backward went Androgeos in panic.
We were all over them in a moment, cut
And thrust, and as they fought on unknown ground,
510 Startled, unnerved, we killed them everywhere.
So Fortune filled our sails at first. Coroebus,
Elated at our feat and his own courage,
Said:

    'Friends, come follow Fortune. She has shown
515 The way to safety, shown she's on our side.
We'll take their shields and put on their insignia!
Trickery, bravery: who asks, in war?
The enemy will arm us.'

                He put on
520 The plumed helm of Androgeos, took the shield
With blazon and the Greek sword to his side.
Ripheus, Dymas—all were pleased to do it,
Making the still fresh trophies our equipment.
Then we went on, passing among the Greeks,
525 Protected by our own gods now no longer;
Many a combat, hand to hand, we fought
In the black night, and many a Greek we sent
To Orcus. There were some who turned and ran
Back to the ships and shore; some shamefully
530 Clambered again into the horse, to hide
In the familiar paunch.

              When gods are contrary
They stand by no one. Here before us came
Cassandra, Priam's virgin daughter, dragged
535 By her long hair out of Minerva's shrine,
Lifting her brilliant eyes in vain to heaven—
Her eyes alone, as her white hands were bound.
Coroebus, infuriated, could not bear it,
But plunged into the midst to find his death.

540 We all went after him, our swords at play,
But here, here first, from the temple gable's height,
We met a hail of missiles from our friends,
Pitiful execution, by their error,
Who thought us Greek from our Greek plumes and shields.

545 Then with a groan of anger, seeing the virgin
Wrested from them, Danaans from all sides
Rallied and attacked us: fiery Ajax,
Atreus' sons, Dolopians in a mass—
As, when a cyclone breaks, conflicting winds

550 Will come together, Westwind, Southwind, Eastwind
Riding high out of the Dawnland; forests
Bend and roar, and raging all in spume
Nereus with his trident churns the deep.
Then some whom we had taken by surprise

555 Under cover of night throughout the city
And driven off, came back again: they knew
Our shields and arms for liars now, our speech
Alien to their own. They overwhelmed us.
Coroebus fell at the warrior goddess' altar,

560 Killed by Peneleus; and Ripheus fell,
A man uniquely just among the Trojans,
The soul of equity; but the gods would have it
Differently. Hypanis, Dymas died,
Shot down by friends; nor did your piety,

565 Panthus, nor Apollo's fillets shield you
As you went down.
                    Ashes of Ilium!
Flames that consumed my people! Here I swear
That in your downfall I did not avoid

570 One weapon, one exchange with the Danaans,
And if it had been fated, my own hand
Had earned my death. But we were torn away
From that place—Iphitus and Pelias too,
One slow with age, one wounded by Ulysses,

575 Called by a clamor at the hall of Priam.
Truly we found here a prodigious fight,
As though there were none elsewhere, not a death
In the whole city: Mars gone berserk, Danaans

In a rush to scale the roof; the gate besieged
580 By a tortoise shell of overlapping shields.
Ladders clung to the wall, and men strove upward
Before the very doorposts, on the rungs,
Left hand putting the shield up, and the right
Reaching for the cornice. The defenders
585 Wrenched out upperworks and rooftiles: these
For missiles, as they saw the end, preparing
To fight back even on the edge of death.
And gilded beams, ancestral ornaments,
They rolled down on the heads below. In hall
590 Others with swords drawn held the entrance way,
Packed there, waiting. Now we plucked up heart
To help the royal house, to give our men
A respite, and to add our strength to theirs,
Though all were beaten. And we had for entrance
595 A rear door, secret, giving on a passage
Between the palace halls; in other days
Andromachë, poor lady, often used it,
Going alone to see her husband's parents
Or taking Astyanax to his grandfather.
600 I climbed high on the roof, where hopeless men
Were picking up and throwing futile missiles.
Here was a tower like a promontory
Rising toward the stars above the roof:
All Troy, the Danaan ships, the Achaean camp,
605 Were visible from this. Now close beside it
With crowbars, where the flooring made loose joints,
We pried it from its bed and pushed it over.
Down with a rending crash in sudden ruin
Wide over the Danaan lines it fell;
610 But fresh troops moved up, and the rain of stones
With every kind of missile never ceased.

Just at the outer doors of the vestibule
Sprang Pyrrhus, all in bronze and glittering,
As a serpent, hidden swollen underground
615 By a cold winter, writhes into the light,
On vile grass fed, his old skin cast away,

Lines 440–473

Renewed and glossy, rolling slippery coils,
With lifted underbelly rearing sunward
And triple tongue a-flicker. Close beside him
620   Giant Periphas and Automedon,
His armor-bearer, once Achilles' driver,
Besieged the place with all the young of Scyros,
Hurling their torches at the palace roof.
Pyrrhus shouldering forward with an axe
625   Broke down the stony threshold, forced apart
Hinges and brazen door-jambs, and chopped through
One panel of the door, splitting the oak,
To make a window, a great breach. And there
Before their eyes the inner halls lay open,
630   The courts of Priam and the ancient kings,
With men-at-arms ranked in the vestibule.
From the interior came sounds of weeping,
Pitiful commotion, wails of women
High-pitched, rising in the formal chambers
635   To ring against the silent golden stars;
And, through the palace, mothers wild with fright
Ran to and fro or clung to doors and kissed them.
Pyrrhus with his father's brawn stormed on,
No bolts or bars or men availed to stop him:
640   Under his battering the double doors
Were torn out of their sockets and fell inward.
Sheer force cleared the way: the Greeks broke through
Into the vestibule, cut down the guards,
And made the wide hall seethe with men-at-arms—
645   A tumult greater than when dykes are burst
And a foaming river, swirling out in flood,
Whelms every parapet and races on
Through fields and over all the lowland plains,
Bearing off pens and cattle. I myself
650   Saw Neoptolemus furious with blood
In the entrance way, and saw the two Atridae;
Hecuba I saw, and her hundred daughters,
Priam before the altars, with his blood
Drenching the fires that he himself had blessed.

Lines 473–502

655   Those fifty bridal chambers, hope of a line
       So flourishing; those doorways high and proud,
       Adorned with takings of barbaric gold,
       Were all brought low: fire had them, or the Greeks.

       What was the fate of Priam, you may ask.
660   Seeing his city captive, seeing his own
       Royal portals rent apart, his enemies
       In the inner rooms, the old man uselessly
       Put on his shoulders, shaking with old age,
       Armor unused for years, belted a sword on,
665   And made for the massed enemy to die.
       Under the open sky in a central court
       Stood a big altar; near it, a laurel tree
       Of great age, leaning over, in deep shade
       Embowered the Penatës. At this altar
670   Hecuba and her daughters, like white doves
       Blown down in a black storm, clung together,
       Enfolding holy images in their arms.
       Now, seeing Priam in a young man's gear,
       She called out:
675   'My poor husband, what mad thought
       Drove you to buckle on these weapons?
       Where are you trying to go? The time is past
       For help like this, for this kind of defending,
       Even if my own Hector could be here.
680   Come to me now: the altar will protect us,
       Or else you'll die with us.'
                     She drew him close,
       Heavy with years, and made a place for him
       To rest on the consecrated stone.
685   Now see
       Politës, one of Priam's sons, escaped
       From Pyrrhus' butchery and on the run
       Through enemies and spears, down colonnades,
       Through empty courtyards, wounded. Close behind
690   Comes Pyrrhus burning for the death-stroke: has him,
       Catches him now, and lunges with the spear.

Lines 503–530

The boy has reached his parents, and before them
Goes down, pouring out his life with blood.
Now Priam, in the very midst of death,
695   Would neither hold his peace nor spare his anger.

'For what you've done, for what you've dared,' he said,
'If there is care in heaven for atrocity,
May the gods render fitting thanks, reward you
As you deserve. You forced me to look on
700   At the destruction of my son: defiled
A father's eyes with death. That great Achilles
You claim to be the son of—and you lie—
Was not like you to Priam, his enemy;
To me who threw myself upon his mercy
705   He showed compunction, gave me back for burial
The bloodless corpse of Hector, and returned me
To my own realm.'
           The old man threw his spear
With feeble impact; blocked by the ringing bronze,
710   It hung there harmless from the jutting boss.
Then Pyrrhus answered:
              'You'll report the news
To Pelidës, my father; don't forget
My sad behavior, the degeneracy
715   Of Neoptolemus. Now die.'
                 With this,
To the altar step itself he dragged him trembling,
Slipping in the pooled blood of his son,
And took him by the hair with his left hand.
720   The sword flashed in his right; up to the hilt
He thrust it in his body.
             That was the end
Of Priam's age, the doom that took him off,
With Troy in flames before his eyes, his towers
725   Headlong fallen—he that in other days
Had ruled in pride so many lands and peoples,
The power of Asia.
           On the distant shore
The vast trunk headless lies without a name.

For the first time that night, inhuman shuddering
Took me, head to foot. I stood unmanned,
And my dear father's image came to mind
As our king, just his age, mortally wounded,
Gasped his life away before my eyes.
Creusa came to mind, too, left alone;
The house plundered; danger to little Iulus.
I looked around to take stock of my men,
But all had left me, utterly played out,
Giving their beaten bodies to the fire
Or plunging from the roof.
                              It came to this,
That I stood there alone. And then I saw
Lurking beyond the doorsill of the Vesta,
In hiding, silent, in that place reserved,
The daughter of Tyndareus. Glare of fires
Lighted my steps this way and that, my eyes
Glancing over the whole scene, everywhere.
That woman, terrified of the Trojans' hate
For the city overthrown, terrified too
Of Danaan vengeance, her abandoned husband's
Anger after years—Helen, that Fury
Both to her own homeland and Troy, had gone
To earth, a hated thing, before the altars.
Now fires blazed up in my own spirit—
A passion to avenge my fallen town
And punish Helen's whorishness.
                                  'Shall this one
Look untouched on Sparta and Mycenae
After her triumph, going like a queen,
And see her home and husband, kin and children,
With Trojan girls for escort, Phrygian slaves?
Must Priam perish by the sword for this?
Troy burn, for this? Dardania's littoral
Be soaked in blood, so many times, for this?

765 Not by my leave. I know
No glory comes of punishing a woman,
The feat can bring no honor. Still, I'll be
Approved for snuffing out a monstrous life,
For a just sentence carried out. My heart
770 Will teem with joy in this avenging fire,
And the ashes of my kin will be appeased.'

So ran my thoughts. I turned wildly upon her,
But at that moment, clear, before my eyes—
Never before so clear—in a pure light
775 Stepping before me, radiant through the night,
My loving mother came: immortal, tall,
And lovely as the lords of heaven know her.
Catching me by the hand, she held me back,
Then with her rose-red mouth reproved me:
780   'Son,
Why let such suffering goad you on to fury
Past control? Where is your thoughtfulness
For me, for us? Will you not first revisit
The place you left your father, worn and old,
785 Or find out if your wife, Creusa, lives,
And the young boy, Ascanius—all these
Cut off by Greek troops foraging everywhere?
Had I not cared for them, fire would by now
Have taken them, their blood glutted the sword.
790 You must not hold the woman of Laconia,
That hated face, the cause of this, nor Paris.
The harsh will of the gods it is, the gods,
That overthrows the splendor of this place
And brings Troy from her height into the dust.
795 Look over there: I'll tear away the cloud
That curtains you, and films your mortal sight,
The fog around you.—Have no fear of doing
Your mother's will, or balk at obeying her.—
Look: where you see high masonry thrown down,
800 Stone torn from stone, with billowing smoke and dust,
Neptune is shaking from their beds the walls

That his great trident pried up, undermining,
Toppling the whole city down. And look:
Juno in all her savagery holds
805 The Scaean Gates, and raging in steel armor
Calls her allied army from the ships.
Up on the citadel—turn, look—Pallas Tritonia
Couched in a stormcloud, lightening, with her Gorgon!
The Father himself empowers the Danaans,
810 Urges assaulting gods on the defenders.
Away, child; put an end to toiling so.
I shall be near, to see you safely home.'

She hid herself in the deep gloom of night,
And now the dire forms appeared to me
815 Of great immortals, enemies of Troy.
I knew the end then: Ilium was going down
In fire, the Troy of Neptune going down,
As in high mountains when the countrymen
Have notched an ancient ash, then make their axes
820 Ring with might and main, chopping away
To fell the tree—ever on the point of falling,
Shaken through all its foliage, and the treetop
Nodding; bit by bit the strokes prevail
Until it gives a final groan at last
825 And crashes down in ruin from the height.

Now I descended where the goddess guided,
Clear of the flames, and clear of enemies,
For both retired; so gained my father's door,
My ancient home. I looked for him at once,
830 My first wish being to help him to the mountains;
But with Troy gone he set his face against it,
Not to prolong his life, or suffer exile.

'The rest of you, all in your prime,' he said,
'Make your escape; you are still hale and strong.
835 If heaven's lords had wished me a longer span
They would have saved this home for me. I call it

More than enough that once before I saw
My city taken and wrecked, and went on living.
Here is my death bed, here. Take leave of me.
840   Depart now. I'll find death with my sword arm.
The enemy will oblige; they'll come for spoils.
Burial can be dispensed with. All these years
I've lingered in my impotence, at odds
With heaven, since the Father of gods and men
845   Breathed high winds of thunderbolt upon me
And touched me with his fire.'

                              He spoke on
In the same vein, inflexible. The rest of us,
Creusa and Ascanius and the servants,
850   Begged him in tears not to pull down with him
Our lives as well, adding his own dead weight
To the fates' pressure. But he would not budge,
He held to his resolve and to his chair.
I felt swept off again to fight, in misery
855   Longing for death. What choices now were open,
What chance had I?

                     'Did you suppose, my father,
That I could tear myself away and leave you?
Unthinkable; how could a father say it?
860   Now if it please the powers above that nothing
Stand of this great city; if your heart
Is set on adding your own death and ours
To that of Troy, the door's wide open for it:
Pyrrhus will be here, splashed with Priam's blood;
865   He kills the son before his father's eyes,
The father at the altars.

                     My dear mother,
Was it for this, through spears and fire, you brought me,
To see the enemy deep in my house,
870   To see my son, Ascanius, my father,
And near them both, Creusa,
Butchered in one another's blood? My gear,
Men, bring my gear. The last light calls the conquered.
Give me back to the Greeks. Let me take up

Lines 642–669

875   The combat once again. We shall not all
Die this day unavenged.'
                 I buckled on
Swordbelt and blade and slid my left forearm
Into the shield-strap, turning to go out,
880   But at the door Creusa hugged my knees,
Then held up little Iulus to his father.

'If you are going out to die, take us
To face the whole thing with you. If experience
Leads you to put some hope in weaponry
885   Such as you now take, guard your own house here.
When you have gone, to whom is Iulus left?
Your father? Wife?—one called that long ago.'

She went on, and her wailing filled the house,
But then a sudden portent came, a marvel:
890   Amid his parents' hands and their sad faces
A point on Iulus' head seemed to cast light,
A tongue of flame that touched but did not burn him,
Licking his fine hair, playing round his temples.
We, in panic, beat at the flaming hair
895   And put the sacred fire out with water;
Father Anchises lifted his eyes to heaven
And lifted up his hands, his voice, in joy:

'Omnipotent Jupiter, if prayers affect you,
Look down upon us, that is all I ask,
900   If by devotion to the gods we earn it,
Grant us a new sign, and confirm this portent!'
The old man barely finished when it thundered
A loud crack on the left. Out of the sky
Through depths of night a star fell trailing flame
905   And glided on, turning the night to day.
We watched it pass above the roof and go
To hide its glare, its trace, in Ida's wood;
But still, behind, the luminous furrow shone
And wide zones fumed with sulphur.

Lines 669–698

910   Now indeed
My father, overcome, addressed the gods,
And rose in worship of the blessed star.

'Now, now, no more delay. I'll follow you.
Where you conduct me, there I'll be.
915   Gods of my fathers,
Preserve this house, preserve my grandson. Yours
This portent was. Troy's life is in your power.
I yield. I go as your companion, son.'
Then he was still. We heard the blazing town
920   Crackle more loudly, felt the scorching heat.

'Then come, dear father. Arms around my neck:
I'll take you on my shoulders, no great weight.
Whatever happens, both will face one danger,
Find one safety. Iulus will come with me,
925   My wife at a good interval behind.
Servants, give your attention to what I say.
At the gate inland there's a funeral mound
And an old shrine of Ceres the Bereft;
Near it an ancient cypress, kept alive
930   For many years by our fathers' piety.
By various routes we'll come to that one place.
Father, carry our hearthgods, our Penatës.
It would be wrong for me to handle them—
Just come from such hard fighting, bloody work—
935   Until I wash myself in running water'

When I had said this, over my breadth of shoulder
And bent neck, I spread out a lion skin
For tawny cloak and stooped to take his weight.
940   Then little Iulus put his hand in mine
And came with shorter steps beside his father.
My wife fell in behind. Through shadowed places
On we went, and I, lately unmoved
By any spears thrown, any squads of Greeks,
945   Felt terror now at every eddy of wind,
Alarm at every sound, alert and worried

Alike for my companion and my burden.
I had got near the gate, and now I thought
We had made it all the way, when suddenly
A noise of running feet came near at hand,
950 And peering through the gloom ahead, my father
Cried out:

      'Run, boy; here they come; I see
Flame light on shields, bronze shining.'

                      I took fright,
955 And some unfriendly power, I know not what,
Stole all my addled wits—for as I turned
Aside from the known way, entering a maze
Of pathless places on the run—

                  Alas,
960 Creusa, taken from us by grim fate, did she
Linger, or stray, or sink in weariness?
There is no telling. Never would she be
Restored to us. Never did I look back
Or think to look for her, lost as she was,
965 Until we reached the funeral mound and shrine
Of venerable Ceres. Here at last
All came together, but she was not there;
She alone failed her friends, her child, her husband.
Out of my mind, whom did I not accuse,
970 What man or god? What crueller loss had I
Beheld, that night the city fell? Ascanius,
My father, and the Teucrian Penatës,
I left in my friends' charge, and hid them well
In a hollow valley.

            I turned back alone
975 Into the city, cinching my bright harness.
Nothing for it but to run the risks
Again, go back again, comb all of Troy,
And put my life in danger as before:
980 First by the town wall, then the gate, all gloom,
Through which I had come out—and so on backward,
Tracing my own footsteps through the night;
And everywhere my heart misgave me: even
Stillness had its terror. Then to our house,

985   Thinking she might, just might, have wandered there.
        Danaans had got in and filled the place,
        And at that instant fire they had set,
        Consuming it, went roofward in a blast;
        Flames leaped and seethed in heat to the night sky.
990   I pressed on, to see Priam's hall and tower.
        In the bare colonnades of Juno's shrine
        Two chosen guards, Phoenix and hard Ulysses,
        Kept watch over the plunder. Piled up here
        Were treasures of old Troy from every quarter,
995   Torn out of burning temples: altar tables,
        Robes, and golden bowls. Drawn up around them,
        Boys and frightened mothers stood in line.
        I even dared to call out in the night;
        I filled the streets with calling; in my grief
1000   Time after time I groaned and called Creusa,
        Frantic, in endless quest from door to door.
        Then to my vision her sad wraith appeared—
        Creusa's ghost, larger than life, before me.
        Chilled to the marrow, I could feel the hair
1005   On my head rise, the voice clot in my throat;
        But she spoke out to ease me of my fear:

        'What's to be gained by giving way to grief
        So madly, my sweet husband? Nothing here
        Has come to pass except as heaven willed.
1010   You may not take Creusa with you now;
        It was not so ordained, nor does the lord
        Of high Olympus give you leave. For you
        Long exile waits, and long sea miles to plough.
        You shall make landfall on Hesperia
1015   Where Lydian Tiber flows, with gentle pace,
        Between rich farmlands, and the years will bear
        Glad peace, a kingdom, and a queen for you.
        Dismiss these tears for your beloved Creusa.
        I shall not see the proud homelands of Myrmidons
1020   Or of Dolopians, or go to serve
        Greek ladies, Dardan lady that I am
        And daughter-in-law of Venus the divine.

Lines 756–787

No: the great mother of the gods detains me
Here on these shores. Farewell now; cherish still
1025 Your son and mine.'
                        With this she left me weeping,
Wishing that I could say so many things,
And faded on the tenuous air. Three times
I tried to put my arms around her neck,
1030 Three times enfolded nothing, as the wraith
Slipped through my fingers, bodiless as wind,
Or like a flitting dream.
                        So in the end
As night waned I rejoined my company.
1035 And there to my astonishment I found
New refugees in a great crowd: men and women
Gathered for exile, young—pitiful people
Coming from every quarter, minds made up,
With their belongings, for whatever lands
1040 I'd lead them to by sea.
                        The morning star
Now rose on Ida's ridges, bringing day.
Greeks had secured the city gates. No help
Or hope of help existed.
1045 So I resigned myself, picked up my father,
And turned my face toward the mountain range.

Lines 788–804

BOOK

III

SEA WANDERINGS
AND STRANGE
MEETINGS

Now our high masters had seen fit to visit
Upon the Asian power of Priam's house
Unmerited ruin, and the seagod's town,
Proud Ilium, lay smoking on the earth,
5   Our minds were turned by auguries of heaven
To exile in far quarters of the world.
By Antander, below Ida's hills, we toiled
To build a fleet, though none could say where fate
Would take or settle us. Then we held muster
10   Of all our able-bodied men.
                                When summer
Had just begun, Anchises gave the word
To hoist sail to the winds of destiny.
Weeping, I drew away from our old country,
15   Our quiet harbors, and the coastal plain
Where Troy had been: I took to the open sea,
Borne outward into exile with my people,
My son, my hearth gods, and the greater gods.

Beyond that water lies the land of Mars—
20   Great plains plowed by the men of Thrace, and ruled
In ancient days by cruel Lycurgus. Guesthood
And common household gods had bound this realm
To Troy while Fortune held. Now making landfall
Under the southwind there, I plotted out
25   On that curved shore the walls of a colony—

Though fate opposed it—and I devised the name
Aeneadae for the people, from my own.

As I made offering to Dionë's daughter,
My divine mother, and to other gods
30 Who give protection to a work begun,
I readied for the knife, there by the sea,
A sleek bull to the overlord of heaven.
Now as it happened the ground rose nearby
In a low hummock, overgrown with cornel
35 And myrtle saplings flickering in a thicket.
I stepped over, trying to tear away
Green stuff out of the mound to make a roof
Of boughs and leaves over the altar. There
I had sight of a gruesome prodigy
40 Beyond description: when the first stalk came torn
Out of the earth, and the root network burst,
Dark blood dripped down to soak and foul the soil.
Shuddering took me, my heart's blood ran slow
And chill with fear. But once more I went forward
45 And fought to pull another stubborn shoot,
To find what cause lay hid there—and again
Dark crimson blood ran out of the ripped bark.
My spirit strove hard; I paid reverence
To nymphs of the wild woods and Father Mars,
50 Guardian of Thrace, that they might make this vision
Turn to good, and lift away the omen.
Then I doubled my effort, a third time
Wrenched at a green shoot, grappling on my knees
Against the sandy ground. Should I tell this
55 Or hold my peace? A groan came from the mound,
A sobbing muffled in the depth of earth,
And words were carried upward:

                                    'Must you rend me,
Derelict that I am, Aeneas? Spare me,
60 Now I am in the grave; spare your clean hands
Defilement. I am no foreigner; old Troy
Gave birth to me; this blood drips from no tree.
Ah, put the savage land behind you! Leave

This shore of greed! For I am Polydorus.
65 An iron hedge of spears covered my body,
Pinned down here, and the pointed shafts took root.'

At this be sure that in a maze of dread
I stopped appalled, my hair stood up, my voice
Choked in my throat. This man, this Polydorus,
70 Ill-starred Priam had sent some years before
In secret, with great weight of gold, to be
Maintained by the Thracian king. That was a time
When Priam's trust in Dardan arms had faltered
As he saw Ilium ringed in siege. The Thracian—
75 After the shattering of Trojan power,
After Fortune had left us—threw in his lot
With Agamemnon's cause and winning arms,
Broke every pact and oath, killed Polydorus,
And took the gold by force. To what extremes
80 Will you not drive the hearts of men, accurst
Hunger for gold!
                        When faintness of dread left me,
I brought before the leaders of the people,
My father first, these portents of the gods
85 And asked their judgment. All were of one mind,
We should withdraw from that earth stained with blood,
With guesthood so profaned, and give our ships
The winds and sea again. For Polydorus
Therefore we held a funeral: on his grave
90 We heaped up earth, and altars to the Dead
Were decked with night-blue bands and cypress gloom,
Round which our women mourned with hair unbound.
We brought up foaming bowls of milk, with shallow
Cups of consecrated blood to pour,
95 And put to rest the spirit in the tomb,
Giving the last loud cry.
                        When seas offshore
Looked promising and smiled back at the wind,
A halyard-snapping land breeze calling seaward,
100 Our men crowded the beaches, launched the ships,
And out we sailed as shorelines fell behind.

Lines 44–72

Midsea a holy island lies, most dear
To Aegean Neptune and the Nereids' mother.
Once in its course afloat from coast to coast
105   The filial Archer God had tied it up
To Myconus, the seamark, and to Gyarus,
Enabling it at rest to scorn the winds.
Here we put in, and the serene island haven
Welcomed our tired men. We went ashore
110   In pilgrimage to Apollo's town. King Anius,
Both king of Delians and priest of Phoebus,
Garlanded in snowy wool and laurel,
Came to meet us, greeting his old friend,
Anchises. We joined hands, then at his side
115   Entered the temple of the god. I paid
My homage to that shrine of ancient stone,
Praying: 'O God of Thymbra, grant a home
And walls to weary men, grant us posterity
And an abiding city; guard our second
120   Tower of Troy, this remnant left alive
By Danaan swords and pitiless Achilles.
Whom should we follow? Or by what sea way
Dost thou direct us? Where may we settle now?
Father, grant us a sign, enter our hearts!'

125   These words were barely uttered, when it seemed
Of a sudden everything shook: doorsills and laurel,
The whole ridge round us quaking; and the caldron
Sang low from the sanctum, now thrown open.
We pitched down prone, and a voice rang in our ears:

130   'Tough sons of Dardanus, the self-same land
That bore you from your primal parent stock
Will take you to her fertile breast again.
Look for your mother of old. Aeneas' house
In her will rule the world's shores down the years,
135   Through generations of his children's children.'

So rang the god's voice. Then our voices rose
In tumult, jubilant; but everyone
Inquired what and where that place could be
To which the god summoned us wanderers
140 And called it a return. Soon then my father,
Calling up memories of ancient men,
Spoke out:
        'Sirs, listen to me and be clear
As to your hopes. Midsea great Jove's great island,
145 Crete, lies southward. There's Mount Ida, there
The cradle of our people. Cretans hold
One hundred cities, fertile and wide domains.
From there, if I recall it well, our first
Forefather, Teucrus, sailed to the coast around
150 Point Rhoeteum and chose it for his kingdom.
As yet no Ilium stood, no citadel;
The settlers lived in lowlands, river valleys.
There was the origin of Mount Cybelus'
Mother goddess, with her Corybantës'
155 Brazen ringing cups, her grove on Ida;
There were her mysteries, devoutly kept,
And the yoked lions of Our Lady's car.
Come then, we'll follow where the gods command,
Court favor of the winds, and lay our course
160 For Cnossus country—no long sail: let Jupiter
Fill our canvas and we beach on Crete
At sunrise the third day.'
                His counsel given,
He slaughtered ritual beasts upon the altars—
165 A bull to Neptune and a bull to thee,
Comely Apollo; to the god of Storm
A black ram, and a white one to the Zephyrs.
Rumor now flew about that Crete's great captain,
Idomeneus, had left his father's kingdom,
170 Driven away, so there were lands abandoned,
Free of our enemies, and homes on Crete
Awaiting settlers. Out from Ortygia's cove
We spread our wings to fly over the sea,
Past Naxos and the Maenad heights, then past

175   Donysa's greenery, Olëaros, and snow-white
       Rifts of Paros—all the Cycladës
       That stud that reach of sea. We sailed along
       Through channels between shore on foaming shore,
       As men vied at ship-handling, shouting out
180   And cheering one another: 'On to Crete!
       On to our ancestors!' And from astern
       The wind blew, freshening, to chase us on.

       At last we ran in to the ancient land
       Of the Curetës. I could barely wait
185   To build our hoped-for city walls, to be
       Called Pergamum, I said. I urged the people,
       Who loved the name, to love their new-found hearths
       And raise a citadel above the town.
       Our ships were not long cradled on dry land,
190   Our men not long engaged in marriages
       Or sowing the new fields, while I gave out
       Homesteads and laws, when, without warning, plague,
       Out of infected air to sap our bodies
       Came on us pitiable to see, and came
195   To blight our trees and crops—a year of death.
       People relinquished their sweet lives or dragged
       Their wasted bodies on; the Dog Star burned
       Our green plantations barren, and our grassland
       Withered; sickly stalks denied us food.
200   Again to Delos' oracle and Phoebus
       Father pressed me—back on our sea-track,
       To beg again the favor of the god:
       What end would he afford our weariness?
       Where might we turn for help, where set our course?

205   Night deepened; sleep on earth held living things;
       But now the sacred images of the gods,
       The Phrygian hearth-gods I had brought with me
       From Troy, out of the fire, seemed to stand
       Before me where I lay in sleep. I saw them
210   Plain in the pure light cast by the full moon
       Edging its way into unshuttered windows.

Lines 125–152

Then it seemed they spoke to comfort me
With these words:

              'All Apollo would have told you,
215   Delos regained, he will deliver here.
See how he sends us here of his own will
Into your room. We are the gods who came
Along with you, and joined your cause, when Troy
Went down in flames; we are the gods who crossed
220   The deepsea swell in ships at your command,
And we are those who will exalt your sons
To starry heaven and give your town dominion.
You must prepare great walls for a great race.
Keep up the long toil of your flight. Your settlement
225   Must be changed. This coast is not the one
Apollo of Delos urged you toward, nor did he
Bid you stay on Crete. There is a country,
Hesperia, as the Greeks have named it—ancient,
Full of man-power in war and fruitful earth;
230   Oenotrians lived there once; then by report
New generations called it Italy
After their leader. Our true home is there,
Dardanus came from there, and Iasius,
Forefathers of our people. Up with you,
235   Be glad, and tell your father full of years
What has been said here, with no room for doubt.
Look for Corythus and Ausonian country;
Lands under Dictë Jupiter denies you.'

Breathless with awe at these appearances,
240   At the divine voice—and all this no dream;
No—for I saw them, large as life, before me,
The veiled heads and the faces near at hand,
So cold sweat soaked me head to foot—
I tore myself from bed; I lifted up
245   My hands and voice to heaven; then I poured
Pure offerings at the fire. These rites performed
To my satisfaction, I recounted all
That strange event in sequence to Anchises.
He saw the ambiguity of the two

250 Ancestral lines, the double parentage,
His late-born error about ancient places.
Then he said:
           'Son (pitted as you are
Against the fates of Ilium) Cassandra
255 Alone made such a prophecy to me.
I call it back now: how she would foretell
This future for our people, saying often
Hesperia, and the realm of Italy.
But who could think the Trojans would migrate
260 To evening lands? Or whom then could Cassandra
Move by foresight? We should yield to Phoebus,
Taking a better course, as we are shown.'

With this we were all happy to comply.
We soon abandoned the new colony,
Leaving few souls behind, and making sail
265 In the decked ships we took to the waste sea.

When we had gained the offing to the west,
No land in sight now, but sky everywhere
And everywhere the sea, a thunderhead
270 Rose high above us, bringing gloom and storm
With crisping dark grey water. Soon the winds
Made the sea rise and big waves came against us.
This way and that we tossed in the great welter;
Low scud muffled daylight; night and rain
275 Wiped out the sky; flash after flash of lightning
Ripped from the burst clouds.
                    We were blown off course
And veered in darkness over the waves. My pilot,
Palinurus himself, could barely tell
280 Day from night, he said, and sighting nothing
But sea about us, could not keep direction.

Lines 180–202

Three days on the deep sea muffled in fog,
Three starless nights we wandered blind. At dawn
On the fourth day we raised land far away
285 In clearing weather, hilltops and then smoke
A-spiral in calm air. Our sails came down,
We took to the oars. No dallying: the seamen
Heaved up whorls of foam on the dark blue sea,
Pulling across it.
290   Safe now from the stormwave,
I took shelter first on the Strophadës—
For so the Greek name goes—islands that lie
In the broad Ionian sea. There nest the vile
Celaeno and her Harpy sisterhood,
295 Shut out, now, from the house of Phineus,
As they were frightened from old banquets there.
No gloomier monster, no more savage pest
And scourge sent by the gods' wrath ever mounted
From the black Stygian water—flying things
300 With young girls' faces, but foul ooze below,
Talons for hands, pale famished nightmare mouths.

When we pulled in to port, what met our eyes
But sleek herds in the meadows everywhere
And flocks of goats, no one attending them.
305 Setting upon them with our swords, we sent up
Shouts to the gods, to Jove himself, to share
The windfall with us; then on the curving beach
We set out couches for a savory feast.
But instantly, grotesquely whirring down,
310 The Harpies were upon us from the hills
With deafening beat of wings. They trounced our meat,
Defiling everything they touched with filth,
And gave an obscene squawk amid the stench.
We tried again. In a secluded gorge
315 Under a cliffside, in thick shade of trees,
We set our tables up, relit our altars.
But the loud horde again, from another quarter,
Came out of hiding, swooped down on the prey

Lines 203–233

With hooked feet, hunched to feed, and spoiled our feast.
320   I then gave orders to resort to arms
And make war on the vicious flock. My men
Did as commanded, laid their swords nearby,
Hidden in grass, and kept shields out of sight.
Now when the birds flew down along the cove
325   Once more with their infernal din, Misenus
From a high lookout sounded the alarm
On his brass horn. Into their midst my men
Attacked and tried a strange new form of battle,
To cut the indecent seabirds down in blood.
330   But they received no impact on their feathers,
Took on their backs no wounding cut: too quick,
They soared away into the upper air,
Leaving the prey half eaten and befouled.
Only Celaeno, perched on a high crag,
335   A ghastly witch, brought words out, croaking down:

'So war is all you give in recompense
For slaughter of bulls and bullocks, can it be,
Heirs of Laömedon? You'd arm for war
To drive the innocent Harpies from their country?
340   Then put your mind on what I prophesy: a thing
Foretold to Phoebus by the almighty father
And by Apollo then to me; now I,
First of the Furies, will disclose it to you.
Italy is the land you look for; well,
345   The winds will blow, you'll find your Italy,
You'll be allowed to enter port;
But you may never wall your destined city
Till deathly famine, for the bloodshed here,
Has made you grind your tables with your teeth!'

350   On this she took wing back into the forest.
But our men of a sudden felt their blood
Run cold, and lost all heart. Not with arms now
But prayers and vows they begged me to make peace,
Whether these foes were goddesses or birds,
355   Obscene and dire. My father, facing seaward,

Hands held out, invoked the heavenly powers
And pledged the rituals due them. 'Gods,' he said,
'Turn back this thing foreboded! Gods, avert
Disaster of that kind! Cherish your faithful!'

360 Hawsers were cast off at his word, and sheets
Paid out to tugging canvas, as the Southwind
Filled the sails. Over the whitecapped waves
We fled while wind and pilot called our course.
And soon out of the sea we raised Zacynthos'
365 Leafy bulk, Dulichium and Samë,
Craggy Neritos; past the rocks of Ithaca,
Laërtes' realm, we ran, and cursed that island
Nurse of cruel Ulysses. Before long
The cloudy peaks of the Leucatan mountain
370 Came in view—Apollo's promontory,
Seamen are wary of. Here we put in
And hauled up, tired, near the little town,
Our anchors out, our sterns high on the shingle.

Then, having gained this land beyond our reckoning,
375 We purified ourselves in the sight of Jove
And lit with offerings our altar fires,
Then on the Actian shore held games of Ilium.
The men, all naked, slippery with oil,
Fought bouts in our traditional wrestling style,
380 Glad to have run past all those Argive towns
And carried out our flight amid our foes.
The sun went slanting round the mighty year,
And freezing winter came, roughing the sea
With northern gales. Against the temple columns
385 I nailed a shield great Abas carried once,
All rounded bronze, and cut this legend on it:
Aeneas from victorious Greeks these arms.

Then I ordered the rowing benches manned,
The harbor left behind. They made a race of it,
390　My men, digging their oars into the swell
And surging on. Phaeacia's airy towers
Hove in sight and dropped away behind.
We passed along the coastline of Epirus
To Port Chaonia, where we put in,
395　Below Buthrotum on the height.
　　　　　　　　　　　　　　And here
An unbelievable story reached our ears:
That Helenus, the son of Priam, now
Ruled over cities of the Greeks, as heir
400　To Pyrrhus' wife and power; Andromachë
Had found again a husband of her nation.
It made me stare, and in my heart I burned
With measureless desire to speak to him,
To learn of that strange turn of life. So upward
405　Inland I went, leaving the port and ships.
And, as it happened, at that hour she,
Andromachë, in a grove outside the city
Beside a brook, thin replica of Simoïs,
Was making from a ceremonial meal
410　Her offerings and libation to the dust,
Calling the great shade at a tomb called Hector's
Made by her—an empty mound of turf
Where she had blessed twin altars for her tears.
But when she saw me coming, saw the men
415　Around me in Trojan arms, her mind misgave,
And, gazing at this ghostliness in terror,
She stood there pale and rigid, till the warmth
Ebbed from her and she swooned. And it was long
Before she spoke, or barely spoke:
420　　　　　　　　　　　　　　'Your face,
Can it be real? And you real, messenger,
Coming before me? Goddess-born? Alive?
Or if sweet daylight left your eyes forever,
Where is my Hector?'
425　　　　　　　　　　Then she wept and filled
The grove with wailing. I had difficulty

Forcing a few words out amid her passion,
So overcome I felt, but murmured to her:

'Alive, oh yes; through every mortal danger
430 This world holds, I carry on my life.
Be sure that what you see is real.
                              Ah, tell me,
Since you were so bereft of such a husband,
What change has come to your relief?
435 What fortune worthy of the wife of Hector,
Andromachë? Then Pyrrhus' wife and slave?'

She bent her head, with eyes downcast, and whispered:

'Happiest of us all was Priam's daughter,
The virgin picked to die at the great tomb,
440 Below Troy wall, of our dead enemy.
She never had to bear the slave's allotment,
Never laid hands on a lord and master's bed.
But when our native city burned, we others
Were shipped out through far seas. I bore the pride
445 And insolence of Achilles' warrior son,
Being brought to bed, in slavery, of his child.
He turned then to a bride in Lacedaemon,
Leda's daughter, Hermionë. He made me
Over to Helenus, to another slave.
450 But now Pyrrhus is dead. Orestes, hot
With lust for her whom he thought stolen from him,
And maddened by the Furies for spilt blood,
Caught Pyrrhus unprepared and cut him down
Before his father's altar.
                              By that death
455 Part of the kingdom passed to Helenus.
He called the plains Chaonian, the realm
Itself Chaonia—from the Trojan Chaon—
And built a Pergamum, a citadel,
460 Called Ilium's, on this ridge. As to yourself,
What winds of destiny gave you this voyage?
Which of the gods impelled you, all unknowing,

Here to our coast? What of your child, Ascanius?
Alive still, nourished still by the world's air?
465   Even at Troy, one thought . .

                    But does the boy
Remember her, the mother who was lost?
And do his father and his uncle Hector
Stir him to old-time valor and manliness?'

470   So she poured out her questions, all in tears,
Her long and vain lament, when the great soldier
And son of Priam, Helenus, approached
From the townside, with many in his train.
In his great joy at knowing us for kindred
475   He led us then to the city gate, by turns
Weeping and speaking. Walking along with him
I saw before me Troy in miniature,
A slender copy of our massive tower,
A dry brooklet named Xanthus . . . and I pressed
480   My body against a Scaean Gate. Those with me
Feasted their eyes on this, our kinsmen's town.
In spacious colonnades the king received them,
And offering mid-court their cups of wine
They made libation, while on plates of gold
485   A feast was brought before them.

                  That day passed,
And other days. Then sailing weather came
When canvas bellied out, filled by a southwind.
Now I put questions to the seer. I said:

490   'Trojan interpreter of the gods' will,
You know the mind of Phoebus, know his tripod,
Know the Apolline laurel; know the stars,
The tongues of birds, and all the signs of birdflight.
Prophesy for me! As you know, the powers
495   Favored me with directions for my sailing:
All the divine speech from the shrines agreed
I must find Italy, must pioneer
In those far lands. The Harpy called Celaeno

Riddled the only strange and evil sign:
500 Of pallid famine, and the wrath of heaven.
What dangers must I steer away from first?
How set my course to conquer that distress?'

Helenus cut down bullocks at his altar
With ceremony, begged the gods for peace,
505 Unbound the sacred ribbons from his head,
And took me by the hand, leading me in
A-tingle at the overshadowing power—
O Phoebus! in thy shrine;
Then with oracular voice the priest addressed me:

510 'Born of the goddess, highest auspices
Are clearly to be seen for your sea faring,
The Lord God deals out destiny so
And turns the wheel of change; so turns the world.
A few things, out of many, shall I tell you,
515 So you may cross the welcoming seas
More safely, to find harbor in Ausonia;
Other details of time to come the Parcae
Keep from Helenus, and Saturn's daughter,
Juno, will not allow him speech of these.

520 That Italy you think so near, with ports
You think to enter, ignorant as you are,
Lies far, past far lands, by untraveled ways.
You are to make the oar bend off Trinacria,
To pass Ausonian water, lakes of the underworld,
525 The island home of Circe the Aeaean,
Before your walls can rise in a safe country.
Here are signs for you to keep in mind:
When in anxiety by a stream apart
Beneath shore oaks you find a giant sow,
530 Snow-white, reclining there, suckling a litter
Of thirty snow-white young: that place will be
Your haven after toil, site of your town.
And have no fear of table-biting times;

Lines 365–394

The fates will find a way for you; Apollo
535   Will be at hand when called.
                            But now avoid
The shoreline to the west, a part of Italy
Lapped by the tide of our own sea: the towns
Are all inhabited by evil Greeks.
540   Here the Locrians founded a colony
And Lyctian Idomeneus with soldiers
Took the Sallentine Plain; here is that town
Of Philoctetes, captain of Meliboea,
Little Petelia, buttressed by her wall.
545   Another thing: when you have crossed and moored
Your ships ashore, there to put up your altars
For offerings, veil your head in a red robe
Against intrusions on your holy fires,
Omen-unsettling sights amid your prayers.
550   You and your company retain this ritual
Veiling in the future, let your progeny
Hold to religious purity thereby.
Now then: at sea again, as the wind takes you
Toward the Sicilian shore, and headlands northward
555   Dwindle up the Narrows of Pelorus,
Steer for the coast to port, the seas to port,
A long sail round, away from shores to starboard.
These land-masses in the past, they say,
Though one unbroken mainland long ago,
560   In cataclysm leaped apart: a change
That the long ages of the past could bring—
The sea rushed in between, to cut away
Hesperia's flank from Sicily, and washed
With narrow tide the sundered shores and towns.
565   Now Scylla haunts the starboard side, Charybdis,
Never appeased, the side to port—and deep
In her whirlpool gulps down the great sea waves
Three times a day and spews them up again,
Sending the whiplash of her spray to heaven.
570   Scylla lies immured in a rocky cave
In clefts of inky darkness, darting out

Lines 395–425

Her faces, pulling ships on to the reef.
First she looks human—a fair-breasted girl
Down to the groin; but then, below, a monster
575 Creature of the sea, a wolvish belly
Merging in dolphins' tails. Better to round
The seamark of Pachynus, and stand out
To sea, taking the long route west, than sight
Weird Scylla in her overhanging gloom
580 And froth of rocks where sea-green hounds give tongue.
Further, if Helenus can look ahead,
If you can trust a seer, and if Apollo
Fills his mind with truth, I have one thing
To tell you, over and over again, one thing
585 To warn you of, son of the goddess: make
Your prayer first of all to Juno's godhead,
Chant with a will your vows to her: secure
With humble gifts the power of that lady,
So in the end in triumph, with Trinacria
590 Left behind, you will be sent to Italy.
Ashore there, when you reach the town of Cumae,
Avernus' murmuring forests, haunted lakes,
You'll see a spellbound prophetess, who sings
In her deep cave of destinies, confiding
595 Symbols and words to leaves. Whatever verse
She writes, the virgin puts each leaf in order
Back in the cave; unshuffled they remain;
But when a faint breeze through a door ajar
Comes in to stir and scatter the light leaves,
600 She never cares to catch them as they flutter
Or to restore them, or to join the verses;
Visitors, unenlightened, turn away
And hate the Sibyl's shrine.
                                              But here no thought
605 Of time spent in delay should count with you—
Though crews reproach you, though the course you set
Call seaward now, and you can fill your sails
With wind in the right quarter, even so
Pray to the prophetess that she herself

Lines 425–456

610 Consent to utter and chant her oracles.
She will inform you of the Italian tribes,
The wars to come, the way you should avoid
Each difficulty, or face it. Do her reverence
And she will bring you through, by sea and land.
615 These are the matters I may warn you of.
Go, and exalt the might of Troy in action.'

When he had said all this in friendliness,
The seer commanded gifts of heavy gold
And carven ivory brought to the ships.
620 He stowed masses of silver between decks
With cauldrons of Dodona, then a cuirass
Woven of chain mail triply laced with gold,
And a magnificent helm plumed at the peak,
The arms of Neoptolemus. Special gifts
625 Went to my father. Then he added horses,
Pilots, too, and oarsmen as required,
And fitted out my fighting men with arms.
Meanwhile Anchises ordered sails unhoused
To catch a favoring wind without delay.
630 Now the diviner of Apollo, bowing
In august deference, said to him:

                                    'Anchises,
Chosen by Venus for the pride of marriage,
Cared for by heaven, brought to safety twice
635 From ruined Pergamum: look toward your land,
Ausonia; make sail for it and take it.
And yet this shoreline you must skirt by sea;
The sector of Ausonia meant by Apollo
Lies far away. Embark now, fortunate
640 In the devotion of your son. Should I
Detain you by more talk while the winds rise?'

Andromachë, too, sad at this last farewell,
Brought out embroidered robes, and cloth of gold,
645 And for Ascanius a Phrygian mantle.
Not to be outdone in courtesy,
She gave armfuls of woven gifts, and said:

Lines 456–485

'Take these things, too, and may they be remembrances
Of my hands, child, and token of my love,
The long love of Andromachë, Hector's dearest.
650   Final gifts of your own people: take them,
You that alone remind me of Astyanax.
His eyes, his hands, his look—all were like yours.
He would be your age, growing up like you.'

I said farewell. and tears came as I spoke:

655   'Be happy, friends; your fortune is achieved,
While one fate beckons us and then another.
Here is your quiet rest: no sea to plow,
No quest for dim lands of Ausonia
Receding ever. Here before your eyes
660   Are replicas of Xanthus and of Troy
Your own hands built—with better auspices,
I pray, and less a challenge to the Greeks.
If one day I shall enter Tiber stream
And Tiber fields and see the walls my people
665   Have in store for them, then of these kindred
Cities, neighboring nations, in Epirus
And in Hesperia, both looking back
To Dardanus as founder, both to one
Sad history, we shall make a single Troy
670   In spirit: may this task await our heirs.'

We set sail for Ceraunia nearby
To cross from there, the short sea-route to Italy.
The sun went west, the hills grew dark. Then down
We threw ourselves upon the welcome land,
675   Assigned the oars for next day, scattered all
Along the dry beach to take food and rest,
And sleep came soft as dew on tired men.

Lines 486–511

Now Night drawn by the Hours had not yet reached
The midpoint of her course when Palinurus
680 Turned out briskly. Studying the winds,
He cupped his ears to catch movements of air;
Observed the slowly wheeling constellations
In the still heaven: bright Arcturus, rainy
Hyades, Great Bear and Little Bear,
685 Orion in his belt of gold. All clear
In cloudless air he made them out to be,
Then gave a trumpet signal from the stern.
So we broke camp, put out to sea, unfurled
Our wings of sails. The stars had vanished, Dawn
690 Was reddening the sky, when far ahead
We saw the blue hills and low-lying plain
Of Italy. Anchises shouted 'Italy!'
And all the men cried 'Italy!' in joy.
My father garlanded a great wine bowl,
695 Filled it with wine, stood on the stern aloft,
And called to the gods:

     'Lords of the land and sea,
Storm powers, ease our way with a stern wind,
Steadily blow for us!'

700   Then as desired
The light airs freshened, and an opening bay
Appeared as we drew in, backed by a temple
Upon an acropolis of Minerva.
The sailors took in sail and rowed for shore.
705 The harbor there, bent like a bow, recoils
From seas out of the East: long rocky spits
Make foaming surf; the port lies hid behind.
Two crags like towers put out arms like walls;
The temple stands back inland.

710   Here I saw
Our first portent: in grassland, horses, four,
As white as snow, at graze in an open field.

'You bring us war, host land,' murmured my father,
'It is for war that horses are caparisoned.
715 These herds mean war for us. Yet the same beasts

Are sometimes trained to take the chariot pole
In harmony, to bear the yoke and bit.
There is, then, hope of peace.'
                                    And there we prayed
720 To the tall Pallas, goddess of clanging arms,
First to receive us on that festal beach;
Then veiled our heads in Phrygian drapery
Before the altars, where by Helenus'
Particular command we made burnt offerings
725 In proper form to Juno of the Argives.
That ritual once complete, we would not stay,
But swung our yardarms and our sails to take us
Out to sea again, leaving behind
Greek territory, treacherous in our eyes.
730 Soon then we saw Tarentum's gulf, or Hercules'
If the old tale be true. There, dead ahead,
Rose the Lacinian goddess on her height.
Then Caulon's towers and Scylaceum,
The coast of shipwreck. On the distant sky
735 Trinacrian Aetna could be seen, and soon
We heard big seas groaning on beaten rocks
And voices of the breakers. Shoals leaped up
Before our eyes, with sand in the sea-swell,
At which my father Anchises cried:
740   'No doubt of it!
Here is Charybdis, that abyss, and those
Perilous points of rock that Helenus
Foretold, with deadly ledges undersea.
Sheer off, men, put your backs into the stroke!'

745 They bent hard to the rowing as commanded,
And Palinurus in the leading ship
Swung his creaking prow over to port.
The whole flotilla followed him in turn
With oars and wind. On every rolling sea
750 We rose to heaven, and in the abysmal trough
Sank down into the world of shades. Three times
The rock cliffs between caverns boomed; three times
We saw the wave shock and the flung spume

Drenching the very stars. The wind at last
755   And sun went down together, leaving us spent,
And in the dark as to our course, we glided
Quietly onward to the Cyclops' shore.

Here was a mighty harbor, in itself
Landlocked and calm, out of the wind's way,
760   But Aetna, just beyond, rumbled and flashed,
Formidable in eruption. Up the sky
She sent a somber cloud of billowing smoke,
A pitch-black turbine full of glowing ash
And balls of fire to lick the stars. Below,
765   She vomited rocks and brought up lava streams,
Entrails of Aetna, boiling in the deep.
The tale goes that the body of Enceladus,
Half consumed by thunderbolt, lies prone
Under that weight, prodigious Aetna piled
770   Above him, jetting flame from broken furnaces,
And when the worn-out giant turns, all Sicily
Rumbles and quakes and weaves a pall of smoke
Against the sky. Under the forest roof
That night we suffered monstrous fears: we could not
775   See what made the din; there were no stars
Or starlight overhead, only the cloud
Obscuring heaven, and the depth of night
Withheld the moon, enwrapt in stormy mist.
At long last rose the morning star; we felt
780   Day's onset as Aurora thinned away
The vapor of the night. Then suddenly
Out of the forest, at the last extremity
Of hunger, came the strange shape of a man,
In pitiful condition, his arms wide
785   To beg for mercy. We took in the sight:
His filth, his uncut beard, his ragged shirt
Pinned up by thorns—but even so, a Greek,

And one sent on an earlier day to Troy
With Greek equipment. Seeing at a distance
790   Dardan clothing, Trojan arms, he cringed
And stopped a while in fear of what he saw,
Then stumbled onward to the shore headlong
With tears and prayers.

                  'In heaven's name,' he said,
795   'By all the powers, I beg you—
Oh, by the light and air we breathe! Take me
With you, Trojans! Anywhere at all
Will be good enough for me. I am, I know it,
One of the Danaans, one from the fleet;
800   I won't deny I fought to take Troy's gods.
For that, if so much harm came of our devilry,
Cut me to bits, scatter me on the water,
Drop me in the sea. If I must die,
Death at the hands of men will be a favor!'

805   With this he took our knees and groveled, kneeling,
Clinging there. We told him to speak out,
Say who he was, born of what blood, what fortune
Put him in such a panic; and my father
After a moment gave the man his hand
810   To calm him by that touch and sign of mercy.
In the end he put aside his fear and said:

'I am an Ithacan, of Ulysses' company—
That man beset by trouble. Achaemenidës
I'm called. My father, Adamastus, lived
815   In poverty, so I shipped out for Troy.
Would god our life of poverty had lasted!
My shipmates left me here, they all forgot me,
Scrambling to get away from the cave mouth
And frightfulness in the cavern of the Cyclops
820   That is a blood-soaked hall of brutal feasts,
All gloom inside, and huge. The giant rears
His head against the stars. Oh heaven, spare earth
A scourge like this—unbearable to see,
Unreachable by anything you say.

825   The innards and the dark blood of poor fellows
    Are what he feeds on: I myself looked on
    When he scooped up two crewmen in his hand
    Mid-cave, and as he lay back smashed them down
    Against the rockface, making the whole floor
830   Swim with spattered blood; I saw him crunch
    Those dead men running blood and excrement,
    The warm flesh still a-quiver in his teeth.
    Not that he did not suffer for the act!
    Not that Ulysses put up with that outrage
835   Or lost his self-possession in the pinch.
    Gorged with feasting and dead-drunk with wine,
    The giant put down his lolling head, lay down
    Enormous on the cave floor. In his sleep
    He dribbled bile and bits of flesh, mixed up
840   With blood and wine. We prayed to the great gods,
    Drew lots for duties, and surrounded him,
    Then with a pointed beam bored his great eye,
    His single eye, under his shaggy brow,
    Big as a Greek shield or the lamp o' Phoebus.
845   So we got back at him—some cause for pride,
    Avenging our friends' shades.
                      As for yourselves,
    Put out to sea, put out to sea, poor fellows;
    Break your hawsers! Tall and dangerous
850   As Polyphemus, penning and milking sheep
    In his rock cave, there are a hundred more
    Unspeakable huge Cyclops everywhere
    At large along these bays and mountain-sides.
    And now three times the long-horned moon has filled
855   With a new glow since I've dragged out my days
    In woods, among the wild things' lonely dens,
    And from a peak spied on the Cyclops there,
    My heart a-tremble at their great footfalls,
    Their shouts. Thin fare I've had, such as the boughs
860   Would yield me: berries, cornel fruit, all stones,
    With roots and grasses. As I looked out seaward
    These were the first ships that I saw put in.

Whatever ships they might turn out to be,
I handed myself over. Boon enough
865 Just to escape these unholy savages.
Better you take this life, by any form
Of death you choose.'

                He had no sooner spoken
Than we all saw, high on the mountainside,
870 The shepherd Polyphemus' giant mass
In motion with his flocks, advancing shoreward.
Vast, mind-sickening, lumpish, heaven's light
Blacked out for him, he held a pine tree staff
To feel his way with, and the woolly sheep
875 Were all his company and all the ease
Or comfort that he had.
On reaching the seashore and the deep water
He washed the fluid from his gouged eye-pit
And gnashed his teeth and groaned, then waded out
880 To the middle depth where still the swell came short
Of dampening his haunches. We made haste
To get away, and far, taking aboard
The suppliant for his pains: in dead silence
We cut our hawsers, launched, and put our backs
885 Into a racing stroke. He heard the splash
And turned back toward it—but he never got
The range of us to reach us, could not breast
The full Ionian sea, wading behind.
At this he sent up an unearthly roar
890 At which the waves on the deep sea were shaken,
Italy was affrighted far inland,
And Aetna's caverns rumbled. Out of the forest,
Out of the mountains, poured the Cyclops tribe
To crowd the bay and shoreline: we could see them
895 Standing there, each with his awful eye
In impotent rage, the brotherhood of Aetna,
Towering heavenward, terrifying peers,
Erect with heads as high as oaks in air
Or evergreen cypresses—great trees of Jove
900 Or those in sacred parklands of Diana.

Lines 652–681

Stung to impetuous action by our fear,
We hoisted sail to a fair wind, paid out sheets
To get searoom, no matter on what course.
But Helenus' commands, his warning stood:
905 No steering between Scylla and Charybdis,
That channel so near death on either side.
Resolved to go about, to take in sail,
We felt—lo and behold—the wind veer northward
Blowing down from the Narrows of Pelorus.
910 We sailed then past Pantagia's river mouth,
Megara Bay, and Thapsus, that low islet—
Coastal places Achaemenidës,
Hard-pressed Ulysses' shipmate, pointed out
As he retraced his wanderings.
915   There's an island
Lying this side of a Sicilian bay,
Facing Plemyrium Point where the waves beat.
Early people called this isle Ortygia.
The tale runs that the Elean stream, Alpheus,
920 Took hidden channels there, under the sea,
And through your fountain, Arethusa, now
Infuses the salt waves. There, as directed,
We worshipped the pure powers of the place,
Then sailed on past Helorus' rich plowlands
925 And ponds. We coasted high crags of Pachynus
With rocky tongues of land, and far away
Shone Camerina, never to be disturbed,
Then the Geloan Plain, Gela itself,
Named for a torrent; then beetling Acragas,
930 Breeder of mettlesome horses in the past,
Displayed her distant massive walls, and helped
By winds I put Selinus of the Palms
Behind us, to sail close to the shoal water
Of Lilybaeum with her hidden reefs.
935 And in the end the port of Drepanum
Took me in, a landing without joy.

Lines 682–708

For after storms at sea had buffeted me
So often, here, alas, I lost my father,
Solace in all affliction and mischance;
940 O best of fathers, in my weariness—
Though you had been delivered from so many
Perils in vain—alas, here you forsook me.
Never had Helenus the seer, who warned
Of many things to make me quail, foretold
945 This grief to me—nor had the vile Celaeno.
Here was my final sorrow, here the goal
Of all my seafaring. When after this
I put to sea, god drove me to your shores."
So in his tale before the attentive crowd
950 Aeneas' single voice recalled the fates
Decreed by heaven, and his wanderings.
He fell silent at last and made an end.

Lines 708–718

BOOK

IV

THE PASSION OF THE QUEEN

The queen, for her part, all that evening ached
With longing that her heart's blood fed, a wound
Or inward fire eating her away.
The manhood of the man, his pride of birth,
5   Came home to her time and again; his looks,
His words remained with her to haunt her mind,
And desire for him gave her no rest.

                                    When Dawn
Swept earth with Phoebus' torch and burned away
10 Night-gloom and damp, this queen, far gone and ill,
Confided to the sister of her heart:
"My sister Anna, quandaries and dreams
Have come to frighten me—such dreams!

                                    Think what a stranger
15 Yesterday found lodging in our house:
How princely, how courageous, what a soldier.
I can believe him in the line of gods,
And this is no delusion. Tell-tale fear
Betrays inferior souls. What scenes of war
20 Fought to the bitter end he pictured for us!
What buffetings awaited him at sea!
Had I not set my face against remarriage
After my first love died and failed me, left me
Barren and bereaved—and sick to death
25 At the mere thought of torch and bridal bed—

I could perhaps give way in this one case
To frailty. I shall say it: since that time
Sychaeus, my poor husband, met his fate,
And blood my brother shed stained our hearth gods,
30   This man alone has wrought upon me so
And moved my soul to yield. I recognize
The signs of the old flame, of old desire.
But O chaste life, before I break your laws,
I pray that Earth may open, gape for me
35   Down to its depth, or the omnipotent
With one stroke blast me to the shades, pale shades
Of Erebus and the deep world of night!
That man who took me to himself in youth
Has taken all my love; may that man keep it,
40   Hold it forever with him in the tomb."

At this she wept and wet her breast with tears.
But Anna answered:
               "Dearer to your sister
Than daylight is, will you wear out your life,
45   Young as you are, in solitary mourning,
Never to know sweet children, or the crown
Of joy that Venus brings? Do you believe
This matters to the dust, to ghosts in tombs?
Granted no suitors up to now have moved you,
50   Neither in Libya nor before, in Tyre—
Iarbas you rejected, and the others,
Chieftains bred by the land of Africa
Their triumphs have enriched—will you contend
Even against a welcome love? Have you
55   Considered in whose lands you settled here?
On one frontier the Gaetulans, their cities,
People invincible in war—with wild
Numidian horsemen, and the offshore banks,
The Syrtës; on the other, desert sands,
60   Bone-dry, where fierce Barcaean nomads range.
Or need I speak of future wars brought on
From Tyre, and the menace of your brother?
Surely by dispensation of the gods

And backed by Juno's will, the ships from Ilium
65   Held their course this way on the wind.
                                        Sister,
What a great city you'll see rising here,
And what a kingdom, from this royal match!
With Trojan soldiers as companions in arms
70   By what exploits will Punic glory grow!
Only ask the indulgence of the gods,
Win them with offerings, give your guests ease,
And contrive reasons for delay, while winter
Gales rage, drenched Orion storms at sea,
75   And their ships, damaged still, face iron skies."

This counsel fanned the flame, already kindled,
Giving her hesitant sister hope, and set her
Free of scruple. Visiting the shrines
They begged for grace at every altar first,
80   Then put choice rams and ewes to ritual death
For Ceres Giver of Laws, Father Lyaeus,
Phoebus, and for Juno most of all
Who has the bonds of marriage in her keeping.
Dido herself, splendidly beautiful,
85   Holding a shallow cup, tips out the wine
On a white shining heifer, between the horns,
Or gravely in the shadow of the gods
Approaches opulent altars. Through the day
She brings new gifts, and when the breasts are opened
90   Pores over organs, living still, for signs.
Alas, what darkened minds have soothsayers!
What good are shrines and vows to maddened lovers?
The inward fire eats the soft marrow away,
And the internal wound bleeds on in silence.

95   Unlucky Dido, burning, in her madness
Roamed through all the city, like a doe

Hit by an arrow shot from far away
By a shepherd hunting in the Cretan woods—
Hit by surprise, nor could the hunter see
His flying steel had fixed itself in her;
But though she runs for life through copse and glade
The fatal shaft clings to her side.

                       Now Dido
Took Aeneas with her among her buildings,
Showed her Sidonian wealth, her walls prepared,
And tried to speak, but in mid-speech grew still.
When the day waned she wanted to repeat
The banquet as before, to hear once more
In her wild need the throes of Ilium,
And once more hung on the narrator's words.
Afterward, when all the guests were gone,
And the dim moon in turn had quenched her light,
And setting stars weighed weariness to sleep,
Alone she mourned in the great empty hall
And pressed her body on the couch he left:
She heard him still, though absent—heard and saw him.
Or she would hold Ascanius in her lap,
Enthralled by him, the image of his father,
As though by this ruse to appease a love
Beyond all telling.

                     Towers, half-built, rose
No farther; men no longer trained in arms
Or toiled to make harbors and battlements
Impregnable. Projects were broken off,
Laid over, and the menacing huge walls
With cranes unmoving stood against the sky.

As soon as Jove's dear consort saw the lady
Prey to such illness, and her reputation
Standing no longer in the way of passion,
Saturn's daughter said to Venus:

                     "Wondrous!
Covered yourself with glory, have you not,
You and your boy, and won such prizes, too.
Divine power is something to remember

135   If by collusion of two gods one mortal
Woman is brought low.

                    I am not blind.
Your fear of our new walls has not escaped me,
Fear and mistrust of Carthage at her height.

140   But how far will it go? What do you hope for,
Being so contentious? Why do we not
Arrange eternal peace and formal marriage?
You have your heart's desire: Dido in love,
Dido consumed with passion to her core.

145   Why not, then, rule this people side by side
With equal authority? And let the queen
Wait on her Phrygian lord, let her consign
Into your hand her Tyrians as a dowry."

Now Venus knew this talk was all pretence,

150   All to divert the future power from Italy
To Libya; and she answered:

                    "Who would be
So mad, so foolish as to shun that prospect
Or prefer war with you? That is, provided

155   Fortune is on the side of your proposal.
The fates here are perplexing: would one city
Satisfy Jupiter's will for Tyrians
And Trojan exiles? Does he approve
A union and a mingling of these races?

160   You are his consort: you have every right
To sound him out. Go on, and I'll come, too."

But regal Juno pointedly replied:
"That task will rest with me. Just now, as to
The need of the moment and the way to meet it,

165   Listen, and I'll explain in a few words.
Aeneas and Dido in her misery
Plan hunting in the forest, when the Titan

Sun comes up with rays to light the world.
While beaters in excitement ring the glens
170 My gift will be a black raincloud, and hail,
A downpour, and I'll shake heaven with thunder.
The company will scatter, lost in gloom,
As Dido and the Trojan captain come
To one same cavern. I shall be on hand,
175 And if I can be certain you are willing,
There I shall marry them and call her his.
A wedding, this will be."
                              Then Cytherëa,
Not disinclined, nodded to Juno's plea,
180 And smiled at the stratagem now given away.

Dawn came up meanwhile from the Ocean stream,
And in the early sunshine from the gates
Picked huntsmen issued: wide-meshed nets and snares,
Broad spearheads for big game, Massylian horsemen
185 Trooping with hounds in packs keen on the scent.
But Dido lingered in her hall, as Punic
Nobles waited, and her mettlesome hunter
Stood nearby, cavorting in gold and scarlet,
Champing his foam-flecked bridle. At long last
190 The queen appeared with courtiers in a crowd,
A short Sidonian cloak edged in embroidery
Caught about her, at her back a quiver
Sheathed in gold, her hair tied up in gold,
And a brooch of gold pinning her scarlet dress.
195 Phrygians came in her company as well,
And Iulus, joyous at the scene. Resplendent
Above the rest, Aeneas walked to meet her,
To join his retinue with hers. He seemed—
Think of the lord Apollo in the spring
200 When he leaves wintering in Lycia
By Xanthus torrent, for his mother's isle
Of Delos, to renew the festival;
Around his altars Cretans, Dryopës,
And painted Agathyrsans raise a shout,

Lines 119–146

205 But the god walks the Cynthian ridge alone
And smooths his hair, binds it in fronded laurel,
Braids it in gold; and shafts ring on his shoulders.
So elated and swift, Aeneas walked
With sunlit grace upon him.
210   Soon the hunters,
Riding in company to high pathless hills,
Saw mountain goats shoot down from a rocky peak
And scamper on the ridges; toward the plain
Deer left the slopes, herding in clouds of dust
215 In flight across the open lands. Alone,
The boy Ascanius, delightedly riding
His eager horse amid the lowland vales,
Outran both goats and deer. Could he only meet
Amid the harmless game some foaming boar,
220 Or a tawny lion down from the mountainside!

Meanwhile in heaven began a rolling thunder,
And soon the storm broke, pouring rain and hail.
Then Tyrians and Trojans in alarm—
With Venus' Dardan grandson—ran for cover
225 Here and there in the wilderness, as freshets
Coursed from the high hills.
                   Now to the self-same cave
Came Dido and the captain of the Trojans.
Primal Earth herself and Nuptial Juno
230 Opened the ritual, torches of lightning blazed,
High Heaven became witness to the marriage,
And nymphs cried out wild hymns from a mountain top.
That day was the first cause of death, and first
Of sorrow. Dido had no further qualms
235 As to impressions given and set abroad;
She thought no longer of a secret love
But called it marriage. Thus, under that name,
She hid her fault.
                 Now in no time at all
240 Through all the African cities Rumor goes—
Nimble as quicksilver among evils. Rumor

Lines 147–174

Thrives on motion, stronger for the running,
Lowly at first through fear, then rearing high,
She treads the land and hides her head in cloud.
245 As people fable it, the Earth, her mother,
Furious against the gods, bore a late sister
To the giants Coeus and Enceladus,
Giving her speed on foot and on the wing:
Monstrous, deformed, titanic. Pinioned, with
250 An eye beneath for every body feather,
And, strange to say, as many tongues and buzzing
Mouths as eyes, as many pricked-up ears,
By night she flies between the earth and heaven
Shrieking through darkness, and she never turns
255 Her eye-lids down to sleep. By day she broods,
On the alert, on rooftops or on towers,
Bringing great cities fear, harping on lies
And slander evenhandedly with truth.
In those days Rumor took an evil joy
260 At filling countrysides with whispers, whispers,
Gossip of what was done, and never done:
How this Aeneas landed, Trojan born,
How Dido in her beauty graced his company,
Then how they reveled all the winter long
265 Unmindful of the realm, prisoners of lust.

These tales the scabrous goddess put about
On men's lips everywhere. Her twisting course
Took her to King Iarbas, whom she set
Ablaze with anger piled on top of anger.
270 Son of Jupiter Hammon by a nymph,
A ravished Garamantean, this prince
Had built the god a hundred giant shrines,
A hundred altars, each with holy fires
Alight by night and day, sentries on watch,
275 The ground enriched by victims' blood, the doors
Festooned with flowering wreaths. Before his altars
King Iarbas, crazed by the raw story,
Stood, they say, amid the Presences,
With supplicating hands, pouring out prayer:

280 "All powerful Jove, to whom the feasting Moors
    At ease on colored couches tip their wine,
    Do you see this? Are we then fools to fear you
    Throwing down your bolts? Those dazzling fires
    Of lightning, are they aimless in the clouds
285 And rumbling thunder meaningless? This woman
    Who turned up in our country and laid down
    A tiny city at a price, to whom
    I gave a beach to plow—and on my terms—
    After refusing to marry me has taken
290 Aeneas to be master in her realm.
    And now Sir Paris with his men, half-men,
    His chin and perfumed hair tied up
    In a Maeonian bonnet, takes possession.
    As for ourselves, here we are bringing gifts
295 Into these shrines—supposedly your shrines—
    Hugging that empty fable."

                        Pleas like this
    From the man clinging to his altars reached
    The ears of the Almighty. Now he turned
300 His eyes upon the queen's town and the lovers
    Careless of their good name; then spoke to Mercury,
    Assigning him a mission:
                   "Son, bestir yourself,
    Call up the Zephyrs, take to your wings and glide.
305 Approach the Dardan captain where he tarries
    Rapt in Tyrian Carthage, losing sight
    Of future towns the fates ordain. Correct him,
    Carry my speech to him on the running winds:
    No son like this did his enchanting mother
310 Promise to us, nor such did she deliver
    Twice from peril at the hands of Greeks.
    He was to be the ruler of Italy,
    Potential empire, armorer of war;
    To father men from Teucer's noble blood
315 And bring the whole world under law's dominion.
    If glories to be won by deeds like these
    Cannot arouse him, if he will not strive
    For his own honor, does he begrudge his son.

Ascanius, the high strongholds of Rome?
320 What has he in mind? What hope, to make him stay
Amid a hostile race, and lose from view
Ausonian progeny, Lavinian lands?
The man should sail: that is the whole point.
Let this be what you tell him, as from me."

325 He finished and fell silent. Mercury
Made ready to obey the great command
Of his great father, and he first tied on
The golden sandals, winged, that high in air
Transport him over seas or over land
330 Abreast of gale winds; then he took the wand
With which he summons pale souls out of Orcus
And ushers others to the undergloom,
Lulls men to slumber or awakens them,
And opens dead men's eyes. This wand in hand,
335 He can drive winds before him, swimming down
Along the stormcloud. Now aloft, he saw
The craggy flanks and crown of patient Atlas,
Giant Atlas, balancing the sky
Upon his peak—his pine-forested head
340 In vapor cowled, beaten by wind and rain.
Snow lay upon his shoulders, rills cascaded
Down his ancient chin and beard a-bristle,
Caked with ice. Here Mercury of Cyllenë
Hovered first on even wings, then down
345 He plummeted to sea-level and flew on
Like a low-flying gull that skims the shallows
And rocky coasts where fish ply close inshore.
So, like a gull between the earth and sky,
The progeny of Cyllenë, on the wing
350 From his maternal grandsire, split the winds
To the sand bars of Libya.
                                        Alighting tiptoe
On the first hutments, there he found Aeneas
Laying foundations for new towers and homes.
355 He noted well the swordhilt the man wore,
Adorned with yellow jasper; and the cloak

Aglow with Tyrian dye upon his shoulders—
Gifts of the wealthy queen, who had inwoven
Gold thread in the fabric. Mercury
360 Took him to task at once:

                "Is it for you
To lay the stones for Carthage's high walls,
Tame husband that you are, and build their city?
Oblivious of your own world, your own kingdom!
365 From bright Olympus he that rules the gods
And turns the earth and heaven by his power—
He and no other sent me to you, told me
To bring this message on the running winds:
What have you in mind? What hope, wasting your days
370 In Libya? If future history's glories
Do not affect you, if you will not strive
For your own honor, think of Ascanius,
Think of the expectations of your heir,
Iulus, to whom the Italian realm, the land
375 Of Rome, are due."

                And Mercury, as he spoke,
Departed from the visual field of mortals
To a great distance, ebbed in subtle air.
Amazed, and shocked to the bottom of his soul
380 By what his eyes had seen, Aeneas felt
His hackles rise, his voice choke in his throat.
As the sharp admonition and command
From heaven had shaken him awake, he now
Burned only to be gone, to leave that land
385 Of the sweet life behind. What can he do? How tell
The impassioned queen and hope to win her over?
What opening shall he choose? This way and that
He let his mind dart, testing alternatives,
Running through every one. And as he pondered
390 This seemed the better tactic: he called in
Mnestheus, Sergestus and stalwart Serestus,
Telling them:

              "Get the fleet ready for sea,
But quietly, and collect the men on shore.
395 Lay in ship stores and gear."

As to the cause
For a change of plan, they were to keep it secret,
Seeing the excellent Dido had no notion,
No warning that such love could be cut short;
400 He would himself look for the right occasion,
The easiest time to speak, the way to do it.
The Trojans to a man gladly obeyed.

The queen, for her part, felt some plot afoot
Quite soon—for who deceives a woman in love?
405 She caught wind of a change, being in fear
Of what had seemed her safety. Evil Rumor,
Shameless as before, brought word to her
In her distracted state of ships being rigged
In trim for sailing. Furious, at her wits' end,
410 She traversed the whole city, all aflame
With rage, like a Bacchantë driven wild
By emblems shaken, when the mountain revels
Of the odd year possess her, when the cry
Of Bacchus rises and Cithaeron calls
415 All through the shouting night. Thus it turned out
She was the first to speak and charge Aeneas:

"You even hoped to keep me in the dark
As to this outrage, did you, two-faced man,
And slip away in silence? Can our love
420 Not hold you, can the pledge we gave not hold you,
Can Dido not, now sure to die in pain?
Even in winter weather must you toil
With ships, and fret to launch against high winds
For the open sea? Oh, heartless!
Tell me now,
425 If you were not in search of alien lands
And new strange homes, if ancient Troy remained,
Would ships put out for Troy on these big seas?
Do you go to get away from me? I beg you,
430 By these tears, by your own right hand, since I
Have left my wretched self nothing but that—
Yes, by the marriage that we entered on,

If ever I did well and you were grateful
Or found some sweetness in a gift from me,
435 Have pity now on a declining house!
Put this plan by, I beg you, if a prayer
Is not yet out of place.
Because of you, Libyans and nomad kings
Detest me, my own Tyrians are hostile;
440 Because of you, I lost my integrity
And that admired name by which alone
I made my way once toward the stars.
                                        To whom
Do you abandon me, a dying woman,
445 Guest that you are—the only name now left
From that of husband? Why do I live on?
Shall I, until my brother Pygmalion comes
To pull my walls down? Or the Gaetulan
Iarbas leads me captive? If at least
450 There were a child by you for me to care for,
A little one to play in my courtyard
And give me back Aeneas, in spite of all,
I should not feel so utterly defeated,
Utterly bereft."
455   She ended there.
The man by Jove's command held fast his eyes
And fought down the emotion in his heart.
At length he answered:
                        "As for myself, be sure
460 I never shall deny all you can say,
Your majesty, of what you meant to me.
Never will the memory of Elissa
Stale for me, while I can still remember
My own life, and the spirit rules my body.
465 As to the event, a few words. Do not think
I meant to be deceitful and slip away.
I never held the torches of a bridegroom,
Never entered upon the pact of marriage.
If Fate permitted me to spend my days
470 By my own lights, and make the best of things
According to my wishes, first of all

Lines 317–342

I should look after Troy and the loved relics
Left me of my people. Priam's great hall
Should stand again; I should have restored the tower
475   Of Pergamum for Trojans in defeat.
But now it is the rich Italian land
Apollo tells me I must make for: Italy,
Named by his oracles. There is my love;
There is my country. If, as a Phoenician,
480   You are so given to the charms of Carthage,
Libyan city that it is, then tell me,
Why begrudge the Teucrians new lands
For homesteads in Ausonia? Are we not
Entitled, too, to look for realms abroad?
485   Night never veils the earth in damp and darkness,
Fiery stars never ascend the east,
But in my dreams my father's troubled ghost
Admonishes and frightens me. Then, too,
Each night thoughts come of young Ascanius,
490   My dear boy wronged, defrauded of his kingdom,
Hesperian lands of destiny. And now
The gods' interpreter, sent by Jove himself—
I swear it by your head and mine—has brought
Commands down through the racing winds! I say
495   With my own eyes in full daylight I saw him
Entering the building! With my very ears
I drank his message in! So please, no more
Of these appeals that set us both afire.
I sail for Italy not of my own free will."

500   During all this she had been watching him
With face averted, looking him up and down
In silence, and she burst out raging now:

"No goddess was your mother. Dardanus
Was not the founder of your family.

Lines 342–365

505 Liar and cheat! Some rough Caucasian cliff
Begot you on flint. Hyrcanian tigresses
Tendered their teats to you. Why should I palter?
Why still hold back for more indignity?
Sigh, did he, while I wept? Or look at me?
510 Or yield a tear, or pity her who loved him?
What shall I say first, with so much to say?
The time is past when either supreme Juno
Or the Saturnian father viewed these things
With justice. Faith can never be secure.
515 I took the man in, thrown up on this coast
In dire need, and in my madness then
Contrived a place for him in my domain,
Rescued his lost fleet, saved his shipmates' lives.
Oh, I am swept away burning by furies!
520 Now the prophet Apollo, now his oracles,
Now the gods' interpreter, if you please,
Sent down by Jove himself, brings through the air
His formidable commands! What fit employment
For heaven's high powers! What anxieties
525 To plague serene immortals! I shall not
Detain you or dispute your story. Go,
Go after Italy on the sailing winds,
Look for your kingdom, cross the deepsea swell!
If divine justice counts for anything,
530 I hope and pray that on some grinding reef
Midway at sea you'll drink your punishment
And call and call on Dido's name!
From far away I shall come after you
With my black fires, and when cold death has parted
535 Body from soul I shall be everywhere
A shade to haunt you! You will pay for this,
Unconscionable! I shall hear! The news will reach me
Even among the lowest of the dead!"

At this abruptly she broke off and ran
540 In sickness from his sight and the light of day,
Leaving him at a loss, alarmed, and mute

Lines 366–390

With all he meant to say. The maids in waiting
Caught her as she swooned and carried her
To bed in her marble chamber.

545   Duty-bound,
Aeneas, though he struggled with desire
To calm and comfort her in all her pain,
To speak to her and turn her mind from grief,
And though he sighed his heart out, shaken still
550 With love of her, yet took the course heaven gave him
And went back to the fleet. Then with a will
The Teucrians fell to work and launched the ships
Along the whole shore: slick with tar each hull
Took to the water. Eager to get away,
555 The sailors brought oar-boughs out of the woods
With leaves still on, and oaken logs unhewn.
Now you could see them issuing from the town
To the water's edge in streams, as when, aware
Of winter, ants will pillage a mound of spelt
560 To store it in their granary; over fields
The black battalion moves, and through the grass
On a narrow trail they carry off the spoil;
Some put their shoulders to the enormous weight
Of a trundled grain, while some pull stragglers in
565 And castigate delay; their to-and-fro
Of labor makes the whole track come alive.
At that sight, what were your emotions, Dido?
Sighing how deeply, looking out and down
From your high tower on the seething shore
570 Where all the harbor filled before your eyes
With bustle and shouts! Unconscionable Love,
To what extremes will you not drive our hearts!
She now felt driven to weep again, again
To move him, if she could, by supplication,
575 Humbling her pride before her love—to leave
Nothing untried, not to die needlessly.

"Anna, you see the arc of waterfront
All in commotion: they come crowding in

Lines 390–417

From everywhere. Spread canvas calls for wind,
580 The happy crews have garlanded the sterns.
If I could brace myself for this great sorrow,
Sister, I can endure it, too. One favor,
Even so, you may perform for me.
Since that deserter chose you for his friend
585 And trusted you, even with private thoughts,
Since you alone know when he may be reached,
Go, intercede with our proud enemy.
Remind him that I took no oath at Aulis
With Danaans to destroy the Trojan race;
590 I sent no ship to Pergamum. Never did I
Profane his father Anchisës' dust and shade.
Why will he not allow my prayers to fall
On his unpitying ears? Where is he racing?
Let him bestow one last gift on his mistress:
595 This, to await fair winds and easier flight.
Now I no longer plead the bond he broke
Of our old marriage, nor do I ask that he
Should live without his dear love, Latium,
Or yield his kingdom. Time is all I beg,
600 Mere time, a respite and a breathing space
For madness to subside in, while my fortune
Teaches me how to take defeat and grieve.
Pity your sister. This is the end, this favor—
To be repaid with interest when I die."

605 She pleaded in such terms, and such, in tears,
Her sorrowing sister brought him, time and again.
But no tears moved him, no one's voice would he
Attend to tractably. The fates opposed it;
God's will blocked the man's once kindly ears.
610 And just as when the north winds from the Alps
This way and that contend among themselves
To tear away an oaktree hale with age,
The wind and tree cry, and the buffeted trunk
Showers high foliage to earth, but holds
615 On bedrock, for the roots go down as far

Into the underworld as cresting boughs
Go up in heaven's air: just so this captain,
Buffeted by a gale of pleas
This way and that way, dinned all the day long,
620 Felt their moving power in his great heart,
And yet his will stood fast; tears fell in vain.

On Dido in her desolation now
Terror grew at her fate. She prayed for death,
Being heartsick at the mere sight of heaven.
625 That she more surely would perform the act
And leave the daylight, now she saw before her
A thing one shudders to recall: on altars
Fuming with incense where she placed her gifts,
The holy water blackened, the spilt wine
630 Turned into blood and mire. Of this she spoke
To no one, not to her sister even. Then, too,
Within the palace was a marble shrine
Devoted to her onetime lord, a place
She held in wondrous honor, all festooned
635 With snowy fleeces and green festive boughs.
From this she now thought voices could be heard
And words could be made out, her husband's words,
Calling her, when midnight hushed the earth;
And lonely on the rooftops the night owl
640 Seemed to lament, in melancholy notes,
Prolonged to a doleful cry. And then, besides,
The riddling words of seers in ancient days,
Foreboding sayings, made her thrill with fear.
In nightmare, fevered, she was hunted down
645 By pitiless Aeneas, and she seemed
Deserted always, uncompanioned always,
On a long journey, looking for her Tyrians
In desolate landscapes—

as Pentheus gone mad
650 Sees the oncoming Eumenidës and sees
A double sun and double Thebes appear,
Or as when, hounded on the stage, Orestës
Runs from a mother armed with burning brands,
With serpents hellish black,
655 And in the doorway squat the Avenging Ones.

So broken in mind by suffering, Dido caught
Her fatal madness and resolved to die.
She pondered time and means, then visiting
Her mournful sister, covered up her plan
660 With a calm look, a clear and hopeful brow.

"Sister, be glad for me! I've found a way
To bring him back or free me of desire.
Near to the Ocean boundary, near sundown,
The Aethiops' farthest territory lies,
665 Where giant Atlas turns the sphere of heaven
Studded with burning stars. From there
A priestess of Massylian stock has come;
She had been pointed out to me: custodian
Of that shrine named for daughters of the west,
670 Hesperidës; and it is she who fed
The dragon, guarding well the holy boughs
With honey dripping slow and drowsy poppy.
Chanting her spells she undertakes to free
What hearts she wills, but to inflict on others
675 Duress of sad desires; to arrest
The flow of rivers, make the stars move backward,
Call up the spirits of deep Night. You'll see
Earth shift and rumble underfoot and ash trees
Walk down mountainsides. Dearest, I swear
680 Before the gods and by your own sweet self,
It is against my will that I resort
For weaponry to magic powers. In secret
Build up a pyre in the inner court
Under the open sky, and place upon it
685 The arms that faithless man left in my chamber,

Lines 469–496

All his clothing, and the marriage bed
On which I came to grief—solace for me
To annihilate all vestige of the man,
Vile as he is: my priestess shows me this."

690   While she was speaking, cheek and brow grew pale.
But Anna could not think her sister cloaked
A suicide in these unheard-of rites;
She failed to see how great her madness was
And feared no consequence more grave

695   Than at Sychaeus' death. So, as commanded,
She made the preparations. For her part,
The queen, seeing the pyre in her inmost court
Erected huge with pitch-pine and sawn ilex,
Hung all the place under the sky with wreaths

700   And crowned it with funereal cypress boughs.
On the pyre's top she put a sword he left
With clothing, and an effigy on a couch,
Her mind fixed now ahead on what would come.
Around the pyre stood altars, and the priestess,

705   Hair unbound, called in a voice of thunder
Upon three hundred gods, on Erebus,
On Chaos, and on triple Hecatë,
Three-faced Diana. Then she sprinkled drops
Purportedly from the fountain of Avernus.

710   Rare herbs were brought out, reaped at the new moon
By scythes of bronze, and juicy with a milk
Of dusky venom; then the rare love-charm
Or caul torn from the brow of a birthing foal
And snatched away before the mother found it.

715   Dido herself with consecrated grain
In her pure hands, as she went near the altars,
Freed one foot from sandal straps, let fall
Her dress ungirdled, and, now sworn to death,
Called on the gods and stars that knew her fate.

720   She prayed then to whatever power may care
In comprehending justice for the grief
Of lovers bound unequally by love.

Lines 496–521

The night had come, and weary in every land
Men's bodies took the boon of peaceful sleep.
725 The woods and the wild seas had quieted
At that hour when the stars are in mid-course
And every field is still; cattle and birds
With vivid wings that haunt the limpid lakes
Or nest in thickets in the country places
730 All were asleep under the silent night.
Not, though, the agonized Phoenician queen:
She never slackened into sleep and never
Allowed the tranquil night to rest
Upon her eyelids or within her heart.
735 Her pain redoubled; love came on again,
Devouring her, and on her bed she tossed
In a great surge of anger.
                                So awake,
She pressed these questions, musing to herself:

740 "Look now, what can I do? Turn once again
To the old suitors, only to be laughed at—
Begging a marriage with Numidians
Whom I disdained so often? Then what? Trail
The Ilian ships and follow like a slave
745 Commands of Trojans? Seeing them so agreeable,
In view of past assistance and relief,
So thoughtful their unshaken gratitude?
Suppose I wished it, who permits or takes
Aboard their proud ships one they so dislike?
750 Poor lost soul, do you not yet grasp or feel
The treachery of the line of Laömedon?
What then? Am I to go alone, companion
Of the exultant sailors in their flight?
Or shall I set out in their wake, with Tyrians,
755 With all my crew close at my side, and send
The men I barely tore away from Tyre
To sea again, making them hoist their sails

To more sea-winds? No: die as you deserve,
Give pain quietus with a steel blade.

760   Sister,
You are the one who gave way to my tears
In the beginning, burdened a mad queen
With sufferings, and thrust me on my enemy.
It was not given me to lead my life

765 Without new passion, innocently, the way
Wild creatures live, and not to touch these depths.
The vow I took to the ashes of Sychaeus
Was not kept."

                              So she broke out afresh

770 In bitter mourning. On his high stern deck
Aeneas, now quite certain of departure,
Everything ready, took the boon of sleep.
In dream the figure of the god returned
With looks reproachful as before: he seemed

775 Again to warn him, being like Mercury
In every way, in voice, in golden hair,
And in the bloom of youth.

                              "Son of the goddess,
Sleep away this crisis, can you still?

780 Do you not see the dangers growing round you,
Madman, from now on? Can you not hear
The offshore westwind blow? The woman hatches
Plots and drastic actions in her heart,
Resolved on death now, whipping herself on

785 To heights of anger. Will you not be gone
In flight, while flight is still within your power?
Soon you will see the offing boil with ships
And glare with torches; soon again
The waterfront will be alive with fires,

790 If Dawn comes while you linger in this country.
Ha! Come, break the spell! Woman's a thing
Forever fitful and forever changing."

At this he merged into the darkness. Then
As the abrupt phantom filled him with fear,

795 Aeneas broke from sleep and roused his crewmen:

"Up, turn out now! Oarsmen, take your thwarts!
Shake out sail! Look here, for the second time
A god from heaven's high air is goading me
To hasten our break away, to cut the cables.
800 Holy one, whatever god you are,
We go with you, we act on your command
Most happily! Be near, graciously help us,
Make the stars in heaven propitious ones!"

He pulled his sword aflash out of its sheath
805 And struck at the stern hawser. All the men
Were gripped by his excitement to be gone,
And hauled and hustled. Ships cast off their moorings,
And an array of hulls hid inshore water
As oarsmen churned up foam and swept to sea.

810 Soon early Dawn, quitting the saffron bed
Of old Tithonus, cast new light on earth,
And as air grew transparent, from her tower
The queen caught sight of ships on the seaward reach
With sails full and the wind astern. She knew
815 The waterfront now empty, bare of oarsmen.
Beating her lovely breast three times, four times,
And tearing her golden hair,

"O Jupiter,"
She said, "will this man go, will he have mocked
820 My kingdom, stranger that he was and is?
Will they not snatch up arms and follow him
From every quarter of the town? and dockhands
Tear our ships from moorings? On! Be quick
With torches! Give out arms! Unship the oars!
825 What am I saying? Where am I? What madness
Takes me out of myself? Dido, poor soul,
Your evil doing has come home to you.
Then was the right time, when you offered him
A royal scepter. See the good faith and honor

Lines 573–597

830 Of one they say bears with him everywhere
The hearthgods of his country! One who bore
His father, spent with age, upon his shoulders!
Could I not then have torn him limb from limb
And flung the pieces on the sea? His company,

835 Even Ascanius could I not have minced
And served up to his father at a feast?
The luck of battle might have been in doubt—
So let it have been! Whom had I to fear,
Being sure to die? I could have carried torches

840 Into his camp, filled passage ways with flame,
Annihilated father and son and followers
And given my own life on top of all!
O Sun, scanning with flame all works of earth,
And thou, O Juno, witness and go-between

845 Of my long miseries; and Hecatë,
Screeched for at night at crossroads in the cities;
And thou, avenging Furies, and all gods
On whom Elissa dying may call: take notice,
Overshadow this hell with your high power,

850 As I deserve, and hear my prayer!
If by necessity that impious wretch
Must find his haven and come safe to land,
If so Jove's destinies require, and this,
His end in view, must stand, yet all the same

855 When hard beset in war by a brave people,
Forced to go outside his boundaries
And torn from Iulus, let him beg assistance,
Let him see the unmerited deaths of those
Around and with him, and accepting peace

860 On unjust terms, let him not, even so,
Enjoy his kingdom or the life he longs for,
But fall in battle before his time and lie
Unburied on the sand! This I implore,
This is my last cry, as my last blood flows.

865 Then, O my Tyrians, besiege with hate
His progeny and all his race to come:
Make this your offering to my dust. No love,
No pact must be between our peoples; No,

But rise up from my bones, avenging spirit!
870 Harry with fire and sword the Dardan countrymen
Now, or hereafter, at whatever time
The strength will be afforded. Coast with coast
In conflict, I implore, and sea with sea,
And arms with arms: may they contend in war,
875 Themselves and all the children of their children!"

Now she took thought of one way or another,
At the first chance, to end her hated life,
And briefly spoke to Barcë, who had been
Sychaeus' nurse; her own an urn of ash
880 Long held in her ancient fatherland.

                              "Dear nurse,
Tell Sister Anna to come here, and have her
Quickly bedew herself with running wate.
Before she brings our victims for atonemen.
885 Let her come that way. And you, too, put on
Pure wool around your brows. I have a mind
To carry out that rite to Stygian Jove
That I have readied here, and put an end
To my distress, committing to the flames
890 The pyre of that miserable Dardan."

At this with an old woman's eagernes.
Barcë hurried away. And Dido's heart
Beat wildly at the enormous thing afoot.
She rolled her bloodshot eyes, her quivering cheeks
895 Were flecked with red as her sick pallor grew
Before her coming death. Into the court
She burst her way, then at her passion's height
She climbed the pyre and bared the Dardan sword—
A gift desired once, for no such need.
900 Her eyes now on the Trojan clothing there
And the familiar bed, she paused a little,
Weeping a little, mindful, then lay down
And spoke her last words:

                              "Remnants dear to me
905 While god and fate allowed it, take this breath

And give me respite from these agonies.
I lived my life out to the very end
And passed the stages Fortune had appointed.
Now my tall shade goes to the under world.
910   I built a famous town, saw my great walls,
Avenged my husband, made my hostile brother
Pay for his crime. Happy, alas, too happy,
If only the Dardanian keels had never
Beached on our coast." And here she kissed the bed.
915   "I die unavenged," she said, "but let me die.
This way, this way, a blessed relief to go
Into the undergloom. Let the cold Trojan,
Far at sea, drink in this conflagration
And take with him the omen of my death!"

920   Amid these words her household people saw her
Crumpled over the steel blade, and the blade
Aflush with red blood, drenched her hands. A scream
Pierced the high chambers. Now through the shocked city
Rumor went rioting, as wails and sobs
925   With women's outcry echoed in the palace
And heaven's high air gave back the beating din,
As though all Carthage or old Tyre fell
To storming enemies, and, out of hand,
Flames billowed on the roofs of men and gods
930   Her sister heard and trembling, faint with terror,
Lacerating her face, beating her breast,
Ran through the crowd to call the dying queen:

"It came to this, then, sister? You deceived me?
The pyre meant this, altars and fires meant this?
935   What shall I mourn first, being abandoned? Did you
Scorn your sister's company in death?
You should have called me out to the same fate!
The same blade's edge and hurt, at the same hour,
Should have taken us off. With my own hands
940   Had I to build this pyre, and had I to call
Upon our country's gods, that in the end
With you placed on it there, O heartless one,

Lines 652–681

I should be absent? You have put to death
Yourself and me, the people and the fathers
945   Bred in Sidon, and your own new city.
Give me fresh water, let me bathe her wound
And catch upon my lips any last breath
Hovering over hers."

               Now she had climbed
950   The topmost steps and took her dying sister
Into her arms to cherish, with a sob,
Using her dress to stanch the dark blood flow.
But Dido trying to lift her heavy eyes
Fainted again. Her chest-wound whistled air.
955   Three times she struggled up on one elbow
And each time fell back on the bed. Her gaze
Went wavering as she looked for heaven's light
And groaned at finding it. Almighty Juno,
Filled with pity for this long ordeal
960   And difficult passage, now sent Iris down
Out of Olympus to set free
The wrestling spirit from the body's hold.
For since she died, not at her fated span
Nor as she merited, but before her time
965   Enflamed and driven mad, Proserpina
Had not yet plucked from her the golden hair,
Delivering her to Orcus of the Styx.
So humid Iris through bright heaven flew
On saffron-yellow wings, and in her train
970   A thousand hues shimmered before the sun.
At Dido's head she came to rest.

                  "This token
Sacred to Dis I bear away as bidden
And free you from your body."

                  Saying this,
975   She cut a lock of hair. Along with it
Her body's warmth fell into dissolution,
And out into the winds her life withdrew.

Lines 681–705

BOOK

V

GAMES AND A CONFLAGRATION

Cutting through waves blown dark by a chill wind
Aeneas held his ships firmly on course
For a midsea crossing. But he kept his eyes
Upon the city far astern, now bright
5   With poor Elissa's pyre. What caused that blaze
Remained unknown to watchers out at sea,
But what they knew of a great love profaned
In anguish, and a desperate woman's nerve,
Led every Trojan heart into foreboding.

10   When they had gained the offing east and north,
No land in sight now, but sky everywhere
And everywhere the sea, a thunderhead
Towered above them, bringing gloom and storm
With shuddering dusky water. Aeneas' helmsman,
15   Palinurus, called from his high stern deck:

"Why have these clouds massed on the height of heaven?
Father Neptune, what are you brewing for us?"

On this he made the seamen shorten sail
And bend to the oars. He trimmed his fluttering canvas
20   More to catch the wind and said:
                              "Aeneas,
Lord commander, even if Jupiter

Should pledge his word for it, I could not hope
To make landfall on Italy in this weather.
25 It's thickening up, and now the wind blows hard
Out of the murky west abeam of us.
No bucking it. We cannot make our northing.
Seeing that Fortune has the upper hand,
I say give in, and follow where she calls.
30 No long reach eastward there's a loyal coast,
I think: the land named for your brother, Eryx,
And the Sicilian ports—if I remember
Rightly my star heights and my miles at sea."

The good commander said:
35   "For some time now
I've noticed what the veering wind demands
And how you fought it uselessly. Change course,
Haul yards and sails around. Could any soil
Be more agreeable to me, or any
40 Where I would rather moor these tired ships,
Than Sicily, home of my Dardan friend,
Acestës, and the ashes of my father?"

With this exchange they headed east for port,
The westwind in their sails. On a following swell
45 The fleet ran free, and happily at last
They turned in toward the shoreline that they knew.
Far off, now, on a high hill top, Acestës
Wondered to see his guest's fleet coming in,
Then hurried down, spiny with javelins,
50 Wearing a Libyan she-bear's hide—Acestës,
Born of a Trojan mother to the river
God Crinisus. As he knew and prized
His parentage, he welcomed their return,
Treated them to the riches of the fields,
55 And comforted with friendship weary men.
When the next day at dawn the brightening sky
Made the stars fade, Aeneas called his crews
Together from all quarters of the shore
And spoke out from a built-up rostrum:

60   "Sons
Of Dardanus, in the high line of gods,
The months are spent, the rounding year fulfilled
Since we interred my godlike father's bones
And mourned and blessed his altars. And if I
65   Am not mistaken, now that day has come
Which I shall hold in bitterness and honor
All my life (gods, you would have it so)
Were I today exiled in Libyan sands
Or caught at sea off Argos, or detained
70   In walled Mycenae, still I should carry out
My anniversary vows and ceremonies,
Heaping the altars, as I should, with offerings.
But now, beyond all expectation, here
We stand beside his ashes and his bones—
75   And surely not, I think, without the great gods'
Will and contrivance—carried here off course
To enter kindly havens. Come then, everyone,
We'll celebrate this holiday in joy.
Let us ask for propitious winds, and when
80   Our city is laid out, our temples blessed
In Father's honor, may he grant each year
That I perform this ritual. Trojan-born
Acestës gives each ship two head of oxen.
Welcome the hearthgods to the feast—our own
85   And those our host Acestës cherishes.
Then, too, if as we trust nine days from now
Dawn lifts for mortals her dear light and bares
The world with sunrays, I shall plan and hold
Contests for Trojans: first a ship-race, then
90   We'll see who wins at running, who stands out
In pride of strength at javelin and archery,
Or dares to fight with rawhide on his hands.
May all compete for prizes and the palm!
Now silence, all. Garland your brows with leaves."

95   At this he shaded his own brows with myrtle,
Loved by his mother. Helymus did the same,
Acestës ripe with age, the boy Ascanius,

And all the young men followed suit. Aeneas
Left the assembly now and made his way
100   With many thousands to the funeral mound,
Walking amid the crowd. Once there, he poured
The ritual libations: two of wine,
Two of fresh milk, and two of victims' blood,
Then cast down purple mourning flowers and said:

105   "I greet and bless you, sacred father, bless you,
Ashes and shade and soul, paternal soul
I vainly rescued once. It was not given me
With you beside me to explore the coasts
And plains of Italy, nor to discover,
110   Whatever it may be, Ausonian Tiber . . ."

So far he had proceeded in his speech
When from the depths of mound and shrine a snake
Came huge and undulant with seven coils,
Enveloping the barrow peaceably
115   And gliding on amid the altars. Azure
Flecks mottled his back; a dappled sheen
Of gold set all his scales ablaze, as when
A rainbow on the clouds facing the sun
Throws out a thousand colors.
120   Aeneas paused,
Amazed and silent, while deliberately
The snake's long column wound among the bowls
And polished cups, browsing the festal dishes,
And, from the altars where he fed, again
125   Slid harmlessly to earth below the tomb.
Now all the more intent, the celebrant
Took up again his father's ritual,
Uncertain whether he should think the snake
The local god, the genius of the place,
130   Or the attendant spirit of his father.
He sacrificed a pair of sheep, a pair
Of swine, a pair of heifers with black hides,
Then poured out shallow bowls of wine and called
The ghost of great Anchises, the death-shade

135   Released from Acheron. Then his companions,
     Each to his capacity, brought in
     Their own glad offerings. They piled the altars,
     Knifed the beasts, placed caldrons on the fires,
     And at their ease upon the grass raked up
140   Live coals under the spits to broil the flesh.

I n due course came the awaited day: the shining
     Sun's team brought a ninth and cloudless Dawn.
     Acestës' influence roused the neighboring folk,
     And now in happy groups they thronged the shore
145   To see Aeneas' men, or to compete.
     But first the prizes were set out on view
     Midfield—blest tripods, fresh green crowns, and palms,
     Rewards for winners; armor, too, and robes
     Infused with crimson dye; gold bars and silver.
150   Next from a central eminence a trumpet
     Sang out for the opening of the games.
     The well matched entrants in the first event
     Were heavy-oared ships, four from the whole fleet:
     Mnestheus' eager oarsmen drove the Seabeast—
155   Mnestheus of Italy he soon would be,
     From whose name came the clan of Memmius.
     Then Gyas captained the Chimaera, huge
     In length and weight, big as a town afloat,
     Which Dardan oarsmen in three tiers drove onward,
160   Surging together at three banks of oars.
     Then he for whom the Sergian house was named,
     Sergestus, rode the great Centaur. Cloanthus,
     From whom your family came, Roman Cluentius,
     Rode in the sea-blue Scylla.
165   Out at sea,
     Well off the foaming beach, there is a rock
     Submerged and beaten by high seas at times
     When Northwest winds in winter hide the stars,

But in calm weather it stands quietly
170   Above the unmoving water, a level perch
And happy sunning place for gulls. Aeneas
Made a green goal here with an ilex bough,
Wishing well-marked for sailors in his charge
The point where they should turn and double back
175   On the long course. Now they drew lots for places,
Captains erect upon the sterns, their gold
And splendid crimson gleaming far around.
The crews, for their part, garlanded with poplar,
Bare to the waist, glistened with rubbing oil,
180   Well settled on their planks, reaching ahead
To oar hafts, listening hard for the starting call.
Throbbing excitement seemed to void their hearts
All beating high in appetite for glory.
Then as the brilliant trumpet gave its note
185   They all surged forward from the starting line,
No lagging: heaven echoed shouts, and channels
Under the crewmen's pulling turned to foam.
Abreast they cleft their furrows, all the sea
Torn up by oarstrokes and the biting prows.
190   The racing cars in a two-horse chariot race
Are not so headlong to consume the field
Once they have left the barriers—not though
The charioteers shake out the rippling reins
To give head to the teams, and hang above them,
195   Bent to the whip. Then with applause and cheers
And partisan shouts the wooded landscape rang,
The shores, embayed, rolled the sound back and forth,
And the reverberant hills gave back the din.
Amid the turbulence, the leader now,
200   Racing ahead at the very start, was Gyas.
Close on him came Cloanthus, better served
By oarsmen, but his ship's weight slowed him up
Behind them at an equal interval
The Seabeast and the Centaur vied for third,
205   And now the Seabeast had it, now the mighty
Centaur took the lead, now both together,
Prows on a line, with their long keels ploughed up

The salt sea water. As they all came near
The offshore rock, the halfway mark, the leader,
210 Gyas, hailed Menoetes at the tiller:

"Why keep so far to starboard, man? This way!
Hug shore, making the turn. What if the oarblades
Graze the rock to port? Let others shear off
Wide to seaward."
215   Heedless, in his fear
Of a hidden ledge, Menoetes swung the prow
Toward the open sea. Gyas again cried out:

"Now why bear off? Stick to the rocks, Menoetes!"
And at that instant looking back he saw
220 Cloanthus just behind on the inner track.
Between the ship of Gyas and the rocks
He shaved his way to port, then suddenly
Shot past him at the turn and got away
Into safe water, leaving the mark behind.
225 Young Gyas flared up now, ablaze
To the bottom of his soul with indignation,
And tears wetted his cheeks. Without a thought
For dignity or the safety of his crew
He tossed cautious Menoetes overboard
230 Into the sea. Then he himself as steersman
Took the tiller, and as captain cheered
His oarsmen as he swung the rudder over,
Heading for shore. When heavy old Menoetes
Slowly at last emerged from the sea bottom
235 Drenched and streaming, up he climbed and sat
Atop the dry ledge. Trojans had laughed to see
His plunge, his swimming, and now laughed again
As he coughed up sea water from his chest.

To the two behind, to Mnestheus and Sergestus,
240 The happy thought had come of passing Gyas,
Now he had lost speed—and Sergestus led,
Nearing the rock, though not by a full boat-length,
For Seabeast by her prow came up alongside.

Lines 158–187

Mnestheus on his catwalk fore and aft
245 Between the oarsmen urged them on:

"Now pull,
Pull for it! Great Hector's companions in arms,
Chosen in Troy's last hour for my crew,
Now bring to bear the strength and nerve you showed
250 In Gaetulan Syrtës, in the Ionian sea,
In the assaulting waves off Malea!
Not for the first place, not for the victory now
Am I, Mnestheus, contending; though I wish—
But let the winners be your choices, Neptune!—
255 Only, to come in last, that's shameful. Fellows,
Win just this, keep us from that disgrace!"

They stretched ahead for strokes and pulled their hearts out,
Making the beaked hull shake at every stroke,
And sheets of sea were yanked, it seemed, from under them.
260 Panting racked them, dry-mouthed, and the sweat
Ran down in streams. But actually, chance
Brought them the wished-for glory. As Sergestus
In his wild zeal entered the danger zone
And turned his prow in toward the rock, his luck
265 Failed and he struck on an outlying reef:
A grinding blow, oars shivered, hitting rock,
And the hull hung tipped up where it went aground.
With a loud shout the sailors heaved together,
Backing water, then brought boathooks out
270 And pikes, retrieving cracked oars from the sea.
Mnestheus meanwhile, more ardent for his luck,
With his fast oars in line, the wind behind him,
Took the shoreward leg through open water.
As a wild dove when startled into flight
275 Beats her affrighted way over the fields—
A dove whose cote and tender nestlings lie
In a rock cranny—with fast clapping wings,
But soon in quiet air goes floating on
With wings extended motionless: just so
280 Mnestheus, just so the Seabeast cleft the sea,

Running for the home stretch, and just so
She glided, borne by her own impetus.

Sergestus was the first she left behind,
Pitted against the ledge in shallow water
285 With pointless cries for help—learning the trick
Of boat-racing with broken oars; ahead
Then Seabeast closed with Gyas' huge Chimaera
That soon, for lack of helmsman, fell away.
Now in the home stretch only one was left,
290 Cloanthus. In his track, with might and main,
Mnestheus pressed on. And now the shouts from shore
Grew twice as loud, as all the watching crowd
Cheered for Mnestheus, filling the air with din.
One crew fought off the shame of losing honor
295 Theirs already, glory won; they'd give
Their lives for fame; but luck empowered the others,
Who felt that they could do it, and so could.
The prows now even, they were close indeed
To winning, had Cloanthus not stretched out
300 His hands to seaward and in bursts of prayer
Called on the gods to hear his vows:
                                          "O gods
Whose power is on the deep sea and whose waves
I'm racing over, I shall place with joy
305 A snow-white bull before your altars, here
Upon this shore, in payment of my vow,
And fling the parts into the sea and pour
A stream of wine!"
                        Under the depth of water
310 All the Nereids, Phorcus' company,
And virgin Panopëa heard his prayer,
And Father Portunus, the harbor god,
With his great hand impelled the Scylla onward.
Swifter than a gust out of the east
315 Or arrow on the wing she ran for land
And took her place in the deep harbor. Then
When all were called together, Anchises' son

Lines 219–244

Proclaimed by the loud crier Cloanthus winner
And veiled his temples with green bay. Moreover,
320 To each contending ship he gave a choice
Of bullocks, three to each, with wine and one
Great bar of silver to be borne away.
Additional rewards went to the captains:
A cloak, woven with gold thread, for the winner,
325 Bordered with a meander's double line
Of Meliboean crimson; pictured there
The royal boy amid the boughs of Ida
Running with javelin, tiring out swift deer,
So lifelike in the chase he seemed to pant.
330 Then Jove's big bird, his weapon-carrier,
Whisked him aloft from Ida in his talons,
While aged guardians held out their hands
To heaven in vain and wild hounds barked at air.
To him whose valor won him second place
335 A triple shirt of mail close-wrought with links
Of polished gold, a trophy of Aeneas'
Victory over Demoleos, near the river
Simoïs under Troy's high wall. This shirt
Aeneas gave to Mnestheus, as an honor,
340 And as protection in the wars to come.
Phegeus and Sagaris, his body servants,
Could barely carry all its folds
On shoulders braced for it, though in other days
Demoleos in this shirt and on the run
345 Had harried straggling Trojans.
                                        The third prize
Aeneas gave was a pair of brazen caldrons
And silver cups embossed in high relief.

All now rewarded, proud of their rich things,
350 Beribboned, garlanded, they were going off,
When back from the rude rock, barely dislodged
By every skill, limping, with missing oars
On one oar-bank, Comedian Sergestus
Brought his long craft ingloriously in.

Lines 245–272

355 Often you'll see a snake on a high road
A felloed wheel has run obliquely over
Or a pedestrian with a heavy stone
Has torn and left half dead: to get away
It sets in motion its long coils, in part
360 Still dangerous with blazing eyes and rearing
Hissing head, in part immobilized
By the crippling wound, writhing upon itself.
So sluggish under oars the ship moved on;
But then she hoisted sail and entered harbor
365 Under full sail. Glad for the rescued ship
And crew, Aeneas gave the promised gift:
A slave woman who knew Minerva's craft,
The Cretan Pholoë, with nursing twins.

Now that the ship race had been run, Aeneas
370 Walked to a grassy field that wooded hills
Curved all around: a vale and an arena.
There with a crowd of thousands the great captain
Betook himself and took a central place,
A seat on a platform. Now he called on those
375 Whom hope for gain led to compete in running,
And set out prizes for them. From all sides
They came up, Teucrians with Sicilians mixed,
Nisus and Euryalus in the lead—
Euryalus exceptional for beauty
380 And bloom of youth, whom Nisus dearly loved.
Next came Diorës of the royal line
Of Priam; then, together, Salius
And Patron, this one an Acarnanian,
The other from Arcadia, a Tegean.
385 Then two Sicilians, Helymus and Panopës,
Men of the woods, henchmen of old Acestës;
And many more whose names are in the dark.
Aeneas spoke among them:

Lines 273–303

"Be aware
390 Of this, now: bear it happily in mind:
Not one goes off without a gift from me.
Two Cretan arrows shod in polished steel
And a double-bladed axe, inlaid in silver,
Await each one of you, the same reward.
395 Then prizes go to the first three finishers
With pale green olive garlands: he who wins
Will get a horse, fully caparisoned;
The runner-up, an Amazonian quiver
Full of Thracian arrows, and a strap
400 Of broad gold, buckled with a well-cut gem.
As for the third place winner, let him go
Contented with this Argive helm."

At this
They toed the line; and when they heard the signal,
405 Suddenly given, broke from the starting post
And made off on the track like an outriding
Rack of storm cloud. As they marked the finish,
Nisus flashed out, sprinting into the lead,
Faster than gale wind or a bolt of thunder.
410 After him, but far behind, came Salius,
And after Salius by a space Euryalus,
Helymus next. But close upon him, look,
Diorës in his flight matched stride with stride,
Nearing his shoulder; if more track remained
415 He would have passed him or come up abreast
In a dead heat. But in the home stretch now
The tired men were making for the finish
When Nisus stumbled by bad luck, in gore—
A slippery place where beasts had been cut down
420 And blood gushed on the turf soaking the grass.
Elated, with the race as good as won,
He staggered there and could not hold his feet
On the trodden ground, but pitched on it headlong
In the mire and blood of offerings.
425 Though beaten,
This man did not forget Euryalus,

Lines 304–334

His beloved, but surging from the spot
Of slipperiness he tripped up Salius,
And he in turn went tumbling head over heels
430 To lie flat, as Euryalus flashed past
By his friend's help running to win first place
Amid applause and cheers. Then Helymus
Came in and then Diorës, third place now.

At this point the whole banked assemblage rang
435 With Salius' clamor, facing the front-row elders,
For the honor stolen from him by a foul.
The crowd's support and his own quiet tears
Were in Euryalus's favor: prowess
Ever more winning for a handsome form.
440 Diorës backed him with loud protestations,
Having won third place all in vain
If the first prize went back to Salius.
Then fatherly Aeneas said:

                              "Your prizes
445 Stand as they are, young fellows. There will be
No change by anyone in the winning order.
Let me console a blameless friend's bad luck."
With this he gave a Gaetulan lion's hide
With shaggy mane and gilded claws to Salius.
450 Nisus now said:

                              "If losers get rewards
As great as that; and you console a fall,
What proper gift will you give Nisus, then?
First prize, the crown, is what I earned by rights
455 Had Fortune not opposed me, taken me out
As it did Salius."

                              While he spoke he showed
His face and body all befouled with mire.
Smiling at Nisus, fatherly Aeneas
460 Ordered a shield brought out, Didymaon's work,
Removed once by Danaans from a portal
Sacred to Neptune: this exceptional prize
He gave to the conspicuous runner.

Lines 334–361

A fter

465   The races had been held and prizes given,
      "Now," said Aeneas, "anyone who has
      A fighting heart and fortitude, step forward,
      Put up your hands for the encasing hide."
      He set a double prize then for the boxing:
470   A bullock for the winner, dressed with gold
      And snowy wool; a sword and a choice helm
      As comfort for the beaten man. Straightway,
      Without an instant's pause, in his huge power,
      Darës got up amid the murmurous crowd—
475   The one man who had held his ground with Paris,
      The man, too, who knocked out the champion, Butës,
      Beside the burial mound where Hector lies:
      Butës, a giant boxer, bragged of coming
      From the Bebrycian tribe of Amycus,
480   But Darës stretched him half dead on the sand.
      So powerful, the man reared up his head
      For combat, showed his shoulders' breadth, his reach
      With left and right, threw punches at the air.
      Who would fight him? Among all those men
485   Not one dared put the leather on his hands.
      Thinking all had withdrawn, yielding the prize,
      He took his stance before Aeneas' feet
      And made no bones of grasping the bull's horn
      In his left hand, and saying:

                            "Son of the goddess,
490   If no one dares commit himself to boxing,
      How long must I stand here? How long may I
      Properly be kept waiting? Say the word,
      And I lead off the prize."

495   Then all the Dardans
      Murmured:

                  "Let the man have what was promised."
      Acestës, though, had hard words for Entellus
      Sitting beside him on a couch of turf:

Lines 362–388

500   "Entellus, what price now that in the old days
You were our strongest fighting man? Will you
Sit here so meek and let a prize like that
Be carried off without a fight? Where now
Is our god, Eryx, whom you call your teacher
505   But let down in the end? What of your fame
Through all Trinacria, and the booty hung
About your hall?"
                Entellus softly answered:
"Not that love of honor or appetite
510   For glory have given way, beaten by fear;
I'm slowed by age, my blood runs feebly now
Without heat, and my strength is spent, my body
Musclebound. Had I that youth again
That I had once, and that this arrogant fellow
515   Counts on, I would need no setting-on,
No prize, no pretty steer, to make me meet him;
Gifts don't concern me."
                After saying this,
He tossed into the ring a pair of gauntlets
520   Monstrously heavy, which the fighter Eryx
Used to bind on his forearms and hands,
Hard rawhide. And the crowd looked on amazed,
So huge they were, of seven oxhides, barred
With lead and iron sewn to stiffen them.

525   Darës himself stared more than anyone
And moved away, reluctant for a bout.
Meanwhile Anchises' great-souled son picked up
And tried the gauntlets, turning their rolled-up weight
This way and that. The veteran Entellus
530   Now spoke up in his deep voice:
                    "What then
If anyone had seen Hercules' gloves
And the grim fight, here on this very shore?
These were the armor worn by your own brother
535   Eryx; even now you see them stained
With blood and spattered brains. In these at last
He faced the great Alcidës, and in these

I used to fight, while hotter blood sustained me
And age had not won out as yet or scattered
540 Snow on my brows. But if this Trojan, Darës,
Refuses our equipment, if Aeneas
In fairness so decides, and my proponent,
Acestës, nods, we'll equalize the fight.
Here, I give up the oxhide gloves of Eryx.
545 Breathe easier, pull off your Trojan gloves."

He threw the double mantle from his shoulders,
Bared his great arms and legs, all thew and bone,
And took his stand, gigantic, in the arena.
Now with paternal care Anchises' son
550 Brought gauntlets of the same weight out
To tie on both men's hands. Then instantly
Each in his stance moved on his toes and put
His fists up high in air, holding his head
Well back out of the range of blows. They sparred
555 With rights and lefts, each trying to sting the other
Into unguarded fighting. One had speed
Of footwork and élan of youth; the other
Giant mass and brawn—but his slow knees
Quivered and buckled, painful gasping shook him,
560 Huge as he was. Often they punched and missed,
Often they hit, thudding on flanks and ribs
Or making chests resound. Then flurrying punches
Pummeled ears and temples, and their jaws
Would crunch at every solid blow. Entellus
565 Gravely stood in the same unshifting stance,
Watchful to roll with punches or to slip them.
Darës, like one assaulting a tall city
Or laying siege to a stronghold on a height,
Tried this approach, then that, explored the ground
570 On all sides cleverly, came on, came in
From various angles, all to no avail.
Then surging up, Entellus poised his right
And threw it, but the other in his quickness
Saw the blow descending and just in time

Lines 414–445

575 Slipped out from under. All Entellus' force
Being spent on air, by his own impetus
The mighty man fell mightily to earth,
As ponderously as, from time to time,
A hollow and uprooted pine will fall
580 On Erymanthus or the range of Ida.
Teucrians and Sicilians in their rivalry
Rose together, as a shout went up,
And, running out, Acestës was the first
To help the old man, his contemporary,
585 Up from the ground.

          Now neither hurt and slowed
Or shaken by the fall, the fighting man
Returned to combat hotter than before,
His power excited by his anger. Shame
590 Aroused him, too, and his own sense of manhood,
So that he went for Darës, driving him
Headlong over the ring, redoubling cuffs
With right and left alike, no pause, no rest.
As thick and fast as hail, drumming on roofs
595 In a big storm, were the old hero's blows
With both hands battering and spinning Darës.
Fatherly Aeneas would not sit by
While this fury went further—so berserk
Entellus was in the rancor of his soul.
600 He stopped the fight, and saved bone-weary Darës,
Saying to comfort him:

          "Poor fellow, how
Could rashness take you this way? Don't you feel
A force now more than mortal is against you
605 And heaven's will has changed? We'll bow to that!"
So, speaking loudly, he broke off the battle,
And loyal shipmates took Darës in hand,
Weak-kneed, his head wobbling from side to side
Spitting out teeth mixed in with gobs of blood.
610 They led him to the ships, and then, recalled,
Received the helm and sword, leaving the palm
And bullock for Entellus. The old champion,

Lines 445–473

Glorying in his courage and his prize,
Spoke out:

615   "Son of the goddess, Teucrians all,
Now see what power was in me in my prime,
And see the death from which you rescued Darës."

He set himself to face the bull that stood there,
Prize of the battle, then drew back his right
620 And from his full height lashed his hard glove out
Between the horns. The impact smashed the skull
And fragmented the brains. Down went the ox
Aquiver to sprawl dying on the ground.
The man stood over it and in deep tones
625 Proclaimed:

            "Here is a better life in place of Darës,
Eryx; here I lay down my gauntlets and my art."

Immediately after this, Aeneas
Invited all so minded to contend
630 With speeding arrows, and he set the prizes.
A mast out of Serestus' ship he raised
With his own giant hand, and at the top
Tethered a dove upon a cord as target
For them to shoot at. When they gathered round
635 A bronze helm took their lots. First shaken out,
And greeted by his partisans with cheers,
Was Hippocoön, son of Hyrtacus;
Then Mnestheus, second-place winner in the ship race,
Wearing his olive garland; and the third
640 Was Eurytion—brother to you, illustrious
Pandarus, who in another day,
When given command to break the truce, led off
With a bow-bent arrow shot amid the Achaeans.
The last one out, deep in the helm, Acestës—

645 He, too, ventured to try the young men's feat.
Now with stout arms they flexed their bows, each man
Hefting his own before him; and then drew
Their shafts from quivers. Right across the sky,
As the bowstring twanged, the first winged arrow, shot
650 By the son of Hyrtacus, whipped through the air
To strike and then stay fixed in the mast's timber.
The long pole trembled and the terrified bird
Fluttered, as all the place rang with applause.
Now Mnestheus took his eager stand, bow bent,
655 And aimed his gaze and full-drawn arrow high,
But by hard luck he missed the bird herself;
His steel point cut the flaxen cord, by which,
Tied to her foot, the bird hung from the mast.
Away she soared, into the south wind, white
660 Against dark clouds. In a flash, Eurytion,
Long ready with his bow bent, arrow drawn,
And whispering to his archer brother's shade
As he tracked the dove delighting in open sky
With clapping wings, now put his arrow through her
665 Under a black cloud. Down she plummeted
And left her life in the upper air of stars,
But brought down with her the transfixing shaft.
Only Acestës now remained, although
The prize escaped him; still he bent his bow
670 And shot into the air, showing them all
His old-time archer's power and bow that sang.
But here before their startled eyes appeared
An omen of great import: afterward
Mighty events made it all clear, and poets
675 Far in the future fabled it in awe.
The arrow flying in thin cloud caught fire
And left a track of flame until, burnt out,
It vanished in the wind—as shooting stars
Will often slip away across the sky
680 Trailing their blown hair. Everyone stood still
And thunderstruck, with prayer to heaven's powers,
Trinacrians and Teucrians alike.

Lines 499–530

Aeneas' great soul soon embraced the sign,
Embraced joyous Acestës, loaded him
685 With handsome gifts, and said:

                    "Here, take them, father,
You are the one the great king of Olympus
Wished by these auspices to be distinguished
Apart from others. You shall have this gift
690 That in his age had been Anchises' own:
A mixing bowl, engraved, that Cisseus
Of Thrace once gave my father, a princely thing,
To keep as a reminder and pledge of love."

With this he bound Acestës' brows with laurel,
695 Proclaiming him the winner before all—
Preferment never grudged by that good fellow,
Eurytion, though he alone had brought
The dove down from the sky. The third-place winner,
He who had cut the cord, came forward next
700 For his reward, and last came he who fixed
His arrow in the timber of the mast.
But even before the finish of this contest
Aeneas called aside Epÿtidës,
Body guard and companion of young Iulus,
705 And spoke into his ear:

                    "Go out and tell
Ascanius—if he has the boys' troop ready
Here along with him, and has maneuvers
Planned for the horses—tell him to lead them on
710 For Grandfather, these squadrons, and to let himself
Be seen in arms."

                    Aeneas now commanded
The whole crowd to withdraw from the long track
And open up the playing field. Then came
715 The riders, boys in even ranks, all shining
Before their parents' eyes, all mounts in hand,
And, as they passed, admiring murmurs rose
From men of Sicily and men of Troy.
The troopers had their hair smartly pressed down
720 By well-trimmed wreaths; each had a pair of lances

Made of cornel, tipped with steel. Some shoulders
Bore glossy quivers. All wore twisted gold
In a pliant necklace on the upper chest.

There were three squadrons—three commanders, weaving
725   Right and left; behind each one there came
Two files of six boy-riders in open column
Bright in the sun, and a trainer to each column.
Number one squadron gloried in its leader,
Little Priam, who bore his grandsire's name—
730   Your noble son, Politës, and a destined
Sire of Italians—riding a Thracian mount
With dappling of white, white pasterns and
Upon his haughty brow a snow-white blaze.
Atys had command of the second squadron,
735   From whom the Latin Atii have their name:
Small Atys, cherished boy-to-boy by Iulus.
Third and last, and handsomest of all,
Came Iulus, riding a Sidonian mount
Given him by the glowing beauty, Dido,
740   To be a keepsake and a pledge of love.
The other troopers rode Sicilian horses
Of old Acestës.
                        Dardans with applause
Now greeted the shy boys and loved their show,
745   Marking in each the features of his forebears.
After the troop had circled the assembly
Before their families' eyes, Epýtidës
From the wings shouted an order prearranged
And cracked his whip. The column split apart
750   As files in the three squadrons all in line
Turned away, cantering left and right; recalled,
They wheeled and dipped their lances for a charge.
They entered then on parades and counter-parades,
The two detachments, matched in the arena,
755   Winding in and out of one another,
And whipped into sham cavalry skirmishes
By baring backs in flight, then whirling round
With leveled points, then patching up a truce

And riding side by side. So intricate
760 In ancient times on mountainous Crete they say
The Labyrinth, between walls in the dark,
Ran criss-cross a bewildering thousand ways
Devised by guile, a maze insoluble,
Breaking down every clue to the way out.
765 So intricate the drill of Trojan boys
Who wove the patterns of their pacing horses,
Figured, in sport, retreats and skirmishes—
Like dolphins in the drenching sea, Carpathian
Or Libyan, that shear through waves in play.
770 This mode of drill, this mimicry of war,
Ascanius brought back in our first years
When he walled Alba Longa; and he taught
The ancient Latins to perform the drill
As he had done with other Trojan boys.
775 The Albans taught their children, and in turn
Great Rome took up this glory of the founders.
The boys are called Troy now, the whole troop Trojan.

Rites for Aeneas' father had reached this point,
When Fortune now first altered and betrayed them.
780 While they were honoring the tomb with games
Saturnian Juno sent her Iris down
From heaven, exhaling winds to waft her far
To the Trojan fleet. Juno had plans afoot,
Her ancient rancor not yet satisfied.
785 So Iris glided on the colored rainbow,
Seen by none, swift goddess, on her way.
She sighted the great crowd, then scanned the shore,
Saw ports deserted and ships unattended;
But on a desolate beach apart, the women
790 Wept for Anchises lost as they gazed out
In tears at the unfathomable sea.

Lines 587–615

"How many waves remain for us to cross,
How broad a sea, though we are weary, weary?"

All had one thing to say: a town and home
795   Were what they dreamed of, sick of toil at sea.
Taking her cue, darting into their midst,
Adept at doing ill, Iris put off
Her aspect as a goddess, and her gown,
To take the form of aged Beroë,
800   Wife of the Tmarian, Dorýclus, blest
With noble birth, a name at Troy, and children.
In this guise she advanced among the mothers.

"Miserable women that we are," she said,
"Whom no Achaean hand dragged out to death
805   Under the walls of our old fatherland!
Unlucky nation, for what final blow
Is Fortune keeping you alive? We've seen
The seventh summer since the fall of Troy,
And all these years we have been driven on
810   By land and sea, by hostile rocks and stars,
To measure the great water in our quest
For Italy—an Italy that recedes
While we endure the roll of the sea-swell.
Here is the land of Eryx, our old brother,
815   Here is our host, Acestës. Who prevents
Our building here a town for town-dwellers?
Country of our fathers, dear hearth gods
Rescued from the enemy to no end,
Will never a wall be called the wall of Troy?
820   Shall I not see on earth Simoïs and Xanthus,
Hector's rivers? Come now, all of you,
Set fire to those infernal ships with me!
I dreamed the clairvoyant Cassandra came
With burning torches, offering them, saying:

825   'Here you may look for Troy! Your home is here!'
Why wait? High time we acted on such portents.

Lines 615–639

See there, Neptune's four altar flames; the god
Has fire for us, the god will give us courage!"

Urging them on, she picked a dangerous brand,
830   Lifted it high and swept it into flame
And threw it. Taken by surprise, the women
Stood bewildered. Then one from the crowd,
The eldest, Pyrgo, royal governess
To Priam's many sons, cried:

835   "Do not take her
For Beroë: this is not she, the Rhoetean,
Wife of Dorýclus, mothers. Just observe
What traits she has of more than mortal beauty,
Her blazing eyes, her audacity, her face,
840   Her voice, her stride. I tell you, I myself
Left Beroë just now, and she is ill;
Vexed, too, that she alone missed our observance
And paid no tribute to Anchises."

                    Thus
845   Pyrgo reported to them. Women of Troy,
They looked now toward the ships, uncertainly,
With animosity, half in unhappy love
Of landscapes there before them, half still bound
To fated realms calling them onward—and
850   The goddess on strong wings went up the sky
Traversing a great rainbow under clouds.
Now truly wrought upon by signs and wonders,
Wrought to a frenzy, all cried out together,
Snatching up fire from hearths, despoiling altars,
855   Taking dry foliage, brush, and brands to throw.
And Vulcan, god of fire, unbridled raged
Through rowing thwarts and oars and piney hulls.

Courier Eumelus brought to Anchises' tomb
And the banked theater news of ships on fire,
860   And looking round they saw the dark smoke cloud
With soaring embers. First to act, Ascanius,

As he had led his troop rejoicing, now
Whipped on his horse to reach the mutinous camp—
And winded trainers could not hold him back.

865 "What unheard-of madness!" the boy shouted.
"Where now, where do you intend to go?
Poor miserable women of our city,
Not the enemy, not the Argive camp,
But your own hopes are what you burn! Look here,
870 I am your own Ascanius."

                    And he hurled
Before their feet his hollow helm, put on
For the sham battles. Meanwhile in all haste
Aeneas came, and the Trojan companies.
875 But the women scattered here and there in fear
Along the beaches, in the woods, wherever
They could take cover in rock caves, ashamed
To face the daylight, face what they had done—
For now they knew their own, and their shocked hearts
880 Were free of Juno. Not on that account
Did fires lit by them lose power or yield
To counter action: under wetted oak
The caulking smouldered and exuded smoke
As the great sluggish heat ate into hulls
885 And the contagion seeped all through the body:
Neither men's force nor streams of water poured
Prevailed on it. Now godfearing Aeneas
Rent the shirt upon his shoulders. Throwing
Wide his hands, he begged high heaven for help:

890 "Almighty Jupiter, unless by now
You loathe all Trojans to the last man,
If divine kindness shown in ancient days
Can still pay heed to mortal suffering,
Grant that our fleet survive this fire, father,
895 Even now: at the last moment save
The frail affairs of Trojans from destruction.
Otherwise, do what now remains to do:

Lines 667–691

With your consuming bolt, with your right hand,
If I deserve it, blast me and overwhelm us."

900   Scarce had he spoken when a black storm broke
      In wild fury with spouting rain, while peals
      Of thunder shook the low lands and high places.
      Down from the whole sky the torrents came
      In dense murk, black as pitch, out of the south.
905   And ships were filled up, half-burnt timbers drenched,
      Till all the fires were out, and all the hulls,
      Except for four, delivered from the burning.
      Aeneas had been stunned by the mischance
      And could not rest, turning this way and that
910   Within him, coping with momentous questions:
      Should he forget the destiny foretold
      And make his home in Sicily, or try
      Again for Italy? Nautës, an older man,
      And one whom Pallas Tritonia had taught
915   His famous thoughtfulness (she gave him answers,
      As to the meaning of the gods' great wrath
      Or what the pattern of the fates required)
      Nautës addressed Aeneas to give him heart:

      "Sir, born of an immortal, let us follow
920   Where our fates may lead, or lead us back.
      Whatever comes,
      All Fortune can be mastered by endurance.
      You have Acestës, a Dardanian
      Divine in lineage: make him your counsellor,
925   Congenial as he is, in all your plans.
      And now these ships are burnt, hand over to him
      The number of those they might have carried: those
      Too weary of your great quest, your sea faring—
      Men who have had long lives, women worn out
930   On shipboard, feeble men, afraid of danger:
      Set them apart, and let them have their city
      Here in this land, the tired ones, and they
      May with permission call their town Acesta."

Lines 691–718

His old friend's plan attracted him, but still
935   Aeneas wondered, all the more torn between
Anxieties of all kinds. As now black Night
Borne upward in her car possessed the sky,
Out of the dark, from heaven, his father's image
Seemed to float suddenly and speak:

940   "My son,
Dearer to me than life while life remained,
And pitted now against the fates of Troy,
I come by Jove's command who drove away
The fire from your ships, being moved to pity
945   In heaven's height at last. Obey the counsel,
Beautiful as it is, now given by Nautës:
Embark for Italy chosen men, the bravest.
In Latium you must battle down in war
A hard race, hard by nurture and by training.
950   First, however, visit the underworld
The halls of Dis, and through profound Avernus
Come to meet me, son. Black Tartarus
With its grim realm of shades is not my home,
But radiant gatherings of godly souls
955   I have about me in Elysium.
To that place the pure Sibyl, after blood
Of many black sheep flows out, will conduct you.
Then you will hear of your whole race to come
And what walled town is given you. Farewell:
960   Night passes midway on her wheeling course,
And cruel Sunrise fanned me with a breath
Her laboring team exhaled."

                         And after speaking
He faded like thin smoke into the air.
965   Aeneas cried: "So soon? Where to, then? Must you
Vanish? Are you taking flight from someone?
Who can forbid you to be held by me?"

So he called out, then turned to poke the embers,
The drowsing fire on his hearth, and paid
970   His humble duty to the Lar of Troy

And Vesta's shrine—the goddess of the hearth—
With ground meal, as in ritual sacrifice,
And a full incense casket. Then at once
He called his captains, told Acestës first
975   Of Jove's command as taught by his dear father,
And what now stood decided in his mind.
No long exchange, no dissent from Acestës.
They listed, for the town, the older women
And set aside men so inclined, who felt
980   No need of winning honor. The remainder
Built new thwarts, replaced burnt timbers, fitted
Oars and rigging: a slim band of men
But brave hearts, keen for war. Meanwhile Aeneas
Marked with a plow the limits of the town
985   And gave home sites by lot. One place should be
Called Ilium, he decreed, one quarter Troy.
Acestës, Trojan that he was, took pleasure
In his new realm, proclaiming an assembly
And giving laws to the senate now convoked.
990   Then on Mount Eryx height a shrine was built,
Hard by the stars, to Venus of Idalia,
And round about Anchises' tomb they left
A hallowed grove, with an attendant priest.

Nine days the people feasted, and the altars
995   Fumed with offerings; light airs lulled the sea
And blowing often from the south renewed
Their call to cross the main. A sound of weeping
Rose on the curving shore, as by a night,
And then a day, embracing, they postponed it.
1000   Even those women, even those men, to whom
The sea's face had seemed harsh, its very name
Intolerable, now desired to go
And bear all exile's toil. Aeneas spoke to them
With kindness and commended them in tears
1005   To their blood-brother Acestës. He decreed
Three calves be slain to Eryx and a lamb
To the Stormwinds. Cables were then cast off,
As he himself, wearing an olive garland,

Standing upon the prow apart, held out
1010 The shallow cup and flung the vitals down
Into the salt surf, then poured out the wine.
Wind coming up astern blew in their wake
As crewmen struck their oars into the swell
And swept a path over the sea.

101.   But now,
Beset with worries, Venus turned to Neptune,
Unfolding from her heart complaints and pleas:
"Juno's anger, and her implacable heart,
Drive me to prayers beneath my dignity.
1020 No length of time, no piety affects her,
Unbroken in will by Jove's commands or Fate,
She never holds her peace. To have devoured
A city from the heart of Phrygia's people
In her vile hatred, this was not enough,
1025 Nor to have dragged the remnant left from Troy
Through all harassment. Now she harries still
Troy's bones and ashes. She alone may know
The causes of such madness. You yourself
Are witness to the giant storm she roused
1030 Not long ago in the sea off Libya,
Mixing sea and sky, with hurricane winds
Of Aeolus her standby—though in vain—
And all this dared in your domain.
But look at her new crime, how she egged on
1035 The Trojan women to their foul ship-burning,
Making the Trojans, for that loss of ships,
Forsake their own folk in a strange country.
But as to what comes next, I beg you, let them
Safely entrust their sailing ships to you
1040 Across the water; let them reach that stream,
Laurentine Tiber—if one may concede
These favors, if the Parcae grant their city."

Lines 775–798

The son of Saturn, tamer of the deep,
Replied:

1045   "Cytherëa, you have every right
To trust my kingdom: you were born from it.
Then, too, I've merited your trust, so often
Have I repressed those mad fits and that fury
Of heavens and the sea. On land as well—
1050 As Xanthus and Simoïs can testify—
I cared for your Aeneas. That day Achilles,
Hot in pursuit, pinned Trojan troops half dead
With fright against their walls and killed a myriad,
Making the rivers, choked with corpses, groan,
1055 So Xanthus could not find his bed or send
His current seaward: then, as Aeneas fought—
Against the odds, against the frown of heaven—
The mighty son of Peleus, it was I
Who caught and saved him in a sack of cloud,
1060 Lust though I did to cast down walls I built
With my own hands—walls of oath-breaking Troy.
To this day my regard for him is the same.
Dispel your fear. He shall, as you desire,
Enter Avernus port. One shall be lost,
1065 But only one to look for, lost at sea:
One life given for many."
                    He assured
And cheered the goddess in this way, then yoked
His team with gold, fitted the foaming bits
1070 In their wild mouths, and let the reins run free,
Flying light on the crests in his blue car.
Waves calmed and quieted, the long sea-swell
Smoothed out under his thundering axle tree,
And storm clouds thinned away in heaven's vast air.
1075 Now came the diverse shapes of his companions,
Enormous whales and Glaucus' hoary troop,
Palaemon, son of Ino, arrowy Tritons,
Phorcus' whole host, Thetis and Mélitë
And virgin Panopëa on the left,
1080 Nesaeë, Spio, Thalia, Cymódocë.

The joys of the fair weather filled in turn
Aeneas' attentive heart.
                              "Up with the masts,"
He ordered. "Sails unfurled from the yard arms!"

1085 The seamen as one man hauled on the sheets
Now port, now starboard, set the bellying canvas
Evenly to the wind, and took the braces,
Veering, this way and that, yard arms aloft
Until the freshening stern-wind filled the sails
1090 And bore them onward. On the leading ship
Palinurus guided the close formation,
All under orders to set course by him.
Now dewy Night had touched her midway mark
Or nearly, and the crews, relaxed in peace
1095 On their hard rowing benches, took their rest,
When Somnus, gliding softly from the stars
Put the night air aside, parted the darkness,
Palinurus, in quest of you. He brought
Bad dreams to you, in all your guiltlessness.
1100 Upon the high poop deck the god sat down
In Phorbas' guise, and said:
                              "Son of Iasius,
Palinurus, the very sea itself
Moves the ships onward. There's a steady breeze.
1105 The hour for rest has come. Put down your head
And steal a respite for your tired eyes.
I'll man your tiller for a while."
                              But Palinurus
Barely looked around. He said:

1110 "Forget my good sense for this peaceful face
The sea puts on, the calm swell? Put my trust
In that capricious monster? Or hand over
Aeneas to the tricky winds, when I
Have been deceived so often by clear weather?"

1115 With this response he held fast to the helm
And would not give it up, but kept his eyes

Lines 827–853

Upon the stars. Now see the god, his bough
A-drip with Lethe's dew, and slumberous
With Stygian power, giving it a shake
1120 Over the pilot's temples, to unfix,
Although he fought it, both his swimming eyes.
His unexpected drowse barely begun,
Somnus leaned over him and flung him down
In the clear water, breaking off with him
1125 A segment of the stern and steering oar.
Headfirst he went down, calling in vain on friends.

The god himself took flight into thin air,
But still the fleet ran safely on its course,
1130 Serene in Father Neptune's promises.
Borne onward, now it neared the Sirens' reef,
That oldtime peril, white with many bones,
Now loud far off with trample of surf on rock.
Here the commander felt a loss of way
1135 As his ship's head swung off, lacking a helmsman,
And he himself took over, holding course
In the night waves. Hard hit by his friend's fate
And sighing bitterly, he said:
                                        "For counting
1140 Overmuch on a calm world, Palinurus,
You must lie naked on some unknown shore."

Lines 853–871

BOOK

VI

THE WORLD
BELOW

So grieving, and in tears, he gave the ship
Her head before the wind, drawing toward land
At the Euboian settlement of Cumae.
Ships came about, prows pointing seaward, anchors
5 Biting to hold them fast, and rounded sterns
Indented all the water's edge. The men
Debarked in groups, eager to go ashore
Upon Hesperia. Some struck seeds of fire
Out of the veins of flint, and some explored
10 The virgin woods, lairs of wild things, for fuel,
Pointing out, too, what streams they found.

                                                    Aeneas,
In duty bound, went inland to the heights
Where overshadowing Apollo dwells
15 And nearby, in a place apart—a dark
Enormous cave—the Sibyl feared by men.
In her the Delian god of prophecy
Inspires uncanny powers of mind and soul,
Disclosing things to come. Here Trojan captains
20 Walked to Diana of the Crossroads' wood
And entered under roofs of gold. They say
That Daedalus, when he fled the realm of Minos,
Dared to entrust himself to stroking wings
And to the air of heaven—unheard-of path—
25 On which he swam away to the cold North

At length to touch down on that very height
Of the Chalcidians. Here, on earth again
He dedicated to you, Phoebus Apollo,
The twin sweeps of his wings; here he laid out
30   A spacious temple. In the entrance way
Androgeos' death appeared, then Cecrops' children
Ordered to pay in recompense each year
The living flesh of seven sons. The urn
From which the lots were drawn stood modeled there.
35   And facing it, upon the opposite door,
The land of Crete, emergent from the sea;
Here the brutish act appeared: Pasiphaë
Being covered by the bull in the cow's place,
Then her mixed breed, her child of double form,
40   The Minotaur, get of unholy lust.
Here, too, that puzzle of the house of Minos,
The maze none could untangle, until, touched
By a great love shown by a royal girl,
He, Daedalus himself, unravelled all
45   The baffling turns and dead ends in the dark,
Guiding the blind way back by a skein unwound.
In that high sculpture you, too, would have had
Your great part, Icarus, had grief allowed.
Twice your father had tried to shape your fall
50   In gold, but twice his hands dropped.

                      Here the Trojans
Would have passed on and gazed and read it all,
Had not Achatës, whom they had sent ahead,
Returned now with the priestess of Apollo
55   And of Diana, goddess of the Crossroads—
Deiphobë, the Sibyl, Glaucus' daughter.
Thus she addressed the king:

                      "The hour demands
No lagging over sights like these. Instead,
60   You should make offering of seven young bulls
From an ungelded herd, and seven again
Well-chosen ewes."

                    With these words for Aeneas—
Orders his men were quick to act upon—

65 The priestess called them to her lofty shrine.
The cliff's huge flank is honeycombed, cut out
In a cavern perforated a hundred times,
Having a hundred mouths, with rushing voices
Carrying the responses of the Sibyl.
70 Here, as the men approached the entrance way,
The Sibyl cried out:

                  "Now is the time to ask
Your destinies!"

           And then:

75   "The god! Look there!
The god!"
             And as she spoke neither her face
Nor hue went untransformed, nor did her hair
Stay neatly bound: her breast heaved, her wild heart
80 Grew large with passion. Taller to their eyes
And sounding now no longer like a mortal
Since she had felt the god's power breathing near,
She cried:
           "Slow, are you, in your vows and prayers?
85 Trojan Aeneas, are you slow? Be quick,
The great mouths of the god's house, thunderstruck,
Will never open till you pray."
                   Her lips
Closed tight on this. A chill ran through the bones
90 Of the tough Teucrians, but their king poured out
Entreaties from his deepest heart:
                   "O Phoebus,
God who took pity on the pain of Troy,
Who guided Paris' hand, his Dardan shaft,
95 Against the body of Aiacidës,
As you led on I entered all those seas
Washing great lands, and then the distant tribe
Of the Massylians at the Syrtës' edge.
Now we take hold at last of Italy
100 That slipped away so long. Grant that the fortune
Of Troy shall have pursued us this far only!
And all you gods and goddesses as well

Who took offence at Ilium and our pride,
At last, and rightly, you may spare
105 Pergamum's children. Most holy prophetess,
Foreknowing things to come, I ask no kingdom
Other than fate allows me; let our people
Make their settlement in Latium
With all Troy's wandering gods and shaken powers.
110 Then I shall dedicate a temple here
To Phoebus and Diana of the Crossroads,
Ordering festal days in Phoebus' name.
A holy place awaits you in my kingdom
Where I shall store your prophecies, your dark
115 Revelations to my people, and appoint
A chosen priesthood for you, gracious one.
But now commit no verses to the leaves
Or they may be confused, shuffled and whirled
By playing winds: chant them aloud, I pray."

120 Then he fell silent. But the prophetess
Whom the bestriding god had not yet broken
Stormed about the cavern, trying to shake
His influence from her breast, while all the more
He tired her mad jaws, quelled her savage heart,
125 And tamed her by his pressure. In the end
The cavern's hundred mouths all of themselves
Unclosed to let the Sibyl's answers through:

"You, sir, now quit at last of the sea's dangers,
For whom still greater are in store on land,
130 The Dardan race will reach Lavinian country—
Put that anxiety away—but there
Will wish they had not come. Wars, vicious wars
I see ahead, and Tiber foaming blood.
Simoïs, Xanthus, Dorians encamped—
135 You'll have them all again, with an Achilles,
Child of Latium, he, too, goddess-born.
And nowhere from pursuit of Teucrians
Will Juno stray, while you go destitute,
Begging so many tribes and towns for aid.

140   The cause of suffering here again will be
A bride foreign to Teucrians, a marriage
Made with a stranger.
                 Never shrink from blows.
Boldly, more boldly where your luck allows,

145   Go forward, face them. A first way to safety
Will open where you reckon on it least,
From a Greek city."
                These were the sentences
In which the Sibyl of Cumae from her shrine

150   Sang out her riddles, echoing in the cave,
Dark sayings muffling truths, the way Apollo
Pulled her up raging, or else whipped her on,
Digging the spurs beneath her breast. As soon
As her fit ceased, her wild voice quieted,

155   The great soldier, Aeneas, began to speak:

"No novel kinds of hardship, no surprises,
Loom ahead, Sister. I foresaw them all,
Went through them in my mind. One thing I pray for:
Since it is here they say one finds the gate

160   Of the king of under world, the shadowy marsh
That wells from Acheron, may I have leave
To go to my dear father's side and see him.
Teach me the path, show me the entrance way.
Through fires, and with a thousand spears behind,

165   I brought him on these shoulders, rescued him
Amid our enemies. He shared my voyage,
Bore all the seas with me, hard nights and days
Of menace from the sea and sky, beyond
The strength and lot of age, frail though he was.

170   Indeed, he prayed this very prayer; he told me
That I should come to you and beg it humbly.
Pity a son and father, gracious lady,
All this is in your power. Hecatë
Gave you authority to have and hold

175   Avernus wood. If Orpheus could call
His wife's shade up, relying on the strings
That sang loud on his Thracian lyre; if Pollux

Redeemed his brother, taking his turn at death,
So often passing back and forth; why name
180 The heroes, Theseus and Hercules?
By birth I too descend from Jove on high—"

While in these terms he prayed and pressed the altar,
Breaking in, the Sibyl said:
185   "Offspring
Of gods by blood, Trojan Anchises' son,
The way downward is easy from Avernus.
Black Dis's door stands open night and day.
But to retrace your steps to heaven's air,
190 There is the trouble, there is the toil. A few
Whom a benign Jupiter has loved or whom
Fiery heroism has borne to heaven,
Sons of gods, could do it. All midway
Are forests, then Cocytus, thick and black,
195 Winds through the gloom. But if you feel such love,
And such desire to cross the Stygian water
Twice, to view the night of Tartarus twice—
If this mad effort's to your liking, then
Consider what you must accomplish first.
200 A tree's deep shade conceals a bough whose leaves
And pliant twigs are all of gold, a thing
Sacred to Juno of the lower world.
The whole grove shelters it, and thickest shade
In dusky valleys shuts it in. And yet
205 No one may enter hidden depths
Below the earth unless he picks this bough,
The tree's fruit, with its foliage of gold.
Proserpina decreed this bough, as due her,
Should be given into her own fair hands
210 When torn away. In place of it a second
Grows up without fail, all gold as well,
Flowering with metallic leaves again.
So lift your eyes and search, and once you find it
Pull away the bough. It will come willingly,
215 Easily, if you are called by fate.
If not, with all your strength you cannot conquer it,

Lines 121–148

Cannot lop it off with a sword's edge.
A further thing is this: your friend's dead body—
Ah, but you *don't* know!—lies out there unburied,
Polluting all your fleet with death
220 While you are lingering, waiting on my counsel
Here at my door. First give the man his rest,
Entomb him; lead black beasts to sacrifice;
Begin with these amends. Then in due course
You'll see the Stygian forest rise before you,
225 Regions not for the living."

She fell silent,
Closing her lips. With downcast face and eyes
Aeneas turned from the cavern to the shore,
Dark matters on his mind. Steadfast Achatës
230 Walked beside him with deliberate pace
And equal anxieties. The two exchanged
In shifting conversation many guesses
As to that friend, now dead, now to be buried,
So the prophetess had said—then suddenly
235 As they came down to the dry beach they saw
Misenus, robbed of life by early death,
Their own Misenus, a son of Aeolus,
Never surpassed at rousing fighting men
With brazen trumpet, setting Mars afire.
240 Once he had been great Hector's adjutant,
Going forward at Hector's side in battle,
Brilliant with trumpet and with spear as well.
After Achilles took the life of Hector,
This gallant soldier joined Dardan Aeneas
245 In allegiance to no lesser cause. That day
By chance, as he blew notes on a hollow shell,
Making the sea sing back, in his wild folly
He dared the gods to rival him. Then Triton,

Envious, if this can be believed,
250 Caught him and put him under in the surf
Amid the rocks off shore.

                                All who were there
Clamored around the body in lament,
Aeneas, the good captain, most of all.
255 In haste then, even as they wept, they turned
To carry out the orders of the Sibyl,
Racing to pile up logs for the altar-pyre
And build it sky-high. Into the virgin forest,
Thicket of wild things, went the men, and down
260 The pitch pines came, the bitten ilex rang
With axe blows, ash and oak were split with wedges,
Mighty rowans were trundled down the slopes.

Aeneas himself went first in all this labor,
Cheering his fellows on, with implements
265 Like theirs in hand; but grimly in his heart
He wondered, studying the unmeasured forest,
And fell to prayer:

                                "If only the golden bough
Might shine for us in such a wilderness!
270 As all the prophetess foretold was true—
Misenus, in your case only too true."

The words were barely uttered when two doves
In casual flight out of the upper air
Came down before the man's eyes to alight
275 On the green grass, and the great hero knew
These birds to be his mother's. Joyously
He prayed:

                                "O be my guides, if there's a way.
Wing on, into that woodland where the bough,
280 The priceless bough, shadows the fertile ground.
My divine mother, do not fail your son
In a baffling time."

                                Then he stood still to see
What signs the doves might give, or where their flight
285 Might lead him. And they fed, and then flew on,

Each time as far as one who came behind
Could keep in view. Then when they reached the gorge
Of sulphurous Avernus, first borne upward
Through the lucent air, they glided down
290 To their desired rest, the two-hued tree
Where glitter of gold filtered between green boughs.
Like mistletoe that in the woods in winter
Thrives with yellowish berries and new leaves—
A parasite on the trunk it twines around—
295 So bright amid the dark green ilex shone
The golden leafage, rustling in light wind.
Aeneas at once briskly took hold of it
And, though it clung, greedily broke it off,
Then carried it to the Sibyl's cave.
300   Meanwhile
The Teucrians on the shore wept for Misenus,
Doing for thankless dust the final honors.
First they built up a giant pyre, enriched
With pitch pine and split oak, with somber boughs
305 Alongside and dark cypresses in front.
On top they made a blazon of bright arms.
One group set water boiling over flames,
Then washed the cold corpse and anointed it,
Groaning loud, and laid it out when mourned
310 On a low couch, with purple robes thrown over it.
A hero's shrouding. Bearers then took up
As their sad duty the great bier. With eyes
Averted in their fathers' ancient way
They held the torch below.
315   Heaped offerings
Blazed up and burned—food, incense, oil in bowls.
And when the flame died and the coals fell in,
They gave a bath of wine to the pyre's remnant,
Thirsty ash; then picking out the bones
320 Corynaeus enclosed them in an urn.
The same priest with pure water went three times
Around the company, asperging them
With cleansing drops from a ripe olive sprig,
And spoke the final words. Faithfully then

325   Aeneas heaped a great tomb over the dead,
    Placing his arms, his oar, his trumpet there
    Beneath a promontory, named for him,
    Misenum now and always, age to age.
    All this accomplished, with no more ado
330   He carried out the orders of the Sibyl.

The cavern was profound, wide-mouthed, and huge,
    Rough underfoot, defended by dark pool
    And gloomy forest. Overhead, flying things
    Could never safely take their way, such deathly
335   Exhalations rose from the black gorge
    Into the dome of heaven. The priestess here
    Placed four black bullocks, wet their brows with wine,
    Plucked bristles from between the horns and laid them
    As her first offerings on the holy fire,
340   Calling aloud to Hecatë, supreme
    In heaven and Erebus. Others drew knives
    Across beneath and caught warm blood in bowls.
    Aeneas by the sword's edge offered up
    To Night, the mother of the Eumenidës,
345   And her great sister, Earth, a black-fleeced lamb,
    A sterile cow to thee, Proserpina.
    Then for the Stygian king he lit at night
    New altars where he placed over the flames
    Entire carcasses of bulls, and poured
350   Rich oil on blazing viscera. Only see:
    Just at the light's edge, just before sunrise,
    Earth rumbled underfoot, forested ridges
    Broke into movement, and far howls of dogs
    Were heard across the twilight as the goddess
355   Nearer and nearer came.
                    "Away, away,"
    The Sibyl cried, "all those unblest, away!
    Depart from all the grove! But you, Aeneas,

Enter the path here, and unsheathe your sword.
360   There's need of gall and resolution now."

She flung herself wildly into the cave-mouth,
Leading, and he strode boldly at her heels.
Gods who rule the ghosts; all silent shades;
And Chaos and infernal Fiery Stream,
365   And regions of wide night without a sound,
May it be right to tell what I have heard,
May it be right, and fitting, by your will,
That I describe the deep world sunk in darkness
Under the earth.
370   Now dim to one another
In desolate night they walked on through the gloom,
Through Dis's homes all void, and empty realms,
As one goes through a wood by a faint moon's
Treacherous light, when Jupiter veils the sky
375   And black night blots the colors of the world.

Before the entrance, in the jaws of Orcus,
Grief and avenging Cares have made their beds,
And pale Diseases and sad Age are there,
And Dread, and Hunger that sways men to crime,
380   And sordid Want—in shapes to affright the eyes—
And Death and Toil and Death's own brother, Sleep,
And the mind's evil joys; on the door sill
Death-bringing War, and iron cubicles
Of the Eumenidës, and raving Discord,
385   Viperish hair bound up in gory bands.
In the courtyard a shadowy giant elm
Spreads ancient boughs, her ancient arms where dreams,
False dreams, the old tale goes, beneath each leaf
Cling and are numberless. There, too,
390   About the doorway forms of monsters crowd—
Centaurs, twiformed Scyllas, hundred-armed
Briareus, and the Lernaean hydra
Hissing horribly, and the Chimaera
Breathing dangerous flames, and Gorgons, Harpies,

Lines 260–289

395   Huge Geryon, triple-bodied ghost.
    Here, swept by sudden fear, drawing his sword,
    Aeneas stood on guard with naked edge
    Against them as they came. If his companion,
    Knowing the truth, had not admonished him
400   How faint these lives were—empty images
    Hovering bodiless—he had attacked
    And cut his way through phantoms, empty air.

    The path goes on from that place to the waves
    Of Tartarus's Acheron. Thick with mud,
405   A whirlpool out of a vast abyss
    Boils up and belches all the silt it carries
    Into Cocytus. Here the ferryman,
    A figure of fright, keeper of waters and streams,
    Is Charon, foul and terrible, his beard
410   Grown wild and hoar, his staring eyes all flame,
    His sordid cloak hung from a shoulder knot.
    Alone he poles his craft and trims the sails
    And in his rusty hull ferries the dead,
    Old now—but old age in the gods is green.

    Here a whole crowd came streaming to the banks,
415   Mothers and men, the forms with all life spent
    Of heroes great in valor, boys and girls
    Unmarried, and young sons laid on the pyre
    Before their parents' eyes—as many souls
    As leaves that yield their hold on boughs and fall
420   Through forests in the early frost of autumn,
    Or as migrating birds from the open sea
    That darken heaven when the cold season comes
    And drives them overseas to sunlit lands.
    There all stood begging to be first across
425   And reached out longing hands to the far shore.

    But the grim boatman now took these aboard,
    Now those, waving the rest back from the strand.
    In wonder at this and touched by the commotion,
430   Aeneas said:

Lines 289–318

"Tell me, Sister, what this means,
The crowd at the stream. Where are the souls bound?
How are they tested, so that these turn back,
While those take oars to cross the dead-black water?"

435 Briefly the ancient priestess answered him:

"Cocytus is the deep pool that you see,
The swamp of Styx beyond, infernal power
By which the gods take oath and fear to break it.
All in the nearby crowd you notice here
440 Are pauper souls, the souls of the unburied.
Charon's the boatman. Those the water bears
Are souls of buried men. He may not take them
Shore to dread shore on the hoarse currents there
Until their bones rest in the grave, or till
445 They flutter and roam this side a hundred years;
They may have passage then, and may return
To cross the deeps they long for."

                                            Anchises' son
Had halted, pondering on so much, and stood
450 In pity for the souls' hard lot. Among them
He saw two sad ones of unhonored death,
Leucaspis and the Lycian fleet's commander,
Orontës, who had sailed the windy sea
From Troy together, till the Southern gale
455 Had swamped and whirled them down, both ship and men.
Of a sudden he saw his helmsman, Palinurus,
Going by, who but a few nights before
On course from Libya, as he watched the stars,
Had been pitched overboard astern. As soon
460 As he made sure of the disconsolate one
In all the gloom, Aeneas called:

                                            "Which god
Took you away from us and put you under,
Palinurus? Tell me. In this one prophecy
465 Apollo, who had never played me false,
Falsely foretold you'd be unharmed at sea
And would arrive at the Ausonian coast.

Is the promise kept?"
                              But the shade said:
470   "Phoebus' caldron
Told you no lie, my captain, and no god
Drowned me at sea. The helm that I hung on to,
Duty bound to keep our ship on course,
By some great shock chanced to be torn away,
475 And I went with it overboard. I swear
By the rough sea, I feared less for myself
Than for your ship: with rudder gone and steersman
Knocked overboard, it might well come to grief
In big seas running. Three nights, heavy weather
480 Out of the South on the vast water tossed me.
On the fourth dawn, I sighted Italy
Dimly ahead, as a wave-crest lifted me.
By turns I swam and rested, swam again
And got my footing on the beach, but savages
485 Attacked me as I clutched at a cliff-top,
Weighted down by my wet clothes. Poor fools,
They took me for a prize and ran me through.
Surf has me now, and sea winds, washing me
Close inshore.
490   By heaven's happy light
And the sweet air, I beg you, by your father,
And by your hopes of Iulus' rising star,
Deliver me from this captivity,
Unconquered friend! Throw earth on me—you can—
495 Put in to Velia port! Or if there be
Some way to do it, if your goddess mother
Shows a way—and I feel sure you pass
These streams and Stygian marsh by heaven's will—
Give this poor soul your hand, take me across,
500 Let me at least in death find quiet haven."
When he had made his plea, the Sibyl said:
"From what source comes this craving, Palinurus?
Would you though still unburied see the Styx
And the grim river of the Eumenidës,
505 Or even the river bank, without a summons?
Abandon hope by prayer to make the gods

Change their decrees. Hold fast to what I say
To comfort your hard lot: neighboring folk
In cities up and down the coast will be
510 Induced by portents to appease your bones,
Building a tomb and making offerings there
On a cape forever named for Palinurus."

The Sibyl's words relieved him, and the pain
Was for a while dispelled from his sad heart,
515 Pleased at the place-name. So the two walked on
Down to the stream. Now from the Stygian water
The boatman, seeing them in the silent wood
And headed for the bank, cried out to them
A rough uncalled-for challenge:
520   "Who are you
In armor, visiting our rivers? Speak
From where you are, stop there, say why you come.
This is the region of the Shades, and Sleep,
And drowsy Night. It breaks eternal law
525 For the Stygian craft to carry living bodies.
Never did I rejoice, I tell you, letting
Alcidës cross, or Theseus and Pirithous,
Demigods by paternity though they were,
Invincible in power. One forced in chains
530 From the king's own seat the watchdog of the dead
And dragged him away trembling. The other two
Were bent on carrying our lady off
From Dis's chamber."
                        This the prophetess
535 And servant of Amphrysian Apollo
Briefly answered:
                    "Here are no such plots,
So fret no more. These weapons threaten nothing.
Let the great watchdog at the door howl on
540 Forever terrifying the bloodless shades.
Let chaste Proserpina remain at home
In her uncle's house. The man of Troy, Aeneas,
Remarkable for loyalty, great in arms,
Goes through the deepest shades of Erebus

545 To see his father.

          If the very image
Of so much goodness moves you not at all,
Here is a bough"—at this she showed the bough
That had been hidden, held beneath her dress—
550 "You'll recognize it."

          Then his heart, puffed up
With rage, subsided. They had no more words.
His eyes fixed on the ancient gift, the bough,
The destined gift, so long unseen, now seen,
555 He turned his dusky craft and made for shore.
There from the long thwarts where they sat he cleared
The other souls and made the gangway wide,
Letting the massive man step in the bilge
The leaky coracle groaned at the weight
560 And took a flood of swampy water in.
At length, on the other side, he put ashore
The prophetess and hero in the mire,
A formless ooze amid the grey-green sedge.
Great Cerberus barking with his triple throat
565 Makes all that shoreline ring, as he lies huge
In a facing cave Seeing his neck begin
To come alive with snakes, the prophetess
Tossed him a lump of honey and drugged meal
To make him drowse. Three ravenous gullets gaped
570 And he snapped up the sop. Then his great bulk
Subsided and lay down through all the cave.
Now seeing the watchdog deep in sleep, Aeneas
Took the opening: swiftly he turned away
From the river over which no soul returns.

575 Now voices crying loud were heard at once—
The souls of infants wailing. At the door
Of the sweet life they were to have no part in,
Torn from the breast, a black day took them off
And drowned them all in bitter death. Near these

580 Were souls falsely accused, condemned to die.
But not without a judge, or jurymen,
Had these souls got their places: Minos reigned
As the presiding judge, moving the urn,
And called a jury of the silent ones
585 To learn of lives and accusations. Next
Were those sad souls, benighted, who contrived
Their own destruction, and as they hated daylight,
Cast their lives away. How they would wish
In the upper air now to endure the pain
590 Of poverty and toil! But iron law
Stands in the way, since the drear hateful swamp
Has pinned them down here, and the Styx that winds
Nine times around exerts imprisoning power.
Not far away, spreading on every side,
595 The Fields of Mourning came in view, so called
Since here are those whom pitiless love consumed
With cruel wasting, hidden on paths apart
By myrtle woodland growing overhead.
In death itself, pain will not let them be.
600 He saw here Phaedra, Procris, Eriphylë
Sadly showing the wounds her hard son gave;
Evadnë and Pasiphaë, at whose side
Laodamia walked, and Caeneus,
A young man once, a woman now, and turned
605 Again by fate into the older form.
Among them, with her fatal wound still fresh,
Phoenician Dido wandered the deep wood.
The Trojan captain paused nearby and knew
Her dim form in the dark, as one who sees,
610 Early in the month, or thinks to have seen, the moon
Rising through cloud, all dim. He wept and spoke
Tenderly to her:
                    "Dido, so forlorn,
The story then that came to me was true,
615 That you were out of life, had met your end
By your own hand. Was I, was I the cause?
I swear by heaven's stars, by the high gods,
By any certainty below the earth,

620 I left your land against my will, my queen.
The gods' commands drove me to do their will,
As now they drive me through this world of shades,
These mouldy waste lands and these depths of night.
And I could not believe that I would hurt you
625 So terribly by going. Wait a little.
Do not leave my sight.
Am I someone to flee from? The last word
Destiny lets me say to you is this."

Aeneas with such pleas tried to placate
The burning soul, savagely glaring back,
630 And tears came to his eyes. But she had turned
With gaze fixed on the ground as he spoke on,
Her face no more affected than if she were
Immobile granite or Marpesian stone.
At length she flung away from him and fled,
635 His enemy still, into the shadowy grove
Where he whose bride she once had been, Sychaeus,
Joined in her sorrows and returned her love.
Aeneas still gazed after her in tears,
Shaken by her ill fate and pitying her.

640 With effort then he took the given way,
And they went on, reaching the farthest lands
Where men famous in war gather apart.
Here Tydeus came to meet him, and then came
Parthenopaeus, glorious in arms,
645 Adrastus then, a pallid shade. Here too
Were Dardans long bewept in the upper air,
Men who died in the great war. And he groaned
To pick these figures out, in a long file,
Glaucus, Medon, Thersilochus, besides
650 Antenor's three sons, then the priest of Ceres
Polyboetës, then Idaeus, holding
Still to his warcar, holding his old gear.
To right and left they crowd the path and stay
And will not have enough of seeing him,

Lines 460–487

655 But love to hold him back, to walk beside him,
And hear the story of why he came.
                                    Not so
Agamemnon's phalanx, chiefs of the Danaans:
Seeing the living man in bronze that glowed
660 Through the dark air, they shrank in fear. Some turned
And ran, as once, when routed, to the ships,
While others raised a battle shout, or tried to,
Mouths agape, mocked by the whispering cry.
Here next he saw Deïphobus, Priam's son,
665 Mutilated from head to foot, his face
And both hands cruelly torn, ears shorn away,
Nose to the noseholes lopped by a shameful stroke.
Barely knowing the shade who quailed before him
Covering up his tortured face, Aeneas
670 Spoke out to him in his known voice:
                                    "Deïphobus,
Gallant officer in high Teucer's line,
Who chose this brutal punishment, who had
So much the upper hand of you? I heard
675 On that last night that you had fallen, spent
After a slaughter of Pelasgians—
Fallen on piled-up carnage. It was I
Who built on Rhoeteum Point an empty tomb
And sent a high call to your soul three times.
680 Your name, your armor, marks the place. I could not
Find you, friend, to put your bones in earth
In the old country as I came away."

And Priam's son replied:
                                    "You left undone
685 Nothing, my friend, but gave all ritual due
Deïphobus, due a dead man's shade. My lot
And the Laconian woman's ghastly doing
Sank me in this hell. These are the marks
She left me as her memorial. You know
690 How between one false gladness and another
We spent that last night—no need to remind you.

When the tall deadly horse came at one bound,
With troops crammed in its paunch, above our towers,
She made a show of choral dance and led
695 Our Phrygian women crying out on Bacchus
Here and there—but held a torch amid them,
Signalling to Danaans from the Height.
Worn by the long day, heavily asleep,
I lay in my unlucky bridal chamber,
700 And rest, profound and sweet, most like the rest
Of death, weighed on me as I lay. Meanwhile
She, my distinguished wife, moved all my arms
Out of the house—as she had slipped my sword,
My faithful sword, out from beneath my pillow—
705 Opened the door and called in Menelaus,
Hoping no doubt by this great gift to him,
Her lover, to blot old infamy out. Why hold back
From telling it? The two burst in the bedroom,
Joined by that ringleader of atrocity,
710 Ulysses, of the windking's line. O gods,
If with pure lips I pray, requite the Greeks
With equal suffering! But you, now tell me
What in the world has brought you here alive:
Have you come from your sea wandering, and did heaven
715 Direct you? How could harrying fortune send you
To these sad sunless homes, disordered places?"

At this point in their talk Aurora, borne
Through high air on her glowing rosy car
Had crossed the meridian: should they linger now
720 With stories they might spend the allotted time.
But at Aeneas' side the Sibyl spoke,
Warning him briefly:

         "Night comes on, Aeneas,
We use up hours grieving. Here is the place
725 Where the road forks: on the right hand it goes
Past mighty Dis's walls, Elysium way,
Our way; but the leftward road will punish
Malefactors, taking them to Tartarus."
Deïphobus answered her:

730   "No need for anger,
     Reverend lady. I'll depart and make
     The tally in the darkness full again.
     Go on, sir, glory of us all! Go on,
     Enjoy a better destiny."

735   He spoke,
     And even as he spoke he turned away.
     Now of a sudden Aeneas looked and saw
     To the left, under a cliff, wide buildings girt
     By a triple wall round which a torrent rushed
740 With scorching flames and boulders tossed in thunder,
     The abyss's Fiery River. A massive gate
     With adamantine pillars faced the stream,
     So strong no force of men or gods in war
     May ever avail to crack and bring it down,
745 And high in air an iron tower stands
     On which Tisiphonë, her bloody robe
     Pulled up about her, has her seat and keeps
     Unsleeping watch over the entrance way
     By day and night. From the interior, groans
750 Are heard, and thud of lashes, clanking iron,
     Dragging chains. Arrested in his tracks,
     Appalled by what he heard, Aeneas stood.

     "What are the forms of evil here? O Sister,
     Tell me. And the punishments dealt out:
755 Why such a lamentation?"
                    Said the Sibyl:
     "Light of the Teucrians, it is decreed
     That no pure soul may cross the sill of evil.
     When, however, Hecatë appointed me
760 Caretaker of Avernus wood, she led me
     Through heaven's punishments and taught me all.
     This realm is under Cretan Rhadamanthus'
     Iron rule. He sentences. He listens
     And makes the souls confess their crooked ways,
765 How they put off atonements in the world
     With foolish satisfaction, thieves of time,
     Until too late, until the hour of death.

Lines 544–569

At once the avenger girdled with her whip,
Tisiphonë, leaps down to lash the guilty,
770   Vile writhing snakes held out on her left hand,
And calls her savage sisterhood. The awaited
Time has come, hell gates will shudder wide
On shrieking hinges. Can you see her now,
Her shape, as doorkeeper, upon the sill?
775   More bestial, just inside, the giant Hydra
Lurks with fifty black and yawning throats.
Then Tartarus itself goes plunging down
In darkness twice as deep as heaven is high
For eyes fixed on etherial Olympus.
780   Here is Earth's ancient race, the brood of Titans,
Hurled by the lightning down to roll forever
In the abyss. Here, too, I saw those giant
Twins of Aloeus who laid their hands
Upon great heaven to rend it and to topple
785   Jove from his high seat, and I saw, too,
Salmoneus paying dearly for the jape
Of mimicking Jove's fire, Olympus' thunder:
Shaking a bright torch from a four-horse car
He rode through Greece and his home town in Elis,
790   Glorying, claiming honor as a god—
Out of his mind, to feign with horses' hoofs
On bronze the blast and inimitable bolt.
The father almighty amid heavy cloud
Let fly his missile—no firebrand for him
795   Nor smoky pitchpine light—and spun the man
Headlong in a huge whirlwind.

                        One had sight
Of Tityos, too, child of all-mothering Earth,
His body stretched out over nine whole acres
800   While an enormous vulture with hooked beak
Forages forever in his liver,
His vitals rife with agonies. The bird,
Lodged in the chest cavity, tears at his feast,
And tissues growing again get no relief.
805   As for the Lapiths, need I tell: Ixion,
Pirithoüs, and the black crag overhead

So sure to fall it seems already falling.
Golden legs gleam on the feasters' couches,
Dishes in royal luxury prepared
810 Are laid before them—but the oldest Fury
Crouches near and springs out with her torch.
Her outcry, if they try to touch the meal.
Here come those who as long as life remained
Held brothers hateful, beat their parents, cheated
815 Poor men dependent on them; also those
Who hugged their newfound riches to themselves
And put nothing aside for relatives—
A great crowd, this—then men killed for adultery,
Men who took arms in war against the right,
820 Not scrupling to betray their lords. All these
Are hemmed in here, awaiting punishment.
Best not inquire what punishment, what form
Of suffering at their last end overwhelms them.
Some heave at a great boulder, or revolve,
825 Spreadeagled, hung on wheel-spokes. Theseus
Cleaves to his chair and cleaves to it forever.
Phlegyas in his misery teaches all souls
His lesson, thundering out amid the gloom:
'Be warned and study justice, not to scorn
830 The immortal gods.' Here's one who sold his country,
Foisted a tyrant on her, set up laws
Or nullified them for a price; another
Entered his daughter's room to take a bride
Forbidden him. All these dared monstrous wrong
835 And took what they dared try for. If I had
A hundred tongues, a hundred mouths, a voice
Of iron, I could not tell of all the shapes
Their crimes had taken, or their punishments."

All this he heard from her who for long years
840 Had served Apollo. Then she said:
                              "Come now,
Be on your way, and carry out your mission.
Let us go faster. I can see the walls
The Cyclops' forges built and, facing us,

Lines 602–631

845   The portico and gate where they command us
To leave the gifts required."

On this the two
In haste strode on abreast down the dark paths
Over the space between, and neared the doors.

850   Aeneas gained the entrance, halted there,
Asperged his body with fresh water drops,
And on the sill before him fixed the bough.

Now that at last this ritual was performed,
His duty to the goddess done, they came

855   To places of delight, to green park land,
Where souls take ease amid the Blessed Groves.
Wider expanses of high air endow
Each vista with a wealth of light. Souls here
Possess their own familiar sun and stars.

860   Some train on grassy rings, others compete
In field games, others grapple on the sand.
Feet moving to a rhythmic beat, the dancers
Group in a choral pattern as they sing.
Orpheus, the priest of Thrace, in his long robe

865   Accompanies, plucking his seven notes
Now with his fingers, now with his ivory quill.
Here is the ancient dynasty of Teucer,
Heroes high of heart, beautiful scions,
Born in greater days: Ilus, Assaracus,

870   And Dardanus, who founded Troy. Aeneas
Marvels to see their chariots and gear
Far off, all phantom: lances fixed in earth,
And teams unyoked, at graze on the wide plain.
All joy they took, alive, in cars and weapons,

875   As in the care and pasturing of horses,
Remained with them when they were laid in earth.
He saw, how vividly! along the grass
To right and left, others who feasted there

And chorused out a hymn praising Apollo,
880   Within a fragrant laurel grove, where Po
Sprang up and took his course to the world above.
The broad stream flowing on amid the forest.
This was the company of those who suffered
Wounds in battle for their country; those
885   Who in their lives were holy men and chaste
Or worthy of Phoebus in prophetic song;
Or those who bettered life, by finding out
New truths and skills; or those who to some folk
By benefactions made themselves remembered.
890   They all wore snowy chaplets on their brows.
To these souls, mingling on all sides, the Sibyl
Spoke now, and especially to Musaeus,
The central figure, toward whose towering shoulders
All the crowd gazed:
895   "Tell us, happy souls,
And you, great seer, what region holds Anchises,
Where is his resting place? For him we came
By ferry across the rivers of Erebus."
And the great soul answered briefly:
900   "None of us
Has one fixed home. We walk in shady groves
And bed on riverbanks and occupy
Green meadows fresh with streams. But if your hearts
Are set on it, first cross this ridge; and soon
905   I shall point out an easy path."
                              So saying,
He walked ahead and showed them from the height
The sweep of shining plain. Then down they went
And left the hilltops.
910   Now Aeneas' father
Anchises, deep in the lush green of a valley,
Had given all his mind to a survey
Of souls, till then confined there, who were bound
For daylight in the upper world. By chance
915   His own were those he scanned now, all his own
Descendants, with their futures and their fates,
Their characters and acts. But when he saw

Aeneas advancing toward him on the grass,
He stretched out both his hands in eagerness
920 As tears wetted his cheeks. He said in welcome:

"Have you at last come, has that loyalty
Your father counted on conquered the journey?
Am I to see your face, my son, and hear
Our voices in communion as before?
925 I thought so, surely; counting the months I thought
The time would come. My longing has not tricked me.
I greet you now, how many lands behind you,
How many seas, what blows and dangers, son!
How much I feared the land of Libya
930 Might do you harm."
                                    Aeneas said:
                                              "Your ghost,
Your sad ghost, father, often before my mind,
Impelled me to the threshold of this place.
935 My ships ride anchored in the Tuscan sea.
But let me have your hand, let me embrace you,
Do not draw back."
                                    At this his tears brimmed over
And down his cheeks. And there he tried three times
940 To throw his arms around his father's neck,
Three times the shade untouched slipped through his hands,
Weightless as wind and fugitive as dream.
Aeneas now saw at the valley's end
A grove standing apart, with stems and boughs
945 Of woodland rustling, and the stream of Lethe
Running past those peaceful glades. Around it
Souls of a thousand nations filled the air,
As bees in meadows at the height of summer
Hover and home on flowers and thickly swarm
950 On snow-white lilies, and the countryside
Is loud with humming. At the sudden vision
Shivering, at a loss, Aeneas asked
What river flowed there and what men were those
In such a throng along the riverside.
955 His father Anchises told him:

Lines 684–713

"Souls for whom
A second body is in store: their drink
Is water of Lethe, and it frees from care
In long forgetfulness. For all this time
960   I have so much desired to show you these
And tell you of them face to face—to take
The roster of my children's children here,
So you may feel with me more happiness
At finding Italy."

965   "Must we imagine,
Father, there are souls that go from here
Aloft to upper heaven, and once more
Return to bodies' dead weight? The poor souls,
How can they crave our daylight so?"

970   "My son,
I'll tell you, not to leave you mystified,"
Anchises said, and took each point in order:

First, then, the sky and lands and sheets of water,
The bright moon's globe, the Titan sun and stars,
975   Are fed within by Spirit, and a Mind
Infused through all the members of the world
Makes one great living body of the mass.
From Spirit come the races of man and beast,
The life of birds, odd creatures the deep sea
980   Contains beneath her sparkling surfaces,
And fiery energy from a heavenly source
Belongs to the generative seeds of these,
So far as they are not poisoned or clogged
By mortal bodies, their free essence dimmed
985   By earthiness and deathliness of flesh.
This makes them fear and crave, rejoice and grieve.
Imprisoned in the darkness of the body
They cannot clearly see heaven's air; in fact
Even when life departs on the last day

Lines 713–735

990   Not all the scourges of the body pass
From the poor souls, not all distress of life.
Inevitably, many malformations,
Growing together in mysterious ways,
Become inveterate. Therefore they undergo
995   The discipline of punishments and pay
In penance for old sins: some hang full length
To the empty winds, for some the stain of wrong
Is washed by floods or burned away by fire.
We suffer each his own shade. We are sent
1000   Through wide Elysium, where a few abide
In happy lands, till the long day, the round
Of Time fulfilled, has worn our stains away,
Leaving the soul's heaven-sent perception clear,
The fire from heaven pure. These other souls,
1005   When they have turned Time's wheel a thousand years,
The god calls in a crowd to Lethe stream,
That there unmemoried they may see again
The heavens and wish re-entry into bodies."
Anchises paused. He drew both son and Sibyl
1010   Into the middle of the murmuring throng,
Then picked out a green mound from which to view
The souls as they came forward, one by one,
And to take note of faces.

                      "Come," he said,
1015   "What glories follow Dardan generations
In after years, and from Italian blood
What famous children in your line will come,
Souls of the future, living in our name,
I shall tell clearly now, and in the telling
1020   Teach you your destiny. That one you see,
The young man leaning on a spear unarmed,
Has his allotted place nearest the light.
He will be first to take the upper air,
Silvius, a child with half Italian blood
1025   And an Alban name, your last born, whom your wife,
Lavinia, late in your great age will rear
In forests to be king and father of kings.

Lines 736–765

Through him our race will rule in Alba Longa.
Next him is Procas, pride of the Trojan line,
1030 And Capys, too, then Numitor, then one
Whose name restores you: Silvius Aeneas,
Both in arms and piety your peer,
If ever he shall come to reign in Alba.
What men they are! And see their rugged forms
1035 With oakleaf crowns shadowing their brows. I tell you,
These are to found Nomentum, Gabii,
Fidenae town, Collatia's hilltop towers,
Pometii, Fort Inuus, Bola, Cora—
Names to be heard for places nameless now.
1040 Then Romulus, fathered by Mars, will come
To make himself his grandfather's companion,
Romulus, reared by his mother, Ilia,
In the blood-line of Assaracus. Do you see
The double plume of Mars fixed on his crest,
1045 See how the father of the gods himself
Now marks him out with his own sign of honor?
Look now, my son: under his auspices
Illustrious Rome will bound her power with earth,
Her spirit with Olympus. She'll enclose
1050 Her seven hills with one great city wall,
Fortunate in the men she breeds. Just so
Cybelë Mother, honored on Berecynthus,
Wearing her crown of towers, onward rides
By chariot through the towns of Phrygia,
1055 In joy at having given birth to gods,
And cherishing a hundred grandsons, heaven
Dwellers with homes on high.
                                        Turn your two eyes
This way and see this people, your own Romans.
1060 Here is Caesar, and all the line of Iulus,
All who shall one day pass under the dome
Of the great sky: this is the man, this one,
Of whom so often you have heard the promise,
Caesar Augustus, son of the deified,
1065 Who shall bring once again an Age of Gold

Lines 766–793

To Latium, to the land where Saturn reigned
In early times. He will extend his power
Beyond the Garamants and Indians,
Over far territories north and south
1070 Of the zodiacal stars, the solar way,
Where Atlas, heaven-bearing, on his shoulder
Turns the night-sphere, studded with burning stars.
At that man's coming even now the realms
Of Caspia and Maeotia tremble, warned
1075 By oracles, and the seven mouths of Nile
Go dark with fear. The truth is, even Alcidës
Never traversed so much of earth—I grant
That he could shoot the hind with brazen hoofs
Or bring peace to the groves of Erymanthus,
1080 Or leave Lerna affrighted by his bow.
Neither did he who guides his triumphal car
With reins of vine-shoots twisted, Bacchus, driving
Down from Nysa's height his tiger team.
Do we lag still at carrying our valor
1085 Into action? Can our fear prevent
Our settling in Ausonia?

                              Who is he
So set apart there, olive-crowned, who holds
The sacred vessels in his hands? I know
1090 That snowy mane and beard: Numa, the king,
Who will build early Rome on a base of laws,
A man sent from the small-town poverty
Of Curës to high sovereignty. After him
Comes Tullus, breaker of his country's peace,
1095 Arousing men who have lost victorious ways,
Malingering men, to war. Near him is Ancus,
Given to boasting, even now too pleased
With veering popularity's heady air.
Do you care to see now, too, the Tarquin kings
1100 And the proud soul of the avenger, Brutus,
By whom the bundled *fasces* are regained?
Consular power will first be his, and his
The pitiless axes. When his own two sons
Plot war against the city, he will call

Lines 793–821

1105 For the death penalty in freedom's name—
Unhappy man, no matter how posterity
May see these matters. Love of the fatherland
Will sway him—and unmeasured lust for fame.
Now see the Decii and the Drusi there,

1110 And stern Torquatus, with his axe, and see
Camillus bringing the lost standards home.
That pair, however, matched in brilliant armor,
Matched in their hearts' desire now, while night
Still holds them fast, once they attain life's light

1115 What war, what grief, will they provoke between them—
Battle-lines and bloodshed—as the father
Marches from the Alpine ramparts, down
From Monaco's walled height, and the son-in-law,
Drawn up with armies of the East, awaits him.

1120 Sons, refrain! You must not blind your hearts
To that enormity of civil war,
Turning against your country's very heart
Her own vigor of manhood. You above all
Who trace your line from the immortals, you

1125 Be first to spare us. Child of my own blood,
Throw away your sword!
                  Mummius there,
When Corinth is brought low, will drive his car
As victor and as killer of Achaeans

1130 To our high Capitol. Paulus will conquer
Argos and Agamemnon's old Mycenae,
Defeating Perseus, the Aeacid,
Heir to the master of war, Achilles—thus
Avenging his own Trojan ancestors

1135 And the defilement of Minerva's shrine.
Great Cato! Who would leave you unremarked,
Or, Cossus, you, or the family of Gracchi,
Or the twin Scipios, bright bolts of war,
The bane of Libya, or you, Fabricius,

1140 In poverty yet powerful, or you,
Serranus, at the furrow, casting seed?
Where, though I weary, do you hurry me,
You Fabii? Fabius Maximus,

You are the only soul who shall restore
Our wounded state by waiting out the enemy.
1145 Others will cast more tenderly in bronze
Their breathing figures, I can well believe,
And bring more lifelike portraits out of marble;
Argue more eloquently, use the pointer
To trace the paths of heaven accurately
1150 And accurately foretell the rising stars.
Roman, remember by your strength to rule
Earth's peoples—for your arts are to be these:
To pacify, to impose the rule of law,
To spare the conquered, battle down the proud."
1155 Anchises paused here as they gazed in awe,
Then added:

    "See there, how Marcellus comes
With spoils of the commander that he killed:
How the man towers over everyone.
1160 Cavalry leader, he'll sustain the realm
Of Rome in hours of tumult, bringing to heel
The Carthaginians and rebellious Gaul,
And for the third time in our history
He'll dedicate an enemy general's arms
1165 To Father Romulus."

      But here Aeneas
Broke in, seeing at Marcellus' side
A young man beautifully formed and tall
In shining armor, but with clouded brow
1170 And downcast eyes:

      "And who is that one, Father,
Walking beside the captain as he comes:
A son, or grandchild from the same great stock?
The others murmur, all astir. How strong
1175 His presence is! But night like a black cloud
About his head whirls down in awful gloom."

His father Anchises answered, and the tears
Welled up as he began:

Lines 846–867

"Oh, do not ask
1180 About this huge grief of your people, son.
Fate will give earth only a glimpse of him,
Not let the boy live on. Lords of the sky,
You thought the majesty of Rome too great
If it had kept these gifts. How many groans
1185 Will be sent up from that great Field of Mars
To Mars' proud city, and what sad rites you'll see,
Tiber, as you flow past the new-built tomb.
Never will any boy of Ilian race
Exalt his Latin forefathers with promise
1190 Equal to his; never will Romulus' land
Take pride like this in any of her sons.
Weep for his faithful heart, his old-world honor,
His sword arm never beaten down! No enemy
Could have come through a clash with him unhurt,
1195 Whether this soldier went on foot or rode,
Digging his spurs into a lathered mount.
Child of our mourning, if only in some way
You could break through your bitter fate. For you
Will be Marcellus. Let me scatter lilies,
1200 All I can hold, and scarlet flowers as well,
To heap these for my grandson's shade at least,
Frail gifts and ritual of no avail."

So raptly, everywhere, father and son
Wandered the airy plain and viewed it all.
1205 After Anchises had conducted him
To every region and had fired his love
Of glory in the years to come, he spoke
Of wars that he must fight, of Laurentines,
And of Latinus' city, then of how
1210 He might avoid or bear each toil to come.

There are two gates of Sleep, one said to be
Of horn, whereby the true shades pass with ease,
The other all white ivory agleam
Without a flaw, and yet false dreams are sent

1215   Through this one by the ghosts to the upper world.
    Anchises now, his last instructions given,
    Took son and Sibyl there and let them go
    By the Ivory Gate.
                    Aeneas made his way
1220   Straight to the ships to see his crews again,
    Then sailed directly to Caieta's port.
    Bow anchors out, the sterns rest on the beach.

Lines 896–901

JUNO SERVED BY A FURY

Nurse Caieta of Aeneas, in death you too
Conferred your fame through ages on our coast,
Still honored in your last bed, as you are,
And if this glory matters in the end
5   Your name tells of your grave in great Hesperia.

When he had seen Caieta's funeral
Performed, her mound of tomb heaped up, Aeneas
Waited until the sea went down, then cleared
Her harbor under sail.
10   Into the night
The soft south wind blew on, the white full moon
Left no sea-reach or path unbrightened for them,
Shimmering on the open sea. They passed
The isle of Circe close inshore: that isle
15 Where, in the grove men shun, the Sun's rich daughter
Sings the hours away. She lights her hall
By night with fires of fragrant cedar wood,
Making her shuttle hum across the warp.
Out of this island now they could hear lions
20 Growling low in anger at their chains,
Then roaring in the deep night; bristling boars
And fenced-in bears, foaming in rage, and shapes
Of huge wolves howling. Men they once had been,
But with her magic herbs the cruel goddess

25   Dressed them in the form and pelt of brutes.
That night, to spare good Trojans foul enchantment—
Should they put in, or near the dangerous beach—
Neptune puffed out their sails with wind astern,
Giving clear passage, carrying them onward
30   Past the boiling surf. Then soon to eastward
Sea began to redden with dawn rays,
And saffron-robed Aurora in high heaven
Shone on her rosy car. Now suddenly
The wind dropped, every breath of wind sank down,
35   And oar-blades dipped and toiled in the sparkling calm.
Still far off-shore, Aeneas on the look-out
Sighted a mighty forest, a fair river,
Tiber, cutting through and at its mouth
Expelling eddies of clay-yellow water
40   Into the sea. Above it, all around,
Birds of myriad colors, birds at home
On river bank and channel, charmed the air
With jargoning and flitting through the trees.
Aeneas called "Right rudder!" to the steersmen,
45   "Turn the prows to land,"
And smiling pulled for shade on the great river.

    Be with me, Muse of all Desire, Erato,
While I call up the kings, the early times,
How matters stood in the old land of Latium
50   That day when the foreign soldiers beached
Upon Ausonia's shore, and the events
That led to the first fight. Immortal one,
Bring all in memory to the singer's mind,
For I must tell of wars to chill the blood,
55   Ranked men in battle, kings by their own valor
Driven to death, Etruria's cavalry,
And all Hesperia mobilized in arms.
A greater history opens before my eyes,
A greater task awaits me.
60   King Latinus,
Now grown old, had ruled his settled towns
And countryside through years of peace. Tradition

Makes him a son of Faunus by a nymph,
Marica of the Laurentines. The father
65 Of Faunus had been Picus, who in turn
Claimed you for sire, old Saturn, making you
The founder of the dynasty. By fate
Latinus had no son or male descendant,
Death having taken one in early youth.
70 A single daughter held that house's hopes,
A girl now ripe for marriage, for a man.
And many in broad Latium, in Ausonia,
Courted her, but the handsomest by far
Was Turnus, powerful heir of a great line.
75 Latinus' queen pressed for their union,
Desiring him with passion for a son,
But heavenly portents, odd things full of dread
Stood in the way. There was a laurel tree
Deep in an inner courtyard of the palace,
80 Venerated for leafage, prized for years,
Having been found and dedicated there—
So the tale went—to Phoebus by Latinus
When he first built a strongpoint on the site;
And from this laurel tree he gave his folk
85 The name Laurentines. Here, for a wonder, bees
In a thick swarm, borne through the limpid air
With humming thunder, clustered high on top
And, locking all their feet together, hung
In a sudden mass that weighted leaves and bough.
90 A soothsayer declared: "In this we see
A stranger's advent, and a body of men
Moving to the same spot from the same zone
To take our fortress." Then came another sign:
While the old king lit fires at the altars
95 With a pure torch, the girl Lavinia with him,
It seemed her long hair caught, her head-dress caught
In crackling flame, her queenly tresses blazed,
Her jewelled crown blazed. Mantled then in smoke
And russet light, she scattered divine fire
100 Through all the house. No one could hold that sight
Anything but hair-raising, marvelous,

Lines 47–78

And it was read by seers to mean the girl
Would have renown and glorious days to come,
But that she brought a great war on her people.
105 Troubled by these strange happenings, the king
Sought out the oracle of his father, Faunus,
Teller of destinies, to listen there
In woodland by Albunea's high cascade
And plashing holy spring—that noblest wood
110 That in cool dusk exhaled a brimstone vapor.
All Italians, all the Oenotrian land,
Resorted to this place in baffling times,
Asking direction; here a priest brought gifts,
Here in the stillness of the night he lay
115 On skins taken from sheep of sacrifice
And courted slumber. Many visions came
Before his eyes and strangely on the air;
He heard their different voices, and took part
In colloquies of gods, in undergloom
120 Addressing the grim powers of Acheron.
Now here in turn Father Latinus came
For counsel. Ritually putting to the sword
A hundred sheep, he lay on their piled fleeces.
Then came a sudden voice from the inmost grove:

125 "Propose no Latin alliance for your daughter,
Son of mine; distrust the bridal chamber
Now prepared. Men from abroad will come
And be your sons by marriage. Blood so mingled
Lifts our name starward. Children of that stock
130 Will see all earth turned Latin at their feet,
Governed by them, as far as on his rounds
The Sun looks down on Ocean, East or West."

So ran the oracle of Father Faunus
In the still night, a warning that Latinus
135 Could not keep to himself, but far and wide
Report of it had reached Ausonian towns

Lines 79–105

Before the sons of Laömedon moored ship
At the grassy riverside.

                        T
                        here with his officers
140   And princely son, Aeneas took repose
      Beneath a tall tree's boughs. They made a feast,
      Putting out on the grass hard wheaten cakes
      As platters for their meal—moved to do this
      By Jupiter himself. These banquet boards
145   Of Ceres they heaped up with country fruits.
      Now, as it happened, when all else was eaten,
      Their neediness drove them to try their teeth
      On Ceres' platters. Boldly with hand and jaw
      They broke the crusted disks of prophecy,
150   Making short work of all the quartered loaves.

      "Look, how we've devoured our tables even!"
      Iulus playfully said, and said no more,
      For that remark as soon as heard had meant
      The end of wandering: even as it fell
155   From the speaker's lips, his father caught it, stopped
      The jesting there, struck by the work of heaven,
      And said at once:
                        "A blessing on the land
      The fates have held in store for me, a blessing
160   On our true gods of Troy! Here is our home,
      Here is our fatherland. You know, my father
      Anchises once foretold this secret token—
      Now I remember—of our destiny.
      He told me then: 'My son, when the time comes
165   That hunger on a strange coast urges you,
      When food has failed, to eat your very tables,
      Then you may look for home: be mindful of it,
      Weary as you are, and turn your hand

To your first building there with moat and mound.'
'70 Here we have felt that hunger, here a last
Adversity awaited us, a limit
Set to our misfortunes. One and all,
At sunrise with high hearts let us find out
About this region and the people here,
175 And where their homes are. We'll fan out in squads
From our ship moorings. Tip your cups to Jove,
Invoke my father Anchises in your prayers,
Put out the winebowls of our feast again."

He twined a leafy sprig into a garland
180 Round his head, then made his formal prayer
To the Glade Spirit there and to the Earth,
First of immortals, to the nymphs, the streams
As yet unknown, to Night and the rising stars
Of Night, to Jove of Ida, to the Mother
185 Goddess of Phrygia, Cybelë, all
Ceremoniously, and then invoked his parents,
One in heaven and one in Erebus.
At this the Father Almighty in high air
Thundered three times out of a brilliant sky
190 And shook before their eyes with his own hand
A cloud ablaze with gold and rays of light.
Now through the Trojan companies quick-silver
Rumor went around: the day had come
For laying down the walls owed them by fate;
195 And each outdid the other as they fell
To feasting and rejoicing in the omen,
Setting the bowls and garlanding the wine.

Next morning when the light of risen day
Shone on the earth, exploring parties sought
200 The Latin city, boundaries, and coasts.
Here was Numicius' fountain, and its pond,
Here Tiber River, here brave Latins lived.

Aeneas ordered to the king's high city
A hundred legates, chosen from all ranks,
205   Their heads shaded by olive shoots of Pallas,
To bear the king gifts and to entreat a state
Of peace for Teucrians. No lingering:
At the command they all moved smartly out
In a quick march. Aeneas marked his line
210   Of walls with a low trench, then toiled away
To deepen it, to throw an earthwork up
With palisades, camp style, around that post,
Their first, on the riverside.
                      Now presently
215   His emissaries reached their journey's end,
Seeing steep roofs and Latin towers ahead
As they approached the wall. In fields outside
Were boys and striplings practising horsemanship,
Breaking in chariot teams in clouds of dust,
220   Pulling taut bows and throwing javelins,
Challenging one another to race or box.
Meanwhile a messenger, riding ahead,
Reported to the old king the arrival
Of tall men in strange costume, and the king
225   Ordered them brought inside. He took his seat
Amid the court, on his ancestral throne.
The royal building, massive and majestic,
Raised on a hundred columns, occupied
The city's height. It had been Picus' palace,
230   Shadowed by trees and history, held in awe.
Here kings by happy omen took the scepter,
Lifted the rods of office up; and here
They had their senate house, a holy place,
A hall for ritual feasts: for a slain ram
235   The city fathers took accustomed seats
On benches at long tables. Here as well
Were sculptures of their old forefathers, ranked
By generations, carved in ancient cedar:
Italus, and Sabinus, planter of vines,
240   Holding as such a pruning hook, and Saturn,
Hoar with age, and the two-faced figure, Janus,

All in the entrance way; and other kings
From earliest times, with men wounded in war
While fighting for their country. There besides
245 Were many arms, hung on the sacred doorposts,
Captured warcars, battle-axes, plumes
Of helmets, massive gate-bars, javelins
And shields, and beaks torn from the prows of ships.
The seated figure of Picus, tamer of horses,
250 In a striped mantle, held a Quirinal staff
And on his left forearm a Shield of Heaven.
Circe his bride, taken with strong desire,
Had struck him with her golden wand, then drugged him
Into a woodpecker and pied his wings.
255 In this interior hall of the holy place,
At ease upon the ancestral throne, Latinus
Called the Teucrians before him, saying
Tranquilly as they entered:
                              "Sons of Dardanus—
260 You see, we know your city and your nation,
As all had heard you laid a westward course—
Tell me your purpose. What design or need
Has brought you through the dark blue sea so far
To our Ausonian coast? Either astray
265 Or driven by rough weather, such as sailors
Often endure at sea, you've broached the river,
Moored ship there. Now do not turn away
From hospitality here. Know that our Latins
Come of Saturn's race, that we are just—
270 Not by constraint or laws, but by our choice
And habit of our ancient god. Indeed,
Though years have dimmed the tale, I can remember
Old Auruncans telling of Dardanus,
How from this country of his birth he went
275 On his long journey to the Idan towns
Of Phrygia and to Thracian Samos, now
Called Samothrace. From this land he set out,
From his old Tuscan home at Corythus.
And now great halls of starry sky enthrone him,
280 To the gods' altars adding one for him."

Lines 181–211

Latinus then fell silent, and in turn
Ilioneus began:
        "Your majesty,
Most noble son of Faunus, no rough seas
285 Or black gale swept us to your coast, no star
Or clouded seamark put us off our course.
We journey to your city by design
And general consent, driven as we are
From realms in other days greatest by far
290 The Sun looked down on, passing on his way
From heaven's far eastern height. Our line's from Jove,
In his paternity the sons of Dardanus
Exult, and highest progeny of Jove
Include our king himself—Trojan Aeneas,
295 Who sent us to your threshold. What a storm
From cruel Mycenae swept across the plain
Of Ida, and what destiny made the worlds
Of Europe and of Asia clash in war,
Has now been heard in the most distant lands
300 Beside the tidal Ocean, and by men
Divided from us by the inclement Zone
Of Sun that burns between the cooler four.
By that storm overwhelmed, and then at sea
So long on the vast waters, now we ask
305 A modest settlement of the gods of home,
A strip of coast that will bring harm to no one,
Air and water, open and free to all.
We will not shame your kingdom. You shall win
No light and passing fame, nor from ourselves
310 A passing gratitude for your kind act.
Ausonians who take Troy to their hearts
Will not regret it. By Aeneas' destiny
I swear, and by his powerful right hand,
Whether tested in covenants or battle,
315 Many a people, many a race—and here
Do not disdain us for this overture
In offering pleas and garlands—many, I say,
Have come to us and wished alliance with us.
But by the will of heaven and heaven's commands

320   Our quest was for your country. Dardanus
    Had birth here, and Apollo calls us back,
    Directing us by solemn oracles
    To Tuscan Tiber, to the sacred waters
    Of the Numician fountain. Here besides
325   Aeneas gives you from his richer years
    These modest gifts, relics caught up and saved
    From burning Troy. This golden cup Anchises
    Used for libations at the altars; Priam
    Bore this accouterment when giving laws
330   To peoples in due form called to assembly:
    Scepter, and holy diadem, and robes
    Woven by Trojan women."

                            Latinus heard
    Ilioneus out, his countenance averted,
335   Sitting immobile, all attention, eyes
    Downcast but turning here and there. The embroidered
    Purple and the scepter of King Priam
    Moved him less in his own kingliness
    Than long thoughts on the marriage of his daughter,
340   As he turned over in his inmost mind
    Old Faunus' prophecy.

                        "This is the man,"
    He thought, "foretold as coming from abroad
    To be my son-in-law, by fate appointed,
345   Called to reign here with equal authority—
    The man whose heirs will be brilliant in valor
    And win the mastery of the world."

                            At length
    He spoke in his elation:
350   "May the gods
    Assist our enterprises as their own!
    What you desire will be granted, Trojan,
    And I accept your gifts. While I am king
    You shall not want for bounty of rich land
355   Or miss the wealth of Troy. Aeneas himself
    Should come, though, if he has such need of us
    And bids for guesthood, for an ally's name.

Lines 239–265

He should not shrink from friendly faces here.
For me a requisite of the peace will be
360 To join hands with your captain.
                                        Now return
To your ship moorings, bring the king my messages.
I have a daughter, whom the oracles
Of Father's shrine and warning signs from heaven
30. Keep me from pledging to a native here.
Sons from abroad will come, the prophets say—
For this is Latium's destiny—new blood
To immortalize our name. Your king's the man
Called for by fate, so I conclude, and so
370 I wish, if there is truth in what I presage."

After this vigorous speech, Father Latinus
Picked out horses for them from his string—
Three hundred who stood glossy in high stalls—
And ordered them led out for all the Trojans,
375 One by one, fast horses, ornamented
With purple saddle cloths, with golden chains
Hung on their breasts, and golden snoods, and yellow
Golden bits they champed between their teeth.
Then for Aeneas, absent though he was,
380 He picked a chariot and a team, a pair
Grown from immortal stock and snorting fire.
Their sire was that stallion crafty Circe
Stole from the Sun, her father, and put to stud
With a mortal mare, getting a bastard breed.
385 Bearing these gifts and offers from Latinus,
Aeneas' legates, mounted now, returned,
And they brought peace.

Only look upward, though,
At Jove's unpitying queen. She at that hour
390 Made her way back from Inachus's Argos,

Holding her course in air. From her great height
Over Pachynus in Sicily to the south,
She could discern Aeneas taking heart,
Ships' companies already building shelters,
395 Leaving the ships, trusting the land they found.
She stayed her flight as pain went through her, then
She tossed her head and cried out from her heart:

"O hateful race, and fate of the Phrygians
Pitted against my own. Could they be killed
400 On the Sigean battlefield? When beaten,
Could they be beaten? Troy on fire, did Troy
Consume her men? Amid the spears, amid
The flames, they found a way. I must, for my part,
Think my powers by this time tired out,
405 Supine, or sleeping, surfeited on hate?
Well, when they were ejected from their country
I had the temerity as their enemy
To dog them, fight them, over the whole sea,
These refugees. The strength of sea and sky
410 Has been poured out against these Teucrians.
What were the Syrtës worth to me, or Scylla,
What was huge Charybdis worth? By Tiber's
Longed-for bed they now lay out their town,
Unworried by deep water or by me.
415 Mars had the power to kill the giant race
Of Lapiths, and the Father of Gods himself
Gave up old Cálydon to Diana's wrath:
And what great sin brought Cálydon or Lapiths
Justice so rough? How differently with me,
420 The great consort of Jove, who nerved myself
To leave no risk unventured, lent myself
To every indignity. I am defeated
And by Aeneas. Well, if my powers fall short,
I need not falter over asking help
425 Wherever help may lie. If I can sway
No heavenly hearts I'll rouse the world below.
It will not be permitted me—so be it—

To keep the man from rule in Italy;
By changeless fate Lavinia waits, his bride.
430 And yet to drag it out, to pile delay
Upon delay in these great matters—that
I can do: to destroy both countries' people,
That I can do. Let father and son-in-law
Unite at that cost to their own! In blood,
435 Trojan and Latin, comes your dowry, girl;
Bridesmaid Bellona waits now to attend you.
Hecuba's not the only one who carried
A burning brand within her and bore a son
Whose marriage fired a city. So it is
440 With Venus' child, a Paris once again,
A funeral torch again for Troy reborn!"

When she had said all this, she dropped to earth
In a shuddering wind. From the dark underworld
Home of the Furies, she aroused Allecto,
445 Grief's drear mistress, with her lust for war,
For angers, ambushes, and crippling crimes.
Even her father Pluto hates this figure,
Even her hellish sisters, for her myriad
Faces, for her savage looks, her head
450 Alive and black with snakes. Now Juno spoke
To excite her:
            "Here is a service all your own
That you can do for me, Daughter of Night,
Here is a way to help me, to make sure
455 My status and renown will not give way
Or be impaired, and that Aeneas' people
Cannot by marriage win Latinus over,
Laying siege to Italy. You can arm
For combat brothers of one soul between them,
460 Twist homes with hatred, bring your whips inside,
Or firebrands of death. A thousand names
Belong to you, a thousand ways of wounding.
Shake out the folded stratagems within you,
Break up this peace-pact, scatter acts of war,

Lines 313–339

465   All in a flash let men desire, demand,
     And take up arms."
                   Without delay Allecto,
     Dripping venom deadly as the Gorgon's,
     Passed into Latium first and the high hall
470   Of the Laurentine king. She took her place
     On the still threshold of the queen, Amata.
     Burning already at the Trojans' coming,
     The plans for Turnus' marriage broken off,
     Amata tossed and turned with womanly
475   Anxiety and anger. Now the goddess
     Plucked one of the snakes, her gloomy tresses,
     And tossed it at the woman, sent it down
     Her bosom to her midriff and her heart,
     So that by this black reptile driven wild
480   She might disrupt her whole house. And the serpent
     Slipping between her gown and her smooth breasts
     Went writhing on, though imperceptible
     To the fevered woman's touch or sight, and breathed
     Viper's breath into her. The sinuous mass
485   Became her collar of twisted gold, became
     The riband of her head-dress. In her hair
     It twined itself, and slid around her body.
     While the infection first, like dew of poison
     Fallen on her, pervaded all her senses,
490   Netting her bones in fire—though still her soul
     Had not responded fully to the flame—
     She spoke out softly, quite like any mother,
     Shedding hot tears at the marriage of her child
     To a Phrygian:
495   "These Trojan refugees,
     Father, are they to take away Lavinia
     In marriage? Have you no pity for your daughter,
     None for yourself? No pity for her mother,
     Who will be left alone by the faithless man,
500   The rover, going to sea at the first north wind
     With a girl for booty? Was that not the way
     The Phrygian shepherd entered Lacedaemon
     And carried Helen off to Troy's far city?

Lines 340–364

What of your solemn word, your years of love
505 For your own people, your right hand so often
Given to Turnus, our blood-kin? Suppose
A son of foreign stock is to be found
For Latins, and this holds, and the command
Your father, Faunus, gave weighs hard upon you,
510 Then I maintain that every separate country
Free from all rule of ours, is foreign land,
And this is what the gods mean. Turnus, too,
If we seek origins, had Inachus
And Acrisius as forebears at Mycenae."

515 Finding Latinus proof against this plea
And holding firm, while in her viscera
The serpent's evil madness circulated,
Suffusing her, the poor queen, now enflamed
By prodigies of hell, went wild indeed
520 And with insane abandon roamed the city.
One sees at times a top that a wound-up thong
Snapped into a spin, when, all eyes for the sport,
Boys drive it round a court in a great circle,
Sweeping curves on the ground, flicked by the whip,
525 While the small boys in fascination bend
Above the rounded boxwood as it whirls,
Given new life at each stroke of the lash.
So restless, wheeling like a spinning top,
Amata sped on, driven through the town
530 Amid her hardy townsmen. Worse, she feigned
Bacchic possession, daring a greater sin
And greater madness. Off to the woods she ran,
Into the leafy hills, and hid her child
To snatch a marriage from the Teucrians
535 Or to postpone the wedding. "Evoë,
Bacchus," she shrilled out, and then cried again
That you alone, the god, deserved the girl,
Who held an ivy thyrsus in your honor
And danced for you, and let her hair grow long,
540 Sacred to you . . . As word of this went round,
Laurentine mothers fired by sudden madness

Lines 365-392

Felt the same passion to acquire new homes.
They left the old ones, baring to the wind
Their necks and hair, while some in fawnskin dress
545   Filled heaven with long quavering cries and bore
Vine-covered wand-spears. In their midst, the queen
Held up a blazing firebrand of pine
And in her fever sang a marriage hymn
For Turnus and her daughter, glancing round
550   With bloodshot eyes. She called out suddenly
And savagely:
                    "Mothers of Latium, listen,
Wherever you may be: if your good hearts
Feel any kindness still for poor Amata,
555   Any concern for justice to a mother,
Shake your headbands loose, take up the revel
Along with me!"
                    To this extreme she went
In the wild wood, the wilderness of beasts,
560   Driven by Allecto with a Bacchic goad.

When to the Fury's mind the first mad fit
Had been whipped up enough—seeing Latinus'
Counsel subverted and his home undone—
Allecto rose up on her somber wings
565   And flew straight to the bold Rutulian's walls,
The city which, they say, Danaë founded
With her Acrisian colonists, blown there
By gale winds from the south. Ardea once
Our early fathers called the place, and still
570   The great name stands, though Ardea's fortune waned.
In his high dwelling there, in darkest night,
Turnus peacefully slept. Allecto stripped
Her savage mask off and her Fury's shape,
To take on an old woman's face: she lined
575   Her forehead with deep seams, put on white hair

And headband, twining there a shoot of olive,
So she became Calybë, thrall in age
To Juno and a priestess of her temple.
Moving near, before the young man's eyes,
580 She wheedled:

        "Turnus, can you bear to see
So many efforts wasted, spilt like water,
And your own rule made over to the Dardan
Colonists? The king withholds your bride,
585 Withholds the dowry that you fought and bled for.
Go into danger and be laughed at for it!
Mow down the Tuscan ranks, shelter the Latins
Under your peace-pact! So? These messages—
While you lay in the stillness of the night—
590 Saturn's almighty daughter ordered me
Herself to bring before you.

                Come then, put
Your young troops under arms, glory in arms,
Prepare a sortie and a fight. These Phrygian
595 Captains in their camp on our fine river,
Give them a burning, burn their painted ships.
Great force in heaven demands it. Let the king
Latinus, too—unless he undertake
To yield your bride and keep his word—let him
600 Feel this, and feel at last the fear of meeting
Turnus in arms."

          Now, making light of her,
The young man gave his answer to the seer:

"News of the squadron making port on Tiber
605 Has not failed, as you think, to reach my ears.
Do not imagine me afraid. Queen Juno
Has not forgotten me. But old age, mother,
Sunk in decay and too far gone for truth,
Is giving you this useless agitation,
610 Mocking your prophet's mind with dreams of fear
And battles between kings. Your mind should be
On the gods' images and on their shrines.
Men will make war and peace, as men should do."

Lines 418–444

Being so dismissed, Allecto blazed in wrath,
615 And sudden trembling ran through the man's body
Even as he spoke, his eyes in a rigid stare,
For now the Fury hissed with all her serpents,
All her hideous faces. Glancing round
With eyes of flame, as the man's faltering tongue
620 Tried to say more, she threw him back and raised
A pair of snakes out of her writhing hair,
Then cracked and cracked her whip and railed at him:

"Look at me now, sunk in decay, see how
Old age in me is too far gone for truth,
625 Deluding me with battles between kings
And dreams of fear! Look at these dreams of mine!
I come to you from the Black Sisters' home
And bring war and extinction in my hand."

With this she hurled a torch and planted it
630 Below the man's chest, smoking with hellish light.
Enormous terror woke him, a cold sweat
Broke out all over him and soaked his body.
Then driven wild, shouting for arms, for arms
He ransacked house and chamber. Lust of steel
635 Raged in him, brute insanity of war,
And wrath above all, as when fiery sticks
Are piled with a loud crackling by the side
Of a caldron boiling, and the water heaves
And seethes inside the vessel, steaming up
640 With foam, and bubbling higher, till the surface
Holds no more, and vapor mounts to heaven.
So, then, in violation of the peace,
He told the captains of his troops to march
On King Latinus, ordering arms prepared,
645 The land defended, and the enemy
Pushed back from the frontiers: he, too, would come,
A match for Teucrians and Latins both.

His orders given, vows made to the gods,
His countrymen cheered one another on,

650 And vied with one another, to make war,
This one admiring Turnus' princeliness,
His figure and his youth; this one the kings,
His ancestors; this one his feats afield.

While Turnus filled these men with recklessness,
655 Allecto beat her way on Stygian wings
Coastward to Trojans, with a fresh design.
Surveying that wild region on the shore
Where shining Iulus trapped or hunted, here
The virgin of the wailing underworld
660 Brought sudden frenzy on the hounds. She touched
Their nostrils with a long familiar scent
So they would run a stag, hot on the track—
This the first cause of turmoil, kindling hearts
Of country folk to war. There was a stag,
665 A beauty, with a giant spread of antlers,
Taken before weaning from a doe
And brought up tame by boys, as by their father,
Tyrrhus, the chief herdsman to the king
And warden of his wide estates. Their sister,
670 Silvia, had trained the beast with love
To do her bidding. She would wreathe his horns
With garlands, groom him, bathe him in a spring
Of limpid water. Placid under her hand,
Accustomed to the table of his mistress,
675 The stag would roam the forest, then return,
However late at night, to the gate he knew.
Now as he wandered far from home, the hounds
Of Iulus on the hunt, furiously barking,
Started the stag. He had been floating down
680 A river, keeping cool by the green bank.
Ascanius himself, now on the chase
And passionate for the honor of the kill,
Let fly a shaft from his bent bow: Allecto's

Guidance did not fail his hand or let him
685 Shoot amiss, and the arrow whizzing loud
Whipped on to pierce the belly and the flank.
Mortally hurt, the swift deer made for home
In the farm buildings. Groaning, he found his stall,
And coated with dark blood he filled the house
690 With piteous cries, as though imploring mercy.
Hugging her shoulders, beating with her hands,
The sister, Silvia, raised a cry for help,
Calling her tough countrymen, who came
Soon, unexpectedly, for the pitiless fiend
695 In the silent wood lay hidden. One was armed
With a burnt-out brand, one with a knotted cudgel,
Each with whatever weapon anger first
Put in his groping hand. Herdsmen for war
Were rounded up by Tyrrhus, breathing fury,
700 Armed with an axe—for he had chanced to be
Splitting an oak four ways with driven wedges.
Now the fierce goddess from her look-out post
Judging the time for further harm had come,
Flapped to the stable roof and from the peak
705 Sounded the herdsman's call: on her curved horn
She sent into the air a blast from hell
At which all groves were set at once a-tremble
And the deep forest rang and rang again.
The lake of Trivia heard it, far away,
710 So did the River Nar, whose current pales
With sulphur, and Velinus of the springs,
And frightened mothers held their children close.
Then truly at the sound, the signal given
By that dire trumpet, weaponed and on the run
715 From every quarter, farmers and foresters
Came together. Trojan troops as well
Poured from the camp through open gates to bring
Ascanius aid, and both sides formed for battle.
No longer now a shindy of country boys
720 With fire-hardened stakes and oaken clubs,
But darkening on a wide field they contended
With two-edged steel, like standing crops in ranks

A-bristle with drawn swords and armor shining,
Struck by the sun and flashing to the clouds,
725   As when under a squall the waves begin
To whiten and the sea, minute by minute,
Heaves and increases, as the swells go higher,
Till from its depths it surges to the sky.

Ahead of the front rank a whizzing arrow
730   Brought down a young man, Almo, eldest son
Of Tyrrhus—as the point lodged in his throat,
Choking the moist channel of his voice
And the frail breath of life with blood. Around him
Many dead soon lay, one old Galaesus,
735   Killed as he interposed and pled for peace,
The fairest-minded of them all, and richest
In those days in Ausonian lands: he owned
Five flocks of bleating sheep, five herds of kine,
A hundred plows that turned his many acres.
740   Now while they fought on the wide field, with Mars
Impartial still, Allecto's promise kept
When she had stained the field with blood and caused
First combat losses, now the feral goddess
Left Hesperia and veered away
745   Through airy sky, proud of her feat, to brag
To Juno:
                "See your quarrel brought to the point
Of grievous war. Now tell them to be friends,
Tell them to make a pact—now that I've splashed
750   The Trojans with Ausonian blood! There's more
If I am sure you want it: I can send out
Rumors to stir the border towns to war,
Fire them with lust for the madness of war,
So they'll be joining in from everywhere.
755   I'll scatter weapons up and down the land."
But Juno said:
                "Terrors and treacheries
We have in plenty. All that may prolong
A war is there: they fight now hand to hand
760   And arms luck gave are running with fresh blood.

There is the marriage, there is the ceremony
Venus' distinguished son and that great king
Latinus may take joy in! As for you,
This roving rather freely in high air
765 Is hardly as the Father wishes, he
Who rules highest Olympus. Down with you.
If any further need to act arises
I myself will manage."
                              At these words
770 From Saturn's daughter, Allecto spread those wings
That hiss with snakes and left the towering air
For underworld again. There is a spot
In central Italy where the mountains are,
A noted place, heard of in many lands,
775 The Valley of Amsanctus. Flanks of forest,
Dark with leaves, close in on either side,
And in the midst a torrent rumbles down
A twisted channel, swirling through the rocks.
Here people show a shuddersome cold cave,
780 An outlet for the breath of cruel Dis,
And an abyss that opens jaws of death
Where Acheron bursts through: between these jaws
The Fury settled in her hateful power,
Giving relief to earth and sky. But still
785 The queenly daughter of Saturn, undeterred,
Gave her last touches to the war. The crowd
Of shepherds as one man rushed from the field
Into the city, carrying the dead—
Young Almo, and Galaesus all disfigured.
790 There they implored the vengeance of the gods
And called upon Latinus to bear witness.
Turnus, at hand now, among men on fire
With rage over the slaughter, made their fears
Redouble, saying rule fell to the Trojans;
795 Italians were to mix with Phrygian stock;
He had been turned away from the king's door.
The kin, then, of those mothers in ecstasy
Who danced for Bacchus in the wilderness—
Amata's name no light encouragement—

800 Came in from everywhere with cries for Mars.
Nothing would do but that, against the omens,
Against the oracles, by a power malign
They pled for frightful war. And they all thronged,
Outshouting one another, round the palace.
805 Latinus, though, like a seacliff stood fast,
Like a seacliff that when the great sea comes
To shatter on it, and the waves like hounds
Give tongue on every side, holds grandly on,
Though reefs and foaming rocks thunder offshore
810 And seaweed flung against it streams away.
But when no power was given him to defeat
Their blinded counsel, and things took their course
At cruel Juno's nod, Father Latinus
Calling upon all the gods, on heaven's
815 Empty air, cried:
                           "I am breached by fate,
Wrecked, swept away by storm. You'll pay the price,
Poor people, with your sacrilegious blood.
This wickedness will haunt you, and the grim
820 Punishment, Turnus, will come home to you,
But it will be too late to pray the gods.
For me, I've earned my rest, though entering haven
I am deprived of happiness in death."

825 He said no more, but shut himself away
And dropped the reins of rule over the state.

There was a custom then in Latium,
Held sacred later in Alban towns, as now
In the world-power of Rome when citizens
First urge the wargod on—
830 To bring the sorrow of war upon the Getae,
Or upon Arabs or Hyrcanians,
Or marching Dawnward toward the Indians

To take the Parthian-captured standards back.
There are two gates, twin gates
835 Of war, as they are called, by long observance
Looked on in awe, for fear of savage Mars.
One hundred brazen bolts keep these gates closed
And the unending strength of steel; then too
Their guardian, Janus, never leaves the portal.
840 Now when the Fathers' judgment holds for war,
The Consul in Quirinal robe and Gabine
Cincture goes to unlock the grating doors
And lifts a call for battle. Fighting men
Then add their voices, and the brazen trumpets
845 Blown together blare their harsh assent.
In that way, now, Latinus was enjoined
To declare war on the people of Aeneas
By setting wide the grim gates. But he would not,
Would not touch them, only turned away
850 From the repellent work, and shut himself
In the interior darkness.

                                    Heaven's queen
At this dropped from the sky. She gave a push
To stubborn-yielding doors, then burst the iron-bound
855 Gates of war apart on turning hinges.
All Ausonian lands as yet unroused,
Unwakened, now took fire. Infantry
Mustered to cross the flatlands, mounted men
Tall on their horses in the dust whirled by,
860 And all must take up arms. With heavy grease
They rubbed shields clean and smooth, made javelins bright,
And whetted axes on the grindstone—thrilled
At standard-bearing, at the trumpet call.
Five sizeable towns, in fact, with anvils cleared,
865 Now turned out weapons: these were tough Atina,
Haughty Tibur, Ardea, Crustumeri,
Towered Antemnae. Workmen fashioned helmets,
Hollow and hard headgear, or for light shields
Bent wicker frames, while others molded breastplates
870 Out of bronze or trim greaves out of silver.
Pride in plowshare and scythe had given way

Lines 606–636

To this, and so had love of plowland labor.
Swords of their fathers in the smithy fires
They forged anew. The trumpet calls went out,
875 The password, sign of war, went round; one fellow
Pulled down his helmet from the wall, another
Yoked his whinnying horses, took his shield,
Put on his mail shirt, triple-linked with gold,
And belted on his good sword.
880   Muses, now
Throw wide the gates of Helicon, your mountain,
Now lift up your song, to tell what kings
Were stirred to war, what troops in each command
Filled all the lowlands, fighting men in whom
885 Even in those days bounteous Italy
Had come to flower, in whom her spirit blazed.
For you remember, you can bring to life
That time, immortal ones, while to ourselves
Faint wraiths of history barely transpire.

890 First to equip a troop and take the field
Was harsh Mezentius of Tuscany,
Who held the gods in scorn. The son who rode
Beside him, Lausus, unexcelled in beauty
Except by Turnus of the Laurentines—
895 Horse-tamer Lausus, conqueror of beasts—
Led from Agylla's town a thousand men,
His followers in vain—he that deserved
More happiness in the father he obeyed,
Deserved indeed no father like Mezentius.
900 Next after these came Aventinus, athlete
Son of the athlete, Hercules; he showed
His palm-crowned chariot and winning team
And put them through their paces on the grassland,
Bearing his father's blazon on his shield—
905 The Hydra wreathed in snakes, a hundred snakes.
In woodland on the Aventine the priestess,
Rhea, in secret brought this child to birth
In the world of daylight. She had mingled limbs
With a strong god in love, in that far time

910 When Tiryns' hero, with Geryon slain,
     Reached the Laurentine land and bathed his kine
     In Tiber's Tuscan water.
                          Soldiery
     That Aventinus led were armed with javelins
915 And thrusting spears: with polished poles and points
     They fought, or hurling shafted Sabine spikes.
     Their captain went on foot, swirling about him
     A giant lion skin with stormy mane
     Still terrible, and the great head for cowl
920 With white fangs in the open maw. So cloaked
     In Hercules' shaggy accouterment,
     He went up to the king's hall.
                              Then twin brothers
     Left Tibur's walls—that town and its townfolk
925 Named for Tiburtus, elder than these two—
     Catillus and fierce Coras, progeny
     Of Argos, by descent from Amphiaraus.
     Ahead of the front line amid the spears
     They raced along, as from a mountain top
930 Two cloud-born Centaurs on the run plunge down
     From Homolë or from the snows of Othrys,
     Making the mighty forest yield and thickets
     Crash before their onset.
                          Then the founder
935 Of the great town, Praenestë, joined the rest,
     He, too, for war—that king whom every age
     Believes a son of Vulcan, Caeculus,
     Born amid the pasturing herds but found,
     An infant, on the hearth.
940   From far and wide
     His country levies came with him: rough hands
     Of high Praenestë and of Gabine Juno's
     Pastures and cold Anio's river side,
     And Hernican rock ledges, wet with streams;
945 Then those you nurtured, wealthy Anagnia,
     Or you, Amasenus Father, by your waters.
     Armor and clanging shields and chariots
     Were not for all, but most with slings let fly

Their bullets of blue lead, while others hefted
950 Pairs of darts. They wore close-fitting caps
Of wolfskin and gripped earth with left foot bare,
The right foot roughly booted.
                              Now Messapus,
Horse-taming son of Neptune, not to be
955 Brought down by any man with fire or steel,
Called out his tribes, long settled in their peace,
Battalions long unused to war, and practiced
Swordsmanship again. Some of his troops
Held land on the Fescennine Heights and some
960 On the Faliscan lowlands, on Soractë's
High points or Flavinium's pasture land,
By Mount Ciminius' lake, Capena's grove.
All marched in equal ranks and hymned their king,
Like snowy swans when sometimes after feeding
965 And taking flight into the lucent clouds,
They cry a choral song from their long throats,
Making Asïa's marsh, the stream below,
Re-echo their high sound. No one who heard
Would think that throng composed of ranks in bronze
970 But rather that a cloud of clamorous birds
Beat landward from the open sea.
                              Imagine
One of the ancient line of Sabines, Clausus,
Leading a host, himself a host of men,
975 From whom in our day throughout Latium—
Since Sabines had an early share in Rome—
The Claudian tribe and family is diffused.
With him came Amiternum's regiment,
And old world Quiritës from Curës came,
980 All troops from Eretum and fair Mutusca's
Olive-bearing land, Nomentum town,
The Rosean countryside around Velinus,
The rugged cliffs of Tetrica, and Mount
Severus, and Casperia and Foruli,
985 Men from Himella's brook, and men who drank
The Tiber and Fabaris river water,
Levies from that cold upland, Nursia,

From Ortina, and the people called Latini,
And those whom Allia—distressful name—
990 Divides by flowing between.

There were as many
As there are waves upon the sparkling sea
Off Libya, when cold Orion sets
In winter, or as ears in fields of wheat
995 When they are warmed by summer's early sun
On Hermus plain or yellowing Lycia.
Clangor of shields and thud of marching feet
Made the earth tremble.

Then a captain hostile
1000 To the very name of Troy, Agamemnon's son
Halaesus, yoked his chariot team and swept
A thousand fighting clans to war for Turnus—
Men who hoed the fertile vineyard slopes
Of Massicus, and men sent by Auruncan
1005 Fathers from the high hills, or, below,
By Sidicina's flatland. Others came
From Calës, or were neighbors of Volturnus'
Fordable waters, and in arms as well
Came harsh Saticulans and bands of Oscans.
1010 Polished clubs were what they used as missiles,
Leashed for recovery, as their practice was;
Light shields protected them on the left side,
And for close combat they had sickle blades.

It will not do for you to go unmentioned,
1015 Oebalus, in our poem, for the nymph
Sebethis bore you, so the story goes,
To Telon when he ruled the Teleboan
Isle of Capri in his age. The father's
Lands did not content the son, who now
1020 Held sway over mainland Sarrastians
On plains the Sarnus watered, and the men
Of Rufrae, Batulum, Celemna's fields,
With those on whom Abella's walls look down
In orchard country—fighters trained to fling
1025 Their boomerangs as the Teutons do. They wore

Headgear of bark stripped from the cork oak tree
And flashed with brazen bucklers, blades of bronze.

Then you, too, Ufens, were sent down to war
From highland Nersae, chieftain as you were
1030 And famed for combat luck among the rugged
Forest hunters, the Aequicoli,
Who worked their stony soil in arms but took
Their joy in cattle raids, freebooter fare.

Just as conspicuous, the priestly Umbro,
1035 Sent from Marruvium by King Archippus,
Came with his helm in olive neatly bound,
A man of power, who had a gift of soothing
Vipers and vile-breathing watersnakes
By a sung rune or stroking into sleep:
1040 He calmed their rabidness and by his skill
Relieved men bitten by them. Yet his lore
Would not enable him to heal the blow
He took from a Dardan spear; no sleepy charms
Or mild herbs gathered in the Marsian hills
1045 Availed against his wounds. Umbro, the wood
Of Angitïa mourned you, and Fucinus'
Mirrors mourned you, the clear quiet lakes.

Hippolytus' handsome son rode out to war,
Sent by Aricia, his mother. Virbius
1050 Had grown up in Egeria's wood, around
The moist bank where Diana's altar stands,
A gracious shrine, and rich. The old tale goes
That when Hippolytus went down to death
By cunning of his stepmother, and paid
1055 The penalty his father claimed in blood,
Torn by stampeding horses, he returned
To the upper air of heaven beneath the stars,
Called back to life by Asclepius' medicines
And by Diana's love. Then the omnipotent
1060 Father, taking it ill that any man
Should rise from undergloom to light and life,

Cast down by his own bolt Apollo's son,
Discoverer of that healing power—Asclepius—
Into the Stygian river. But the goddess
1065 Trivia, kind Diana, hid Hippolytus
In a place apart, and sent him to the nymph
Egeria in her retired wood.
There he would live his obscure life alone
In Italy's deep forest, and his name
1070 Would now be Virbius. This is the reason
Horses with hooves are banned from Trivia's shrine
And all her sacred groves: that on the shore
In fright from sea-beasts they had wrecked the chariot
And killed the man Hippolytus. Even so,
1075 Over the plain behind a fiery team
His son rode in a chariot to war.

Turnus himself came on, a mighty figure
Moving among the captains blade in hand
And by a head the tallest. His high helm
1080 With triple plume bore a Chimaera's head
Exhaling Aetnean fires—raging the more
With savage heat the more blood flowed, the wilder
Grew the battle. On his polished shield,
In gold emblazonry, Io appeared
1085 With lifted horns and hair grown coarse—that instant
Changed, in the huge blazon, into a cow.
There stood her escort, Argus, and her father,
Inachus, the rivergod, poured out
A stream from a figured urn. And following Turnus
1090 Marched a cloud of infantry, as all
The plain filled up with troops in arms—Argive
Ardea's men, Auruncan bands, Rutulians,
Old time Sicani, Sacrani in ranks,
Labici carrying painted shields—all those
1095 Who plowed in time of peace your sacred shores,
Numicius, or your woodland pastures, Tiber,
Or who turned clods on the Rutulian hills
And Circe's ridge, those lands presided over
By Jupiter of Anxur and Feronia,

1100   Lady of wild beasts, blithe in her green grove.
    Satura's black marsh lies there, and the chill
    Ufens river winds through bottomlands
    To find peace in the sea.
                       Besides all these

1105   Camilla of the Volscian people came,
    Riding ahead of cavalry, her squadrons
    Gallant in bronze. A warrior girl whose hands
    Were never deft at distaff or wool basket,
    Skills of Minerva, she was hard and trained

1110   To take the shock of war, or to outrace
    The winds in running. If she ran full speed
    Over the tips of grain unharvested
    She would not ever have bruised an ear, or else
    She might have sprinted on the deep sea swell

1115   And never dipped her flying feet. To see her,
    Men and women pouring from the fields,
    From houses, thronged her passage way and stared
    Wide-eyed with admiration at the style
    Of royal purple, robing her smooth shoulders,

1120   Then at the brooch that bound her hair in gold,
    Then at the Lycian quiver that she bore
    And shepherd's myrtle staff, pointed with steel.

Lines 800–817

BOOK

VIII

ARCADIAN ALLIES

That day when Turnus raised the flag of war
Over Laurentum tower, and his trumpets
Blared hoarse-throated, when he laid the whip
On fiery teams, making bright armor clang—
Then hearts were stirred by fear, then all of Latium
Joined in distracted tumult, and young men
Grew bloody-minded, wild. The high commanders,
Messapus and Ufens, and that one
Who held the gods in scorn, Mezentius,
From every quarter drew repeated levies
And laid the wide fields waste of their field hands.
Dispatched to Diomedes' distant city,
Venulus went to ask for aid: to state
That Trojans had a foothold in Latium,
That, landing there, Aeneas had brought in
His conquered gods and claimed to be a king
Called for by destiny; that many tribes
Made league with the Dardanian, and his name
Reverberated far and wide through Latium;
What he might build on this first enterprise,
What he desired as outcome of the war
Should fortune favor him: that would be clearer
To Diomedes than to either king,
Turnus or Latinus.

25   Thus affairs
Took shape in Latium. And Laömedon's heir,
Who saw the whole scene, weltered in his trouble,
Wave after wave of it. This way and that
He let his mind run, passing quickly over
30 All he might do, as when from basins full
Of unstilled water, struck by a ray of sun
Or the bright disk of moon, a flickering light
Plays over walls and corners and flies up
To hit high roofbeams and a coffered ceiling.
35 Now it was night, and through the lands of earth
Deep slumber held all weary living things
Of bird and beast kind, when the Trojan prince,
Aeneas, heartsick at the woe of war,
Lay down upon the riverside
40 In the cold air, under the open sky,
And gave his body at long last repose.
Before him as he slept the very god
Of that place, Tiberinus of fair waters,
Lifting his hoary head through poplar leaves,
45 Appeared all veiled in cobweb cloak of grey
And crowned with shady sedge. He seemed to speak
In these words to relieve the burdened man:

"Sir, born of heaven, in whose care Troy city
Now comes back to us from its enemies,
50 And in whose keeping high and everlasting
Pergama stands: you whom Laurentine soil
And Latin countryside have long awaited,
Here is your home, your hearth gods, fixed and sure.
Now is no time to let go, or give way
55 To fear at threats of war. Angers that rose
Among the gods have passed. And I can tell you—
Lest you suppose this nothing but a dream—
Under the shoreside oaks a giant sow
Will be discovered, lying on the ground,
60 With her new farrow, thirty young all told,
A white sow, with white sucklings at her teats.

Lines 18–45

And by this portent, after thirty years
Ascanius will found the famous town
Called Alba, or White City. I foretell

65 No doubtful matter. But just now, as to
What lies ahead and how you may win through it,
Listen, and I'll explain in a few words.
In this country an Arcadian tribe, descended
From a forebear called Pallas, colonists

70 With King Evander, followers of his flag,
Marked out a spot and founded on the hills
A town they named for Pallas, Pallanteum.
Always at war with Latins, as they are,
Join forces with them, make them your allies.

75 I myself between my banks will take you
Straight upstream, so you'll make way with oars
Against the current.
                                    Son of Venus, rise.
Now, while the early stars of evening set,

80 Address your prayers in proper form to Juno,
Melt with your pleas her menaces and anger.
You'll make return to me when you prevail.
I am that river in full flood you see
Cutting through farmland, gliding past these banks,

85 The sea-blue Tiber, heaven-delighting stream,
My mansion's here, my fountainhead far north
Amid the hilltop cities."
                                    Having spoken,
He sank away into the watery depths

90 At the river-bottom. From Aeneas then
Night-time and sleep departed, and he rose.
Facing the light that fanned up in the east
From the pure sun, he cupped his ritual hands
To lift clear water from the stream, then spoke

95 His heartfelt prayer to heaven:
                                    "Nymphs of the springs,
Laurentine nymphs, mothers of river kind,
And Father Tiber with your sacred stream,
Take in Aeneas as your guest, at last

100 Shield him from peril. By whatever source
     The ponds lie that embrace you in your pity
     For our ill fortune, from whatever ground
     You well up in your loveliness, you'll be
     Forever honored and adorned forever
105 With gifts from me, O potent stream, great lord
     Of waters in the west. Only be with me,
     And give me confirmation of your will."

     He finished, then selected from his squadron
     Two biremes and had them manned and armed,
110 But something suddenly caught his eye—a sign
     To marvel at: snow-white in the green wood,
     Snow-white as her own litter, lay the sow
     Upon the grassy bank, where all could see
     And grave Aeneas dedicated her
115 To thee, Juno the great, to thee indeed,
     Lifting both sow and brood before the altar
     In sacrifice. Then all that night's long hours
     The Tiber quieted his swollen stream
     And countering his current with still water
120 Slackened so, that like a tranquil pool
     Or placid marsh he smoothed his whole expanse
     And left no toil for oars. Once underway,
     Therefore, cheered on, they made good speed upstream.
     Their tarry hulls with bubbling wakes behind
125 Slipped through the water, and the waves were awed,
     The virgin woods were awed at this new sight:
     The soldiers' shields that flashed in distant air,
     The painted ships afloat upon the river.
     Oarsmen outwearied night and day in rowing,
130 Passed the long bends, shaded by differing trees,
     And cleft green forests in the mirroring water.
     At that hour when the fiery sun had climbed
     To heaven's midpoint, distant still they saw
     Wall, citadel, a few house tops—the town
135 Built heavenward by Roman power now
     But meager then, and poor, held by Evander.
     In toward the settlement they swung their prows.

By chance that day the Arcadian king paid honor
To Hercules, great son of Amphitryon,
140 And to the other gods in festival
Outside the town, in a green grove. With him
Were his son Pallas and his leading men
And homespun senate. They made offerings
Of incense while hot blood fumed on the altars.
145 When they caught sight of the tall ships and saw
The strangers gliding through the woodland shade,
Rowing in silence, they were caught by fear
At the sudden apparition, and all sprang up,
Leaving the feast. But Pallas with high heart
150 Forbade them to disrupt the ritual.
Taking a spear, he ran toward the newcomers
And called out, while still distant, from a mound:
"Soldiers, what brought you this strange way? Where **bound?**
What is your nation? Where is your home?" he said.
155 "Do you bring peace or war?"

                    Then Lord Aeneas
From his high poop called back, as he held out
A branch of olive signifying peace:

"You see before your eyes men born in Troy,
160 Enemy lances to the Latins—those
Who arrogantly attacked us in our exile.
We come to find Evander. Take this message:
Say chosen captains of Dardania
Have come proposing partnership in war."
165 Struck by that far away great name, young Pallas
Called:

            "Disembark, whoever you may be,
And speak directly to my father . . . Come,
You'll be the guest of our hearth gods tonight."
170 He took Aeneas' hand in a strong grip,
And up the grove they went, leaving the river.

Then, for the king, Aeneas had friendly words:
"Most noble son of Greece, Fortune would have me
Make my appeal to you with suppliant boughs.
175 I have not feared you as Arcadian
Or captain of Danaans, or blood-kin
Of the Atridae. No, my own manhood
And heaven's holy words, our ancestry
In common, and your fame through all the world,
180 Have brought me here by destiny, and gladly,
To join my strength with yours. The Greeks maintain
Electra bore the founding father of Troy,
Old Dardanus, who sailed to the Teucrians.
Electra was the child of that prodigious
185 Atlas who upholds the heavenly sphere
On a snowy shoulder. Father of your line
Was Mercury, whom snow-white Maia bore
On the cold summit of Cyllenë—Maia,
Fathered, if we can trust these tales,
190 By that same Atlas, pillar of starry sky.
So both our lines are branches of one blood.
Putting my trust in this, I sent no legates,
Made no round-about approaches to you,
But have exposed myself, and my own life,
195 In coming as a suppliant. The Daunians,
The race that harries you, now harries us
In savage war. If they defeat and rout us,
Nothing, so they believe, stands in the way
Of their subduing all Hesperia,
200 Ruling the seas that bathe her, north and south.
Trust us as we trust you. We have the stamina
For warfare, and we have the spirit for it.
In difficulties our men have proved themselves."

Here Aeneas paused. For all this time,
205 Evander's gaze had slowly swept the speaker,
His eyes, his countenance, and his whole figure.
Now he replied:
            "Most gallant Teucrian,
How happily I welcome you and know you;

210 How you remind me of your father's speech,
The voice of great Anchises, and his look!
For I remember how Prince Priam, son
Of old Laömedon, Salamis-bound
To the kingdom of Hesionë, his sister,
215 Visited the cold Arcadian land.
The bloom of youth was on me. I admired
The Trojan leaders, and admired Priam,
But tallest in that company by far
Your father passed. With a boy's adoration
220 I longed to speak to him, to shake his hand,
So I approached. Then all aglow I led him
Into Pheneus town. His parting gifts
Were a fine quiver full of Lycian arrows,
A gold-brocaded cloak, and two gold bits,
225 Those that my Pallas owns now.
                              Well, then, here
Is what you ask, my right hand in a pact.
And when first light returns to earth tomorrow
I'll send you back with a fresh increment
230 Of troops to gladden you, and fresh supplies.
Now, since you come as friends, be kind enough
To join us at our feast, one held each year
And not to be postponed. Become acquainted,
Even so soon, with how your allies fare."

235 On this he called for dishes and winecups
Already taken off to be brought back,
As he himself gave the guests grassy seats
And led Aeneas to the place of honor—
A maple chair cushioned with lionskin.
240 Then picked men and the priest who served the altar
Vied with one another to bring roast meat,
To load bread-baskets with the gifts of Ceres,
Milled and baked, and to pour out the wine.
Aeneas with his Trojans feasted then
245 On a beef chine and flesh of sacrifice.
When they were fed, their appetites appeased,
Royal Evander spoke:

No empty-headed
Superstition, blind to the age-old gods,
250   Imposed this ritual on us, and this feast,
This altar to a divine force of will.
No, Trojan guest, we carry out these rites,
Renewed each year, as men saved from barbaric
Dangers in the past. Look first of all
255   At this high overhanging rocky cliff;
See how rock masses have been scattered out,
Leaving a mountain dwelling bare, forsaken
Where the crags fell in avalanche. Here was once
A cave with depths no ray of sun could reach,
260   Where Cacus lived, a bestial form, half man,
And the ground reeked forever with fresh blood,
While nailed up in vile pride on his cave doors
Were men's pale faces ghastly in decay.
Vulcan had fathered this unholy brute
265   Who as he moved about in mammoth bulk
Belched out the poisonous fires of the father.

After long prayers, time brought even to us
A god's advent and aid.
                            The great avenger,
270   Hercules, appeared, still flushed with pride
In spoils he took when slaughtering Geryon,
The triple-bodied giant, and as conqueror
He drove the giant's bulls this way before him,
While the mild herds grazed in our river valley.
275   Cacus' blood-thirsty mind, madly aroused
To leave no crookedness untried, no crime
Unventured, turned four bulls out of their grounds,
Four heifers, too, all of the handsomest.
But not to leave their hoof-tracks going away,
280   He held their tails and pulled the cattle backward—
Traces of passage thus reversed—and hid
The stolen beasts in the cave's rocky darkness.

Caveward, then, no sign would lead a searcher.
Now when Amphitryon's heroic son
285 Had got his well-fed cattle on the move
Out of their pasture, ready to depart,
The oxen bellowed at this leave-taking,
Filling the wood with protest, crying loud
To the hills they left. One answer came: one heifer
290 Out of the cave-depth lowed, out of her prison,
Foiling Cacus' hopes. For now indeed
The affront of it set Hercules ablaze
With black bile of anger. Taking arms,
Taking in hand his knotted massy club,
295 He ran for the mountain top. Our people then
Saw for the first time fear in Cacus' eyes
As faster than the eastwind he made off
To reach his cave—and terror winged his feet.
He shut himself inside, breaking the chain
300 Wrought there in iron by his father's hand
To keep a boulder hanging. Down it crashed
To block the entrance—none too soon. Imagine
Hercules of Tiryns in his fury
Facing that wall! This way and that he turned
305 And stared to measure every access point,
And ground his teeth, and in his rage three times
Went over all Mount Aventine; three times
In vain pitted himself against the rock,
And rested three times, wearied, in the valley.
310 But from the ridge over the cave arose
A flinty pinnacle, sheer on all sides,
A towering home for nests of carrion birds.
As to the left this leaned over the river
The hero strained against it from the right
315 And shook it, till the rock-embedded roots
Were loosened, then torn free; and all at once
He heaved it over. At that fall great heaven
Thundered, river margins leapt apart,
And the shocked stream in flood surged backward. **Then**
320 The cavern, Cacus' huge domain, unroofed,
Lay open to its gloomy depth, as though

Lines 212–243

Earth, by some force cracked open to its depth,
Unlocked the underworld and brought to view
The ghastly realm the gods hate, the abyss
325   Now visible from above, and ghosts atremble
At the daylight let in. Caught by the light
Unlooked for, and closed in by stone, the giant
Bellowed as never in his life before,
While from above with missiles Hercules
330   Let fly at him, calling on every mass
At hand to make a weapon, raining down
Dry boughs and boulders like millstones. But then
The monster, seeing no escape was left,
Wonderful to relate, belched from his gullet
335   Clouds of smoke, blanketing all the place
In blinding haze that took sight from the eyes
And thickened in the cave to smoky night,
Profound gloom laced with fire. Hercules'
Great heart could not abide this trick, but down
340   He plunged headlong in one leap through the flames
Where the smoke billowed thickest, and the cavern
Seethed in that black cloud. Down there he caught
And pinioned Cacus as the monster belched
His fires in vain: fastening on his throat
345   He choked him till his eyes burst out, his gullet
Whitened and dried up with loss of blood.
Soon the black den was cleared, the doors torn off,
The stolen cattle—loot their tracks denied—
Revealed in the light of day, and the misshapen
350   Carcass dragged out by the heels. Our people
Could not be sated by the spectacle
But gazed long at the dreadful eyes, the face,
The shaggy bristling chest of the half-beast,
His gorge's fiery breath put out. Since then
355   This feast is held, and younger men are glad
To keep the memory of the day—in chief
Potitius, the founder, and the house
Of the Pinarii, custodians
Of rites to Hercules. Here in the grove
360   He placed this altar, ever to be called

The Greatest by ourselves, and be the Greatest.
Come then, soldiers, honor that great feat,
Garland your heads with leaves, hold out your cups,
Invoke the god we share, and tip your wine
365 Most heartily."

              At this with poplar leaves
Of shifting color, Herculean shade,
He veiled his hair, and the leafy braided wreath
Hung down as the blest winecup filled his hand.
370 Tipping their wine at once over the table
The others made their prayer. Meanwhile Olympian
Heaven downward turned, evening came on,
And soon the priests, led by Potitius,
After their ancient mode, belted in furs,
375 Went round with torches. They renewed the feast,
Bringing a welcome second course, and heaped
The altar tops with dishes. For a hymn
At the lit altars came the Salii,
All garlanded with poplar—files of dancers,
380 Here of the young, there of the elder men,
Who praised in song the feats of Hercules,
His story: how he grappled monsters first,
Choking his step-mother's twin snakes, and how,
Again by might, he ruined tall towns in war,
385 Troy-town and then Oechalia, and endured
A thousand bitter toils under Eurystheus,
Doomed to these by Juno's enmity.

"O thou unconquered one, who slew the centaurs,
Pholus and Hylaeus, born of cloud,
390 And broke the Terror of Crete by thy right hand
And killed the lion under Nemea's crag!
Before thee shook the Stygian lakes, the Keeper
Of Orcus shook, sprawled in his gory cave
On bones partly devoured. No monstrous form
395 Affrighted thee, even Typhoeus' self
Though mountainous in arms. And Lerna's hydra
Coiling about thee with a swarm of heads
Attacked no guileless warrior. Hail to thee,

True son of Jove, new glory of the gods,
400   With friendly stride come join us, join thy feast!"

So ran the hymns they sang, and crowning all
A song of Cacus' cave and breath of fire—
Voices that filled the leafy wood, and rang,
And sprang back from the echoing hill-sides.

405   When they had carried out the ritual
They turned back to the town. And, slowed by age,
The king walked, keeping Aeneas and his son
Close by his side, with talk of various things
To make the long path easy. Marveling,
410   Aeneas gladly looked at all about him,
Delighted with the setting, asking questions,
Hearing of earlier men and what they left.
Then King Evander, founder unaware
Of Rome's great citadel, said:

415   "These woodland places
Once were homes of local fauns and nymphs
Together with a race of men that came
From tree trunks, from hard oak: they had no way
Of settled life, no arts of life, no skill
420   At yoking oxen, gathering provisions,
Practising husbandry, but got their food
From oaken boughs and wild game hunted down.
In that first time, out of Olympian heaven,
Saturn came here in flight from Jove in arms,
425   An exile from a kingdom lost; he brought
These unschooled men together from the hills
Where they were scattered, gave them laws, and chose
The name of Latium, from his latency
Or safe concealment in this countryside.
430   In his reign were the golden centuries
Men tell of still, so peacefully he ruled,
Till gradually a meaner, tarnished age
Came on with fever of war and lust of gain.
Then came Ausonians and Sicanians,

Lines 301–328

435 And Saturn's land now often changed her name,
   And there were kings, one savage and gigantic,
   Thybris, from whom we afterborn Italians
   Named the river Tiber. The old name,
   Albula, was lost. As for myself,
440 In exile from my country, I set out
   For the sea's end, but Fortune that prevails
   In everything, Fate not to be thrown off,
   Arrested me in this land—solemn warnings
   Came from my mother, from the nymph Carmentis,
445 Backed by the god Apollo, to urge me here."

   Just after this, as he went on he showed
   The altar and the gate the Romans call
   Carmental, honoring as of old the nymph
   And prophetess Carmentis, first to sing
450 The glory of Pallanteum and Aeneas'
   Great descendants. Then he showed the wood
   That Romulus would make a place of refuge,
   Then the grotto called the Lupercal
   Under the cold crag, named in Arcadian fashion
455 After Lycaean Pan. And then as well
   He showed the sacred wood of Argiletum,
   "Argus' death," and took oath by it, telling
   Of a guest, Argus, put to death. From there
   He led to our Tarpeian site and Capitol,
460 All golden now, in those days tangled, wild
   With underbrush—but awesome even then.
   A strangeness there filled country hearts with dread
   And made them shiver at the wood and Rock.

   "Some god," he said, "it is not sure what god,
465 Lives in this grove, this hilltop thick with leaves.
   Arcadians think they've seen great Jove himself
   Sometimes with his right hand shaking the aegis
   To darken sky and make the storm clouds rise
   Towering in turmoil. Here, too, in these walls
470 Long fallen down, you see what were two towns,

Lines 329-355

Monuments of the ancients. Father Janus
Founded one stronghold, Saturn the other,
Named Janiculum and Saturnia."

Conversing of such matters, going toward
475   Austere Evander's house, they saw his cattle
Lowing everywhere in what is now
Rome's Forum and her fashionable quarter,
Carinae. As they came up to the door,
Evander said:
480   "In victory Hercules
Bent for this lintel, and these royal rooms
Were grand enough for him. Friend, have the courage
To care little for wealth, and shape yourself,
You too, to merit godhead. Do not come
485   Disdainfully into our needy home."

Even as he spoke, he led under the gabled
Narrow roof Aeneas' mighty figure
And made him rest where on strewn leaves he spread
A Libyan bearskin. Swiftly Night came on
490   To fold her dusky wings about the earth.

Now Venus, as a mother sorely frightened,
And with good reason, moved by the menaces
Of the Laurentines and their hostile rising,
Turned to Vulcan. In her bridal chamber
495   All of gold, putting divine desire
In every word, she said:
                  "While Argive kings
Lay their due victim, Pergama, waste—her towers
Doomed to fall in fires her enemy set—
500   Never did I demand for the desperate
Any relief at all, no weapons forged
By your skill, in your metal. Most dear husband,

I never wished to tax you, make you toil
In a lost cause, however much I owed
505   To Priam's sons, however long I wept
Over Aeneas' ordeals. Now, however,
By the command of Jove he has made good
His landing on the Rutulian shore, and so
I do come now, begging your sacred power
510   For arms, a mother begging for her son.
The daughter of Nereus moved you, and Tithonus'
Consort moved you by her tears to this.
Look now, and see what masses throng together,
See what cities lock their gates and whet
515   The sword against me, to cut down my own!"
The goddess spoke and wrapped her snowy arms
This way and that about him as he lingered,
Cherishing him in her swansdown embrace.
And instantly he felt the flame of love
520   Invading him as ever; into his marrow
Ran the fire he knew, and through his bones,
As when sometimes, ripped by a thunder peal,
A fiery flash goes jagged through the clouds.
His wife, contented with her blandishment,
525   Sure of her loveliness, perceived it all.
Lord Vulcan, captive to immortal passion,
Answered her:

        "Why do you go so far
Afield for reasons? Has your trust in me
530   Gone elsewhere, goddess? If concern like this
Had moved you in the old days, even then
I might have armed the Trojans lawfully—
For neither Jove almighty nor the Fates
Forbade Troy to endure, Priam to live,
535   Ten further years. If you are ready now
To arm for war and have a mind to wage it,
All the devoted craft that I can promise,
All that is forgeable in steel and molten
Alloy by the strength of a blast-fire—
540   You need not beg me for these gifts. Have done
With doubting your own powers!"

Lines 378–404

He said no more,
But took her in his arms as she desired
And gave himself, infused in her embrace,
545 To peace and slumber.

When his first repose
Came to an end in the mid-course of night
Now on the wane, and waked him, at that hour
When a poor woman whose hard lot it is
550 To make a living by her loom and spindle,
Pokes up the embers, wakes the sleeping fire,
Adding some night-time to her morning's work,
And by the firelight keeps her household maids
Employed at their long task—all to keep chaste
555 Her marriage bed and bring her children up—
At that same hour, no more slothful than she,
The Lord of Fire rose from his soft bed
To labor at the smithy.

Near the coast
560 Of Sicily and Aeolian Lipari
A steep island rises, all of rock
And smoking. Underneath, a mammoth cave
And vaulted galleries of Aetna, burned
Away by blast-fire from the Cyclops' forge,
565 Rumble in thunder: mighty blows are heard
Reechoing and booming from the anvils,
Chalybian bars of iron hiss in the caverns,
Vulcan's workshop, named for him Vulcania.
To this the Lord of Fire came down from heaven.

570 Working with iron in the enormous cave
Were Cyclops Thunderclap and Anvilfire
And Flash, stripped to the waist. They had a bolt
In hand, such as from open sky the Father
Often hurls to earth—this one part done,
575 Part still unfinished. First the smiths had added
Twisted hail, three rays, three rays of raincloud,
Three of red fire and the flying southwind.
Now they were mixing in terrifying lightning,
Fracas, and fear, and anger in pursuit

580 With flares. Elsewhere they strove to finish
A chariot of Mars, and flying wheels
On which he might stir fighting men and cities.
Then to an aegis, cuirass bringing dread
Of Pallas when aroused, they gave a polish,
585 Vying to shine the golden serpent scales,
The knot of vipers and the Gorgon's head—
For the goddess' very breast—with severed neck
And rolling eyes.
              "Put all these things away,"
590 Commanded Vulcan. "Cyclops under Aetna,
Drop the work begun. Here is our task:
Armor is to be forged for a brave soldier.
Now we can use your brawn, and your deft hands,
Your craft, your mastery. Shake off
595 All reluctance."
              Vulcan said no more,
But they for their part buckled down as one,
Allotting equal tasks to each. In streams
The molten brass and gold flowed. Iron that kills
600 Turned liquid in the enormous furnace heat.
They shaped a vast shield, one that might alone
Be proof against all missiles of the Latins;
Fastened it, layer on layer, sevenfold.
Some smiths drew pulsing in and blasted out
605 The air with bellows, others plunged the metal
Screeching in fresh water, and the cavern
Groaned under the anvils they set down.
Now this, now that one, for a mighty stroke
Brought up his arms in rhythm, as they hammered,
610 Shifting the metal mass with gripping tongs.

While in Aeolia Vulcan, Lord of Lemnos,
Pressed that fiery task, mild morning light
With birdsong under eaves awoke Evander,

And the old man arose. He slipped his arms
615 Into his tunic and bound on his trim
Tyrrhenian sandals, then by shoulder and flank
Slung his Arcadian blade. A mantling hide
Of panther, where it hung down on the left,
He tossed back. Then his two awakened watchdogs
620 Preceded him out of the entrance way
And kept close to their master. He went on
To visit the secluded place his guest,
Aeneas, occupied, and he remembered
What had been said, what favors he had promised.
625 Just as early, Aeneas had come outside,
And one man had his son beside him, Pallas,
The other had Achatës. When they met
They joined hands and sat down in the open court
To enjoy the talk at last permitted them.
630 The king began, saying:

                    "Greatest of Trojan captains,
Never while you live shall I consider
Troy to be conquered and her kingdom gone,
But, though our name is great, our power is slight
635 To strengthen you in war. We are confined
On this side by the river, and on that
The Rutulians bring pressure on our wall
With noisy forays. No, I plan for you
A league with a great host, an army rich
640 In many kingdoms. Here by unforeseen
Good fortune your salvation now appears.
Fate called for your coming. No long way
From here men live in the city of Agylla,
Built of ancient stone. The Lydians,
645 Renowned in war, in the old days settled there
On the Etruscan ridges, and for years
The city flourished, till an arrogant king,
Mezentius, ruled it barbarously by force.
How shall I tell of carnage beyond telling,
650 Beastly crimes this tyrant carried out?
Requite them, gods, on his own head and on

Lines 457–484

His children! He would even couple carcases
With living bodies as a form of torture.
Hand to hand and face to face, he made them
655   Suffer corruption, oozing gore and slime
In that wretched embrace, and a slow death.
But at long last the townsmen, sickening
Of his unholy ways, took arms and laid
Siege to the madman and his house. They killed
660   His henchmen and threw fire on his roof,
But in the midst of slaughter he escaped,
Took refuge in Rutulian territory,
And got himself defended by the arms
Of Turnus, host and friend. On this account
665   Etruria's people have risen as one man
In righteous anger, threatening war at once,
Demanding the king back for punishment.

Now I will make you leader of these thousands,
Aeneas: for in fact while ships of theirs
670   Are crowded on the shore and fret for action,
Calling for ensigns to go forward, still
A soothsayer of great age holds them all back,
Forewarning them:
               'Picked men of Maeonia,
675   Flower and heart of an old heroic race,
Though justly moved by your past suffering
Against your enemy, and though Mezentius·
Fires you with rightful anger, no Italian
May have command of this great people's cause.
680   Choose leaders from abroad.'
                    Taking alarm
At heaven's warning, the Etruscan ranks
Rest on their arms, here in this plain, and Tarchon
Sends me envoys with his crown and scepter,
685   Badges of regal power. He asks that I
Go up to camp and take the Tyrrhene throne.
But slow and cold old age, weakened by years,
Forbids command; an old man's vigor falls

Behind in action. I should urge my son
690 To accept, if he were not of mingled blood,
Through a Sabine mother heir to her fatherland
No, you are he whose age and foreign birth
The fates approve, and whom the gods desire.
Enter on your great duty now, great heart,
695 Commander of Trojans and Italians both!
I shall, besides, commit to you my Pallas,
All my comfort and my hope, to learn
With you as master how to weather battle,
Mars' dead serious work. May he become
700 Familiar with your actions, look to you
As his exemplar from his early years.
I'll add two hundred horsemen, all Arcadians,
Picked for ruggedness. In his own name
Pallas will give two hundred more."

705   In silence
After this speech, Anchises' son, Aeneas,
And faithful at his side Achatës sat
With downcast eyes. They would have pondered long
And grimly on the many trials to come,
710 Had not the Cytheran queen from open heaven
Given a sign—one utterly unforeseen:
A quivering flash out of the upper air,
A thunder crack, and in that instant all
The sky seemed falling, as it seemed on high
715 A Tyrrhene trumpet gave a rumbling blast.
They all looked up. Again and yet again
Tremendous crashes came. Between the clouds
In sunlit air they saw red glare of armor
Clashing, thundering at the shock. The others
720 Sat still, mystified, but Troy's great captain
Recognized the sound, and knew the promise
Made by his goddess mother. Then he said:

"My friend, you need not, truly need not ask
What new event's portended. I am the man
725 Whom heaven calls. This sign my goddess mother
Prophesied she would send if war broke out,

Lines 509–535

And said, too, she would bring out of the sky
Arms made by Vulcan to assist me. Ai!
What carnage is at hand for poor Laurentines.
730 What retribution you will make to me,
Turnus. Many a shield, many a helm,
And many brave men's bodies you'll take under,
Father Tiber. Let them insist on war,
Let them break treaties!"

735   After saying this,
He rose from his high seat and first revived
The fires for Hercules on slumbering altars,
Gladly revisiting, as yesterday,
The guardian Lar and humble household gods.
740 Likewise Evander and the men of Troy
Made sacrifice of chosen ewes. Thereafter
Back to his ships and comrades went Aeneas,
And chose among them soldiers known for bravery
To follow him to war. The rest were carried
745 Effortlessly downstream on the current
To bring Ascanius news of these affairs
And of his father.

                              Those Etruria-bound
Were now supplied with horses. For Aeneas
750 They led a special mount, all blanketed
With a lionskin, gleaming with gilded claws.
Then suddenly a rumor flew about
The little town that horsemen were departing
Quickly for the Etrurian king's domain.
755 Mothers in fright doubled their prayers: fear
Brought danger nearer, and the specter of war
Grew larger in their eyes. But Lord Evander
Clung to the hand of his departing son
And could not have enough of tears. He said:
760

"If only Jupiter would give me back
The past years and the man I was, when I
Cut down the front rank by Praeneste wall
And won the fight and burned the piles of shields!
I had dispatched to Hell with this right hand

765   King Erulus, to whom Feronia,
    His mother, gave three lives at birth—a thing
    To chill the blood—three sets of arms to fight with,
    So that he had to be brought down three times.
    Yet this hand took his lives that day, took all,
770   And each time took his arms. I should not now
    Be torn from you and from your dear embrace,
    My son, and neither would Mezentius
    Have shown contempt for me, his bordering power,
    Putting so many cruelly to the sword
775   And widowing his town of citizens.
    But O high masters, and thou, Jupiter,
    Supreme ruler of gods, pity, I beg,
    The Arcadian king, and hear a father's prayer:
    If by thy will my son survives, and fate
780   Spares him, and if I live to see him still,
    To meet him yet again, I pray for life;
    There is no trouble I cannot endure.
    But, Fortune, if you threaten some black day,
    Now, now, let me break off my bitter life
785   While all's in doubt, while hope of what's to come
    Remains uncertain, while I hold you here,
    Dear boy, my late delight, my only one—
    And may no graver message ever come
    To wound my ears."
790   These were the father's words,
    Poured out in final parting. He collapsed
    Completely, and the servants helped him in.

    And now indeed through open gates the horsemen
    Left the town, Aeneas at their head,
795   Achatës at his right hand, then the others,
    Trojan officers, and Pallas himself
    Mid-column in short cloak with blazoned arms,
    A sight as brilliant as the Morning Star

Whom Venus loves above all stellar fires,
800   When from the bath of Ocean into heaven
He lifts his holy visage, making Night
Dissolve and wane. Mothers with quaking breasts
Were standing on the walls, watching the cloud
Of dust, the burnished gleams of cavalry,
805   As the armed riders picked their way through scrub
Cross-country toward their goal. A shout went up,
And, forming into column, they rode on,
Hoofbeat of horses shaking the dust of the plain.

Near the cold stream of Caerë there's a grove
810   Immense and deep, awesome to our forebears.
The hills encircle it with dark fir trees.
The tale goes that the old Pelasgians,
Who held this Latin country who knows when,
Made grove and feast day sacred to Silvanus,
815   God of the fields and herds. Not far from there
Tarchon and his Tyrrhenians had encamped
On favorable ground, and one could see
From a high hill the tents of all the army
On the wide plain. Now Lord Aeneas came
820   To this place with his soldiers picked for battle.
Here they refreshed their weariness and gave
Their horses pasture. Venus the gleaming goddess,
Bearing her gifts, came down amid high clouds
And far away still, in a vale apart,
825   Sighted her son beside the ice-cold stream.
Then making her appearance as she willed
She said to him:
               "Here are the gifts I promised,
Forged to perfection by my husband's craft,
830   So that you need not hesitate to challenge
Arrogant Laurentines or savage Turnus,
However soon, in battle."
                      As she spoke
Cytherëa swept to her son's embrace
835   And placed the shining arms before his eyes
Under an oak tree. Now the man in joy

Lines 589–617

At a goddess' gifts, at being so greatly honored,
Could not be satisfied, but scanned each piece
In wonder and turned over in his hands
840 The helmet with its terrifying plumes
And gushing flames, the sword-blade edged with fate,
The cuirass of hard bronze, blood-red and huge—
Like a dark cloud burning with sunset light
That sends a glow for miles—the polished greaves
845 Of gold and silver alloy, the great spear,
And finally the fabric of the shield
Beyond description.
          There the Lord of Fire,
Knowing the prophets, knowing the age to come,
850 Had wrought the future story of Italy,
The triumphs of the Romans: there one found
The generations of Ascanius' heirs,
The wars they fought, each one. Vulcan had made
The mother wolf, lying in Mars' green grotto;
855 Made the twin boys at play about her teats,
Nursing the mother without fear, while she
Bent round her smooth neck fondling them in turn
And shaped their bodies with her tongue.
                       Nearby,
860 Rome had been added by the artisan,
And Sabine women roughly carried off
Out of the audience at the Circus games;
Then suddenly a new war coming on
To pit the sons of Romulus against
865 Old Tatius and his austere town of Curës.
Later the same kings, warfare laid aside,
In arms before Jove's altar stood and held
Libation dishes as they made a pact
With offering of swine. Not far from this
870 Two four-horse war-cars, whipped on, back to back,
Had torn Mettus apart (still, man of Alba,
You should have kept your word) and Roman Tullus
Dragged the liar's rags of flesh away
Through woods where brambles dripped a bloody dew.

Lines 617–645

875　　There, too, Porsenna stood, ordering Rome
　　　　To take the exiled Tarquin back, then bringing
　　　　The whole city under massive siege.
　　　　There for their liberty Aeneas' sons
　　　　Threw themselves forward on the enemy spears.
880　　You might have seen Porsenna imaged there
　　　　To the life, a menacing man, a man in anger
　　　　At Roman daring: Cocles who downed the bridge,
　　　　Cloelia who broke her bonds and swam the river.

　　　　On the shield's upper quarter Manlius,
885　　Guard of the Tarpeian Rock, stood fast
　　　　Before the temple and held the Capitol,
　　　　Where Romulus' house was newly thatched and rough.
　　　　Here fluttering through gilded porticos
　　　　At night, the silvery goose warned of the Gauls
890　　Approaching: under cover of the darkness
　　　　Gauls amid the bushes had crept near
　　　　And now lay hold upon the citadel.
　　　　Golden locks they had and golden dress,
　　　　Glimmering with striped cloaks, their milky necks
895　　Entwined with gold. They hefted Alpine spears,
　　　　Two each, and had long body shields for cover.
　　　　Vulcan had fashioned naked Luperci
　　　　And Salii leaping there with woolen caps
　　　　And fallen-from-heaven shields, and put chaste ladies
900　　Riding in cushioned carriages through Rome
　　　　With sacred images. At a distance then
　　　　He pictured the deep hell of Tartarus,
　　　　Dis's high gate, crime's punishments, and, yes,
　　　　You, Catiline, on a precarious cliff
905　　Hanging and trembling at the Furies' glare.
　　　　Then, far away from this, were virtuous souls
　　　　And Cato giving laws to them. Mid-shield,
　　　　The pictured sea flowed surging, all of gold,
　　　　As whitecaps foamed on the blue waves, and dolphins
910　　Shining in silver round and round the scene
　　　　Propelled themselves with flukes and cut through billows.

Lines 646–674

Vivid in the center were the bronze-beaked
Ships and the fight at sea off Actium.
Here you could see Leucata all alive
915   With ships maneuvering, sea glowing gold,
Augustus Caesar leading into battle
Italians, with both senators and people,
Household gods and great gods: there he stood
High on the stern, and from his blessed brow
920   Twin flames gushed upward, while his crest revealed
His father's star. Apart from him, Agrippa,
Favored by winds and gods, led ships in column,
A towering figure, wearing on his brows
The coronet adorned with warships' beaks,
925   Highest distinction for command at sea.
Then came Antonius with barbaric wealth
And a diversity of arms, victorious
From races of the Dawnlands and Red Sea,
Leading the power of the East, of Egypt,
930   Even of distant Bactra of the steppes.
And in his wake the Egyptian consort came
So shamefully. The ships all kept together
Racing ahead, the water torn by oar-strokes,
Torn by the triple beaks, in spume and foam.
935   All made for the open sea. You might believe
The Cyclades uprooted were afloat
Or mountains running against mountain heights
When seamen in those hulks pressed the attack
Upon the other turreted ships. They hurled
940   Broadsides of burning flax on flying steel,
And fresh blood reddened Neptune's fields. The queen
Amidst the battle called her flotilla on
With a sistrum's beat, a frenzy out of Egypt,
Never turning her head as yet to see
945   Twin snakes of death behind, while monster forms
Of gods of every race, and the dog-god
Anubis barking, held their weapons up
Against our Neptune, Venus, and Minerva.
Mars, engraved in steel, raged in the fight

Lines 675–701

950   As from high air the dire Furies came
      With Discord, taking joy in a torn robe,
      And on her heels, with bloody scourge, Bellona.

      Overlooking it all, Actian Apollo
      Began to pull his bow. Wild at this sight,
955   All Egypt, Indians, Arabians, all
      Sabaeans put about in flight, and she,
      The queen, appeared crying for winds to shift
      Just as she hauled up sail and slackened sheets.
      The Lord of Fire had portrayed her there,
960   Amid the slaughter, pallid with death to come,
      Then borne by waves and wind from the northwest,
      While the great length of mourning Nile awaited her
      With open bays, calling the conquered home
      To his blue bosom and his hidden streams.
965   But Caesar then in triple triumph rode
      Within the walls of Rome, making immortal
      Offerings to the gods of Italy—
      Three hundred princely shrines throughout the city.
      There were the streets, humming with festal joy
970   And games and cheers, an altar to every shrine,
      To every one a mothers' choir, and bullocks
      Knifed before the altars strewed the ground.
      The man himself, enthroned before the snow-white
      Threshold of sunny Phoebus, viewed the gifts
975   The nations of the earth made, and he fitted them
      To the tall portals. Conquered races passed
      In long procession, varied in languages
      As in their dress and arms. Here Mulciber,
      Divine smith, had portrayed the Nomad tribes
980   And Afri with ungirdled flowing robes,
      Here Leleges and Carians, and here
      Gelonians with quivers. Here Euphrates,
      Milder in his floods now, there Morini,
      Northernmost of men; here bull-horned Rhine,
985   And there the still unconquered Scythian Dahae;
      Here, vexed at being bridged, the rough Araxes.

Lines 701–729

All these images on Vulcan's shield,
His mother's gift, were wonders to Aeneas.
Knowing nothing of the events themselves,
990   He felt joy in their pictures, taking up
Upon his shoulder all the destined acts
And fame of his descendants.

Lines 729–731

BOOK

IX

A NIGHT SORTIE,
A DAY ASSAULT

While all these differing actions were afoot
In the far distance, Juno from high air
Sent Iris down to Turnus. As it chanced,
That day the rash prince rested in the grove
5   Of his forebear, Pilumnus, in a valley
Blest of old. There Iris, rose-lipped child
Of Thaumas, told him:

             "Turnus, what no god
Would dare to promise you—your heart's desire—
10   The course of time has of itself brought on.
Leaving his town and ships and followers
Aeneas journeyed to the Palatine
Court of Evander. Still unsatisfied,
He's gone to distant hamlets of Corythus
15   To rally and arm the Lydian countrymen.
Why hesitate? Now is the time to sound
The call for cavalry and war-cars, now!
Break off this lull, strike at their flurried camp,
Take it by storm!"

20   On even wings she rose
Into the sky, inscribing her great bow
In flight upon the clouds. He knew her sign,
And lifting both his hands to starry heaven
Sent these words after her:

25   "Glory of the sky,
Who brought you down to me, cloudborne to earth?

What makes the sudden brilliance of the air?
I see the vault of heaven riven, and stars
That drift across the night-sky. I'll obey
30 This great presage, no matter who you are
Who call me to attack."

               Then riverward
He took his way and from the surface drew
Pure lustral water, then he heaped his vows
35 Plenteously on heaven. Soon his army
At full strength moved out through open land,
Studded with riders, with dyed cloaks and gold,
Messapus commanding the forward units,
Tyrrhus' sons the rear, Turnus the center—
40 As Ganges fed by seven tranquil streams
Flows high and quietly, or Nile goes full
In a seaward channel when the enriching flood
Ebbs from the fields at last.

               A distant cloud
45 In black dust mounting up, a darkness rising
Suddenly on the plain came to the eyes
Of Trojan lookouts. Then Caïcus yelled
From the rampart facing inland:

                    "Countrymen,
50 What is the mass of men there on the plain
In a dark cloud of dust? Take arms, be quick,
Hand missiles out, and spears, and man the walls.
Here comes the enemy. On guard!"

                  In tumult
55 Back to the camp through all the gates retiring
Trojans took position on the walls—
For so on his departure their best soldier,
Aeneas, had instructed them: if any
Emergency arose, not to do battle,
60 Not to entrust their fortunes to the field,
But safe behind their walls to hold the camp.
Therefore, though shame and anger tempted them
To a pitched battle, even so they barred
Their gates as he commanded, and compact
65 In towers, armed, awaited the enemy.

Turnus, riding hard, had left the slow
Main column far behind. Now he turned up
Before the camp, with twenty chosen horsemen.
A Thracian piebald was his mount, his helm
70 All golden with a crimson plume. He shouted:
"Who will it be, men? Who will join with me
To open the attack? Look here!"
                                        He cast
High in the air his spinning javelin—
75 First in that fight. Then the tall horseman rode
Straight onward in the open field. His troop
Took up the cry and galloped after him
With a wild din, yelling astonishment
At Trojans' faint hearts.
80   "They won't risk themselves
In the open in a fair fight, won't come down
To stand up to us. How they hug the camp!"

Now Turnus furiously this way and that
Rode round the walls and looked for a way in
85 Where there was none. As a wolf on the prowl
Round a full sheepfold howls at crevices,
Enduring wind and rain at dead of night,
While nestled safe under the ewes the lambs
Keep up their bleating; he, beside himself,
90 Tormented by accumulated hunger,
Jaws athirst for blood, in all his fury
Cannot reach them, rend them: so the Rutulian
Flared up with helpless rage at what he saw
Of walls and camp, a fever in his bones.
95 How could he work an entrance? By what course
Dislodge the shut-in Trojans from their rampart,
Get them to issue on the plain? The fleet!
Next to the camp it lay, shielded by earthworks
On the land side and by the running stream.
100 He rode for it, calling his cheering men
To bring up fire, and he, himself enflamed,
Took up a blazing pine torch in his hand.
Then as his presence urged them on, they all

Lines 47–74

Rode to and fro in earnest to arm themselves
105   With evil torches, tearing camp-fires apart
As fuming brands gave off a pitchy glare
And Vulcan clouded heaven with smoke and ash.

Now which of the immortals, Muse, dispelled
That cruel conflagration from the Trojans?
110   Who turned those fires from the ships? Tell me
The old belief and the eternal tale.
In those days when Aeneas shaped his fleet
On Phrygian Ida and prepared to sail
The deep sea, then the mother of the gods,
115   The Berecynthian, addressed great Jove:

"Son, now Olympus owns your mastery,
Grant your dear mother what she asks of you.
There was a forest of pines I loved for years,
A grove high on a mountain crest, where men
120   Brought offerings to me—a dusky place
With dark pine trees and a tall stand of maple.
These I gladly gave to the Dardan prince
When he required a fleet. But now a pang
Of fear has made my heart contract. Relieve
125   My anguish, let your mother's plea avail
In this: that those ships' timbers not be breached
Or swamped on any course by any storm,
But let their birth and growth here on our mountains
Prosper them all."
130   But in reply her son
Who makes the firmament revolve demurred:
"What swerving, Mother, do you ask of fate?
What privilege for these, your ships? Shall hulls
That mortal hands have made enjoy a right
135   That only immortals have? And shall Aeneas

Lines 74–97

Go secure through insecurities
And dangers? Which of the gods can wield that power?
Rather, when they have done their work and moored
In the Ausonian ports one day, those ships
140 That have escaped the storm waves and brought home
The Dardan hero to Laurentine lands,
Then I shall strip away their mortal shape
And make them, at my bidding, goddesses
Of the great deep, like Doto, Nereus' child,
145 And Galatëa, in the midsea foam
Breasting their way."

             So ran the pledge of Jove,
Ratified when by his Stygian brother's
Rivers, boiling banks, and black whirlpool
150 He took oath nodding, making all Olympus
Tremble at his nod.

                Now, then, the promised
Hour had come, the overshadowing Fates
Had filled the appointed time. Now havoc planned
155 By Turnus roused the Mother to keep away
His firebrands from her blessed hulls. Fresh light
Shone in men's eyes, a great cloud from the East
Appeared to storm across the sky with Ida's
Retinue of Cybelë. Then a voice
160 To chill the blood came falling through the air
And reached all ranks, Rutulian and Trojan:

"No desperate rallying to defend my ships,
You Trojans, no equipping men for that.
Turnus may sooner fire the sea itself
165 Than hulls of holy pine. Ships, now go free,
Go as sea-goddesses. Your Mother sends you."

Each broke her hawser instantly; their bows
Went under like a school of dolphins diving
Into the depths, then wondrously came up,
170 So many virgin forms now seaward bound.
The astounded troop drew back; as horses reared,

Messapus, even he, was terrified.
The river halted with a raucous noise
As Tiber turned back from the sea. But Turnus'
175   Fiery confidence held; in quick response
He blazed at them to give them heart:

                        "These wonders

Are all aimed at the Trojans! Jove himself
Has robbed them of their usual ally,
180   Not waiting for our swords and fires to do it.
The open sea is closed to Trojans now,
Now they have no way out. That element
Is taken from them, and dry land is ours,
Where all the tribes of Italy, men in thousands,
185   Take up arms. Those fateful oracles,
So-called, on which the Phrygians plume themselves,
Terrify me not in the least: enough
And more has now been granted Fate and Venus,
Seeing the Trojans reached Ausonian lands.
190   I have my fate as well, to combat theirs,
To cut this criminal people down, my bride
Being stolen. Pain over such a loss is not
For the Atridae only, nor may only
Mycenae justly have recourse to arms.
195   Enough that Trojans perished once? Their sin
That once had been enough, were they not still
Given to hatred of all womankind.
They get their courage from a wall between us,
Ditches to put us off—a paltry space
200   From massacre for them. Did they not see
The walls of Troy, built up by Neptune's hand,
Collapse in flames? Which one of you picked men
Is ready with his blade to breach their wall
And rush their flustered camp with me? I need
205   No arms from Vulcan, nor a thousand ships,
To take these Trojans on. Let the Etruscans
All be quick to join them as allies.
They need not fear sneak thievery by night
Of their Palladium, guards on the height cut down,

210 Nor will we hide in a horse's pitch-dark belly.
Openly by day I'll have their ramparts
Ringed with flame, by god: I'll see to it
They won't suppose they're fighting with Danaans,
Pelasgian troops Hector held off ten years.

215 Now, though, seeing the day's best hours are gone,
Be of good cheer, men; after the day's good action,
Rest and be fed. A fight's in preparation,
You can be sure of that."

In the interim

220 Messapus had the duty of placing men
Outside the gates, and watch-fires round the ramparts.
Fourteen officers were assigned to guard
The perimeter, with a hundred men to each
In crimson helmet-plumes and glinting gold.

225 Scattering to their posts, they manned the watch
By turns, and settled on the grass at ease
To drink their wine, tipping the brazen bowls.
The campfires gave them light, and wakeful sentries
Passed the night in gaming.

230 From their ramparts
Overlooking the scene, the Trojans watched.
Anxiously they had tried and braced the gates,
Joined catwalks to their battlements and brought
Fresh missiles up. Mnestheus had charge of this

235 With grim Serestus—for the lord Aeneas
Appointed them, if a crisis called for it,
To keep order in troops and settlement.
On the alert along the walls, the legion
Faced the danger, each his share of it,

240 Guarding in turn what each one had to guard.

Nisus guarded a gate—a man-at-arms
With a fighting heart, Hyrtacus' son. The huntress
Ida had sent him to Aeneas' side,

A quick hand with a javelin and arrows.
245 Euryalus was his comrade, handsomer
Than any other soldier of Aeneas
Wearing the Trojan gear: a boy whose cheek
Bore though unshaven manhood's early down.
One love united them, and side by side
250 They entered combat, as that night they held
The gate on the same watch. And Nisus said:

"This urge to action, do the gods instil it,
Or is each man's desire a god to him,
Euryalus? For all these hours I've longed
255 To engage in battle, or to try some great
Adventure. In this lull I cannot rest.
You see how confident the Rutulians are.
Their watchfire lights wink few and far between,
They've all lain down in wine and drowsiness,
260 And the whole place is quiet. Now attend
To a thought I'm turning over in my mind,
A plan that grows on me. 'Recall Aeneas,'
Everyone, seniors, all our folk, demand:
'Dispatch men to report to him.' Will they
265 Now promise the reward I ask for you?
The glory of the feat's enough for me.
Below that rise of ground there I can find,
I think, a way through to Fort Pallanteum."

Taken aback, his love of glory stirred,
270 Euryalus replied to his ardent friend:

"And me? Are you refusing me my place
Beside you in this great affair? Must I
Send you alone into such danger? Born
For that, was I, and trained for that, amid
275 The Argive terror, those hard hours of Troy,
By a true fighter, one inured to battle,
My father, Opheltës? Never till now have I
Behaved so at your side, and as a soldier
Pledged to see Aeneas' destiny through.

280   Believe me, here's a spirit that disdains
      Mere daylight! I hold life well spent to buy
      That glory you aspire to."
                              Nisus answered:
      "Not for a minute had I any qualms
285   About you on that score. Unthinkable!
      Witness great Jupiter—or whoever else
      May favor this attempt—by bringing me
      In triumph back to you. But if some god
      Or accident defeats me—and one sees
290   Miscarriage of bold missions many a time—
      You must live on. Your age deserves more life.
      If I am dragged free from a fight or ransomed,
      Let there be someone who can bury me.
      Or if, as often, bad luck rules that out,
295   Someone who can carry out the ritual
      For me, though I'm not there, and honor me
      With an empty tomb.
                              Then too, I would not bring
      Such grief on your poor mother, one who dared
300   As many mothers did not, child, to come
      This far with you, taking no care for shelter
      Behind Acestës' walls."
                              But the boy said:
      "Your reasoning is all a waste of breath.
305   Not by an inch has my position changed.
      Let us be off."
                              With this he roused the watch,
      Men who came up to stand guard in their turn,
      As he took his relief, matching his stride
310   With Nisus', and they sought the prince of Troy.
      Earth's other creatures now had given over
      Care in sleep, forgetful of their toil,
      But the high Trojan captains, chosen men,
      Held council on the realm's pressing affairs:
315   What action should they take? Or who should be
      Their messenger to Aeneas? In the open
      Midcourt of the camp, leaning on spears,
      Gripping their shields, they stood. And Nisus came,

Euryalus beside him, eager men
320 Who begged for a quick hearing, saying how grave
The matter was, worth a commander's time.
Iulus moved first to hear the excited pair,
Ordering Nisus to speak out. He did so,
Saying:

325   "Soldiers of Aeneas, listen
With open minds, and let what we propose
Be looked on without reference to our years.
The Rutulians have quieted down. Their wine
Has put them all to sleep. But we make out
330 An opening for a sortie where the road
Divides there at the gate nearest the sea,
A gap at that point in their line of fires
With only black smoke rising. If you let us
Take advantage of this to find our way
335 To Aeneas and Pallanteum, you'll see us back
With plunder before long, and slaughter done.
No fear the path will fool us: many times,
Hunting these valleys, we have come in view
Of the town's outposts, and we know the river,
340 The whole course of it."

                    Bowed by weight of years
And ripe of mind, Aletës here exclaimed:
"Gods of our fathers, in whose shadow Troy
Forever lives, you are not after all
345 Intent on wiping out the Teucrians,
Seeing you've given our fighters daring souls
And resolute hearts like these."

                    And as he spoke
He took each by the shoulder, took his hand,
350 While tears ran down his cheeks.

                    "What fit rewards
For this brave action, soldiers, shall I reckon
We can make to you? The best of all
The gods will give, and your own sense of duty.
355 Then our devout Aeneas will recompense you
In other ways, and soon; so will Ascanius,
Young as he is: never will he forget

A feat of this distinction . . ."

                              Here Ascanius
360 Broke in:
              "Never indeed, as my well-being
     Wholly depends on Father's coming back.
     By our great household gods, by our hearthgod,
     Lar of Assaracus, by whitehaired Vesta's
365 Holy chapel, Nisus, hear my vow:
     Whatever fortune I may have, whatever
     Hope, I now commit to both of you.
     Recall my father, bring him before my eyes.
     With him recovered, nothing can be grim.
370 Then I shall give two cups well shaped in silver,
     Rough with embossing, that my father took
     The day Arisba fell; twin tripods, too,
     Two gold bars and an ancient winebowl, gift
     Of Dido the Sidonian. More than this:
375 If it should happen that my father wins
     The land and throne of Italy, and divides
     By lot the captured booty—well, you've seen
     The mount that Turnus rode, the arms he bore,
     All golden: I exempt that mount, that shield
380 And crimson-crested helmet from allotment,
     Even now, to be your trophies, Nisus.
     Father will reward you, too, with twelve
     Deep-breasted beauties and twelve captive men,
     Each with his armor; beyond these, whatever
385 Private lands the king, Latinus, owns.
     But as for you whose age my own approaches,
     Young but so admirable, I embrace you
     With my whole heart, and say you'll be my friend
     In all future adventures. There shall be
390 No labor for distinction in my life
     In wartime or in time of peace without you.
     Whether in speech or action, all my trust
     Goes now to you."

                              Euryalus answered him:
395 "The day will never come when I shall prove
     Unequal to this kind of mission, hard

And daring as it is—if only fortune
Turns to our benefit and not against us.
One gift above all gifts I ask of you.
400 My mother comes of the old stock of Priam,
And she is here: poor lady, Ilium,
Her homeland, could not keep her, neither could
Acestës' city walls, from following me.
I leave her ignorant of the risks I run,
405 With no leave-taking. Let the present night
And your sword-arm be witness, I could not
Endure my mother's tears! Will you, I beg,
Console her in her deprivation, help her
If she is left without me. Let me take
410 This expectation of your care along—
I shall face danger with a lighter heart."
This moved the Dardan officers to tears,
Iulus most of all. Thoughts of his own
Devotion to his father wrung his heart.
415 When he had wept, he said:

                              "Be sure of it.
All here will be conducted worthily
Of the great thing you undertake. That mother
Will be mine—only the name Creusa
420 Wanting to her—and I shall not stint
In gratitude for parenthood so noble.
Whatever comes of your attempt, I swear,
As once my father did, by my own life
That all I promise on your safe return
425 Holds likewise for your mother and your kin."

So he spoke out in tears, and from his shoulder
Lifted on its belt his gilded sword,
A marvel of craft. It had been forged and fitted
To an ivory sheath by the Gnosian, Lycaon.
430 To Nisus Mnestheus gave a lion's pelt
And shaggy mane, and steadfast old Aletës
Made an exchange of helmets. Both now armed,
They set out, followed to the gate by all
The company of officers, with prayers

435 From young and old; and in particular
Princely Iulus, thoughtful, responsible
Beyond his years, gave many messages
To carry to his father. These the winds
Of heaven scattered, every one, unheard,
440 And puffed them to the clouds.

The messengers
Now issued from the gate, traversed the trench,
And made their way through darkness toward the encampment
Deadly to them. Still, before the end,
445 They were to bring a bloody death on many.
Now everywhere they saw in drunken sleep
Lax bodies on the grass, up-tilted chariots
Along the river, forms of men at rest
Amid the reins and wheels, arms lying there
450 Where winecups also lay. The first to speak
Was Nisus, and he said:

"Euryalus,
Here I must dare to use my sword: the case
Cries out for it; our path lies there. But you
455 Keep watch, keep well alert all round about
For any stroke against us from behind.
Ahead, I'll devastate them right and left
And take you through."

He broke off whispering
460 To lunge at Rhamnes, the proud man propped up
On rugs and snoring loud, lungs full of sleep.
A king himself and augur to King Turnus,
Now by no augury could he dispel
His evil hour. Three of his bodyguards
465 Who lay nearby at random by their spears
Nisus dispatched, then Remus' armorer
And then his charioteer, discovered prone
Under the very horses' feet: the swordsman

470 Slashed their drooping necks. Then he beheaded
Remus himself, their lord, and left the trunk
To spout dark blood. By the warm blood the ground
And bedding were all soaked. Next Lamyrus
And Lamus died, and so did Serranus,
475 A handsome soldier who had played at dice
That night for hours and now lay undone
By abundant Bacchus. Lucky this man had been
If he had made his gambling last the night
Into the dawn. Think of an unfed lion
480 Havocking crowded sheepfolds, being driven
Mad by hunger: how with his jaws he rends
And mauls the soft flock dumb with fear, and growls
And feeds with bloody maw.
                              Euryalus
485 Carried out equal slaughter, all inflamed,
As he too fell upon the nameless ranks
Of sleeping soldiery. Then he attacked
Fadus, Herbesus, Rhoetus, Abaris,
Unconscious men—but Rhoetus came awake
490 And took in everything, struck dumb with fear,
Trying to hide behind a huge wine bowl.
Full in the chest as he arose the Trojan
Plunged his blade up to the hilt and drew it
Backward streaming death. Dying, the man
495 Belched out his crimson life, wine mixed with blood,
As the hot killer like a cat pressed on.
He came then to Messapus' company,
Their fires burning low, their tethered horses
Grazing the meadow. But now Nisus spoke
500 In a curt whisper—for he saw his friend
Carried away by slaughter and lust for blood—
"Let us have done," he said. "The Dawn's at hand
And dangerous. We've made them pay enough,
We've cut our way through." Turning now, they left
505 A quantity of booty, solid silver
Armor, wine bowls, handsome rugs. Euryalus
Took medals and a golden studded belt
From Rhamnes—gifts the rich man, Caedicus,

In the old days had sent to Remulus
Of Tibur as a distant guest-friend's pledge,
510 And Remulus at death had passed them on
To his own grandson, at whose death in war
The Rutulians had got them. These the boy
Tore off and fitted to his torso—tough
And stalwart as it was, though all in vain—
515 Then donned Messapus' helm with its high plume
As the marauders put the camp behind them,
Making for safety.
                    At that hour, horsemen
Sent ahead from the city of Latinus—
520 Other troops being halted on the plain—
Came bringing answers to the prince, to Turnus,
Horsemen three hundred strong, all bearing shields,
With Volcens in command. Nearing the camp
And riding toward the rampart, they caught sight
525 Of the two Trojans over there who veered
On the leftward path. Euryalus's helmet
In the clear night's half-darkness had betrayed him,
Glimmering back, as he had not foreseen,
Dim rays of moonlight. And the horsemen took
530 Sharp notice of that sight. Troop-leader Volcens
Shouted:
          "Soldiers, halt! What's this patrol?
Who are you two in arms there, and where bound?"

They offered no reply to him, but made
535 All speed into a wood, putting their trust
In darkness there. Troopers rode left and right
To place themselves at the familiar byways
Until they had the wood encircled, every
Exit under guard. The wood itself
540 Covered much ground, all bristling underbrush,
Dark ilex, and dense briars everywhere,
The path a rare trace amid tracks grown over.
Deep night under the boughs, and weight of booty,
Slowed Euryalus, and fear confused him
545 As to the pathway. Nisus, unsuspecting,

Got free of the wood, escaped the foe,
Ran past the places later known as Alban,
Latinus' high-fenced cattle pastures then.
But all at once he stopped and looked around
550 In vain for his lost friend.

                "Euryalus,
Poor fellow, where did I lose you? Where shall I
Hunt for you? Back all that winding way,
That maze of woodland?"

555   Backward in his tracks,
As he recalled them, now he went, and strayed
Through silent undergrowth. He heard the horses,
Heard the clamor and calls of the pursuit,
And after no long interval a cry
560 Came to his ears: Euryalus now he saw
Set upon by the whole troop—first undone
By darkness and the treacherous terrain,
Now overwhelmed by the sudden rush of men
Who dragged him off, though right and left he strove.
565 Now what could Nisus do? What strength had he,
What weapons could he dare a rescue with?
Should he then launch himself straight at the foe,
Through many wounds hastening heroic death?
His arm drawn back, hefting his javelin,
570 He glanced at the high quiet moon and prayed:

"Thou, goddess, thou, be near, and help my effort,
Latona's daughter, glory of the stars
And guardian of the groves. If Hyrtacus,
My father, ever brought gifts to thy altars,
575 Votive gifts for me; if I myself
Have honored thee out of my hunting spoils
With offerings, hung in thy dome or fixed
Outside upon thy sacred roof, now let me
Throw this troop into confusion: guide
580 My weapon through the air."

                    He made the cast,
With all the force and spring of his whole body.
And through the darkness of the night the javelin,

Whipping on, hit Sulmo's back and snapped there,
585 Putting a splinter through his diaphragm.
The man rolled on the ground and vomited
A hot flood, even as he himself grew chill,
With long convulsions. All the rest peered round
This way, then that way. All the more savagely
590 The assailant hefts a second javelin
Back to his ear. Now see commotion, hear
The whizzing shaft! It splits the skull of Tagus
Side to side and sticks in the cleft hot brain.
Now Volcens in a wild rage nowhere saw
595 The man who threw the missile, could not tell
In what quarter to hurl himself.
                                    "All right,"
He said, "You, then—you'll pay with your hot blood
For both my men."
600   And with his sword unsheathed
He went straight for Euryalus. Now truly
Mad with terror, Nisus cried aloud.
He could not hide in darkness any longer,
Could not bear his anguish any longer:

605 "No, me! Me! Here I am! I did it! Take
Your swords to me, Rutulians. All the trickery
Was mine. He had not dared do anything,
He could not. Heaven's my witness, and the stars
That look down on us, all he did was care
610 Too much for a luckless friend."
                                    But while he clamored,
Volcens' blade, thrust hard, passed through the ribs
And breached the snow-white chest. Euryalus
In death went reeling down,
615 And blood streamed on his handsome length, his neck
Collapsing let his head fall on his shoulder—
As a bright flower cut by a passing plow
Will droop and wither slowly, or a poppy
Bow its head upon its tired stalk
620 When overborne by a passing rain.

Now Nisus
Plunged ahead into the crowd of men
And made for Volcens only, of them all,
Concerned only with Volcens. All around him
625 Enemies grouped to meet him, fend him off
To left and right, but onward all the same
He pressed his charge, swirling his lightning blade
Until he sank it in the yelling visage
Straight before him. So he took that life
630 Even as he died himself. Pierced everywhere,
He pitched down on the body of his friend
And there at last in the peace of death grew still.
Fortunate, both! If in the least my songs
Avail, no future day will ever take you
635 Out of the record of remembering Time,
While children of Aeneas make their home
Around the Capitol's unshaken rock,
And still the Roman Father governs all.

The Rutulians, now victors, with their trophies
640 Bore the dead Volcens into camp with tears,
And tears flowed in the camp as well, at finding
Rhamnes bled to death, and many captains
Taken off at one stroke in that slaughter,
Even as Numa and Serranus were.
645 A great crowd pressed around the dead and dying,
Pressed toward the ground still fresh with carnage, foaming
Rills of blood. The men could recognize
The trophies there, and point them out: Messapus'
Shining helm, and medals now regained
650 That had cost toil and sweat in the attack.
By this time early Dawn, leaving Tithonus'
Yellow bed, scattered first rays of light
Over the lands of earth: down poured the sun,
The world stood clear.

655   And Turnus in full armor
     Roused his men to arm. Each officer
     Drew up his line of battle, all in bronze,
     And soldiers gave their anger a fighting edge
     With divers versions of the night attack.
660   The attackers' heads, indeed—a ghastly sight—
     They fixed on spears, and lifted, and bore out
     In taunting parade: Euryalus and Nisus.
     Aeneas' men-at-arms on the left flank
     Formed their defending line along the walls,
665   The right enclosed by river. On high towers,
     Having the ditch before them, broad and deep,
     They stood in sorrow, moved by those grim heads,
     Impaled and dripping gore—heads too well known
     To their unhappy fellows. In the meantime,
670   Rumor on strong wings flying went about
     The settlement in dread, until it whispered
     Close by Euryalus's mother's ears.
     Then all at once warm life drained from her body,
     Shuttle and skein unwound dropped from her hands.
675   She flew outdoors, all wretchedness, and wailed
     As women do, tearing her hair, and ran
     To reach the rampart, in mad haste, to reach
     The front line, paying soldiers there no heed,
     No heed to danger, none to missiles. Then
680   She filled heaven's air with keening: "Must I see you
     Even like this, Euryalus? You that were
     In these last days the comfort of my age
     Could leave me, could you, cruel boy, alone?
     Sent into danger so, had you no time
685   For your poor mother's last farewell? Ah, god,
     You lie now in a strange land, carrion
     For Latin dogs and birds, and I your mother
     Never took you—your body—out for burial,
     Nor closed your eyes nor washed your wounds nor dressed you
690   In the fine robe I had been weaving for you
     Night and day, in haste, before the loom,
     Easing an old woman's pain. But where
     Shall I go now? Where is the earth that holds

Your trunk dismembered, all your mangled body?
695 This—is this all of yourself, my son,
That you bring back to me? By sea and land
Did I keep this beside me?
                                    Put your spears
Into me, Rutulians, if you can be moved,
700 Let fly your javelins all at me, and let me
Be the first you kill. Or else take pity,
Father of the great gods, with your bolt
Dispatch this hateful soul to the abyss.
I cannot else break off my tortured life."
705 All hearts were shaken by her cries, and groans
Of mourning came from all, their strength for battle
Broken and benumbed. At the behest
Of Ilioneus and Iulus, weeping hard,
The woman, as she fanned the flame of grief,
710 Was brought inside, supported on the arms
Of Actor and Idaeus, and given rest.

But now a far-off trumpet sang in bronze
Heart-chilling clamor, and a battle shout
Re-echoed from the sky, as Volscians charged
715 Under cover of shields evenly locked
To fill the moat and tear the rampart down.
Some tried to find a way over and in
With scaling ladders at points lightly manned,
Where gaps showed in the high line of defenders,
720 Not so close-packed. But the Trojans, trained
In their long war, knew how to hold a wall.
They rained all kinds of missiles down, and used
Tough poles to push off climbers. Stones as well
Of deadly weight they rolled and tumbled over
725 To crack the shield-roofed ranks. Nevertheless,
Beneath a "tortoise shell" so thick, those troops
Were glad to take their chances. Yet the time

Came when they could not. Where the massed attackers
Threatened, Trojans trundled a mass of stone
730 And heaved it down to fell men in a swathe
And smash their armored shell. Now Rutulians
No longer cared to fight blind under shields
But strove to clear the wall with archery.
Mezentius in his quarter of the field,
735 A sight to quail at, shook his Etruscan pine,
His firebrand, and lobbed in smoking darts.
Messapus, Neptune's child, tamer of horses,
Breached a wall and called for scaling ladders.

Calliopë, I pray, and Muses all,
740 Inspire me as I sing the bloody work,
The deaths dealt out by Turnus on that day,
And tell what men each fighter sent to Orcus:
Help me to spread the massive page of war.
There was one tower of commanding height
745 And served by catwalks, in a strategic place.
Italian troops with might and main
Struggled to conquer this or bring it down
With every trick of siege. And for their part
The Trojans held it with a hail of stones
750 And shafts they shot through loopholes. Turnus now
Became the first with his thrown torch
To lodge a fire in the tower's side.
Blazing up there with wind, it caught the planks
And clung around the portals it consumed.
755 The garrison, in panic at this horror,
Having no exit, herded to that side
Still free of deadly fire; but the tower
Under the sudden shift of weight went down,
All heaven thundering with its crash. Men dropped
760 Half-dead with all that mass of ruin to earth,
Impaled on their own weapons, or run through

Lines 515–543

By cruel splinters. Lycus and Helénor
Barely escaped, the only ones: the young
Helénor, whom a slave, Licymnia,
765   Had borne in secret to Maeonia's king
And sent to Troy—although forbidden arms—
With naked sword and shield blank, bare of deeds.
Now as he saw himself amid a thousand
Troops of Turnus, ranks of Latins waiting
770   Here and others there, as a wild beast
Pinned by a band of hunters in a ring
Will rage against their spears and hurl himself
Upon sure death, with one leap on the spearpoints:
In the same way the young man facing death
775   Rushed at the enemy, and where he saw
The spears were thickest, there he aimed his charge.
But Lycus, being far quicker on his feet,
Made for and gained the wall amid the enemy,
Amid their missiles, trying to reach the top
780   And outstretched hands of friends. But on his heels
Ran Turnus with his spear, and won the race,
Taunting him:

> "Did you hope to get away,
You madman, from our hands?"

785   And taking hold
Of the man hanging there he tore him down
With a big chunk of wall—as when the bird
Who bears Jove's bolt takes wing, lugging a hare
Or snowy swan aloft in crooked talons,
790   Or when Mars' wolf steals from the fold a lamb
Whose mother, bleating, seeks it. Everywhere
The shouting rose as Rutulians fought onward,
Filling the moat with piled up earth, while some
Tossed high upon the rooftops burning brands.
795   Casting a stone, a piece of mountain crag,
Ilioneus brought down Lucetius
As he approached a gate carrying fire.
Liger killed Emathion, and Asilas
Killed Corynaeus: a javelin man won
800   Over a bowman's deftness from a distance.

Lines 543–572

Caeneus brought Ortygius down, and Caeneus,
Even as he triumphed, fell to Turnus. Turnus
Then killed Itys and Clonius, Dioxippus
And Promolus, then Sagaris and Idas
805 High on the battlement. But Capys killed
Privernus. First, Themilla's point had grazed him
So that he lost his head and threw his shield down,
Bringing his hand up to the wound: therefore
The winging arrow sank in his left side
810 And, deeply embedded, broke the inner vents
Of breath with a mortal wound.
In great style fitted out, the son of Arcens
Stood in his cloak with figured needlework
All vivid Spanish blue—a brilliant sight.
815 Brought up in Mars Wood by Symaethus stream
And where Palicus' altar stands, enriched
By offerings, appeasable and mild,
The young man had been sent to war by Arcens.
Mezentius dropped his spears, then made a sling
820 Go whipping round his head three times as he
Put stress upon it, and he split the adversary's
Temples with a molten leaden slug,
Knocking him down asplay on a bank of sand.
At this point, it is said, Ascanius
825 First aimed a shaft in war. In days before
He had been used to scare wild game in flight.
Now with one shot he brought a strong man down,
Numanus, Remulus by added name,
Who late had married Turnus' younger sister.
830 Now this captain strode ahead and shouted
Boasts that had or had not dignity,
Inflated as he was by his new status.
He swashbuckled and cried:

                              "What, not ashamed
835 To be besieged again, pinned by a rampart,
Walling yourselves away from death? You Phrygians
Twice-conquered! Look, see those who claim
Our wives, prizes of war! What god, what madness
Brought you to Italy? Here are no Atridae,

840   Here is no artful talker like Ulysses.
      Tough pioneer's our stock. Our new-born sons
      We take to the river first to harden them
      In wilderness waves, ice-cold. Our boys are keen
      At hunting, and they wear the forests out;
845   Their pastimes are horse-taming and archery.
      Hard labor, too, and a life of poverty
      Our young men are inured to: they can crumble
      Earth with hoes or shake walled towns in war.
      Our life is worn away with iron. A spear
850   Reversed will goad an ox. And slow old age
      Enfeebles no man's bravery or vigor.
      No, we press down helms on our white hair,
      And all our days delight in bringing home
      Fresh plunder, and in good freebooter fare.
855   You people dress in yellow and glowing red,
      You live for sloth, and you go in for dancing,
      Sleeves to your tunics, ribbons to your caps.
      Phrygian women, in truth, not Phrygian men!
      Climb Mount Dindyma where the double pipes
860   Make song for the effete, where the small drums
      And the Idaean Mother's Berecynthian
      Boxwood flute are always wheedling you!
      Leave war to fighting men, give up the sword."

      As he broadcast these insults and hard words,
865   Ascanius could not abide the man.
      He turned and set a shaft on his bowstring,
      Taut horse-gut, and he drew his arms apart,
      Then stood to make petition to high Jove:

      "Almighty Jupiter, only give consent
870   To this attempt, this venture. I shall bring
      Thy temple gifts in my own hands each year
      And place a snowy bullock at thy altar,
      Gold leaf on his brow, grown up to hold
      His head high as his mother's, then to charge
875   With lowered horns and paw the sand with hooves."

Lines 602–629

This prayer the Father heard. From a clear sky
He thundered on the left, just as the bow
Sang out, freighted with doom. The springing shaft
Under high tension made a fearful whistle
880 Flying to pass clean through the head of Remulus,
Cleaving both temples with its shank of steel.

"Go on, please, mock our courage with windy talk.
Twice-conquered Phrygians return
This answer to the Rutulians."
885   Only this
Ascanius called out. The Trojans cheered,
Echoing him in joy, lifting up their hearts.
At that moment in the quarter of high air
Apollo with flowing hair, from a throne of cloud,
890 Looked down upon Ausonian troops and town.
He spoke to the victor, Iulus:
                                        "Blessèd be
Your new-found manhood, child. By striving so
Men reach the stars, dear son of gods
895 And sire of gods to come. All fated wars
Will quiet down, and justly, in the end
Under descendants of Assaracus,
For Troy no longer bounds you."
                                        As he spoke
900 He put himself in motion out of heaven,
Parting the smoothly blowing winds
To make his way down to Ascanius.
And then he changed into an ancient man,
Butës, the armor-bearer of Anchises
905 And faithful door-keeper in the old days, now
An aide given Ascanius by his father.
Apollo walked like Butës to the life—
He had his voice, his coloring, his white hair,
His grimly clinking arms. And now he said
910 To Iulus in his ardor:
                                        "Let it suffice
That Numanus met death by your good shot

Without retaliation, son of Aeneas.
This feat of arms, your first, mighty Apollo
915 Grants you, and he feels no jealousy
For the weapon matched with his. Only refrain
From other acts of war . . ."

                              But even as he thus
Broke into words, midway in speech, Apollo
920 Quitted mortal vision, fading fast
Into thin air and distance. Dardan captains
Glimpsed the god and the god's bow and heard
His quiver clanging as he went away.
Therefore despite his eagerness for battle
925 They kept Ascanius from it, by command
And will of Phoebus, while they all, themselves,
Pushed forward once again to join the fight
And put themselves in danger. Battle cries
Ran tower to tower along the entire wall
930 As men bent springing bows, or twisted thongs
On javelins to whip them out. The ground
Was littered with flung missiles. Shields and helms
Rang out as they were hit, and the fierce fight
Mounted as when a storm out of the west—
935 When the Young Goats, the rainy stars, arise—
Lashes the earth, or as when clouds descend
In thick hail on the deep, and Jupiter
Goes rough with southwind, making the downpour veer,
And bursts the cloudy arches of the sky.
940 Two brothers, sons of Alcanor of Ida,
Pandarus and Bitias, whom Iaera,
Nymph of the woods, in Jove's wood, reared to manhood,
Tall as their native pines and hills,
Relying on their arms alone, unbarred
945 And opened the gate their captain had assigned them,
Daring the enemy to come in. The two
Then took their stand inside, to right and left,
Before the gate-towers. They were mailed in steel,
Their heads adorned with high and windy crests,
950 As hard by rivers, on the banks of Po
Or near the lovely Adige, twin oaks

Lines 654–680

Go soaring high in air and lift their heads
Into the sky with foliage uncut
And nod their utmost tops.

955   The Rutulians
Now stormed the entrance when they saw it clear,
And in a moment Quercens and Aquiculus,
A handsome soldier, and foolhardy Tmarus,
Haemon as well, a son of the god Mars,
960 With all their men were turned and put to flight
Or else lay down their lives at the very gate.
Then anger grew in fighting hearts. The Trojans
Shoulder to shoulder closed in on that place
For combat hand to hand, and dared to sortie.
965 Elsewhere, as he raged and scattered foes,
The commander, Turnus, heard from a messenger
That, blooded with fresh kills, his adversaries
Were offering combat at an open gate.
He dropped his action, in a towering rage,
970 To rush the entry and the insolent brothers.
First to be brought down by his javelin cast—
The first to sortie—was Antiphatës,
Bastard of tall Sarpedon by a Theban.
Winging through the soft air the Italian
975 Cornel shaft sank in, deep in the chest,
Stuck there, and the black wound's open chasm
Yielded a foaming wave of blood; the steel
Grew warm in the transfixed lung. Then with his blade
He brought down Meropës and Erymas
980 And then Aphidnus: finally Bitias,
The fiery-eyed, all energy of heart,
Not with a javelin—for he would not give
His life up to a javelin—no, a pike,
A great beam given a spin, with a rushing noise
985 That struck with impetus like a thunderbolt.
His shield's two bulls' hides were not proof against it,
Nor was his coat of trusty mail with lapping
Scales of gold. Giant-like he reeled and fell,
Earth groaned, and his great shield came thundering down.
990 Just as at Baiae, on the Euboean shore,

A rocky pier, first built of massive blocks,
Goes over as men up-end it in the sea,
Creating surface havoc with its plunge
To rest deep on the sea-floor, as the water
995 Seethes around it and the black sands rise;
And at the crashing sound that high-peaked isle,
Procida, shakes, and so does Ischia,
Typhoeus' flint bed, fixed by Jove's command.
On this the god of warfare, Mars, instilled
1000 New heart and vigor in the Latin troops,
Goading them on, and sent among the Trojans
Rout and black Dread. The attackers flowed
From every quarter, now their chance had come,
And he, the god of battle, swept their souls.
1005 Pandarus, seeing his brother in the dust,
Seeing where Fortune lay, how the tide turned,
Pushed to shut the gate with his broad shoulders,
Turning it with a great heave on its hinge.
He left outside a number of his own
1010 In desperate combat, but took others in
As they turned back, pell-mell. Demented man,
Not to have seen the Rutulian prince burst in
Among them, close-packed there! By his free act
He shut the prince inside the town, a tiger
1015 Mingling with cowed cattle. Turnus' eyes
Shone out with new light, as a deadly clang
Came from his armor. On his helmet crest
The plume shook, red as blood, and from his shield
He flashed out rays like lightning. Taken aback,
1020 Aeneas' soldiers knew that hated face
And that gigantic figure. Pandarus
Flared up, hot with rage for his dead brother,
Calling:
        "Here is no bridegroom's royal house
1025 From Amata, no Ardean inner court
To comfort Turnus with his native walls.
Your enemy's fortress-camp is what you see,
And not the faintest chance of getting away."
But smiling calmly at him Turnus answered:

1030 "Step forward if you have the heart for it.
Come within range. You will be telling Priam
Achilles has been found again, and here."
That was all. And the other man let fly
His knotty spear-shaft, bearing bark untrimmed,

1035 With his whole strength. But only the blowing air
Incurred its flight, for Juno warded off
Impact and wound. It stuck fast in the gate.
"Not from this blade, the stroke of my sword-arm,
Will you escape. The man responsible

1040 For wound and weapon is no·bungler."
                                    Turnus
Spoke and rose to full height, sword in air,
Then cleft the man's brow square between the temples
Cutting his head in two—a dreadful gash

1045 Between the cheeks all beardless. Earth resounded
Quivering at the great shock of his weight
As he went tumbling down in all his armor,
Drenched with blood and brains; in equal halves
His head hung this and that way from his shoulders.

1050 Trojans, aghast, turned round in a stampede,
And if the thought had come to the champion
To break the gate-bars, to admit his friends,
That would have been the last day of the war,
The last for Trojans. But high rage and mindless

1055 Lust for slaughter drove the passionate man
Against his enemies. He caught Phaleris
First, and Gyges, slashing from behind
Their leg tendons, then he took their spears
To throw at the backs of men in flight, and Juno

1060 Gave him heart and force. Next he dispatched
Halys to join the rest, and Phegeus,
His shield run through, and men still on the walls,
Unwary there and urging on the fight—
Alcandrus, Helius, Noemon, Prytanis.

1065 As Lynceüs came against him, shouting out
To his companions, Turnus on the rampart
Whirled from the right a great sword-stroke and struck him
One blow, as he closed, taking off his head,

Which dropped still helmeted at a distance. Next
1070　He killed Amycus, nemesis of game,
Unmatched at poisoning lance and arrow points,
And Clytius, a son of Aeolus,
And Cretheus, familiar of the Muses,
Ever in love with gittern harp and song
1075　And tuning notes on strings, forever chanting
War-horses and wars and feats of arms.
The Teucrian commanders, at long last,
Hearing of carnage wrought among their people,
Came on the scene—Mnestheus and grim Serestus,
1080　Finding their troops distraught, the enemy
At large inside. And Mnestheus shouted at them:

"Where do you think you'll run, then, after this?
What walls, what fortress have you in reserve?
Is a single man, hemmed in by your own ramparts
1085　On all sides, countrymen, going to cause
A massacre like this throughout the town
And not be stopped? Will he dispatch so many
Of our best men to Orcus? You poltroons,
Have you no shame, no pity for your own
1090　Unhappy country, for the gods of old,
For great Aeneas?"
　　　　　　　　　　Burning at these words,
They stiffened and stood fast in close array.
Now Turnus gradually edged away
1095　From combat, moving toward the riverside,
Where the stream closed the camp. Fiercer at this,
The Trojans with a battle cry began
To advance against him, massing ranks—as when
A crowd with deadly lances at the ready
1100　Corners a savage lion: in his fear
Still dangerous and glaring balefully,
He backs away, as neither wrath nor courage
Allow him to turn tail, yet he's unable,
Yearn though he may, to charge the men and weapons.
1105　Likewise of two minds, Turnus kept stepping
Backward in no haste, seething with rage,

Lines 771–798

And even twice he turned to charge his foes,
Put them to flight twice, broken, along the walls.
But then the entire garrison on the run
1110 Formed up in a solid mass, and Juno dared not
Give him power to match theirs. Jupiter
Sent out of heaven Iris, borne on air,
To tell his sister his unkind decrees
Should Turnus not depart the Trojan ramparts.
1115 Therefore neither his shield nor his sword arm
Availed the man to hold out in the end,
Stormed at by missiles from all sides: his helm
Rang out around his head with constant blows,
The bronze dented by stones, the horsehair crest
1120 Knocked off; and neither could his shield-boss take
That battering. Now with redoubled force
The Trojans cast their spears, Mnestheus himself,
A lightning spearman, cast. Down Turnus' body
Streaming sweat made rivers black as pitch,
1125 He could not get his breath, his gasping shook
His arms and shoulders, wearied out. At last,
Headfirst in all his armor, down he plunged
Into the river in one leap. Old Tiber
Welcomed the diver in his yellow depth,
1130 Buoyed him up to the surface in mild water
With carnage washed away, and floated him
Exultant to his fellow soldiers' hands.

Lines 799–818

BOOK

X

THE DEATH OF
PRINCES

The Olympian hall of Jove admitted morning,
And there the father of gods and king of men
Convoked a council, in that starry court
From which he viewed the bright lands far below,
5   The Dardan fortress-camp, the Latin races.
When all the gods had taken seats together
In the great court, with gates to east and west,
He said to them:
                        "Lords of the open sky,
10 Why this reversion to old thoughts and aims
And bitter strife again? I had forbidden
Italy to engage in war with Trojans.
Under that ban, what does this conflict mean?
What fear made those on this side and on that
15 Resort to arms, incite to arms? The time
For war will come—you need not press for it—
That day when through the Alps laid open wide
The savagery of Carthage blights the towns
And towers of Rome. Then men may strive in hate,
20 Then havoc one another. Now refrain.
Be pleased to endorse the league I have decreed."
Jupiter's words were few. Not so the words
Of golden Venus in reply:
                        "O Father,
25 Eternal lord of men and their affairs—

What other power may one call on now?—
Don't you see how Rutulians gloat, how Turnus
Rides in his car among them, all puffed up
With his good luck in war? Closed walls no longer
30   Shield the Trojans; no, inside the gates
They must do battle on their very ramparts,
And moats run high with blood. All unaware,
Aeneas is far away. Now will you never
Let that siege be raised? Once more an enemy
35   Looms at the walls of budding Troy, once more
A host of soldiers! And once more the son
Of Tydeus, this time from Aetolian Arpi,
Rises against the Trojans. Yes, I think
My wounds are yet in store for me, and I,
40   Your child, but keep the mortal spearman waiting!
If without your consent, your heavenly will,
The Trojans crossed to Italy, then let them
Pay for their sins, afford them no relief;
But if they had those many oracles,
45   Heaven's and the underworld's, behind them,
Why can the first who comes ignore your will
And form new destinies? Must I recall
The burning ships on Eryx shore,
The king of tempests, and the gales unleashed
50   Out of Aeolia, or Iris borne
From cloudland? Even the powers of Hell are stirred
By Juno now—that third part of the world
Remained untried: Allecto has been ushered
Suddenly into the upper world and goes
55   In frenzy through Italian towns. No thought
Of empire moves me now; one only hoped
For that while fortune held. Let those you favor
Conquer. If there is no place on earth
Your pitiless consort will allow the Trojans,
60   Then by the smoking rubble of fallen Troy
I beg you, Father, let me send Ascanius
Unharmed out of the war, let him live on,
My grandson! Granted Aeneas may be tossed

On strange waters again and lay his course
65   Where fortune shows the way. But let my strength
Only protect this child and save him now
From deadly combat. Amathus is mine,
And Paphos height, Cythera and Idalia.
There let him put his arms away and spend
70   His life ingloriously. Ordain that Carthage
Crush beneath her sway Ausonia's power—
No hindrance there to the city-states of Tyre!
What use then to escape the plague of war,
To take flight through the midst of Argive fires,
75   To taste all bitter perils of the sea
And the vast earth, looking for Latium—
For Pergama reborn? And would it not
Have served them better to have made a home
Upon the ashes of their land, the soil
80   Where Troy once was? Just give them Xanthus back
And Simoïs, I beg: let the poor Trojans
Live through Ilium's hard hours again."
Then queenly Juno, stung to fury, said:
"Why force me to break silence, long and deep,
85   And put abroad in words my hidden pain?
Of men and gods, did any drive Aeneas
To choose war, to march as an enemy
Against the Latin king? 'He sailed for Italy
Under the Fates' direction.' Let it be so—
90   And spurred on by the mad fits of Cassandra!
Did he leave camp, trust life to the wild winds,
Under my influence? Or give a boy
Authority in war, command of ramparts?
Or trouble Etruscan loyalty, or the lives
95   Of peaceful folk? What god, what cruelty
Of mine impelled him to this harm? Where, now,
Is Juno to be found in this, or Iris
Down from the clouds? Intolerable that Italians
Ring your budding Troy with flames, that Turnus
100   Sets foot on the soil of his fatherland—
Whose grandfather was Pilumnus and whose mother

Lines 48–76

Divine Venilia. What, then, of the torch
The Trojans carry smoking against Latins,
What of their subjugating others' fields
105 And driving off their herds? What shall we say
Of how they take their pick of fathers-in-law
And drag the betrothed girl from her lover's arms?
How with their hands outstretched they pray for peace
And armor their beaked ships? Oh, you, of course,
110 Can steal Aeneas from the hands of Greeks
And spread in the man's place ground-mist and air,
And change a fleet into so many nymphs;
That I, for my part, helped the Rutulians
Somewhat, is this abominable? 'All unaware,
115 Aeneas is far away.' All unaware
And far away let him remain. Your homes
Are Paphos, Idalium, and Cythera's height;
Why go afield to a walled town rife with war
And rugged fighting hearts? Am I the one
120 Who has attempted to bring Phrygia's
Frail kingdom down? Am I? Or is it not
The man who pitted the poor Trojans once
Against Achaeans? What is the cause that made them,
Europe and Asia, break the peace and rise
125 In arms—through treachery? Guided by me
Did the adulterous Dardan make his conquest
Over Sparta, or did I supply
The weapons, or foment the war with lust?
You should have feared then for your people. Now
130 Late in the day you rise to make your moan,
Unfounded too, and bait me pointlessly!"
So ran the plea of Juno, and the lords
Of sky, each to his mind, murmured assent,
As when the early gusts caught in a forest
135 Murmur, and the rustling unseen wind
Rolls on, the harbinger of gales to come
For men at sea. The Almighty Father then,
Chief power of the world, began to speak,
And as he spoke the great hall of the gods
140 Fell silent, and earth quaked, and silence reigned

In highest air, the west-winds went to rest,
The deep sea stilled his waters into calm.
"Take heed then, and keep faſt in memory
These words of mine. Whereas Ausonians
145 Are not allowed to league themselves with Trojans
And it is not acceptable to you
To end your discord, therefore I shall hold
Without distinction Rutulians and Trojans,
Whatever fortune each may have today,
150 Whatever hope may guide him; whether the camp
Lies under siege as fated for Italians
Or through Troy's blunder, and through prophecies
Malign and dark. Neither do I exempt
The Rutulians. The effort each man makes
155 Will bring him luck or trouble. To them all
King Jupiter is the same king. And the Fates
Will find their way."
                              Then by his Stygian brother's
Rivers, boiling banks, and black whirlpool
160 He took oath nodding, making all Olympus
Tremble at his nod. There was an end
Of speaking. Jupiter from his golden throne
Arose, and lords of heaven on either hand
Escorted him to the threshold of his hall.

T hat day the Rutulians beset all gates,
165
Fighting to kill, to ring the walls with flame.
The Aenean legion could but bear the siege,
Immured within, and had no hope of flight.
Poor soldiers, helpless to break out, they stood
170 On towers aloft and thinly manned the ramparts.
There were Asius, Imbrasus' son,
Thymoetes, Hicetaon's son, and both
Assaraci, with Castor and old Thymbris

In the front line; Sarpedon's brothers, then,
175 Clarus and Thaemon from high land of Lycia.
There Acmon of Lyrnesus—great in bulk
As Clytius, his father, or his brother,
Menestheus—with all his might lifted a stone
So huge it seemed the fragment of a mountain.
180 Some with javelins fought the besiegers off,
Some with stones, or throwing firebrands
And fitting arrows to the bowstring.

See,
Enclosed by them, the Dardan prince himself,
185 Most fitting ward of Venus, his fair head
Uncovered, as a jewel shines out, inset
In yellow gold, a jewel for throat or brow,
Or as pale ivory glows, inlaid by craft
In boxwood or Orician terebinth:
190 Upon his milky nape the flowing hair,
Caught in a pliant golden band, came down.
And, Ismarus, you too were seen by young
High-hearted kinsmen as you aimed your shots
And armed your shafts with poison, well-born son
195 Of a Maeonian house, where plowmen turn
Rich earth, Pactolus waters with its gold.
And Mnestheus, too, was there, exalted still
By yesterday's great feat, when he fought Turnus
Down from the rampart; Capys, too, whose name
200 Descends to us in the Campanian city.
That day all these fought on in bitter war.
But in the middle of that night Aeneas
Plowed the coastal sea. When he had left
Evander and reached the camp of the Etruscans,
205 He sought the king, told him his name and race,
What help he looked for and what help he brought;
Informed him of the levies that Mezentius
Won over, and the violent heart of Turnus,
Reminded him of how unsure the plans
210 Of men are and, so reasoning, made his plea.
No time was lost; Tarchon joined forces with him,
Sealed a pact; and, freed from fate's delay,

The Lydian host, pledged to a foreign captain,
At the command of heaven, went to sea.
215 Aeneas' ship sailed first in line; her beak
Showed Phrygian lions below a figurehead
Of Ida, welcome sight to exiled Trojans.
There great Aeneas sat and inwardly
Reflected on the fortunes of the war.
220 And Pallas, at his left hand, questioned him,
Now of the stars, the course laid through the night,
Now of adventures met by land and sea.
Muses, throw wide the gates of Helicon
And lift your song of all that host that sailed
225 Beneath Aeneas' flag from Tuscan shores
And manned the ships and rode the sea.
                                        Massicus
First, in the bronze-beaked Tiger, cleft the waves,
Commander of a thousand men who left
230 The walls of Clusium and Cosa city,
Arrows their weapons, quivers lightly slung
And deadly bows.
                        Along with him sailed Abas,
Grizzled and grim, his whole ship's company
235 In richest armor, and his ship agleam
With gilt Apollo for a figurehead.
His Populonian motherland had sent
Six hundred practiced fighters, and three hundred
Came from the isle of Elba, rich in ore,
240 In inexhaustible mines of the Chalybës.
Third came the interpreter of gods to men,
Asilas, who commanded all presage
Of entrails at the altar, stars in heaven,
Flight of birds, prophetic lightning fires.
245 He hurried aboard ship a thousand men
In close formation, rugged ranks of spears,
Placed under him by the Tuscan town of Pisa,
Settled from Greece, from Alpheus river-side.
Astyr came next, the handsomest of captains,
250 Confident horseman, bearing motley arms.
Three hundred soldiers more had been dispatched—

Like-minded in their zeal—by those at home
In Caerë and the plains of Minio,
In ancient Pyrgi, fever-prone Graviscae.
255 Cunerus, never could I pass you by,
Bravest in war of the Ligurian captains,
Nor you with your scant following, Cupavo
Plumage of swan upon your crest: a sign
Reproaching Amor and his goddess mother
260 With your own father's change of form.
Cycnus, they say, when mourning Phaëthon
In Phaëthon's young sisters' poplar shade
Among the new leaves, quieting with song
His woe for love lost, dressed himself
265 In softest plumage as in snowy age
And left the earth and chanting sought the stars.
With crewmen young as he, the son, Cupavo,
Drove ahead with oars the giant Centaur,
Figurehead that towered, threatening
270 The waves with a great boulder: the tall ship,
With long keel driven, furrowed the open sea.
Then Ocnus came, who roused his company
From the paternal waterways: a son
Of sibylline Manto and the Tuscan river.
275 Mantua, it was he who gave you walls
And named you for his mother—Mantua,
Rich in forebears, not of a single stock,
But three distinct tribes, each with four communes,
The chief one Mantua, whose vigor came
280 From Tuscan blood. Mezentius' cruelty
Had there aroused five hundred sturdy men
To take up arms against him. These were led
By a pine-timbered fighting ship whose prow
Showed Mincius River flowing out of Garda,
285 Father Garda, in grey veil of sedge.
Then heavy in the waves Aulestes came
Surging ahead, as a hundred tree-trunk oars
Lashed at the sea and turned it up in foam.
Huge Triton bore him, and the blue sea quailed
290 Before the figure's conch: the dipping torso

Down to the flanks a shaggy man, his belly
Merging with a monster of the sea.
Beneath the semi-human breast the foaming
Groundswell murmured. All these many captains
295 In thirty ships had sailed for Troy's relief
And sheared the expanse of brine with brazen prows.

Now daylight left the sky, and the mild moon,
In mid-heaven, rode her night-wandering car,
But duty would not give Aeneas rest:
300 He held the tiller still, still shifted sail.
Then look: halfway upon his course, a band
Of old companions hove in sight: the nymphs
Whom kind Cybelë had, by her command,
Transformed from ships to nymphs and given power
305 Over the sea. Swimming abreast they came,
Parting the waves—as many as one time
Had prows of bronze and moored ashore. Far off
They knew their king, and, like a dancing chorus,
Veered around his ship. One most adept
310 At speaking, Cymodocea, in his wake
Took hold of the ship aft with her right hand
And pulled herself up, as her left hand kept
Her stroke in quiet water. Then she spoke
To the still unwitting captain:
315   "Still awake,
Aeneas, kin to gods? Be wakeful, then,
And slacken off your sheet. We are those pines
From Ida's holy crest, and once your fleet,
Now become sea nymphs. When the base Rutulian
320 Bore down on us with sword and fire, headlong
We broke our cables, though against our will.
All through the sea we looked for you. This form
The Mother of Gods in pity fashioned for us,
Allowing us as goddesses to spend

325 Our lives under the waves. Now learn from us:
  The boy, Ascanius, is pinned down behind
  His wall and moat, amid attacking spears
  Of Latins, rough in onslaught. Even now
  Arcadian horse, mingled with brave Etruscans,
330 Hold their appointed place; but Turnus plans
  To throw his squadrons in between, to keep
  The Arcadians from your camp.
         Now up with you,
  As Dawn comes order a call to arms for all
335 Your troops, and take the shield the Lord of Fire
  Himself supplied you, made unconquerable,
  And rimmed with gold. If you'll trust what I say,
  The new day sees heaps of Rutulians slain."

  When she had said this, as she slipped away
340 With her right hand she sped the tall ship onward,
  Having the skill of it: the ship more swift
  Than javelin or arrow down the wind
  Took flight over the waves. The ships behind
  Lifted the pace. Anchises' Trojan son,
345 Amazed and baffled, even so took heart
  And comfort from the omen. Raising his eyes
  To heaven's vault, briefly he prayed:
          "Benignant
  Lady of Ida, Mother of Gods, to whom
350 Mount Dindymus is dear, and towered cities,
  And lions yoked in tandem under harness,
  Be my first patroness in combat; bring
  Fulfilment of the augury; come near
  Thy Phrygian soldiers, goddess, and advance
355 With friendly stride."
         He prayed thus, as the day
  Came swiftly round again with ripened light
  And routed darkness. First he gave his people
  Orders to act on signals, to devote
360 Their minds to war and fit themselves for action.
  By now, as he stood high upon the stern,
  He had the Trojans and the camp in view.

On his left arm holding the shield ablaze,
He raised it up now. From the walls the Trojans
365 Shouted to heaven. Hope reawakened wrath,
And they hurled missiles, clamoring as when
The cranes that home on Strymon through the clouds
Call back and forth as they traverse the heavens,
Leaving the South behind with cheerful cries.
370 Rutulian prince and captains of Ausonia
Marvelled first at all this, till they turned
And saw the sterns already nearing shore,
The whole sea moving landward with the ships.
Aeneas' helmet blazed; flames from the crest
375 Gushed upward; the gold boss of his great shield
Shot out vast firelight, even as when
Blood-red, ill-omened, through transparent night
A comet glows, or Sirius comes up,
That burning star that brings drought and disease
380 To ill mankind, and makes all heaven drear
With baleful shining.

      Not for that did Turnus
Fail in audacity, in his confident hope
To occupy the shore first and drive back
385 The invaders from the beach.

        "Here is the chance
You've prayed for: now to hack them up with swords!
The battle is in your hands, men. Let each soldier
Think of his wife, his home; let each recall
390 Heroic actions, great feats of our fathers.
Down to the surf we go, while they're in trouble,
Disembarking, losing their footing. Fortune
Favors men who dare!"

        Now he took thought
395 For what troops he should lead in the assault,
And those to leave, pressing the siege.

         Meanwhile
Aeneas put men off on landing ramps
From the high sterns. They waited, many of them,
400 For the slack water in a breaker's ebb
And leapt into the shallows. Some held on

To oars for steadiness. Now Tarchon sighted
Shoreline without a sandbar or long breakers,
Only the sea swell mounting, going in
405 Unhindered to a line of surf and smother.
He swung his prows at once and begged his men:
"Picked oarsmen, now give way with your good oars,
And lift the bow with every stroke, then split
This enemy land wide open with your beaks.
410 Let each keel plow the shingle. It's all one
With me if we break up, beaching her here,
Once the dry land is under us."

          At this,
The crew surged at the oars and drove the ships
415 In spume against the mainland, till the prows
Crunched in, and keels in safety came to rest.
But not yours, Tarchon. Grounded in shoal water,
She hung tipped over on a sloping reef,
A long time, balancing, tiring the swell,
420 Until she came apart and spilled her crew
Into the waves. Oar hafts and floating thwarts
Impeded seamen; undertow pulled back
Their feet from under them.

          At the same time
425 No sluggishness held Turnus. On the double
He brought his line of battle down upon
The Trojans and disposed it on the shore.
Now trumpets gave their signal. In the lead
Aeneas broke through troops from the countryside—
430 A first good omen for the fight to come—
And mowed the Latins down. He killed the giant
Theron, who left ranks to encounter him,
Bent on meeting the enemy champion.
A sword-blade driven through his bronze chain-mail
435 And tunic stiff with gold drank from his side
Slashed open. Next Aeneas struck Lichas down,
A man excised from his dead mother's womb
And held then consecrate to thee, Apollo,
As one who had been granted immunity
440 In infancy from the perilous knife. Nearby,

Aeneas hurled to death tough Cisseus
And Gyas the gigantic; these with clubs
Had bludgeoned ranks of men. But Hercules'
Old weapon in their powerful hands could not
445 Help them win through, nor could their sire, Melampus,
Comrade of Hercules in those days when Earth
Afforded him hard labors. Then, as Pharus
Babbled oaths, Aeneas sent his javelin
Spinning—look!—into his yelling mouth.

450 You, too, unlucky Cydon, at the side
Of Clytius, your latest joy, whose cheeks
Were goldening with down, might have succumbed
To the Dardan's blow and lain, pitiful sight,
Free of the loves you ever bore young men,
455 Had not your band of brothers in a mass
Come forward, Phorcus' sons, all seven of them,
Hurling seven javelins. A number
Glanced ineffectual from helm and shield,
And others kindly Venus turned aside
460 So they should only graze him. Aeneas spoke
To loyal Achatës:

                    "Hand me still more spears.
Of those lodged in the Greeks at Ilium
My throwing arm will not send one astray."

465 He took a heavy spear and cast it hard,
Winged in the air, so that it crashed clean through
The brazen shield of Maeon, then stove in
His breastplate and his breast. Alcanor, who
Had run to help, held up his falling brother,
470 But passing onward on its bloody way
The spear went through his arm, and the arm hung
Lifeless on its tendons from his shoulder.
Numitor, then, pulling the spear away
Out of his brother Maeon's body, threw it
475 Back at Aeneas, but had not the luck
To hit him, only grazed Achatës' thigh.
Now up came one from Curës, Clausus, bold
In the first flush of youth: putting his back

Into a long shot with his rigid spear
480 He hit Dryops just under the chin; the point
Passed through his throat and took his life and voice
Upon the instant as he gave a cry.
His forehead smote the ground and he spewed gore.
By various strokes Clausus brought down as well
485 Three Thracians, men of Boreas' high house,
And three whom Father Idas and their country,
Ismarus, had sent. Then came Halaesus,
Then the Auruncan troops; Messapus then,
The cavalry leader, Neptune's son. First these
490 Then those fought hard to push the landing parties
Back, and on Ausonia's very threshold
The pitched battle raged. As in wide heaven
Contrary winds do battle, matched in force
And impetus; and neither will give way
495 To the other, nor will clouds nor sea give way;
The fight hangs in the balance, power to power
Locked in stalemate: even so the ranks
Of Troy with ranks of Latins met in combat,
Foot to foot, unbudging, man to man.
500 At another point a stream in flood had rolled
A scattering of stones and trees uprooted.
Here where the rough watercourse had made them
Leave their mounts and fight on foot
Against their custom, Pallas saw Arcadians
505 Turn their backs on Latins in pursuit.
In that crisis he had but one recourse:
To sting them by appeals and bitter chiding:

"Friends, where are you bound? I beg you now
By all the brave things you have done,
510 The wars fought through, your leader, great Evander,
With my own hopes of emulating him,
Put no faith in retreat. The way ahead
Has to be cleared by cold steel through the enemy.
There where the mass of them is heaviest
515 Your proud land calls you forward, and calls me,
Pallas, your captain. No unearthly powers

Stand in our way; we are hemmed in by soldiers
Mortal as we are mortal. Just as many
Lives, as many hands, belong to us.
520 Look, how the deep sea's barrier behind us
Cuts us off: no land there for retreat.
Is it the camp we head for, or the water?"

With this he charged the clump of enemy center.
First to meet him, led by cruel fate,
525 Was Lagus: as this man tore from the ground
A heavy boulder, Pallas put a javelin
Through him where the spine divides the ribs,
Then pulled it from the cage of bone it clung to.
There, as he bent over, Hisbo failed
530 To hit him, though he hoped to, running up
In reckless rage at a comrade's cruel death;
Pallas received him with a sword thrust, deep
In his expanded lung. Next he went after
Sthenius and the scion of Rhoetus' line,
535 Anchemolus, who dared his stepmother's
Incestuous bed. And you twin brothers, too,
Laridës, Thymber, fell on the Rutulian field,
Identical sons of Daucus, so alike
Their parents, happily bemused, could never
540 Tell the two apart. Now Pallas made
A grim distinction: now Evander's blade
Cut Thymber's head off, while for you, Laridës,
Dying fingers of your right hand, severed,
Fluttered as they groped for the sword hilt.
545 Made hot by his reproach, and seeing him fight
With such distinction, the Arcadians
Were armed by rage and shame against the foe.
Then Pallas put a spear through Rhoeteus
As he sped past him in his car, escaping
550 You, noble Teuthras, and your brother, Tyres.
That gave a breathing space to Ilus, target
Of Pallas' spear, which Rhoeteus intercepted.
Down from his car he rolled and kicked the earth
Of Italy as he died.

Lines 375–404

555 　　　　　　　　When the winds rise,
Longed for in summer, a shepherd kindles fires
In woods at scattered points; then in a rush
The spaces in between blaze up, and Vulcan's
Line of battle spreads without a break
560 In ragged flame across the countryside;
And seeing he has brought it off, the man
Looks down on the triumphant fires: just so
Brave acts of comrades came together, Pallas,
In one tableau of bravery for your sake.
565 But now against them came Halaesus, keen
In warfare, braced in armor. First he killed
Ladon, then Pheres, then Demodocus.
With a sword flash he lopped off the right hand
Strymonius had raised, aimed at his throat.
570 Then with a stone he smashed the face of Thoas,
Shattering the skull-bones, mixed with brains and blood.
His father had foretold Halaesus' fate
And hidden him in woodland, but the day
The old man closed his glazing eyes in death
575 The Parcae took the son in hand, to be
Cut down, blood sacrifice, by Evander's spear.
Thus it was that Pallas prayed before
He threw against him:
　　　　　　　　"Grant, O Father Tiber,
580 Luck to the steel of this shaft I let fly,
A passage through the hard chest of Halaesus.
Then these arms that I shall strip from him
Shall be your oak's to hold."
　　　　　　　　This the god heard,
585 For while Halaesus held his shield for Imaon,
He left his chest bare to the Arcadian spear.
Now Lausus, a great figure in the battle,
Would let no troops of his be terrified
By all the carnage heroic Pallas wrought.
590 His first exploit was bringing Abas down—
Abas who faced him, knotty bastion
Of Trojans in the fight. Arcadians fell,
Etruscans fell, and you, too, Trojan soldiers,

Bodies the Greeks had left unscathed. The lines
595 Of troops met, matched in strength and officers,
Crowded by rear ranks till the congested front
Allowed no elbow-room for weaponry.
Here Pallas strove and pressed; against him, Lausus,
Not much disparate in age, and both
600 Splendid in height and build; but fortune gave
Neither a homecoming to his native land.
Now, though, the mighty ruler of Olympus
Would not let them encounter one another.
Their fates awaited them, each at the hands
605 Of a still greater foe.

The nymph Juturna,
Turnus' loving and immortal sister,
Counselled him to go to Lausus' aid.
From his command post to the battle's heart
610 In a flying chariot he cut his way
And seeing his own men cried:

                              "The time has come
To interrupt this battle. I take Pallas,
Pallas falls to me. I wish his father
615 Stood here to watch."

                              At his command the troops
Drew off, clearing the ground. As they gave way,
The Arcadian, struck by the arrogant command,
Stood amazed at Turnus. Casting his eyes
620 Upon the giant form he took his measure,
All at a distance still, with a grim stare,
Then countered thus the tyrant's brutal words:

"Either I win the honor of taking spoils
From the enemy commander, or I die
625 A noble death. My father will bear alike
One destiny or the other. No more threats."

He strode into the open, and the blood
Turned cold in hearts of the Arcadians.
Down from his chariot Turnus leapt and lunged
630 On foot to closer quarters, as a lion
After he sights from some high place a bull
Far off, spoiling for combat on the plain,
Goes bounding forward: such was the look of Turnus
As he came on.

635   When he seemed near enough
For a spear-cast, Pallas opened the engagement.
Hoping his daring would bring luck to him,
Outmatched in power as he was. He cried
To the open air above him:

640   "By my father's
Welcome and the feast to which you came
A stranger, Hercules, now lend your help
To my great effort here, I pray. Let Turnus,
Dying, see me take his blood-stained arms,
645 And bear the sight of me, his conqueror."

Hercules heard him. Deep in his heart he quelled
A mighty groan, and let the vain tears flow.
At this the Olympian father addressed his son
In kindness:

650   "Every man's last day is fixed.
Lifetimes are brief, and not to be regained,
For all mankind. But by their deeds to make
Their fame last: that is labor for the brave.
Below the walls of Troy so many sons
655 Of gods went down, among them, yes, my child,
Sarpedon. Turnus, too, is called by fate.
He stands at the given limit of his years."

So saying, Jupiter turned his eyes away
From the land of the Rutulians.

660   On the field
With all his might, Pallas let fly his spear,
Then drew his flashing blade out of the sheath.

Lines 451–475

Onward the shaft flew till it punched its way
Through layers of the shield rim, then struck home
665 There where the cuirass lapped the ridge of shoulder,
Grazing Turnus' great torso in the end.
But after balancing for a long time
His oaken shaft with whetted head of steel,
Pointed at Pallas, Turnus hurled it, saying:
670 "Watch this, and see if my spearhead has not
More penetrating power."

                      With quivering shock
His point ripped through the center of the shield,
Through all the skins of steel and bronze and bull's hide
675 Outer integuments, and then punched through
The cuirass armor and the stalwart chest.
Pallas pulled from the wound the warm spearhead
In vain, for blood and life came out as well
By the same passage. Forward on his torn breast
680 He plunged, his armor clanging over him,
And bit the hostile earth with bloody mouth
As he gave up his life.

                      Looming above him,
Turnus called:
685   "Arcadians, note well
And take back to Evander what I say:
In that state which his father merited
I send back Pallas. And I grant in full
What honor tombs confer, what consolation
690 Comes of burial. No small price he'll pay
For welcoming Aeneas."

                      As he spoke
He pressed with his left foot upon the dead
And pulled away the massive weight of swordbelt
695 Graven with pictured crime: that company,
Aegyptus' sons, killed by Danaus' daughters,
Young men murdered on one wedding night,
Their nuptial beds blood-stained. Eurytus' son,
Clonus, had chased the images in gold.
700 Now Turnus gloried in it, in his winning.

The minds of men are ignorant of fate
And of their future lot, unskilled to keep
Due measure when some triumph sets them high.
For Turnus there will come a time
705 When he would give the world to see again
An untouched Pallas, and will hate this day,
Hate that belt taken.

                  Now on the battleground
Pallas's troops in tears with many groans
710 Thronged to bear off the prince, laid on his shield.
O grief, O glory, destined for your father!
This, your first day, gave you to the war
And took you from it, even though you leave
Windrows of Rutulian dead.

715   No rumor only
Of this great loss, but a sure messenger
Ran to Aeneas, telling how his men
Were now within an ace of being destroyed,
How he must lose no time stemming the rout.
720 Near enemies he cut down with his blade,
Then made a swathe before him in the ranks,
Driving on Turnus where the man stood, proud
Of his new kill.

                Pallas, Evander, all
725 Their history rose before Aeneas' eyes:
The first feast he had come to as a stranger,
The right hands joined in friendship. Now he took
Four sons of Sulmo, four more Ufens reared,
Took them alive to offer to the shades
730 In sacrifice, wetting with captive blood
The flames of Pallas' pyre. Magus, at whom
He made a spearcast, cleverly dodged ahead
So all aquiver the shaft passed over him.
Embracing then the spearman's knees he pled:

Lines 501–523

735 "I pray you by your father's ghost and by
Your hope of Iulus' rising power, preserve
A life here, for a father and a son.
I have a great house. Hidden deep within
Are bars of enchased silver, weights of gold
740 Both finished and unfinished. Victory
For Trojans cannot hinge on this one case;
This one life cannot weigh so much."

                                        Aeneas

Retorted in this way:

745   "Those bars of gold
And silver that you tell of, spare for your sons.
Turnus has already done away
With all such war-trade, Pallas being lost.
My father Anchises' ghost feels as I say,
750 And so does Iulus."

                        And with this he took
The man's helm in his left hand, bent the neck
Backward, still begging, and drove home the sword
Up to the hilt.

755   Next, not far off, he met
Haemonidës, a sacred minister
Of Phoebus and Diana of the Crossroads,
Wearing the holy headband, all in white
And shining priestly robes. Over the field
760 Aeneas drove him till the man went down,
Then stood, his mighty shadow covering him,
And took his life in sacrifice. Serestus
Bent for his arms and shouldered them to be
Your trophy, Mars Gradivus, battle-king.
765 The Italians rallied, led by Caeculus
Of Vulcan's line, and Umbro from the Marsian
Mountains, as the Dardan still raged on
Against them. With his blade he cut away
Anxur's left arm with all his round of shield.
770 This man had made some loud threat, thinking words
Would summon prowess, carried away, perhaps,
And sure long years would bring him hoary age.

Then to confront Aeneas' fiery course
Tarquitus came, elate with flashing arms,
775 A son the nymph Dryopë bore to Faunus,
God of woodland. Spear drawn back and thrust,
Aeneas pinned his big shield to his cuirass,
Putting him out of action. As Tarquitus
Vainly pled, and would have pled again,
780 The Trojan struck his head off to the ground,
Then with his foot made the warm trunk roll over,
Speaking above him from his pitiless heart:
"Lie there now, fearsome as you are. No gentle
Mother will ever hide you in the earth
785 Or weight your body with a family tomb.
Either you stay here for the carrion birds
Or the sea takes you under, hungry fishes
Nibble your wounds."

                    Aeneas then ran onward
790 After Antaeus and Lucas, front-rank men
Of Turnus, Numa the brave and tawny Camers,
Son of great-hearted Volcens, wealthiest
Landowner in Ausonia once, who ruled
The silent town, Amyclae. As men say
795 The titan Aegaeon had a hundred arms,
A hundred hands, and sent out burning breath
From fifty mouths and breasts when he opposed
Jove's thunderbolt, clanging his fifty shields
And drawing fifty swords, just so Aeneas
800 Multiplied savagery over the whole field
Once his sword-point warmed.

                        Now see him rushing
Niphaeus' four-horse team, their breasts against him:
When they catch sight of him with his long strides
805 And murderous moaning, they wheel round in fear,
Careering backward, spilling out their driver,
Whirling the chariot along the shore.
At the same time Lucagus and his brother
Liger drove their white team into action,
810 Liger at the reins, while grim Lucagus

Made play with his sword. Far from inclined
To await their fiery onset, Aeneas rushed them,
Looming with his spear aimed. Liger called:

"This is not Diomedes' team you see
815　And not Achilles' war-car, not the field
Of Phrygia. Here and now on Latin ground
You'll have an end of war, an end of life."

So in his madness he proclaimed. The Trojan
Warrior called out nothing in reply
820　But sent his javelin spinning. Hanging on
And bending to the stroke, using his blade
To goad the team, left foot ahead, Lucagus
Settled himself to fight, just as the spear
Broke through his gleaming shield's rim at the bottom,
825　Penetrating his left groin. Pitched from the car,
He rolled out dying on the field. Aeneas,
That grave captain, mocked him bitterly:

"No panic of your team lost you your footing,
No mere shadows of enemy ahead
830　Made them shy backward. No, you've tumbled out
And left them of your own accord."
　　　　　　　　　　　　　　With this,
He took hold of the horses' heads. Lucagus'
Luckless brother slid from the chariot
835　And held his hands out helplessly. He said:
"I beg you in your own name, in the name
Of those who gave you life, great as you are,
Soldier of Troy, let this life be; in mercy
Hear my prayer."
840　　　　　　　　　　He prayed on, but Aeneas
Said:
　　　　　"Your speech was not like this just now.
Die and be brotherly, stay with your brother."
He slashed open the breast where life is hid.
845　And deaths like these all over the battlefield

The Dardan captain brought about, in fury
Wild as a torrent or a dark tornado.
Finally Ascanius and the troops,
Besieged in vain, broke out and left the camp.

850   At this point Jupiter slyly said to Juno:

"Sister and wife, too, most delightful wife,
As you were thinking—not amiss, that thought—
It must be Venus who sustains the Trojans,
Not their good right arms in war, their keen
855   Combativeness and fortitude in danger."
In low tones Juno answered:
                              "Darling husband,
Why provoke me, heartsick as I am,
And fearing as I do your grim decrees?
860   If my love mattered to you as it did
And should, you would not, O Omnipotent,
Deny me this: the power to spirit Turnus
Out of the battle and to keep him safe
For his father, Daunus. Well then, let him perish,
865   Give Trojans quittance with his gentle blood!
And yet he took his name from our own stock,
His sire Pilumnus, four generations gone,
And generously has he often heaped your shrine
With offerings."
870   The king of high Olympus
Briefly answered:
                    "If a reprieve is asked
From imminent death, more time for the young man
Before he falls—if you so understand me—
875   Take Turnus off in flight, wrest him away
From fate that stands before him. There is room
For that much lenience. If some greater favor

Lines 602–625

Lies hid in your mind beneath your prayer,
If you imagine the whole war affected,
880 Changed by this, you cherish a vain hope."
Then Juno said in tears:

"Oh, if at heart
You meant to grant what you begrudge in words,
And life were still ahead, assured for Turnus!
885 Now heavy doom's ahead for him, the innocent!
Else I'm adrift from truth. Oh, let me be
Deluded, let my fear be baseless, change
Your purpose for the better, as you can!"

890 With this, from heaven straightway she launched herself
In a tucked-up robe of cloud, driving a storm
Before her through the air. She made her way
To the Ilian lines and the Laurentine camp,
Then made a bodiless shade of spectral mist
895 In likeness of Aeneas, weird and strange,
Adorned the image with Dardanian arms
And matched the godlike hero's shield and plume,
Gave unreal words, a voice without a mind,
A way of walking, modeled after his.
900 This form was like the ghosts that after death
Are said to hover and haunt, or shapes of dream
Deluding sight and touch in sleep. Now, then,
Before the front line sprang the happy phantom,
Angering Turnus with a threat of arms
905 And shouted challenges. Turnus attacked,
At the extreme range hurling a whizzing spear.
The phantom wheeled, turning its back, and ran.
At this, thinking in truth his enemy
Had given ground, Turnus in his confusion
Drank deep of an empty hope. He called:

910 "Where bound, Aeneas? Come, don't leave behind
Your wedding vows. That earth you sailed to find
You'll get from my sword arm." And shouting this
He pressed on after, making his drawn sword flash,

Not seeing that his jubilation now
915   Was at the mercy of the wind.

                    One ship,
It happened, stood there moored to a high rock ledge,
Ladders and gangway out: King Osinius
Had sailed in it from Clusium. The distraught
920   Phantom of Aeneas in flight ran here
To fling itself aboard and under cover.
Hard on its heels, past every obstacle,
Turnus bounded over the steep gangway.
He had scarce reached the prow when Juno broke
925   The mooring line and wrenched the ship away
Adrift on the ebb of surf. Ashore, Aeneas
Called for the absent man to stand and fight,
While he sent down to earth many a soldier
Met on the field.

930   But now the weightless phantom
Looked for a lair no longer. Soaring up,
It mingled with a black cloud, as high wind
Bore Turnus out to sea. And he gazed back,
Bewildered at this business, giving no thanks
935   For safety. Then he spread his hands to heaven
And cried out:

              "Father Almighty, have you found me
So to be deplored, and so chastised?
Where am I sea-borne? And from where? And why
940   This flight, or what am I, to be so taken?
Shall I see my encampment, or Laurentum's
Walls again? What of that company
Of men who rode with me, followed my flag?
Monstrous that I have left them all to face
945   A death unspeakable. Now must I see them
Leaderless, and hear the wounded groaning?
What shall I do? What chasm on earth is deep
Enough to hide me? Better, winds be merciful,
Drive this ship on a rocky coast, a reef,
950   With all my heart I beg you; put her aground
In savage sandbanks where no Rutulians
Or news of my disgrace can come."

Lines 652–679

                                        He prayed,
And in his spirit swayed this way and that,
955 Whether for madness at so great a shame
To fit his breast upon his blade and drive it
Bloody through his ribs, or else to plunge
Amid the waves and swim for shore—
That curving shore where he could meet again
960 The Teucrians in arms. Three times he moved
To try each way, three times almighty Juno
Held him back, pitying him in her heart,
And curbed the young man's passion. Smoothly onward
Cutting a wake in the deep sea he sailed,
965 With favoring swell and current, carried home
To the ancient city of his father, Daunus.

Meanwhile, hot-hearted Mezentius joined the fight,
Being by Jove alerted, and he drove
Against the cheering Trojans. But the Etruscan
970 Lines converged on him with all their hatred,
On him alone, on him alone with all
Their javelins cast in a continual shower.
He weathered it the way a rocky headland,
Jutting into the waste sea, bare to gales,
975 Bare to the sea-surge, taking all the blows
And fury of sky and sea, remains unshaken,
Buffeting back. So he brought Hebrus down,
Dolichaon's son, then Latagus, with Palmus
On the run: one smashed in mouth and face
980 By a huge stone, a bit of mountain crag;
The other hamstrung, left to his slow writhing,
Even while Mezentius handed Lausus
Shoulder armor and a plume to wear
Upon his crest. He killed Evanthës then,
985 The Phrygian, and Mimas, peer and friend
Of Paris. Theäno bore him to Amycus

On the same night that Cisseus' royal daughter,
Hecuba, pregnant with a fire-brand,
Bore Paris. Paris lies in Priam's town.
990   The Italian beach holds Mimas the forgotten.
Think of a wild boar, one Mount Vesulus
Kept safe in his pine forests many years
Before the nipping hounds harried him out—
Or one the Laurentine marsh for long has fed
995   On reedy undergrowth—now ringed by hunters
Ready with nets, he stands at bay and snorts,
Ferocious with his bristling hump, and no one's
Blood is up enough to go in closer:
They keep safely away as they attack
1000 With darts and shouts, while he turns on them all,
Undaunted, waiting for the time to charge,
Gnashing his tusks and shrugging off the darts.
So men who justly hated Mezentius
Had not the gall to meet him, blade to blade,
1005 But harried him with darts and wild shouts
At a safe distance.

                    There was a man named Acron,
Come from Corythus' old country, a Greek
Exile who left his marriage unfulfilled.
1010 As he drove Rutulians into disarray,
In crimson plumes, in rose-red of his bride,
Mezentius caught sight of him apart.
An unfed lion prowling in the bush
And ravenous, catches sight of a wild goat
1015 Or a tall-antlered stag: then he exults,
And gaping terribly ruffles up his mane
Before he kills and cleaves to a feast of flesh,
While blood bathes and befouls his cruel jaws.
With such a spring Mezentius fell upon
1020 The dense-ranked enemy. Unlucky Acron
Crumpled first and kicked the black earth, dying,
Splashing with blood the spear-shaft broken off.
But when Orodës turned to run, the killer
Scorned to hit him from behind, to cast

1025 Unseen and wound him. No, he caught and turned him,
Facing him man to man—proving the better
By force of arms, not by an unfair shot.
With foot pressed on the dying where he lay
He pulled his spear out, calling:

                                                    "Here's no mean
1030 Partaker in this battle, men. Here lies
Orodës, once so high."

                                        The Italian troops
Shouted together, echoing in ovation.
1035 Then, however, as he expired, Orodës
Whispered:

                            "Whoever you are, you'll not take joy
In this death long, for it will be avenged.
An equal destiny awaits you here.
1040 The same field will be yours to lie in soon."
Mezentius answered smiling in hard anger:
"Die now. But as for my fate, let the father
Of gods and king of men attend to it."

He pulled the spearhead from Orodës body.
1045 Harsh repose oppressed his eyes, a sleep
Of iron, and in eternal night they closed.

Now Caedicus cut Alcathoüs down,
Sacrator killed Hydaspës, Rapo killed
Parthenius and Orsës, man of brawn;
1050 Messapus finished Clonius and Ericetës,
Lycaon's son—one fallen from his unbridled
Mount and lying prone, the other on foot.
On foot the Lycian, Agis, too, came forward
Only to be hurled in the dust by one
1055 Who had his grandfather's bravery, Valerus.
Next Thronius fell to Salius, Salius fell
Before Nealcës, dead shot with a javelin
And the sly arrow striking at long range.
In the battle now Mars evenly dealt out
1060 To both sides heavy grief and mutual death,

Lines 733–756

Both killing, both going down in equal numbers,
Winners and losers, neither any longer
Knowing the meaning of retreat.

                                    The gods
1065 In Jove's long hall pitied the empty rage
Of these two armies, and the painful toil
Mankind must bear. For here Venus looked on,
There her opponent, Juno, while death-pale
Tisiphonë in savagery roamed
1070 The field amid the soldiers in their thousands.
Yes, and Mezentius shook a giant spear
An he stormed over the field: tall as Orion
When he wades through expanses of the sea
With shoulders unsubmerged, or when he brings
1075 As aged ash-tree staff from mountain heights
And treads the earth, head hidden in the clouds.
So giant-like Mezentius came on
In his enormous armor.

                            Sighting him
1080 In the long battle-line, Aeneas made
His way toward him. Mezentius stood fast,
Utterly fearless, biding his gallant foe,
Immobile, massive, measuring with his eye
The distance needed for his throw. He said:

1085 "My right arm, only god I have, and shaft
I now let fly, be on my side! I pledge
You, Lausus, armed in what I strip from him,
From this free-booter's body, you shall be
My trophy of Aeneas."

                            After his speech,
1090 He made a long cast, and the whistling spear
Winged on, clanged on the shield, but sprang away
To fix itself between the flank and groin
Of Antarës, a distinguished soldier there,
1095 Hercules' old companion. Sent from Argos,
He stayed close to Evander and made his home
In an Italian town. Killed by a stroke

That missed another, now he lay and skyward
Turned his eyes in death, remembering
1100   The sweet land, Argos.
                   Then the godfearing captain
Aeneas made his throw. Through the round shield,
Convex with triple bronze, layers of linen
Worked with triple bull's hide, the spear passed
1105   And stuck low in the groin. Yet at the end
It lost force. Cheered at seeing Etruscan blood,
Aeneas in a flash drew sword from hip
And closed with his shocked enemy. Now Lausus
Groaned at the sight for love of his dear father,
1110   And down his cheeks the tears rolled.
                      Here indeed
I shall not fail to tell of that hard death
You came upon, and of your heroism—
If ancientness for a great act wins belief—
1115   And of your memorable self, young soldier.
Mezentius had begun to back away,
Disabled, hampered, dragging on his shield
The enemy spear, when in a lightning move
The young man threw himself into the fight:
1120   Just as Aeneas rose for a downward cut
He beat aside the blade, and for a space
Put the man off. Italian troops came up
With shouts, while under cover of Lausus' shield
The father limped away. The soldiers' javelins
1125   Harassed Aeneas and kept him back, so he
Took shelter behind his shield in a black rage.
As when the stormclouds pour down hail in showers,
Every farmer and plowman leaves his field,
And every traveler takes cover, snug
1130   In some good shelter, overhanging bank
Or rock-vault, while the rain falls: they defer
The day's work till the sun comes out again;
So, swamped by missiles left and right, Aeneas
Suffered the war-cloud till its thunder passed
1135   And meanwhile had harsh words and threats for Lausus:

Lines 781–810

"Why this rush deathward, daring beyond your power?
Filial piety makes you lose your head."

But Lausus all the same leapt to the clash,
Beside himself. Now in the Dardan captain
1140 Anger boiled up higher. The Parcae wound
The thread of Lausus to the end: Aeneas
Drove his tough sword through the young man's body
Up to the hilt—for it pierced the half-shield, light
Defense for one so menacing—and the shirt
1145 His mother had woven him, soft cloth of gold,
So blood filled up the folds of it. His life
Now left his body for the air and went
In sorrow to the shades. But seeing the look
On the young man's face in death, a face so pale
1150 As to be awesome, then Anchises' son
Groaned in profound pity. He held out
His hand as filial piety, mirrored here,
Wrung his own heart, and said:

                                          "O poor young soldier,
1155 How will Aeneas reward your splendid fight?
How honor you, in keeping with your nature?
Keep the arms you loved to use, for I
Return you to your forebears, ash and shades,
If this concerns you now. Unlucky boy,
1160 One consolation for sad death is this:
You die by the sword-thrust of great Aeneas."

Then giving Lausus' troops a sharp rebuke
For hanging back, he lifted from the ground
1165 The dead man as he lay, his well-combed hair
Soaking with blood.

                              By rippling Tiber now
His father slowed the bleeding of his wound
With river water and eased himself, his back
1170 Against a tree-trunk. His bronze helm nearby
Hung from the boughs, and on the grass in peace
His heavy armor lay. Men of his choosing
Stood in a circle; he himself, in pain,

His flowing beard combed forward on his chest,
Panted and tried to rest, to ease his neck.

1175 Repeatedly he asked for news of Lausus,
Repeatedly sent messengers to recall him
Bearing his gloomy father's word. But weeping
Troops bore Lausus lifeless on his armor,
A mighty prince brought down by a mighty wound.

1180 Mezentius' heart knew well for whom they wept
When still far off. Gouging up dust he soiled
His white hair, spread his hands to heaven; and when
The body came, he clung to it.

                "Did such pleasure

1185 In being alive enthrall me, son, that I
Allowed you whom I sired to take my place
Before the enemy sword? Am I, your father,
Saved by your wounds, by your death do I live?
Ai! Now at the end exile is misery to me,

1190 Now the wound of it goes deep! There's more:
My son, I stained your name with wickedness—
Driven out as I was, under a cloud,
From throne and scepter of my ancestors.
Long since I owed my land, my hating folk,

1195 Punishment for my sins. I should have given
My guilty life up, suffering every death.
I live still. Not yet have I taken leave
Of men and daylight. But I will."

                         At this

1200 He stood up on his anguished thigh, and though
Strength ebbing and the deep wound made him slow,
Undaunted he commanded that they bring
His mount, his pride and stay, on which he rode
From all his wars victorious. Then he said

1205 To the mournful animal:

                  "Rhaebus, we two
Have had a long life now, if lives are ever
Long for mortals. Either you win today
And bring that armor yonder back, blood-smeared,

1210 Aeneas' head, too, and avenge with me
What Lausus had to bear, or if no force

Can clear that way, you'll die as I must die.
Brave heart, I know you will not bend the neck
To strangers' orders or to Trojan masters."

1215 He eased himself on the warm back of the horse,
Astride him as before, and took a sheaf
Of javelins in each hand, his bronze helm shining,
Horse-hair plume a-bristle, and off he galloped
Into the battle-lines. In that one heart
1220 Shame seethed amain, and madness mixed with grief.
Three times with a great voice he called Aeneas,
Who knew the voice and prayed in joy:

                                "So be it!
So may the father of gods and high Apollo
1225 Bring it on! Begin the fight!"

                                At this
He moved on up to meet him with his spear.
Mezentius in his turn said:

                                "Hard enemy,
1230 How can you think to terrify me, now
My son is lost? That was the only way
You could destroy me. Neither do I quail
At death nor act in deference to any god.
So drop your talk, I come resolved to die.
1235 But first there are these gifts I bring for you."

At once he hurled a javelin at his enemy,
Then sent another and another still
Straight to the mark, as he rode wide around
In a great circle. But the golden boss
1240 Held intact. Leftward the assailant rode
Three times around. Aeneas faced the shots
And three times turned a thicket of javelins
On the bronze shield. The contest, long drawn out,
The toil of plucking steel points from his shield,
1245 The disadvantages of fighting on foot,
Grew wearisome. Racking his brains, at last
He burst from his position to hurl a spear
Squarely between the temples of the war-horse.

Lines 864–891

The beast reared back and high, pawing the air
1250 With his forefeet; then on his rider thrown
The horse came down, entangling the man,
And with his shoulder out of joint, headlong
He plunged and pinned him. Trojan and Latin shouts
Flared to heaven. Aeneas on the run
1255 Came up, pulling his sword out of the sheath,
Stood over him and said:
                                              "Where is the fierce
Mezentius now, and his bloodthirsty soul?"

The Etruscan with his eyes cast up regained
1260 His senses, drinking in the air of heaven,
Answering:
                      "Bitter as gall, my enemy,
Why pillory me and hold up death before me?
Taking my life you do no wrong; I had
1265 No other expectation, coming to battle.
Lausus, my son, made no compact with you
That you should spare me. One request I'll make
If conquered enemies may ask a favor:
Let my body be hid in earth. I know
1270 On every hand the hatred of my people.
Fend off their fury and allow me room
In the same grave with my son."
                                              This said, he faced
With open eyes the sword's edge at his throat
1275 And poured his life out on his armored breast
In waves of blood.

Lines 892–908

BOOK

XI

DEBATERS AND A WARRIOR GIRL

When Dawn came up from Ocean in the east,
Though Pallas' death had left Aeneas shaken,
And duty pressed him to give time
For burial of the dead, he first
5 In early light discharged his ritual vows
As victor to the gods. A big oak trunk
Lopped of its boughs, he planted on a mound
And dressed it with Mezentius' bright gear
To make a trophy, god of war, to thee.
10 He fitted it with a crest still oozing blood,
With javelins of the warrior, and his cuirass,
Twelve times cut and breached. On the left side
He tied the bronze shield, and he slung the ivory
Scabbard and sword around the figure's neck.
15 Then he addressed the officers who thronged
About him in elation:

                "One great mission
Stands accomplished, men. For what remains
Let all our fears depart from us. I stripped
20 These arms from a proud king—my offering now,
First trophy in the war: Mezentius,
Become this figure at my hands. The road
Before us leads to the Latin town and king.
Look to your gear, and courage. Think ahead
25 With good cheer of the war to come, and when

By will of the high gods our flag is raised,
Our troops led from the camp, nothing amiss
Or unforeseen will cumber or delay us,
No heavy heartedness will slow us down.
30   Meanwhile let us give over to the earth
Our friends' unburied bodies: the one honor
Possible for them now in Acheron.
Go," he continued, "and make beautiful
The funeral rites for those heroic souls
35   Who won this land for us. Let Pallas first
Be sent to Evander's grieving town. He lacked
No valor when the black day took him off
And sank him in death's bitterness."

                    He wept
40   As he said this, then made his way again
To his own threshold, where the corpse of Pallas
Lay in care of old Acoetës, once
Arcadian Evander's armor-bearer,
Chosen under less happy auspices
45   To be companion of a cherished ward.
Their household stood around, with men of Troy,
And Trojan women, hair unbound in mourning.
Then as Aeneas entered the tall doorway
Everyone there groaned mightily to heaven,
50   Beating their breasts. The prince's lodge rang out
With sobs and lamentation. When he saw
The head at rest, the snow-white face of Pallas,
The smooth chest and the open wound
The Ausonian spearhead made, his tears welled up
55   With grim words:

                "Was it you, poor boy, that Fortune
Would not let me keep when she came smiling?
You who were not to see our kingdom won,
Or ride in victory to your father's house?
60   This was not the pledge I made Evander
On your behalf, on leaving him, when he
Embraced me and gave godspeed to my quest

For country-wide command. Anxiously, too,
He warned of battle with a rugged race,
65   With savage fighting men.
                     Even at this hour
Prey to false hope, he may be making vows
And heaping altars with his gifts, while here
We gather with a soldier, young and dead,
70   Who owes no vows to heaven any longer;
Here is our helpless ritual and our sorrow.
Father ill-fated, you will see his funeral.
Can this be our return, our longed-for triumph,
This my great pledge carried out? Enough.
75   Evander, you will see no shameful wound
Of one who ran, hit from behind; you'll pray
For no hard death because a son lives on
Disgraced. What a defence Ausonia lost
And you, too, Iulus!"
80   Having wept his fill,
He had the forlorn body taken up
For journeying, and from the army chose
A thousand men to march as retinue
At Pallas' funeral; these would take part
85   In mourning with his father—for great pain
Small consolation, but the poor king's due.
Deft hands now made a pliant bier of wicker,
Arbutus shoots and oak twigs interwoven,
Shading the piled-up couch with screens of leaves.
90   Here on his rustic bed they lay the prince,
Most like a flower a girl's fingers plucked,
Soft-petaled violet or hyacinth
With languid head, as yet not discomposed
Or faded, though its mother earth no longer
95   Nourishes it and makes it stand in bloom.
Aeneas brought two robes all stiff with gold
Embroidery and purple. Dido of Sidon
Herself had loved the toil of making these
With her own hands one day for him, inweaving

100   Golden thread into the fabric. One
      Of these the sorrowing man wrapped round the prince
      In final honor, and he spread the other,
      Mantling the hair soon to be set aflame.
      He heaped the many prizes Pallas won
105   In the Laurentine battle, to be borne
      In a long file, and added mounts and weapons
      Taken in his own fights from the enemy.
      Then came, hands bound behind their backs, the prisoners
      He sent as offerings to the shades below,
110   Intending that when slain they should bedew
      The pyre's flames with blood. And he commanded
      Officers themselves to carry trophies—
      Tree-trunks in foemen's gear—with names attached.
      Acoetës had to be led, far gone in age
115   And misery, his breast stung by his blows,
      His cheeks torn by his nails; at times he fell,
      Full-length, flinging himself to earth. War cars
      They also led, a-glisten with Rutulian blood.
      The war-horse Aethon, bare of insignia,
120   Came behind, with big tears rolling down
      To wet his cheeks, then men who bore the spear
      And helm of Pallas—for his belt and sword
      Were held by Turnus the victorious.

      And now the whole sad column marched: the Trojans,
125   All the Etruscans, the Arcadians,
      With arms reversed.
                          When the long file had gone
      A distance on its way, Aeneas halted,
      Sighed from the heart, and spoke a final word:
130   "More of the same drear destiny of battle
      Calls me back to further tears. Forever
      Hail to you, my noble friend, my Pallas,
      Hail and farewell forever."
                          That was all.
135   Then he turned backward toward the parapets
      And made his way to camp.

Lines 75–99

From the Latin city
Spokesmen wearing chaplets of olive boughs
Had now arrived with a petition for him:
140 Let him give back their dead, felled by the sword,
Who lay upon the field; let him permit
Interment of them under an earthen mound.
There was no combat with defeated men
Who breathed the air no longer. Let him spare them,
145 Hosts, he called them once, and fathers-in-law.
This request the good heart of Aeneas
Could not spurn but granted, and he added:

"What unmerited misfortune, Latins,
Could have embroiled you in so sad a war
150 That now you turn your backs on us, your friends?
Do you ask peace from me for those whose lives
Were taken by the cast of Mars? Believe me,
I should have wished to grant it to the living.
Never should I have come here had not Fate
155 Allotted me this land for settlement,
Nor do I war upon your people. No,
Your king dropped our alliance, lent himself
Instead to Turnus' fighting. In all fairness,
Turnus should have faced death on this field.
160 If he would end the war by force, and drive
The Trojans out, he should have fought me, fought
My weapons; then the one for whom great Mars—
Or his own sword—prevailed would have lived on.
Go now, light fires beneath your wretched dead."

165 He finished, and they stood stricken and still,
Turning their eyes to look at one another.
Drancës, an aging man, forever hostile
To the young Turnus, whom he blamed and hated,
Spoke in reply:
170   "Great man by fame, and proven

Greater in warfare, prince of Troy, how can I
Match your godly nobleness with praise?
Shall I admire the just man first, or first
His deeds of war? Surely in gratitude
175 We'll take your generous words back to our city,
Then, Fortune willing, we shall see that you
And King Latinus reunite. Let Turnus
Look for his own ally! Our happiness
Will be to raise your destined bulk of wall
180 And bear the stones of Troy upon our shoulders."

To this the rest as one man spoke assent,
And so they made a twelve-day truce, while peace
Should hold between them, Teucrians and Latins
Mingling without harm as they traversed
185 The wooded ridges. Lofty ash-trees rang
With strokes of double-bladed axes, pines
That towered starward toppled and came down,
And men with wedges all day long
Split oak and fragrant cedar logs, or hauled
190 The trunks of mountain ash on groaning wains.

Rumor already flown ahead inland
Had heralded the mournful news: it filled
Evander's ears, his house, his city walls—
Rumor that only lately had reported
195 Pallas victorious in Latium.
Arcadians crowding to the gates by night
Took up the funeral torches custom called for:
Flames whose glare in a long line moved out
Along the road, between the fields. The Phrygian
200 Column came to meet and join that line
Of men lamenting. When the women saw them
Near the walls, they made the darkened town
Blaze up with wailing cries. As for Evander,
Nothing could hold him, but he took his way
205 Amid them all to where they set the bier,
Then threw himself on Pallas. Clinging there

With tears and sobs, he barely spoke at last
When pain abated:

              "This you had not promised,
210   Pallas, telling your father with what care
You would go into action, facing Mars.
I knew how heady it could be to draw
First blood, to taste the wine of victory
In your first combat—manhood's bitter gain,
215   War's hard initiation, close at hand,
My vows, my prayers unheard by any god.
O blessed wife, so lucky in your death,
Not kept alive to suffer this! For my part,
I have outlived my time to linger on,
220   Survivor of my son. Would god Rutulians
Had found me side by side with Trojan troops
And pinned me to the earth with spears. I should
Myself have given up my life. Would god
This cortège brought me and not Pallas home.
225   Not that I blame you or decry our compact,
Trojans—and our hand-grip, guest and host.
This lot awaited me in my old age.
But if my son had early death before him
I can rejoice that first he took the lives
230   Of countless Volscians, that he met his end
Leading the Trojans into Latium.
Besides, I could not wish a funeral
More noble for you, Pallas, than this one
Aeneas in his piety performs,
235   With Phrygian leaders and Etruscan captains,
All the Etruscan army. Men to whom
Your sword-arm dealt out death are here as trophies,
Great ones; you, too, Turnus, would stand here,
A huge trunk hung with arms, had age and strength
240   And seasoning of years matched him with you.
But in my misery why do I hold back
The Trojans from the war? March on; remember
This, my message to your king: 'If I
Live out my hateful life now, Pallas gone,

245   Your sword-arm keeps me—Turnus' life the debt
   You see it owes to father as to son.
   In this alone your greatness and your fortune
   Now have scope. I ask no joy in life—
   I may not—but to take word to my son
250   Far down amid the shades.' "

                        Dawn at that hour
   Brought on her kindly light for ill mankind,
   Arousing men to labor and distress.
   By now Aeneas and Tarchon had built up
255   Their pyres along the curving shore. On them
   In the old-time ritual each bore and placed
   The bodies of his men. The smoky fires
   Caught underneath and hid the face of heaven
   In a tall gloom. Round pyres as they blazed
260   Troops harnessed in bright armor marched three times
   In parade formation, and the cavalry
   Swept about the sad cremation flame
   Three times, while calling out their desolate cries.
   Tears fell upon the ground, fell upon armor.
265   High in air rose the wild yells of men,
   The metal knell of trumpets. There were some
   Who hurled gear taken from the Latin slain
   Into the fire, helmets and ornate swords,
   And reins and chariot wheels. Others tossed in
270   Gifts more familiar to the dead, their spears and shields
   Which luck had not attended. On all sides
   Death received burnt offerings of oxen,
   Throats of swine were bled into the flames
   With cattle commandeered from all the fields.
275   Then over the whole shore they stood to see
   Their fellow-soldiers burning, and kept watch
   On pyres as they flared: men could not be
   Torn from the scene till dew-drenched night came on
   And a night sky studded with fiery stars.
280   The wretched Latins, also, in their quarter,
   Built countless pyres, and of their many dead
   They buried some, took some inland, or home
   Into the city. All the rest they burned,

Heaped up in mammoth carnage, bodies jumbled,
285 Numberless and nameless. Everywhere
Field strove with field in brightness of thick fires.

A third day lightened heaven of cold and gloom
Before the mourners raked from the deep ash
Scattered bones and piled warm earth upon them.
290 That day, in the city, within the walls
Of rich Latinus, high-pitched wailing rose,
The climax of long mourning. Mothers, brides
Bereft, and tender hearts of sisters grieving,
Orphaned boys—all cursed the war, the marriage
295 Hope of Turnus. "Let him fight alone,"
They called, "and fight it out to a decision,
He who demands kingship in Italy
And highest honors for himself." Then Drancës
Gave his weight to this, fiercely avowing
300 Turnus alone was called to single combat.
At the same time, many declared themselves
In one way or another on Turnus' side;
The queen's great name protected him; renown
And trophies fairly won stood in his favor.

305 Amid these hot exchanges, as the tumult
Reached its height, who should arrive in gloom—
One more misfortune—but the emissaries
Back from Diomedes' city, bearing
His reply: and nothing had been gained
310 By all their effort and expense; their gifts,
Their gold, their long entreaties had not moved him;
Latins must look elsewhere for reinforcement
Or ask for peace terms from the Trojan prince.
Now King Latinus at this grievous blow
315 Lost heart, he too, for the gods' anger shown
In burial mounds before his eyes had told him

Aeneas came as one ordained,
Brought by palpable will of the unseen.
Therefore he called together his high council,
320   Principal men of Latium, in his court,
And in all haste they came to the royal house,
Through the full streets. Eldest among them, first
In power of the scepter, grim in aspect,
King Latinus took his chair, commanding
325   Those returned from the Aetolian town
To tell their tale, their answers, point by point.
Silence being enjoined on all the rest,
Obediently Venulus began:

"We have seen Diomedes, fellow townsmen,
330   Seen the Argive camp. We made the journey,
Won through all the dangers, gripped the hand
That brought the realm of Ilium down. We saw him
Laying the foundations of his city,
Named Argyripa for his father's race,
335   In Iapyx country, hard by Mount Garganus.
When we were in the camp, with leave to speak
Before him, tendering our gifts, we told
What name was ours, what fatherland, what enemy
Made war upon us, and what urgent cause
340   Drew us to Arpi. First he heard us out,
Then answered peaceably:

                  'Fortunate race
And realm of Saturn, men of old Ausonia,
What happened to disturb your quiet life
345   And make you rouse the unknown that is war?
We who did violence to the Ilian land
With cold steel—and I now pass over pain
Endured in warfare under those high walls
And soldiers the Simoïs there holds under—
350   All of us have paid throughout the world
Beyond belief in suffering for our crimes.
Priam himself might pity the lot of us.
Witness Minerva's deadly star and storm,
Euboean crags, vengeful decoying lights;

355 Then too, after our conquest, driven far
To strange landfalls, Menelaus Atrides
Tastes exile near the pillars of Proteus,
Ulysses has beheld Aetnean Cyclops.
Neoptolemus' realm—shall I tell of that,
360 And hearth gods of Idomeneus destroyed?
Of Locrians, now displaced in Libya?
Even that marshal of the great Achaeans,
The Mycenaean, entering his home
Met death at his unspeakable consort's hands.
365 The adulterer lay in wait at Asia's fall.
And must I add all that the gods denied me:
Return to the altars of my fatherland,
My longed-for wife, Calydon's loveliness?
At this hour still, portents I dread to see
370 Pursue me: lost companions, turned to birds,
Have taken to the air and roam the streams—
What torture for my soldiers—as they fill
The seacliffs with their cries, their mewing cries.
These punishments were all to be expected
375 From that day when I so far lost my mind
As to attack a being formed in heaven,
Wounding, defiling, Venus' hand.

                                    No, no.
Invite me to no warfare such as this.
380 Troy fallen, I have had no quarrel with Trojans,
No delight in calling up evil days.
The gifts you bring me from your country, take
Instead to Aeneas. I have stood my ground
Against his whetted spear, fought him with swords.
385 Trust one who knows the surging mass of him
Behind his shield, the whirlwind of his cast!
Had Ida's land borne two more men like him,
Troy would have marched upon the towers of Argos,
Greece would be mourning a contrary fate.
390 As to our stalemate before stubborn Troy,
The sword arm of Aeneas, with Hector's, halted
Dominance of the Greeks for ten long years;
Both known for courage, both for skill in arms,

Aeneas first in reverence for the gods.
395 Your right hands and your forces should be joined
And well may be. Take care they do not clash
In combat.'

        Now your majesty has heard
Both Diomedes' responses and his views
400 Of our great war."

        Barely had the legates
Finished their story when a hubbub rose,
And turbulence among the listening faces,
As when rock-beds that stem a rushing stream
405 Make the roiled current roar, and banks re-echo
Foam-lash of the waves. But soon the council's
Mood grew calm, excited tongues were stilled,
And calling on the gods from his high throne
The king spoke out:

410   "Much earlier than this
I should have wished—and wiser it would have been—
To meet and take decisions in this crisis,
Not with the enemy at our walls, as now.
My countrymen, we make ill-omened war
415 With men of heavenly birth, unconquerable,
Untired by battle, and even in defeat
Unable to put up the sword. What hope
You had of brothers-in-arms, Aetolians,
You must dismiss. Each man may have his hope,
420 But this how narrow now you see. Then too
All that we had, now visited with ruin,
Lies before your eyes and in your hands.
But I accuse no one. What bravery
Could do was done. The whole strength of our kingdom
425 Fought the battle. It is over. Now
Let me disclose the plan formed in my mind
Still tentatively. Give me your attention.
I shall be brief. There is an old domain
Of mine along the Tuscan stream, extending
430 Far toward sundown, well beyond Sicanian
Boundaries. Auruncans and Rutulians
Sow crops there, plow the stony hills, or graze

Lines 292–319

The wildest of them. Let this region all
Be ceded now in friendship to the Trojans,
435 With a pine-forested zone of mountain heights.
Let us make equitable treaty terms
And in the realm call them co-citizens.
Here let them settle and here build their walls
If such desire is in them. If their hearts
440 Are set on other lands and other races,
And they are able to leave our soil, why then
Twice ten good ships of stout Italian oak
We'll build them; if they muster crews for more,
The timber lies at the sea's edge. They may
445 Prescribe the number and rig, and we shall give
The bronze, the labor, and the launching ways.
It will content me, further, that one hundred
Emissaries chosen from our best
Shall bring our terms and sign the pact and offer
450 Olive boughs of peace, carrying gifts—
Gold bars and ivory, and throne and robe,
Insignia of our kingship. All take counsel
Here and now. Shore up our tired strength."

Then Drancës rose, belligerent as before.
455 The fame of Turnus galled him, made him smart
With envy unconfessed, this wealthy man,
A lavish spender and an orator
But a cold hand in battle; held to be
No empty counselor; a strong party man.
460 His mother's nobility made him arrogant,
Though he had no certain father. Now he spoke
To add to and to aggravate their anger:

"Excellency, it is all clear as day,
The situation you address: no need
465 For us to enlarge on it. All here concede

They know what these events mean for our people,
Yet they keep silent.
              Let the man we know
Allow us liberty to speak, and let him
470   Hold his bluster. His unlucky star,
His baleful influence—and I shall say it,
Threaten as he may to run me through—
His whim put out so many shining lights
Among our captains that we see our city
475   Founder in grief—while at the Trojan camp
He skirmishes, being sure to get away,
Frightening the air with javelins.
                      One more gift,
Your gracious majesty, include with all
480   You'd have us send or offer to the Trojans,
One gift more; and let no violence
From any man prevail on you to yield
A father's right: betrothal of your daughter
Fittingly to an exceptional son,
485   By that eternal bond to accomplish peace.
But if our minds and hearts are so oppressed
By terror, let us plead with Turnus here
Himself to do this kindness to us all:
Resign his marital rights to king and country.
490   Why must you, sir, send into open peril
Time and again your suffering countrymen,
You, chief of woes to Latium, cause of all?
In war there's no salvation. We require
Peace of you, Turnus, and along with it
495   The one pledge that makes peace inviolable.
Look: I whom you pretend to be your rival—
I will not linger on that—I first of all
Come to beg you: pity your own people!
Cool your hot head, being beaten; leave the field.
500   In our defeat we have seen enough of death
And made a landscape desolate. If glory
Is on your mind still, iron self-conceit,
Or a royal house for dowry charms you so,
Then take the risk and brave the enemy!

Lines 344–370

505 Must I suppose that for the sake of Turnus'
Royal marriage we poor common souls
Should strew the field, unburied and unwept?
Come, sir, if any fighting blood is in you,
Any native legacy from Mars,
510 Go face the man who calls you out to combat!"

Under this taunting Turnus' fiery temper
Flared up; but he gave a groan of scorn,
Then broke out in his deep voice:
                              "Plenty of talk
515 You always have when contests call for action.
Summon a senate, you are the first one there.
No need to fill this hall with words, big words
You can let fly in safety, keeping walls
Between you and the enemy, no moats
520 As yet running with blood. Hammer away
With all your rhetoric. Say I'm afraid
When your own sword has left the dead in heaps,
The field brilliant with trophies everywhere.
What bravery in action can achieve
525 You are still free to experience; no need
To hunt for enemies; they ring the walls.
Go out to meet them, shall we? Why hang back?
Will all your skill for battle rest forever
In a windbag's breath and in those flying feet?
530 Beaten, am I? Can anyone have cause
To utter that word, beaten, you foul wretch,
Seeing the Tiber risen with Ilian blood
And all Evander's house, his line, brought low,
Arcadians killed and stripped? I should not say
535 I seemed a beaten man to Bitias
And Pandarus, that giant, or the throngs
I sent to hell on one victorious day,
Shut between walls, at that, with enemy
Earthworks to right and left of me. In war
540 There's no salvation? Sing that to your Trojan
Chief and your own prospects, you mad fool!
Go on confusing everything with fear,

Exalt a race twice-conquered and their strength,
Cry down Latinus' power. Nowadays
545 The Myrmidons tremble at Phrygian spears,
Diomedes and Achilles tremble—
Yes, and Aufidus torrent flows uphill
In flight from the Adriatic.

                                 Take him now
550 Pretending to be frightened when I blast him,
The artful devil, just to add that touch—
Intimidation—to his case against me.
You'll never lose that life, such as it is,
To this right hand, don't worry: let it stay
555 Long resident in that tame breast of yours.
Now, Father, I revert to you, to your
Large-scale proposal. If you put no further
Hope in our fighting power; if we are left
So unsupported; if our army corps
560 By one reversal has gone all to pieces,
Our fortune reached the point of no return,
Then let us beg for peace with beggar's hands.
Yet, oh, had we a spark of our old spirit!
The luckiest of men in this hard time,
565 The finest man, to my mind, would be he
Who bit the dust, once and for all, and died
To avoid a sight like this! But if in fact
We have resources, fresh reserves of men,
Italian states and peoples with us still,
570 And if the Trojans won at a great cost
In blood—they have their burials as well,
The storm struck all alike—why then give up
Like cowards on the threshold? Why allow
Our knees to shake before a trumpet blows?
575 Days passing and the changing work of time
Have often righted things. Fortune returns
To put on solid ground those she derided.
Say the Aetolian will not help, nor Arpi,
Messapus will, so will that lucky seer,
580 Tolumnius, so will chiefs whom many nations

Sent to us—and no small fame will come
To the picked men of Latium and Laurentum—
Yes, and Camilla of the noble Volsci,
Leading her cavalry, splendid in bronze.

585 But if the Trojans call on me alone
For combat, and if you approve, and I
Am blocking something for the good of all,
Then Victory has not so bitterly
Hated these hands and so eluded them

590 That I should not, in such a hopeful cause,
Make my attempt. And cheerfully I'll go
Against him, though he overshadow Achilles,
And wear gear made, like his, by Vulcan's hands.
This life of mine I, Turnus, not outdone

595 In valor by the men of old, have sworn
In service to my father-in-law and you.
'Aeneas calls on him alone.' Call on,
I pray. If this brings anger of the gods,
May Drancës not appease it with his death,

600 Nor if it brings honor and feats of arms
May he bear off the palm for these."
                                    The two
Debated the obscure future in this way,
In bitter strife. Meanwhile Aeneas left camp

605 And took the field. Now see a messenger
Hastening through the palace with hue and cry
To alarm the town. He brought word that the Trojan
Battle-line, and the Tuscan complement
Had left the Tiber to move down the plain.

610 Their minds in tumult, shaken by the news,
The common people felt their anger roused
As by a goad. With oaths their hands went out
For arms, and then the young men yelled "To arms!"
Even as their despondent fathers wept.

615 Everywhere now clamor and discord rose
Into the air above the town, as when
Bird-flocks come down in a tall grove, or swans
Where the Padusan Channel teems with fish

Lines 430–458

Give their hoarse-throated cries on echoing pools.
620　But Turnus caught the moment and made it his.
He said:

　　　　"Just so, my townsmen. Hold your council.
Sit and praise the name of peace. And they?
Their army sweeps to attack our capital."
625　That was all. He leapt up and away,
Quitting the council hall with rapid stride,
Then gave commands:

　　　　　　"Volusus, it's for you
To make the Volscian squadrons arm. You lead
630　The Rutulians. Messapus, arm your horsemen. Coras, you
And your twin brother see our cavalry
Deployed across the plain. One foot battalion
Reinforce the approaches to the city
And man the towers. All the rest, prepare
635　With me for action, as and where I order."

Running crowds made for the city walls,
And King Latinus, prey to the dark hour,
Left the council chamber and postponed
All he had set afoot. Bitterly now
640　He blamed himself for having failed to welcome
Aeneas the Dardanian to his realm
As son-in-law.

　　　　　　Before the city gates
Deep pits were dug, big stones and pikes brought up;
645　A vibrant trumpet sang bloodshed and war.
In long uneven lines mothers and boys
Appeared atop the ring of walls: the final
Effort drew them all. The queen as well
Rode in her carriage with a company
650　Of mothers to the shrine of Pallas, high
Above the town, with gifts, and close beside her
The young princess, Lavinia, rode—the cause
Of so much suffering, lovely eyes downcast.
The women, entering, beclouded all
655　That shrine with smoke of incense, and sad voices
Rose from the portal in a tide of prayer:

"O power over battle, our protectress,
Virgin, Tritonia, shatter in thy hand
The spearhaft of the Phrygian corsair!
660 Throw him headlong to earth, let him lie dead
Below our high gates!"
                              Turnus, furiously
On edge for battle, pulled his armor on,
First his cuirass, glowing red, with scales
665 A-quiver; then he encased his legs in gold,
His head still bare; then belted on his sword
And ran down from the citadel, his figure
Glittering, golden, while his heart beat high,
At grips with foemen even now in thought—
670 As a stallion breaks his tether and goes free
At last out of the stall, and down the meadow,
Gaining the open land: there he may turn
To a grazing herd of mares, or canter on
To a stream he knows well for a cooling plunge,
675 Neighing and frisking, tossing back his head,
His mane at play over his neck and shoulders.

Square in his path, her Volscian squads behind her,
Camilla came, hard-riding warrior queen.
Before the gates she leapt down from her mount,
680 And her whole troop, taking the cue, dismounted
At the same instant slipping to the earth.
She spoke then, saying:

"Turnus, as confidence goes hand in hand
With bravery that earned it, now I dare
685 And undertake to meet Aeneas' horsemen,
Charging the Tuscan cavalry alone.
Let me first risk the combat at close quarters;
You with your infantry stand by the walls
Meanwhile, and guard the city."
690   His eyes intent
Upon the awesome virgin, Turnus answered:
"Virgin, glory of Italy, how tell
My gratitude, or how repay my debt?

Courageous spirit, towering above all here,
695 Now share the toil with me. Rumor, confirmed
By scouts I send, informs me that that dog
Aeneas dispatched his light-armed horse ahead
To scour the plain, while on the mountain track
Through the wild land, crossing the ridge, he makes
700 His own descent upon the town. I'll set
An ambush where the path is arched by forest,
Soldiers to close both ends of the defile.
You take the field, engage the Tuscan horse;
Messapus and the Latin cavalry
705 Will be there with you, and Tiburtus' troop.
Plan your battle as my co-commander."

With corresponding orders he dispatched
Messapus, with his Latins, to that fight,
While he himself marched on his enemy.

710 The mountain road curves in a pass, designed
By nature for entrapment and surprise,
Heavily wooded, dark on either hand.
The road thins out here, and the narrowing gorge
Begrudges a way through. But on high ground
715 Amid the look-out posts along the crest
There's a concealed plateau, a safe retreat,
Whether you plan a rush from right or left
Or stand fast on the ridge and roll down boulders.
Here by familiar shortcuts Turnus came,
720 Pre-empted the high ground, and lay in wait
In woods made dangerous.

In heaven meanwhile
Diana spoke to Opis, the fleet huntress,
One of the divine virgins in her train.
725 Her lips opened in sadness, and she said:

"Sister, now Camilla goes her way
To the cruel war, equipped with bow and quiver,
Weapons of ours, but all in vain,
Cherish her as I may beyond the rest.
730 No new love, this, come just now to Diana,
Moving my heart with pleasure.
                                    Years ago
When haters of his insolent power drove him
Out of Privernum, ancient realm and town,
735 Metabus took along his infant child
In flight amid the struggles of that war
To share his exile. By her mother's name,
Casmilla, changed a bit, he called the child
Camilla. Now he carried her before him
740 Close to his breast, and toiled for refuge on
Long ridges in the wilderness, though spears
Of grim pursuit were everywhere behind,
And Volscian patrols cast a wide net.
Lo and behold, square in his path, in flood,
745 The torrent Amasenus, foaming high,
Ran over banks and brim, filled by so wild
A cloudburst. As the man prepared to swim it,
Love for his infant stayed him, and he feared
For his dear burden. Weighing all the choices
750 Possible, he settled suddenly
And desperately on this: in his tough hand
He chanced to carry a battle-spear of oak,
Knotted and seasoned; now to this he tied
His child, encased in cork-tree bark, and bound her
755 Trimly in the middle of the shaft.
He balanced it in his big hand and prayed
To the air of heaven:
                          'Daughter of Latona,
Diana, kindly virgin of the groves,
760 I, her father, swear this child shall be
Thy servant—the first weapon she embraces
Thine, as by thy mercy through the air
She escapes the enemy. I beg thee, goddess,

Take her as thine own, this girl committed
765   Now to the veering wind.'

                Then he drew back
His arm and let the spun shaft fly. The waters
Dinned below, and over the rushing stream
Small and forlorn Camilla soared across
770   Upon the whistling spearshaft. Well aware
Of troops in force approaching from behind,
Metabus took to the river. Spear and child
In triumph he recovered from the turf,
His offering to the Virgin of the Crossroads.

775   Now not a city gave him sanctuary,
Public or private—nor would he himself,
Because of his fierce nature, yield to any—
So he lived out his life upon the shepherds'
Lonely mountains. Here in undergrowth
780   Amid rough haunts of beasts he nursed his daughter,
Putting her to the breast of a wild mare
Whose teats he milked into her tender mouth.
When the small child took her first steps, he armed
Her hands with a sharp javelin, and hung
785   A bow and quiver from her infant shoulder.
No gold headband, no flowing outer garment
Covered her, but a tiger skin hung down
Her back from head to foot; and as a child
She flung play darts with her soft hand and whirled
790   A sling-stone on a strap around her head
To fell a crane of Strymon or a swan.
Then many mothers in the Tuscan towns
Desired her in vain to be their daughter.
All her contentment being with Diana,
795   The girl remained untouched and ever cherished
Passion for arms and for virginity.
I wish that she had not been swept away
In this campaign, or tried to challenge Trojans,
She would be still my dear, one of my sisters.
800   Come, though, granted harsh fate is at hand,
Go gliding out of heaven, nymph, and visit
Latin lands where, with unlucky omen,

Battle is begun. Here are my weapons.
Take one vengeful shaft out of the quiver.
805 By this let any Trojan or Italian,
One or the other, who may violate
Her sacred body with a wound, pay back
In blood an equal penalty to me.
Then I shall carry, pillowed in a cloud,
810 The body of the pitiable one—
Her war-gear intact—to her final rest
In her own land and tomb."

                  When she had finished,
Opis dropped from heaven through light airs
815 With a rushing sound, wrapt in a dark whirlwind.

The Trojan column now approached the town,
With Tuscan chiefs and all their cavalry
In numbered squadrons. Over the level ground
With thudding hoofs the war-horse trots and snorts
820 And rears up, tugging at the check of rein,
And curvets here and there. The wide, steel-glinting
Field bristles with lances; the long vista
Teems with upright arms. Against them soon
Messapus and the headlong Latin horse,
825 Coras, his brother, and Camilla's wing
Came into view, defenders in the field,
With lances drawn back, then in forward thrusts,
And with a brandishing of javelins.
The onward rush of men and horses neighing
830 Blazed in the sunlight. When they came within
Spear-throw of one another, Trojan and Latin
Pulled up in a halt; then, all at once,
With shouts they spurred their furious mounts and flung
Their javelins in showers from both sides
835 As thick as snow-flakes, making a daytime dusk.
Now shaft to shaft, Tyrrhenus and the savage

Latin horseman, Aconteus, met head-on
With a mighty crash that caused the first downfall
From shock of horses, breast to bursting breast:
840 Aconteus, pitched off like a thunderbolt
Or stone out of a catapult, came down
Far off, his life dispersed into the air.
At this, their lines disordered, Latin troopers
Turned and, tossing shields behind their shoulders,
845 Rode off toward the town. Asilas led
The Trojan squadrons in pursuit. But then
When near the walls, again the Latins shouted,
Yanked the horses' yielding necks about
And wheeled to fight. Now Trojans fled in turn
850 At a full gallop, as in full retreat—
Just as the sea with alternating rush
Now runs ashore in foam above the ledges
And lapping soaks the sand high on the beach,
Now in a rapid seething ebb recedes
855 And glides from land and pulls the rolling pebbles—
Twice the Tuscans drove the Rutulians
Headlong to the walls, but thrown back twice
They fled, glancing behind, their shoulders covered.
Now, when they came together a third time
860 The two formations mingled, man to man,
And then indeed groans of the dying rose,
Then arms and bodies in a mire of blood
Went down, and dying horses, with their riders
Butchered, as the bitter fight surged on.
865 Orsilochus, in dread of meeting Remulus,
Hurled his javelin at the other's mount
And left the steel point under its ear; at this
The war-horse reared in fury, forelegs high,
To shake the wound away, with towering chest,
870 And Remulus was thrown to earth. Catillus
Brought down Iollas, then Herminius,
Great-souled, great-bodied warrior, his bare head
Flowing with tawny locks, his shoulders bare.
Wounds held no terrors for him, great as he was,

875 Fighting uncovered—but the driven lance
A-quiver passed clean through his shoulders' breadth
And made him double up in agony.

Dark blood spilt everywhere. Men dealt out death
By cold steel as they fought and strove by wounds
880 To win the beauty of courageous death.

Amid the carnage, like an Amazon,
Camilla rode exultant, one breast bared
For fighting ease, her quiver at her back.
At times she flung slim javelins thick and fast,
885 At times, tireless, caught up her two-edged axe.
The golden bow, Diana's weapon, rang
Upon her shoulders: yes, when she gave ground,
Forced to retreat, with bow unslung in flight
She turned and aimed her arrows. At her side
890 Rode chosen comrades, virgins all: Larina,
Tulla, Tarpeia shaking her bronze axe.
These were the girls of Italy that she,
Divine Camilla, picked to be her pride,
Her staunch handmaidens, both in peace and war.
895 So ride the hardened Amazons of Thrace
With drumming hooves on frozen Thermodon,
Warring in winter, in their painted gear,
Sometimes around Hippolyta, the chieftain,
Or when the daughter of Mars, Penthesilëa,
900 Drives her chariot back victorious
And women warriors bearing crescent shields
Exult, riding in tumult with wild cries.

Savage girl, whom did your lance unhorse,
What victims, first and last,
905 How many thrown down on the battlefield,
Torn bodies dying? Eunaeus, Clytius' son,
Came first: he faced her with unarmored breast,
And with her shaft of pine she ran him through.
He tumbled, coughing streams of blood, took bites

Lines 644–669

910 Of bloody earth, and dying writhed on his wound.
Then she brought Liris down, and then Pagasus.
Liris, his mount stabbed under him, spun off
And tried to gather up the reins; Pagasus,
Coming to help, put out his hand, unarmed;
915 And both alike went down. She sent to join them
Hippotas' son, Amastrus. At a distance,
Pressing on with couched lance, she rode after
Tereus, Harpalycus, Demophoön.
And Chromis. And for every javelin
920 She twirled and cast a Phrygian trooper fell.
Still out of range, Ornytus, a hunter, rode
A Iapygian horse, in strange war-gear:
His broad shoulders covered by bullock's hide,
His head by a huge wolf's muzzle gaping wide
925 With gleaming fangs. In his right hand he held
A forester's bladed hunting spear. This man
Now wheeled about, the tallest by a head
Amid his company; but soon Camilla
Caught him from behind—no effort there,
930 Since all were in retreat—and ran him through.
Then from above, heart full of hate, she said:

"In forests, were you, Tuscan, flushing game?
The day has come when boasts of all your kind
Are proven wrong, by women under arms.
935 You'll take no light fame to your fathers' shades:
To have been killed by the lance-head of Camilla."

She killed next two of the very tallest Trojans,
Orsilochus and Butës. Butës' head
Being turned, she put her lancehead in the gap
940 Between his helm and cuirass, where the neck
Showed white, above the shield on the left arm.
Then running as Orsilochus gave chase
In a wide circuit, tricking him, she closed
A narrowing ring till she became pursuer;
945 Then to her full height risen drove her axe

Lines 668–696

Repeatedly through helmet and through bone
As the man begged and begged her to show mercy.
Warm brains from his head-wound wetted his face.
One who came upon her at that moment
950 Reined in, taken aback at the sudden sight—
The son of Aunus, Appennine mountaineer.
Not the least guileful of Ligurians
This man was, while fate allowed him guile.
Seeing he could not spur away from combat,
955 Could not deflect the queen from her attack,
Resorting to a cunning ruse, he said:

"What's so remarkable if, to a girl's taste,
Your mainstay is your horse? No running away!
Take me on, hand to hand, on level ground;
960 Get ready for a fight on foot, and learn
Whose blown-up vanity will have a fall."

Now bitter anger made her burn at this.
She gave a friend her mount and faced the man
Fearlessly, on foot with equal arms:
965 A naked blade, a shield without device.
But he, who thought his ruse had worked, rode off
Without a pause, reining his mount around,
Goading him into a run with iron spurs.

"Ligurian fool, too cocksure, much too soon,
970 Your slippery native trickery has failed.
No chance it will return you in your skin
To Aunus, the old deceiver."
                                                    So the girl
Called out as in a sprint with lightning pace
975 She came abreast and passed the running horse,
Then whirled and yanked the reins and met the shock
Of the Ligurian's onset, making him pay
Her penalty in hated blood. So easily
A falcon, sacred bird, from his rock tower
980 Will strike a soaring dove high in a cloud

Lines 696–722

And grip her as he tears her viscera
With crooked talons; blood and plucked-out feathers
Fall from the sky.
                But on that scene the father
985   Of gods and men kept no indifferent watch
From his aerial seat high on Olympus.
He roused the Tuscan, Tarchon, to the mêlée,
Instilling anger in him, far from mild,
So that amid the carnage, where the companies
990   Of horse were giving way, Tarchon rode out,
With one shout or another rallying
The left and right wings, calling men by name,
Putting new fight in routed cavalry.

"Incapable of shame, poltroons forever!
995   Tuscans, what is this fright, what cowardice
Has entered into you? Shall a single woman
Drive you out of line, break your formations?
What do we carry swords for? Why hold on
To useless lances? None of you is tame
1000 When it comes to making love, bed wars at night,
Or when a flute preludes the dance of Bacchus.
Look for a feast, and cups on laden tables
(All you care for, all you're keen for), yes,
When some dependable reader of the entrails
1005 Heralds an offering, and a fatted lamb
Is calling you into the sacred wood!"

With this he gave rein to his mount, prepared
To face death, he as well, in the battle's heart,
And straight for Venulus went storming on.
1010 With his right arm he swept him from the saddle,
Hugged him to his chest, and spurring hard
With a great effort lugged the man away.
A yell went up to heaven as all the Latins
Turned to watch. And like a streak of lightning
1015 Tarchon with his load of man and weapons
Flew over open ground. Then he broke off
The steel point of the enemy lance and groped

For an opening where he could wound and kill him.
But fighting back the other warded off
1020 The hand aimed at his throat, met force with force
As when a golden eagle flapping skyward
Bears a snake as prey—her feet entwined
But holding fast with talons, while the victim,
Wounded as it is, coils and uncoils
1025 And lifts cold grisly scales and towers up
With hissing maw; but all the same the eagle
Strikes the wrestler snake with crooked beak
While beating with her wings the air of heaven
Just so, out of the Latin squadron, Tarchon
1030 Triumphing bore off his prey. And Tuscans
Heeding the example their captain gave,
His daring that came off, at once attacked.

One Arruns, a man marked by fate, rode wide
Around Camilla, javelin at the ready,
1035 Waiting his chance, ahead of her in cunning.
Wherever in the mêlée the girl rode
In her wild forays, Arruns kept behind,
Silently stalking her; when she turned back
Blooded from the enemy, he drew rein
1040 In stealth and swung his nimble mount away.
Now this way, looking for an opening,
Now that, he shadowed her, going about
A circuit on all sides, the dangerous man,
A dead shot, hefting clear his pointed shaft.
1045 By chance Chloreus, Mount Cybelus' votary,
Once a priest, came shining from far off
In Phrygian gear. He spurred a foaming mount
In a saddle-cloth of hide with scales of bronze
As thick as plumage, interlinked with gold.
1050 The man himself, splendid in rust and purple
Out of the strange East, drew a Lycian bow

To shoot Gortynian arrows: at his shoulder
Golden was the bow and golden too
The helmet of the seer, and tawny gold
1055 The brooch that pinned his cloak as it belled out
And snapped in wind, a chlamys, crocus-yellow.
Tunic and trousers, too, both Eastern style,
Were brilliant with embroidery. Camilla
Began to track this man, her heart's desire
1060 Either to fit luxurious Trojan gear
On a temple door, or else herself to flaunt
That golden plunder. Blindly, as a huntress,
Following him, and him alone, of all
Who took part in the battle, she rode on
1065 Through a whole scattered squadron, recklessly,
In a girl's love of finery.
                                        Now at length
From where he lurked, seeing the time had come,
Arruns went into action, let his javelin
1070 Come alive, and prayed aloud to heaven:

"Supreme god, holy Soractë's guardian,
Above all others we are blest in thee,
For whom the pine-chips' glowing pile is fed.
Assured by our devotion, in thy cult
1075 We step through beds of embers without harm.
Mighty Apollo, grant that we wipe out
With arms this ignominy. I want no spoils,
No trophy of a beaten girl. My actions
Elsewhere will bring me honor. May this dire
1080 Scourge of battle perish, when hit by me.
Then to the cities of my ancestors
With no pretence of glory I'll return."

Phoebus heard, and felt disposed to grant
His prayer in part; the rest he gave the winds
1085 To blow away. Granted, Arruns should fell
Camilla in the shock of death; denied
That Arruns' land should see the man return:
That plea the gale winds wafted to the South.

So when the javelin whistled from his hand
1090 The Volscians to a man, fiercely intent,
Looked toward their queen. Oblivious of the air
Around her, of the whistling shaft, the weapon
Gliding from high heaven, she remained
Until the javelin swooped and thudded home
1095 Beneath her naked breast. There, driven deep,
The shaft drank the girl's blood. In consternation
Fellow troopers gathered on the run
To catch and hold their captain as she dropped.
But Arruns on the instant galloped off
1100 In a daze, in fearful joy; he put no further
Trust in his lance nor in himself to meet
The warrior girl in arms. Just as a wolf
Who killed a shepherd or a full-grown steer
Makes off cross-country for the hills, to hide
1105 Before the arrows chase him—knowing well
His kill was reckless—tail curved down between
His legs to his quaking belly, off he goes;
Just so, Arruns in panic made himself scarce,
Well out of it amid a crowd of horsemen.
1110 Dying, Camilla tugged at the javelin,
But the steel point between the ribs held fast
In the deep wound. She drooped from loss of blood,
Her eyelids drooped, chill with approaching death,
And the fresh glow of youth drained from her cheeks.
1115 With halting breath she whispered now to Acca,
One of her company, equally young,
Her confidante, most faithful of them all,
And said:
          "Until now, sister, I was able.
1120 Now this wound galls me and finishes me.
Everything around is growing dark.
Make your escape and take my last command
To Turnus: that he join the battle here
To keep the Trojans from the town. Farewell."

1125 Even while speaking she let slip the reins
And slid fainting to earth. Little by little,

Growing cold, the girl detached herself
From her whole body and put down her head,
Death's captive now, upon her strengthless neck,
1130 And let her weapons fall.
Then with a groan for that indignity,
Her spirit fled into the gloom below.
Now, spreading measureless, a shout went up
To strike the golden stars. Camilla gone,
1135 The fight became more savage. Massed for battle,
Trojans in all their force pressed on, with Tuscan
Captains and the Arcadians of Evander.

As for the sentinel of Diana, Opis,
Resting all this time on a mountain top,
1140 She had been watching without fear. But now
She sighted, far off in the furious din
Of cavalries, Camilla beaten down
And pitifully dead. Then from her heart
The nymph said, groaning:
1145   "It is too cruel, girl,
Your punishment—too cruel for having tried
To challenge Trojans in the war. Devotion
Paid to Diana in your solitude,
In the wild wood, our arrows on your shoulder,
1150 Did not avail you. Yet your queen has left you
Not without honor at the hour of death,
Nor will your end be unrenowned
Among earth's peoples, nor will it be known
As unavenged. Whoever dared to pierce
1155 Your body, impiously, pays with his life
And justly."
                    On a mound in a mountain's shade
The ancient king, Dercennus of Laurentum,
Had an ilex-darkened massive tomb.
1160 Here with an easy spring, most beautiful,
The goddess mounted and looked down on Arruns.
Seeing him bright in arms and puffed with pride,
"Why turn aside?" she said. "Step this way, come
And perish here; enjoy the fit reward

1165   Camilla brings. You wretch, will even you
      Die by Diana's arrows?"
                    Then she picked
      A feathered shaft out of the gilded quiver
      And, taking deadly aim, drew the bow back
1170   Full circle, till the tips could almost meet.
      Her hands aligned, the left hand felt the point,
      The right hand, and taut bowstring, touched her breast.
      All in one instant Arruns heard the arrow
      Whistle in the ripped air and the arrowhead
1175   Thud in his body. As he moaned and died
      His fellow troopers rode off, unaware,
      And left him in the dust, a spot unknown
      On the wide terrain. Opis, taking wing,
      Went soaring to the high Olympian air.

1180   Now first to leave the field, their mistress lost,
      Were Camilla's light-armed cavalry. Then routed
      Rutulians made off, and fierce Atinas.
      Captains torn from squadrons, troops astray
      Wheeled toward the town and looked for safety there.
1185   No one at all could hold or make a stand
      With javelins against the Trojan onset.
      Bows were unstrung on slumping shoulders, galloping
      Hooves shook up the loose dry mire of the field.
      A dusky cloud of churned-up dust rolled on
1190   To the city walls, where mothers on the towers
      With beaten breasts lifted their women's cry
      To the stars of heaven. Hard on the heels of men
      First breaking through the open gates, a crowd
      Of enemy pressed, or men of both sides mingled,
1195   So there was no escape from piteous death,
      But in the very entry, amid the walls
      Of their own city, their protecting houses,
      Lanced from behind, they gave up life and breath.
      Then after some had shut the gates, they dared not
1200   Open a way in for their friends, or take them
      Into the town, beg as they would. Now came
      A wretched slaughter, as the gates' defenders

Shot at the crowd that rushed upon their shots.
Kept out before the eyes of weeping parents,
1205   Some of those borne onward in the rout
Plunged headlong in the moat, and others rode
In blind panic to batter at the gates,
Unyielding, barred against them. On the walls
Even older women, mothers—as true love
1210   Of homeland taught them, and as they had seen
Camilla fight—outdid each other now
At hurling missiles with unsteady hands,
In place of steel, hard oaken balks and pikes
With fire-hardened points. For their town wall
1215   They dared, they burned, to be the first to die.

In the mountain wood, meanwhile, the cruel news
Filled Turnus' thoughts, as Acca brought him word
Of the great tumult: Volscian troops destroyed,
Camilla fallen, foes in Mars' good graces
1220   Carrying all before them, riding on,
Panic already at the city walls.
Raging, as Jove's hard will required, Turnus
Left the heights that he had manned and left
The rough wood. Hardly was he out of sight
1225   And holding level ground, when Lord Aeneas
Entered the pass, unguarded now, and crossed
The ridge and issued from the woodland shade.
Then both, with no time lost, marched on the city,
Two whole hosts, not many miles apart.
1230   Aeneas viewed the plain smoking with dust
Far off, and saw the army of Laurentum;
Turnus at the same time recognized
Aeneas, pitiless captain in the field,
And heard the tramp of feet, the neigh of horses
1235   Coming behind. In moments they would skirmish,
Go to the test of battle, had not reddened
Phoebus already dipped his weary team
In the Spanish sea and, as the bright day ebbed,
Brought on the night. One army strengthened walls,
1240   The other encamped in quiet before the town.

Lines 886–915

BOOK

XII

THE FORTUNES
OF WAR

Turnus now saw how Latin strength had failed,
How the day's fight was lost and they were broken;
Saw that they held him to his promise now
All eyes upon him. But before they spoke
His passion rose, hot and unquenchable.
As in the African hinterland a lion,
Hit in the chest by hunters, badly hurt,
Gives battle then at last and revels in it,
Tossing his bunch of mane back from his nape;
All fighting heart, he snaps the shaft the tracker
Put into him, and roars with bloody maw.
So Turnus in the extremity flared up
And stormed at the old king:

"No one waits
While Turnus shirks a battle. No pretext
Allows Aeneas' riffraff to renege
Or take their challenge back. By god, I'll fight him.
Father, bring sacred offerings and state
The terms of combat. Either by this right arm
I send to hell that Dardan prince who left
His Asia in the lurch—and let the Latins
Rest and look on! while I alone disprove
With my sword-point the charge against us all—
Or else let him take over a beaten people,
Let Lavinia be the winner's bride."

To this Latinus answered steadily:

"Soldier without a peer, as you surpass
The rest in heroism, all the more
Must I labor to think, and weigh my fears,

30 Taking account of all that may occur.
You have your father Daunus' realm, you have
Your many conquered towns. Gold and the heart
To spend it are not lacking to Latinus.
Here in Latium, in the Laurentine land,

35 Are other girls of noble blood unmarried.
Allow me these reflections, painful, yes,
But open and above-board. Take to heart
This fact: it was not right that I should pledge
My daughter to a suitor of other days:

40 Gods, and prophecies of men, forbade.
Affection for you, our Rutulian kinsman,
Won me over—and my wife in tears.
I broke my bonds of duty, stole the girl,
Though promised, from her husband, and took arms

45 Against the will of heaven. You see what followed,
Turnus: the bloody wars and the defeats,
The bitter days you, most of all, endure.
Beaten in two great battles, barely alive
We keep Italian hopes within our town,

50 The Tiber's currents warm still with our blood,
The open land white with our bones. And why,
Again and yet again, am I pulled back
From action? What mad dream blurs my resolve?
Granted with Turnus dead I am prepared

55 To make them partners in the realm, why not
Stop fighting, rather, while he lives unharmed?
What will Rutulians of your family say,
What will all Italy say, if I betray you—
Heaven forbid!—to death while you contend

60 For marriage to my daughter? Only give thought
To the veering ways of war, take pity on
Your aged father whom Ardea keeps
At home, secluded from us and forlorn."

All that he said affected Turnus' fury
65 Not in the least: it mounted, all the more
Fevered at words of healing. When the man
Could speak at last, he said:

               "My lord, I beg you,
Put this reckoning for my sake aside
70 For my sake; let me bid my death for honor.
Father, I too can make a rapid cast
Of javelins, not puny when they strike.
Blood flows from wounds I, too, can give. This time
His goddess-mother, she who, when he runs,
75 Hides him in womanish cloud, who hides herself
In empty phantoms—she'll be far away."

But now the queen, Amata, terrified
By the new hazard of the single combat,
Wept and pale as death clung to her ardent
80 Son-in-law:

              "Turnus, I beg you by these tears.
By all you hold at heart for me, Amata—
You our one hope, our stay in grim old age—
Latinus' honor and authority
85 Rest in your hands, all our declining house
Now leans upon you: this one thing I beg:
Refrain from single combat with the Trojans.
Any mischance that may await you there
Awaits me, too; for with you I'll forsake
90 This hostile daylight. Never as a captive
Shall I look on Aeneas as my son."

Lavinia, listening to her mother, streamed
With tears on burning cheeks; a deepening blush
Brought out a fiery glow on her hot face.
95 As when one puts a stain of crimson dye
On ivory of India, or when
White lilies blush, infused with crimson roses,
So rich the contrast in her coloring seemed.
Desire stung the young man as he gazed,

100 Rapt, at the girl. He burned yet more for battle,
Briefly answering Amata:
                                      "Please,
Mother, no tears for me, no parting omen
So unpromising, as I go out
105 To combat ruled by iron Mars. No longer
Is Turnus free to put off risk of death.
Idmon, come, be my messenger, say this
To the Phrygian tyrant—words not to his liking.
When Dawn tomorrow, borne from the Ocean stream
110 On crimson chariot wheels, reddens the sky,
He need not lead the Trojans in attack
On the Rutulians. Let all Trojan weapons
Rest, Rutulians rest. With our own blood
Let us two put an end to war, and there
115 On that field, let Lavinia be the prize."

With this he whirled away into his quarters,
Called for his team, and smiled with joy at horses
Whinnying before him. These were the two
That Orithyia, consort of the North Wind,
120 Gave as a glory to Pilumnus: horses
Rivaling snow in whiteness, wind in speed;
And, flanking them, the nimble charioteers
Clapped hollow palms to chests and combed their manes.
Then round his shoulders Turnus donned his cuirass
125 Glinting with golden and pale copper scales,
Made ready sword and shield, and helm with horns
To bear his crimson plume. The sword was one
The Fire God himself had forged for Daunus,
Dipping it white-hot in the wave of Styx.
130 And finally, from where it leaned against
A pillar of the hall, he picked a spear,
His powerful hand gripping that hardy shaft
He took in battle from Auruncan Actor.
Shaking it, making it vibrate, he cried out:

135 "Spear, that never failed me once when called on,
Now the time has come. A champion once

Carried you; Turnus bears you now. See to it
That I smash down that body and tear away
With my strong hand the breastplate of the Phrygian
140 Eunuch, and befoul in dust those lovelocks
Curled with hot iron, drenched with liquid myrrh."

To this length driven by passion, he gave off
A sparkling glow from his whole face, and fire
Flashed from his eyes, as a wild bull at bay
145 Will give a fearsome bellow and whet his horns
To fury on a tree-trunk, striking blows
Against the wind, kicking up spurts of sand
In prelude to the fight.
                  Likewise, meanwhile,
150 Aeneas, fierce in his maternal armor,
Whetted his edge for war, and roused himself
To anger, full of joy that, by the terms
He offered, war should cease. He comforted
His officers, allayed pale Iulus' fear,
155 Recalling fate's design, then ordered men
To take Latinus an assured reply
And set conditions for the coming peace.

T he next day's dawn had barely cast its glow
On mountain tops—at that hour when the Sun's
160 Heaven-climbing team strives from the deep, exhaling
Light from flaring nostrils—when Rutulian
Troops and Trojans, under the city walls,
Laid out a field for combat. Some built hearths
And grassy altars for their common gods,
165 While fire and fresh spring water were brought out
By priests in cloaks, rosemary round their brows.
The compact legion of Ausonians
Debouched now from the crowded city gates;
The Trojan-Tuscan army from the plain

170 Streamed up in various accouterment,
Ranks glinting steel, as though rough work of Mars
Had called them, and amid their numbers captains
Wheeled about in pride of gold and crimson:
Mnestheus of Assaracus's line,
175 Valiant Asilas, and the master of horse,
Messapus, Neptune's son. At a trumpet note
Each side retired to its appointed zone
With lances fixed in earth and shields at rest.
Then matrons and townspeople, pouring out
180 With old men and infirm, thronged towers and roofs,
While others clustered at the tall gateways.

But gazing from the height we now call Alban—
Nameless then, it had no fame or glory—
Juno surveyed the plain, the facing lines,
185 Troy's and Laurentum's, and Latinus' town.
Promptly she turned, immortal to immortal,
And spoke to Turnus' sister, nymph of ponds
And purling streams. Heaven's king Jupiter
For the maidenhead that he had ravished, gave
190 This divine dignity: rule over limpid things.

"Nymph," she said, "and loveliness of rivers,
Cherished by me, you know I honor you
Above all Latin girls who ever entered
Great-hearted Jove's unwelcome bed: I've kept
195 Most happily for you a place in heaven.
Now let me tell you of your grief-to-be,
Lest you think me the cause. While Fortune seemed
Compliant, and the Fates let power rest
With Latium, your brother and your city
200 Had my protection. Now I see the soldier
Meeting a destiny beyond his strength:
His doom's day, mortal shock of the enemy,
Are now at hand. I cannot bear to watch
This duel, this pact. If you dare help your brother
205 More at close quarters, do it, and well done.
A better time may follow present pain."

Lines 123–153

The words were barely out before Juturna's
Eyes brimmed over tears; with her clenched hand
She thrice or four times beat her comely breast.

210   "This is no time for tears," the goddess said,
"Be quick, go snatch your brother back from death
If there's a way. Or else renew the war,
Cast out the pact which they drew up. I'll be
Sponsor to your audacity."

215   With this
Last urgent word she left her wondering, torn,
In turmoil from the pang her heart had suffered.
Meanwhile the kingly men appeared: Latinus
Mighty in aspect in a four-horse car,
220   His shining brow crowned with twelve golden rays
In token of the Sun, his ancestor,
While Turnus rode behind his snowy team,
Handling a pair of spears, broad in the blade.
Then from his quarters Lord Aeneas came—
225   The father of the Roman race—aglow
With starry shield and armor forged by heaven,
Close at his side the second hope of Rome,
Ascanius. A priest in a clean robe
Brought out a boar's young and a sheep unshorn
230   To place before the altar fires. These men
With eyes turned to the rising sun, bestowed
Their handfulls of salt meal, took knives to mark
The foreheads of the beasts, and poured from shallow
Ritual cups libations on the altars.
235   Aeneas, the god-fearing, with drawn sword
Spoke out his vows:
                "Sun be my witness now
And this land for whose sake I could endure
Hard days and many; then the almighty Father
240   Also, and his lady—thou, Saturnia,
More kindly to us, goddess, now, I pray;
And thou, too, famous Mars, whose hand hurls down
On men all wars according to thy will;
I call on springs and streams, and all the powers

245   Both of high heaven and the deep blue sea:
        Should victory fall to the Ausonian, Turnus,
        It is agreed that in defeat we shall
        Retire upon Evander's town, that Iulus
        Quit this region, and Aeneas' people
250   Never afterward return in war
        Or send this kingdom challenges to arms.
        If on the other hand the day is ours,
        Conferred by divine Victory, as I think—
        And may the gods confirm it by their will—
255   I shall not make Italians underlings
        To Trojans. For myself I ask no kingdom.
        Let both nations, both unconquered, both
        Subject to equal laws, commit themselves
        To an eternal union. I shall give
260   Rituals and gods to both. My father-in-law
        Latinus, let him keep his arms, and keep
        His royal authority. My share will be
        A town with walls, laid out and built by Trojans.
        Lavinia will give that town her name."

265   In these terms first Aeneas declared himself.
        Latinus followed, with a skyward look,
        His right hand lifted to the stars.
                              "Aeneas,
        I swear by the same powers—by earth and sea
270   And stars, by the twin children of Latona,
        Janus' two faces, and the nether powers,
        Shrines of pitiless Dis: let this be heard
        By the Sky Father who with lightning bolts
        Can seal inviolate the pacts of men.
275   Here as I touch the altars I appeal
        To ritual fires, and mediating gods,
        Never shall that day dawn that sees our peace,
        Our treaty, ruptured by my countrymen,
        However things fall out. No force on earth
280   Can make me swerve from my intent, no force,
        Though it embroil the earth and water in flood

To pour land into sea, heaven into hell.
Just as this scepter here in my right hand
Will never put out foliage or shade,
285 Once cut from the live tree-bole in the forest,
Torn from that mother, and laid bare by steel
Of branching arms and leaves. This one-time bough
The artificer's hand has fitted well
In a bronze sheath and given to our Latin
290 Lords to carry."
                    By these spoken vows
They sealed the pact between them in the sight
Of captains on both sides, then cut the throats
Of duly hallowed beasts over the flames
295 And tore the living entrails out, to heap
In freshly loaded platters on the altars.

On the Rutulian side the coming match
Seemed more unfair, however, as time went on.
Fears came and went, troubling them all the more
300 When, seeing the contenders close at hand,
They saw their strength unequal. This disquiet
Multiplied now as Turnus walked in silence
Reverently and humbly to the altars,
Eyes downcast, his cheeks drawn, his flesh pale.

305 Now when Juturna saw troops in commotion,
Whispering ever louder, and losing heart,
She moved into the ranks, disguised as Camers—
An officer whose ancestry was noble,
His father's valor a matter of renown
310 And he himself assiduous in arms—
Taking this form, amid the ranks she went,
Aware of their condition, putting out
One rumor and another, asking them:

Lines 205–228

"Does no one blush, Rutulians, to expose
315 One life, one soldier, for so large a force?
In numbers of good men, in fighting power,
Are we no match for them? Look: all are here,
Trojans, Arcadians, fate-driven Tuscans,
Foes to Turnus. If we take them on
320 With merely every other man, we barely
Find a foe for each. Turnus will rise
In fame to those high gods upon whose altars
He makes the offering of his life: he'll be
Alive upon the lips of men. Not so
325 With all the rest! Losing our fatherland,
Proud masters on our backs, we'll be enslaved
For never stirring on this field today."

This fueled the fire of what the soldiers thought,
And louder murmuring crept through the ranks,
330 Laurentine, too, and Latin. Their mood changed,
And men who lately hoped for rest from combat,
Safety for their way of life, now felt
A hankering for weapons, wished the pact
Could be unmade, and pitied Turnus' lot
335 As underdog. To add to all this, then,
Juturna gave a more insidious stroke,
For high in heaven she produced a sign
Most potent to confuse Italian minds,
A strange, deceitful tableau. Winging down
340 Through rosy dawnlit air, Jove's golden bird
Came chasing offshore seafowl, noisy flocks,
And with a swoop upon the waves caught up
In crooked talons a surpassing swan.
The Italians gazed, enthralled. Then all the birds
345 In flight wheeled round with screams—wondrous to see—
Their wings darkening heaven, and in a cloud
Harried the enemy through the air until
Their pressure and the swan's weight broke his grip:
His talons dropped the prey into the river,
350 Then gaining depth of cloud he soared away.
Cheers at this omen broke from Rutulian ranks,

And hands were freed for arms. Tolumnius,
The augur, gave a cry:
           "Here was the sign!
355 The sign I often looked for in my prayers.
I welcome it, I see the gods behind it.
Arm with me! Follow my lead! poor countrymen
On whom that vulture from abroad has come
To scare like light-winged terns or gulls in war
360 And to lay waste your seaboard. He'll be gone,
His canvas wide-winged toward horizon cloud!
It is for you to take heart, all together,
Close your formations, and fight on to save
The prince this raiding stranger took for prey."

365 He finished, then ran forward with a spear
To launch it at the facing enemy.
The whistling shaft of cornel sang ahead
Unwavering through the air. At the same time
A great shout sounded from all companies,
370 Their hearts grown hot with turmoil, as the spear
Flew on toward where nine handsome brothers stood—
All of them borne to the Arcadian
Gylippus by his faithful Tuscan wife.
The spear hit one of them just at the waist
375 Where the sewn belt rubbed on his upper belly,
And a brooch clamped the strap from either side.
The spear that passed from rib to rib brought down
This well-built soldier, all a-gleam in armor,
Pitching him on the tawny sand. His brothers,
380 Brave men, now as one, in shock and grief,
Some with swords out, some with steel to throw,
Came in a blind rush forward. But Laurentine
Squads moved out to meet them, double-quick.
Then from the other side again came Trojans,
385 Tuscans from Agyllina, Arcadians
In painted gear, now charging side by side.
One passion took possession of them all:
To make the sword their arbiter. They ripped
The altars to get firebrands, missiles flew

390 In darkening squalls over the whole sky,
A rain of steel, while sacrificial bowls
And hearth fires of the peace were snatched away.

His treaty void, Latinus took to flight
With images of his defeated gods.
395 Others caught up their chariot reins or vaulted
Into the saddle, drawing blades, advancing.
Avid to break the pact, Messapus rode
Against Aulestes, the Etruscan prince
Who wore a prince's blazon. This poor captain
400 Flinched aside, then stumbled as he whirled
Amid the obstructing altars and went down
On head and shoulders. In a flash Messapus
Rode up with his spear, high on his horse,
And even as the prone man begged for mercy
405 Thrust hard downward with his beam-like shaft.
Then he called out.
                    "That does for him. A richer
Carcase for the great gods!"
                                And Italians
410 Running up despoiled the still-warm body.
Out of one altar Corynaeus pulled
A half-burnt firebrand, facing Ebysus
As he came lunging for a stroke; he hit him
Between the eyes with flames; his bush of beard
415 Flared up and gave a smell of burning flesh.
Corynaeus closed, and caught in his left hand
His staggered enemy's hair, then struck a knee
Into his groin and bent him to the ground
To be dispatched with a sword-thrust in the side.
420 With naked blade Podalirius rose behind
The shepherd Alsus, as he ran along
The front through spears, but Alsus whirled his axe
Backward and split the skull of his enemy
From brow to chin. Gore splattered on his armor;
425 Harsh repose oppressed his eyes, a sleep
Of iron, and in eternal night they closed.

Lines 284–310

Meanwhile the man of honor, Aeneas, stood
Bare-headed with his right hand out, unarmed,
And called his troops:

430   "Where bound? Are you a mob?
Why this outbreak of brawling all at once?
Cool your hot heads. A pact has been agreed to,
Terms have been laid down. I am the one
To fight them. Let me do so. Never fear:
435 With this right hand I'll carry out the treaty.
Turnus is mine, our sacrifice obliged it."

But even as he called out, as he spoke,
A winging shaft—look!—whizzed and struck the man,
440 Sped by who knows what hand, what spinning gust—
What stroke of luck, what god won this distinction
For the Rutulians. Glory for the shot
Went afterward suppressed; no claims were made
By anyone of having hit Aeneas.

When Turnus saw Aeneas in retreat,
445 Leaving his troops, and saw the Trojan captains
Thrown into disarray, he seethed again
With sudden hope and called for team and weapons.
Flashing aboard his car in one proud leap,
He pulled hard at the reins and went careering,
450 Handing over to death dozens of men
And bringing others down half-dead. Whole files
He smashed under his wheels. He wrested spears
From men who fled and killed them on the run.
Like blood-stained Mars himself he rode, when Mars
455 Goes headlong by the frozen Hebrus river,
Beating out claps of thunder on his shield
And lashing on his furious team for war—
That team that on the open ground outruns

Lines 311–334

The south and west winds, while the farthest land
460 Of Thrace re-echoes to their drumming hooves;
And riding with him go black visages
Of Fright, Ambush, and Anger, Mars' companions.
That was the way of Turnus, lashing on
A team that smoked with sweat amid the battle,
465 Trampling foes in wretchedness brought down.
His running hooves kicked up a bloody spray
And pocked the mire of sand and gore. The rider
Cut down Sthenelus with a long throw,
Thamyrus and then Pholus at close quarters;
470 With a long throw, again, Imbrasus' sons
Glaucus and Ladës, whom their father reared
In Lycia and richly fitted out
To fight on foot or to outride the wind.
Elsewhere on the field Eumedës charged
475 Into the mêlée—a man famed in war,
Son of the fabled Dolon—having his name
From his old grandfather, his recklessness
And deft hand from his father, who had dared
To ask Achilles' team as his reward
480 For spying on the Danaan camp at Troy.
For that audacity Diomedes gave
A different reward: all hope expired
For horses of Achilles. Now when Turnus
Caught sight of Eumedës at a distance
485 Across the plain, he had a shot at him
With a light javelin over the open space,
Drove after it, reined in, and vaulted down
To where the man had fallen and lay dying.
With one foot on his neck he wrenched away
490 The sword from his right hand, then sank the blade
Shining but soon encrimsoned in his throat.
Then from above he said:
                       "Here's good land, Trojan,
The western land you thought to take in war.
495 Lie there and measure it. See what is gained
By daring to face up to me in arms.
See how far you go in founding cities."

To bear him company he brought Asbytës
Down with a spear-cast, then killed Chloreus,
500 Sybaris, Darës, and Thersilochus,
Thymoetës too, thrown when his horse shied.
As Thracian Northwind, Boreas, in a gale
Roars on Aegean deeps and shoreward surf
Where squalls roll down the dark and the scud flies,
505 Just so, wherever Turnus cut his way,
Formations yielded to him, ranks turned tail
And ran before him. His own impetus
Carried him on; the wind his chariot made
Whipped back and forth his flying crest. One man,
510 Phegeus, hated the sight
Of Turnus tall before him thundering on.
Square in the chariot's path he flung himself
And yanked aside the galloping horses' jaws
That foamed upon the bits. While he hung on
515 To the yoke, borne onward, Turnus' broad spearhead,
Now thrust at his unshielded flank, broke through
His mail of double mesh and grazed his body.
None the less, turning his shield around,
Resorting to his blade, he made a lunge,
520 Only to go down headlong as the wheel
And axle spinning struck and laid him low.
Then by a stroke between the helmet rim
And breastplate, Turnus cut his head away,
Leaving his trunk mired in sand.
525   While all these
Deaths were being brought about by Turnus,
Mnestheus and Achatës, ever faithful,
Accompanied by Ascanius, helped Aeneas
Into the camp, bleeding, putting his weight
530 With every other step on his long spear.
He strove in rage to extract the arrowhead
With snapped-off shaft, and asked for the quickest way:
A sword-cut, making a deeper and open wound
To expose the embedded point, then send him back
535 Into the battle. But now Iapyx came,
Son of Iasus, and most dear to Phoebus.

Captured one time by sharp desire, Apollo
Made him gifts of skills that were the god's—
Augury and the lyre and speeding arrows.
540 Iapyx, however, to postpone the death
Of a father desperately ill, preferred
To learn the powers of herbs, a healer's ways,
And practice without glory silent arts.
Aeneas, bitterly impatient, stood
545 And leaned on his great spear, unmoved
By tears of soldiers gathering in a crowd
And Iulus grieving. In Paeonian style
The old man rolled his cloak back carefully
And worked with his physician's hand, with herbs
550 Of potency from Phoebus—all in vain,
In vain trying to worry out the barb
Or grip and tug the embedded steel with tongs.
No luck guided his probes, and no help came
From Phoebus, the arch-healer. More and more
555 Savage the terror of the field grew; nearer
Came the calamitous end. By now they saw
A wall of dust that stood against the sky,
Horsemen approaching, arrows falling thick
Into the middle of the camp; and skyward
560 Rose the shouts of men who fought, the cries
Of men who fell, cut down by pitiless Mars.
Now, shaken by the pain unmerited
Her son bore, mother Venus picked a stalk
Of dittany from Cretan Ida—dittany
565 With downy leaves and scarlet flower, a plant
That wild goats know about when stuck with arrows.
Venus now brought this down, veiling her face
In a dark cloud, and for a secret poultice
Dipped the leaves to imbue a shining bowl
570 Of Tiber water, sprinkling in ambrosia's
Health-giving juices and the fragrant Heal-all.
Quite unaware of her, old Iapyx used
The medicated fluid to lave the wound.
Then, sure enough, all anguish instantly
575 Left Aeneas' body, all his bleeding

Lines 392–422

Stopped, deep in the wound. The arrowhead
Came out, unforced and ready to his hand.
New strength renewed his old-time fighting spirit.

"Here, be quick, and give the man his armor,"
580 Iapyx exclaimed. "Why stand there?"

                            First to speak.
He fired their hearts against the enemy.
"No mortal agency brought this about,
No art however skilled, not my own hand
585 Preserves you, but a greater power, Aeneas.
A god is here at work. He sends you back
To greater actions."

Avid for battle now,
The captain sheathed his left leg and his right
590 In golden greaves, hating the minutes lost,
And hefted his long spear. Once he had fitted
Shield to flank, harness to back, he hugged
Ascanius, embracing him with steel,
Then through his vizor brushed his lips and said:

595 "Learn fortitude and toil from me, my son,
Ache of true toil. Good fortune learn from others.
My sword arm now will be your shield in battle
And introduce you to the boons of war.
When, before long, you come to man's estate,
600 Be sure that you recall this. Harking back
For models in your family, let your father,
Aeneas, and uncle, Hector, stir your heart."

This said, his powerful figure passed the gates,
His long spear flashing in his hand. With him
605 Antheus and Mnestheus and a dense battalion
Sortied en masse, and all reserves inside
Flowed outward from the abandoned camp. The field

Went dark with blinding dust, the marching feet
Awakened crumbled earth and made it tremble.
610 Turnus from the rampart opposite
Saw them coming; so did the Ausonians,
And felt a chill of dread run through their bones.
First of them all to hear and know the sound,
Juturna trembled and turned back. Aeneas
615 With flying feet led through the open field
His dark battalion at high speed—as when
A stormcloud out at sea moves toward the land
And cuts the sunlight off; then farmers know,
Alas, what's coming, shivering in their hearts,
620 For it will bring down trees, devastate crops,
And flatten all things far and wide. The winds
Fly in ahead and bring the tempest roar.
Just so the captain from the Troad led
His troops in close formation, swarming on,
625 Against the enemy. With his long blade
Thymbraeus cut massive Osiris down,
Mnestheus killed Arcetius, Épulo
Fell to Achatës, Ufens fell to Gyas,
Tolumnius, the augur, too, succumbed,
630 He who had made the first spear-cast against them.
Skyward the shouting rose as in their turn
Rutulians turned their dusty backs and fled
Across the fields. Aeneas held aloof
From fugitives and would not chase or kill
635 Those met on foot or mounted men with lances.
In the dense murk he tracked Turnus alone,
Called on Turnus alone to stand and fight him.

Stricken with dread of this, Juturna, now
Nerved as a man for combat, made Metiscus,
640 Turnus' charioteer, tumble headfirst
Along the reins and fall from the chariot pole.
Then she left him far behind as she
Drove onward, swerving, reins in hand, and took
The entire guise, voice, armor of Metiscus.

Lines 444–472

645 About a rich landowner's farm a black-winged
Swallow flits through lofty rooms and picks
A meal of scraps and crumbs for her loud nestlings;
Now she is heard in empty colonnades,
Now skimming over ponds. Just so, Juturna,
650 Borne by that team amid her enemies,
In her swift car traversed the field: now here,
Now there she showed her brother glorying
And would not let him fight but flew far onward.

Aeneas all the same kept after him,
655 Following his twists and turns, and calling out
In a loud voice among the scattered troops.
But each time that he glimpsed his enemy
And tried to match on foot the speed in flight
Of the racing team, Juturna whirled away.
660 He groaned. What could he do? As in a cross-rip
Weltering without headway, in his heart
He felt desires clash. But now against him
Messapus came, light on his feet, with two
Steel-pointed and tough spears in his left hand.
665 He twirled and threw one, aimed for a direct hit,
And, halting, falling to one knee, Aeneas
Crouched behind his shield. The driven spear
Still carried off the apex of his helm
And knocked away his plume.
670   At this attack,
A tide of battle-fury swept the Trojan,
Overcome by Rutulian bad faith.
The team and car of his great adversary
Being out of range, he called on Jove and called
675 On altars of the broken peace to witness,
Many times, then into the mêlée
He raced, most terrible to see, with Mars
Behind him, rousing blind and savage slaughter,
All restraints on wrath cast to the winds.
680 What god can help me tell so dread a story?
Who could describe that carnage in a song—

Lines 473–503

The captains driven over the plain and killed
By Turnus or in turn by Troy's great hero?
Was it thy pleasure, Jupiter, that peoples
685 Afterward to live in lasting peace
Should rend each other in so black a storm?
One duel briefly stayed the Trojan charge,
When Sucro, the Rutulian, held Aeneas;
Then on that side where fate is quickest, Aeneas
690 Drove his raw steel through the man's rib-cage.
Turnus unhorsed Amycus and his brother,
Diorës, and dismounted then to strike them,
Killing with his spear the one who came
Against him, and the other with his sword.
695 He cut their heads away and bore them off,
Dripping blood, hung to his chariot rail.
Aeneas consigned Talos and Tanaïs
To bloody death, and brave Cethegus—three
In one fight; then Onitës as he mourned them,
700 A son of Peridía from fabled Thebes.
Turnus killed certain brothers sent from Lycia,
Apollos's highlands, and went on to kill
Menoetës. hater of war—his hatred vain.
A fisherman in his Arcadian youth,
705 He had his poor hut near the brooks of Lerna.
Crowded with perch, and knew no seats of power
His father tilled a plot of rented land.

The two assailants were like fires begun
On two sides of a dry wood, making laurel
71c Thickets crackle, or like snow-fed streams
That foam and roar seaward down mountain-sides
And leave, each one, a watercourse laid waste.
With no less devastating power these two,
Aeneas and Turnus, cut their way through battle.
715 Now with fury rising, now again
With bursting hearts and reckless of defeat,
They spent their whole strength running upon danger.
Here came Murranus, and he boasted loud

Lines 503–529

Of grandfathers, and grandfathers of theirs,
720 Of old names, and one family entire
That came down through the Latin kings. Aeneas
Tumbled him headlong with a whirlwind cast
Of a big stone and bashed him to the ground.
Under the yoke and reins, his own wheels knocked him
725 Rolling where with beating hooves his team,
Oblivious of their master, trampled him.
Then Hyllus charged ahead in boundless rage,
But Turnus met him with a javelin flung
Against his gilded brow, and through his helm
730 The shaft stuck in his brain.

                    Bravest of Greeks,
Cretheus, neither could you, by your sword arm,
Be saved from Turnus. Nor when Aeneas came
Did gods protect their minister, Cupencus.
735 Facing the blade thrust at his breast, he could not
Fend it with his brazen shield, poor soldier.
Then the Laurentine fields witnessed your death,
Aeolus, yours too, sprawled on the earth,
Whom once the Argive columns and Achilles,
740 Bane of Priam's realm, could not bring down.
Here was your finish. Though your manor stood
In Ida's shade, your manor at Lyrnesus,
Laurentine earth would be your sepulchre.

Each army's total strength was now engaged,
745 All Latins and all Trojans, every man:
Mnestheus and brave Serestus, too; Messapus,
Master of horse, valiant Asilas; ranks
Of Tuscans, and Arcadians of Evander,
Each putting all he had into the struggle,
750 Never a let-up, never a breathing spell;
In the vast combat every man fought on.

Lines 529–553

Here, though, Aeneas' lovely mother sent
The captain a new thought: to approach the walls,
To bring his troops to bear upon the city
755 Quickly, and take the Latins by surprise,
Threatening sudden ruinous assault.
Following Turnus down the long front, he viewed
The city from one vantage or another
And saw how quiet it lay, immune, untouched
760 By the wild battle. Now in his mind's eye,
Afire, he saw a greater fight to come.
He called his officers, Mnestheus, Sergestus,
Brave Serestus, and climbed a rise of ground
Round which the Trojan legion came together,
765 Crowding, shields and spears held at the ready.
Standing amid them on the mound, he said:

"There will be no time lost in carrying out
What I shall say now. Jupiter stands with us.
Granted this change of action unforeseen,
770 On that account let no man lag behind.
Unless our enemies accept our yoke
And promise to obey us, on this day
I shall destroy their town, root of this war,
Soul of Latinus' kingdom. I shall bring
775 Their smoking rooftops level with the ground.
Must I go on, awaiting Turnus' whim
To face and fight me once again in battle,
Beaten already as he is? I think not.
Countrymen, this town is head and heart
780 Of an unholy war. Bring out your firebrands!
Make terms, this time, with a town in flames!"

On this he ended. Vying with one another
High-hearted troops formed up in echelon,
A compact mass, and headed for the walls.
785 Now scaling ladders all at once appeared,
Now spurting fires. One company rushed the gates
And cut down the first guards they met; another

Lines 554–578

Launched their missiles, darkening the sky.
Aeneas himself, among the foremost, held
790　His right hand up in shadow of the walls
With shouted accusations of Latinus,
Calling the gods to witness that once more
The fight was forced upon him, that Italians
Twice had turned his foes, that a second pact
795　Had now been broken. Amid the townspeople
Panic and discord grew: some said the town
Should be unbarred, gates opened to the Dardans;
These would hale to the walls the king himself.
The rest ran to fetch arms and man the ramparts.
800　As when a shepherd, tracking bees, has found
Their hive in tufa, he fills up the cleft
With acrid smoke; inside, roused in alarm,
The bees clamber about their waxen quarters,
Buzzing loud and growing hot with rage
805　As black and reeking puffs invade their home,
And deep in rocky dark their hum resounds
While smoke goes up in the clear air.
　　　　　　　　　　　　　　More trouble
Came now to weary Latins, a new grief
810　That shocked the whole town to its heart.
When Queen Amata from her window saw
The enemy at hand, the walls besieged,
Flames flying to the roofs, she saw no soldiers
Drawn up against them, no Rutulians
815　Under Turnus' command—and thought, poor woman,
Her prince had been destroyed in the mêlée.
Her mind riven by this thunderclap, she cried
That she had been the cause, the source of evil,
And many such laments in her sad frenzy.
820　Maddened now, wishing to die, she rent
Her crimson gown and knotted round a beam
The noose that strangled her in hideous death.
When Latin women heard of this disaster,
Doubling their sorrow, princess Lavinia first
825　Tore her flowerlike hair and scored her cheeks,

Then all the rest crowded about her, mad
With horror and grief. The palace rang with wailing.
Everywhere in the town the black news ran
And hearts grew sick. Ripping his robe, Latinus
830 Fouled his snowy hair with dust and filth,
Stunned by his wife's death and the city's fall.
Fighting his war meanwhile, and far away
At the edge of the battlefield, Turnus pursued
A straggling few, but now more sluggishly,
835 Less and less joyous in his winning team.
Faint outcries, with dark overtones of terror,
Came to him on the breeze; he cupped his ears
And heard the sound of turmoil in the city,
A joyless uproar.

840   "Sink, heart. What great loss
Has brought on this commotion, this wild cry
Borne from the distant city on the wind?"

With this, distraught, he took the reins and halted.
Then his sister, who seemed his charioteer,
845 Metiscus, driver of his team and car,
Bent toward him and protested:
                                "Turnus, this way
For our pursuit of Trojans! Victory
Opened the way here first. And there are others
850 Able over there to defend their homes.
Aeneas is attacking the Italians
In pitched battle; let us play our part
By massacring Teucrians. Your death-toll
And feats of war will be no less than his."

855 But Turnus answered:
                                "Sister—yes, I knew you
Long since, when you spoiled the pact by guile
And gave yourself to this war. Now again
You need not try to hide your divinity
860 But who has wished you sent down from Olympus
To take this rough work on? That you should see

The painful end of your unhappy brother?
What am I to do? What stroke of luck
Can guarantee my safety now? I saw
865 Before my eyes, and calling on my name,
Murranus downed—great soul by a great wound—
And none survives more dear to me. Poor Ufens
Died as though to avoid seeing my shame;
The Trojans have his body and his gear.
870 But now destruction of our homes—the one thing
Lacking to my desperate case—can I
Face that? Should I not give the lie to Drancës?
Shall I turn tail? Will this land know the sight
Of Turnus on the run? To die—is that
875 So miserable? Heaven has grown cold;
Shades of the underworld, be friendly to me.
As a pure spirit guiltless of that shame
I shall go down among you—never unfit
To join my great forefathers."

880 Just as he finished, here came Sacës riding
At a dead run amid the enemy,
His mount foaming, his face torn by a wound,
Crying out "Turnus!" as he rode, and then:

"Turnus, our last chance rests with you: be moved
885 For your own people. Like a thunderbolt
Aeneas falls on us. He means to topple
The citadels of Italy in ruin.
Firebrands even now fly to the roofs.
The Latins turn their faces toward you, turn
890 Their eyes to you; the king himself, Latinus,
Mutters in doubt, unsure whom to call sons,
What alliance to turn to. Worst of all,
The queen who put such trust in you is gone,
Dead by her own hand, fleeing daylight in fear.
895 Only Messapus and Atinas still
Maintain a fighting line before the gates.
In close formation on both flanks the enemy

Lines 636–663

Bristles with spearheads like a crop of steel.
And yet you keep your chariot in play
900　On this deserted meadow."

　　　　　　　　　　Stunned and confused
By one and another image of disaster,
Turnus held stock-still with a silent stare.
In that one heart great shame boiled up, and madness
905　Mixed with grief, and love goaded by fury,
Courage inwardly known. When by and by
The darkness shadowing him broke and light
Came to his mind again, wildly he turned
His burning eyes townward and from his car
910　Gazed at the city.

　　　　　　　　Look now: billowing
Flames went up from floor to floor and twined
About a defensive tower that he himself
Had built and braced, fitted with wheels and ramps.

915　"Ah, sister, see, fate overpowers us.
No holding back now. We must follow where
The god calls, or implacable Fortune calls.
My mind's made up on what remains to do:
To meet Aeneas hand to hand, to bear
920　All that may be of bitterness in death.
You'll find no more unseemliness in me.
Let me be mad enough for this mad act,
I pray, before I die."

　　　　　　　　He left his car
925　In one swift leap upon the field and coursed
Away from his sad sister. Then, amid
The spear-casts of the enemy, on the run,
He broke through the attacking Trojan line.
As when a crag dislodged by wind rolls down
930　From a mountain-top—for either a storm of rain
Washed earth from under it or time and age
Had undermined it—and it goes headlong,
A mass ungovernable, bounding on
In huge descent, sweeping along with it

Lines 663–689

93.   Trees, herds, and men: so through the broken ranks
To the city walls went Turnus in his rush.
With blood spilled there the ground was drenched, the air
A-swish with javelins cast. His hand held up
To arrest the fighting, with a great shout he called:

940   "Rutulians, hold! Put up your weapons, Latins!
The outcome here, for good or ill, is mine.
Better that single-handed in your stead
I pay for a broken truce and fight it out
To a decision."
945   When Aeneas heard
The name of Turnus, he forsook the walls,
Forsook the high point of the citadel,
Threw off all hindrance, cut all action short,
In joy, clanging in arms a fearsome thunder,
950   Grand as Mount Athos or Mount Eryx or
Old Father Appennine himself, when high
Oak forests flash and roar, and into heaven
He rears his crown of snow.
                       Now, sure enough,
955   Rutulians and Trojans and Italians
All outdid each other, dropping combat,
Craning to see; now those men on the ramparts,
Those at the battering ram low on the walls,
Put down their shields. Even Latinus marveled,
960   Seeing two giant men of action, born
In countries so far distant, come together,
Vowed to a decision by the sword.

O nce a space on the open ground was cleared,
The combatants ran forward, hurling spears
965   At a distance first, then closing hand to hand.
Their brazen shields and harness rang; the earth
Groaned under them; redoubling stroke on stroke,

Lines 689–714

They fought with swords, and prowess merged with luck
In the fighting power of each.

970   On Sila's flank
Of mighty mountain, or Taburnus' height,
When two bulls lower heads and horns and charge
In deadly combat, herdsmen blanch and scatter.
Then cattle all stand mute
975   As heifers muse on a new forest lord
Whom all the herds will follow. The contenders,
Compact of shocking force, with lowered horns
Gore one another, bathing necks and humps
In sheets of blood, and the whole woodland bellows.
980   Just so Trojan Aeneas and the hero
Son of Daunus, battering shield on shield,
Fought with a din that filled the air of heaven.
Jupiter held the two pans of a scale
In balance and placed in each a destiny—
985   Doom for him whose weight would bring death down.
Turnus, thinking himself secure, flashed out
To his full height, blade lifted overhead,
And struck. The Trojans and the anxious Latins
Raised a cry, both ranks of men on edge,
990   But then the treacherous blade on impact broke
And left the man undone, enraged, his one
Recourse in flight. Swifter than wind he fled
And stared at the strange sword-hilt in his hand,
Disarmed now. Legend tells that when he first
995   Stepped up behind his team for headlong combat,
Haste made him leave his father's blade behind
And snatch that of his charioteer, Metiscus.
This for a long time had sufficed, while he
Rode down the Trojan stragglers from behind;
1000   But now, encountering the armor forged
By the god Vulcan, the mere mortal blade
Snapped into fragments like an icicle,
And shattered bits shone on the yellow sand.
Crazed by the loss, in search of open ground,
1005   Turnus ran, weaving circles at a loss
This way and that—for the dense crowd of Trojans

Ringed and shut him in, and on one side
A broad marsh, on the other high stone walls
Made limits to his flight. As for Aeneas,
1010   Slowed though his knees were by the arrow wound
That hampered him at times, cutting his speed,
He pressed on hotly, matching stride for stride,
Behind his shaken foe. As when a stag-hound
Corners a stag, blocked by a stream, or by
1015   Alarm at a barrier of crimson feathers
Strung by beaters, then the dog assails him
With darting, barking runs; the stag in fear
Of nets and the high river-bank attempts
To flee and flee again a thousand ways,
1020   But, packed with power, the Umbrian hound hangs on,
Muzzle agape: now, now he has him, now,
As though he had him, snaps eluded jaws
And bites on empty air. Then he gives tongue
In furious barking; river banks and pools
1025   Echo the din, reverberant to the sky.
As Turnus ran he raged, raged at Rutulians,
Calling their names, demanding his own sword.
Aeneas countered, threatening instant death
For any who came near; he terrified them,
1030   Promising demolition of their city,
And pressed the chase, despite his wound. Five times
They ran the circular track and five again
Reran it backward, this way and now that.
They raced for no light garland of the games
1035   But strove to win the life and blood of Turnus.

Now on this field there happened to have stood
An old wild olive, bitter-leaved, a tree
Sacred to Faunus, with a trunk revered
By seamen long ago: those who survived
1040   Shipwreck or storm fixed votive offerings there
And hung their garments to Laurentum's god.
The Trojans, treating it like any other,
Had left a stump but lopped away the tree,
So they could fight on a clear field. The spear

Lines 744–772

1045   Thrown by Aeneas had stuck in that tough stump
        Where winging force had carried it and held it.
        The Dardan bent to extract the weapon now
        And cast it at the man he could not catch.
        At this, Turnus grew mad with fear. He said:

1050   "Faunus, have pity, I entreat you! Gracious
        Earth, hold fast the steel, if I have honored you
        All my life, whereas Aeneas' men
        Warred on you and profaned you."

                                        So he prayed
1055   And asked divine assistance, not in vain,
        For pausing at the stump, and struggling long,
        Aeneas, using all his power, could not
        Pry apart the bite of stubborn oak.
        As bitterly he braced and strove, Juturna
1060   Ran up, once again changed to Metiscus,
        Giving her brother back his sword. At this,
        Indignant that the nymph had made so free,
        Venus came forward, and she tore away
        Aeneas' weapon from the deep oak root,
1065   So both men were rearmed. They towered up,
        One confident of his own blade, the other
        Tall and savage, with a spear to throw,
        And both now, panting, faced the duel of Mars.

        Omnipotent Olympus' king meanwhile
1070   Had words for Juno, as she watched the combat
        Out of a golden cloud. He said:

                                "My consort,
        What will the end be? What is left for you?
        You yourself know, and say you know, Aeneas
1075   Born for heaven, tutelary of this land,
        By fate to be translated to the stars.

        Lines 772–795

What do you plan? What are you hoping for,
Keeping your seat apart in the cold clouds?
Fitting, was it, that a mortal archer
1080 Wound an immortal? That a blade let slip
Should be restored to Turnus, and new force
Accrue to a beaten man? Without your help
What could Juturna do? Come now, at last
Have done, and heed our pleading, and give way.
1085 Let yourself no longer be consumed
Without relief by all that inward burning;
Let care and trouble not forever come to me
From your sweet lips. The finish is at hand.
You had the power to harry men of Troy
1090 By land and sea, to light the fires of war
Beyond belief, to scar a family
With mourning before marriage. I forbid
Your going further."
                                So spoke Jupiter,
1095 And with a downcast look Juno replied:

"Because I know that is your will indeed,
Great Jupiter, I left the earth below,
Though sore at heart, and left the side of Turnus.
Were it not so, you would not see me here
1100 Suffering all that passes, here alone,
Resting on air. I should be armed in flames
At the very battle-line, dragging the Trojans
Into a deadly action. I persuaded
Juturna—I confess—to help her brother
1105 In his hard lot, and I approved her daring
Greater difficulties to save his life,
But not that she should fight with bow and arrow.
This I swear by Styx' great fountainhead
Inexorable, which high gods hold in awe.
1110 I yield now and for all my hatred leave
This battlefield. But one thing not retained
By fate I beg for Latium, for the future
Greatness of your kin: when presently

Lines 796–821

They crown peace with a happy wedding day—
1115 So let it be—and merge their laws and treaties,
Never command the land's own Latin folk
To change their old name, to become new Trojans,
Known as Teucrians; never make them alter
Dialect or dress. Let Latium be.
1120 Let there be Alban kings for generations,
And let Italian valor be the strength
Of Rome in after times. Once and for all
Troy fell, and with her name let her lie fallen."

The author of men and of the world replied
1125 With a half-smile:
                    "Sister of Jupiter
Indeed you are, and Saturn's other child,
To feel such anger, stormy in your breast.
But come, no need; put down this fit of rage.
1130 I grant your wish. I yield, I am won over
Willingly. Ausonian folk will keep
Their fathers' language and their way of life,
And, that being so, their name. The Teucrians
Will mingle and be submerged, incorporated.
1135 Rituals and observances of theirs
I'll add, but make them Latin, one in speech.
The race to come, mixed with Ausonian blood,
Will outdo men and gods in its devotion,
You shall see—and no nation on earth
1140 Will honor and worship you so faithfully."

To all this Juno nodded in assent
And, gladdened by his promise, changed her mind.
Then she withdrew from sky and cloud.
                                      That done,
1145 The Father set about a second plan—
To take Juturna from her warring brother.
Stories are told of twin fiends, called the Dirae,
Whom, with Hell's Megaera, deep Night bore
In one birth. She entwined their heads with coils
1150 Of snakes and gave them wings to race the wind.

Before Jove's throne, a step from the cruel king,
These twins attend him and give piercing fear
To ill mankind, when he who rules the gods
Deals out appalling death and pestilence,
Or war to terrify our wicked cities.
Jove now dispatched one of these, swift from heaven,
Bidding her be an omen to Juturna.
Down she flew, in a whirlwind borne to earth,
Just like an arrow driven through a cloud
From a taut string, an arrow armed with gall
Of deadly poison, shot by a Parthian—
A Parthian or a Cretan—for a wound
Immedicable; whizzing unforeseen
It goes through racing shadows: so the spawn
Of Night went diving downward to the earth.

On seeing Trojan troops drawn up in face
Of Turnus' army, she took on at once
The shape of that small bird that perches late
At night on tombs or desolate roof-tops
And troubles darkness with a gruesome song.
Shrunk to that form, the fiend in Turnus' face
Went screeching, flitting, flitting to and fro
And beating with her wings against his shield.
Unstrung by numbness, faint and strange, he felt
His hackles rise, his voice choke in his throat.
As for Juturna, when she knew the wings,
The shriek to be the fiend's, she tore her hair,
Despairing, then she fell upon her cheeks
With nails, upon her breast with clenched hands.

"Turnus, how can your sister help you now?
What action is still open to me, soldierly
Though I have been? Can I by any skill
Hold daylight for you? Can I meet and turn
This deathliness away? Now I withdraw,
Now leave this war. Indecent birds, I fear you;
Spare me your terror. Whip-lash of your wings
I recognize, that ghastly sound, and guess

1155
1160
1165
1170
1175
1180
1185

Lines 849–877

Great-hearted Jupiter's high cruel commands.
Returns for my virginity, are they?
He gave me life eternal—to what end?
Why has mortality been taken from me?
Now beyond question I could put a term
To all my pain, and go with my poor brother
Into the darkness, his companion there.
Never to die? Will any brook of mine
Without you, brother, still be sweet to me?
If only earth's abyss were wide enough
To take me downward, goddess though I am,
To join the shades below!"

                              So she lamented,
Then with a long sigh, covering up her head
In her grey mantle, sank to the river's depth.

Aeneas moved against his enemy
And shook his heavy pine-tree spear. He called
From his hot heart:

                    "Rearmed now, why so slow?
Why, even now, fall back? The contest here
Is not a race, but fighting to the death
With spear and sword. Take on all shapes there are,
Summon up all your nerve and skill, choose any
Footing, fly among the stars, or hide
In caverned earth—"

                    The other shook his head,
Saying:

        "I do not fear your taunting fury,
Arrogant prince. It is the gods I fear
And Jove my enemy."

                    He said no more,
But looked around him. Then he saw a stone,
Enormous, ancient, set up there to prevent
Landowners' quarrels. Even a dozen picked men
Such as the earth produces in our day
Could barely lift and shoulder it. He swooped
And wrenched it free, in one hand, then rose up
To his heroic height, ran a few steps,

Lines 877–902

And tried to hurl the stone against his foe—
But as he bent and as he ran
And as he hefted and propelled the weight
He did not know himself. His knees gave way,
1230   His blood ran cold and froze. The stone itself,
Tumbling through space, fell short and had no impact.

Just as in dreams when the night-swoon of sleep
Weighs on our eyes, it seems we try in vain
To keep on running, try with all our might,
1235   But in the midst of effort faint and fail;
Our tongue is powerless, familiar strength
Will not hold up our body, not a sound
Or word will come: just so with Turnus now:
However bravely he made shift to fight
1240   The immortal fiend blocked and frustrated him.
Flurrying images passed through his mind.
He gazed at the Rutulians, and beyond them,
Gazed at the city, hesitant, in dread.
He trembled now before the poised spear-shaft
1245   And saw no way to escape; he had no force
With which to close, or reach his foe, no chariot
And no sign of the charioteer, his sister.
At a dead loss he stood. Aeneas made
His deadly spear flash in the sun and aimed it,
1250   Narrowing his eyes for a lucky hit.
Then, distant still, he put his body's might
Into the cast. Never a stone that soared
From a wall-battering catapult went humming
Loud as this, nor with so great a crack
1255   Burst ever a bolt of lightning. It flew on
Like a black whirlwind bringing devastation,
Pierced with a crash the rim of sevenfold shield,
Cleared the cuirass' edge, and passed clean through
The middle of Turnus' thigh. Force of the blow
1260   Brought the huge man to earth, his knees buckling,
And a groan swept the Rutulians as they rose,
A groan heard echoing on all sides from all
The mountain range, and echoed by the forests.

Lines 902–929

The man brought down, brought low, lifted his eyes
1265 And held his right hand out to make his plea:

"Clearly I earned this, and I ask no quarter.
Make the most of your good fortune here.
If you can feel a father's grief—and you, too,
Had such a father in Anchises—then
1270 Let me bespeak your mercy for old age
In Daunus, and return me, or my body,
Stripped, if you will, of life, to my own kin.
You have defeated me. The Ausonians
Have seen me in defeat, spreading my hands
1275 Lavinia is your bride. But go no further
Out of hatred."
              Fierce under arms, Aeneas
Looked to and fro, and towered, and stayed his hand
Upon the sword-hilt. Moment by moment now
1280 What Turnus said began to bring him round
From indecision. Then to his glance appeared
The accurst swordbelt surmounting Turnus' shoulder,
Shining with its familiar studs—the strap
Young Pallas wore when Turnus wounded him
1285 And left him dead upon the field; now Turnus
Bore that enemy token on his shoulder—
Enemy still. For when the sight came home to him,
Aeneas raged at the relic of his anguish
Worn by this man as trophy. Blazing up
1290 And terrible in his anger, he called out:

"You in your plunder, torn from one of mine,
Shall I be robbed of you? This wound will come
From Pallas: Pallas makes this offering
And from your criminal blood exacts his due."

1295 He sank his blade in fury in Turnus' chest.
Then all the body slackened in death's chill,
And with a groan for that indignity
His spirit fled into the gloom below.

Lines 930–952

POSTSCRIPT

I

There once was a Troy, or Ilium, a walled city given over to fire and sword around 1250 B.C. You can see the fortress mass of stonework, unearthed during the last century, a few miles inland south of the Hellespont, looking west toward Tenedos and the Aegean. But the Troy of Homer was far less historical than mythical. Composing in Greek around 750 B.C., he imagined a heroic world drawn from the storytellers who preceded him and elaborated it in his *Iliad* and *Odyssey*. The Greeks were spellbound, and so later were the Romans. Composing in Latin in the decade after 29 B.C., Virgil chose the mythical age of Homer as the setting of his narrative.

Those were early days indeed, and there had been days earlier still, at the limit of Greco-Roman memory or reference, when the ancestors of Homer's heroes lived their primordial and shadowy lives near the gods. The god Atlas, both titanic personage and snow-covered mountain, had a daughter named Electra, beloved of the sky-god, Zeus, the Roman Jupiter. Their sons were Dardanus and Iasius. From the western land later known as Italy Dardanus journeyed to Asia Minor and founded Dardania.

Dardanus espoused a daughter of a neighboring king, Teucer, and begot Erichthonius. Erichthonius begot Tros, whence the name Troy. Tros had three sons, Assaracus, Ilus (whence Ilium), and Ganymede. Assaracus begot Capys, who begot Anchises. Ilus begot Laömedon, who begot Priam. In the royal house of Troy, accordingly, Anchises and Priam were second cousins. Their sons, respectively Aeneas and Hector, were cousins once further removed. Anchises had had the privilege of lying with the goddess Venus, who bore him Aeneas. Aeneas married Creusa, a sister of Hector.

In Book XX of *The Iliad*, Aeneas faces Achilles in single combat and acquits himself well but not so well as to quiet the fears of the sea-god, Poseidon, who proposes to save him, saying to the other gods:

". . . Come now, we ourselves
may take him out of danger, and make sure
that Zeus shall not be angered by his death
at Achilles' hands. His fate is to escape
to ensure that the great line of Dardanus
may not unseeded perish from the world.
For Zeus cared more for Dardanus, of all
the sons he had by women, and now Zeus
has turned against the family of Priam.
Therefore Aeneas and his sons, and theirs,
will be lords over Trojans born hereafter."

According to this, Aeneas will escape not only the sword of Achilles—as he
does when Poseidon spirits him off to another part of the field—but the
doom already known to impend for Troy and the family of Priam. We hear
further that not all Trojans will be killed or enslaved when the city falls but
that there will be survivors, and Trojans "born hereafter," over whom Aeneas
and his sons (the plural is worth noting) will be lords. Here is the germ of
The Aeneid.

II

In post-Homeric storytelling the prophecy of Poseidon would be borne out
with respect to the survival of Aeneas, a datum undisputed in otherwise
differing versions. Perhaps Homer's authority prevailed to this extent, his
poem foretold this much of the truth. The possibility of foreknowledge and
accurate prophecy enthralled the ancient mind. So did its logical corollary,
the notion of fate and fated events. It is not too much to say that *The Aeneid*
is charged with notions of fate and instances of prophecy.

On his way back from Greece, where he had become ill, Virgil died at
Brundisium in 19 B.C. with his work unfinished. He had hoped to spend
three more years on his poem and then to devote himself to philosophy. If
this were not known we might have guessed it. *Felix qui potuit rerum cognos-
cere causas* he had once written, and meant it, though perhaps with a shade
of irony, of his predecessor, the atomist Lucretius: "Happy the man who has
learned the causes of things." Things known and felt by Virgil in his lifetime
included extremes of experience almost as great as those of our own century.
His mind certainly dwelt on the possible causes, or what later thinkers would
call a Sufficient Cause, of those extremes. Seen from the outside, as it were,
are events as unalterably fixed beforehand as they are in retrospect? If so, or
nearly so, by what power, and to what end?

Virgil gave his poem the Greek title *Ainêis*, thus expressly invoking, as with his prior *Eclogues* and *Georgics*, the older poetry, the parent poetry, of Greece. He re-created a Homeric hero in the Homeric age; he also deliberately echoed Homer in many details of narrative, in many conventions and features of style. But his purpose was totally un-Homeric and drastically original: to enfold in the mythical action of *The Aeneid* foreshadowings and direct foretellings of Roman history, more than a thousand years of it between Aeneas and his own time. Most of all, the apparent Homeric pastiche, the ancient story, was to refer at times explicitly but more often by analogy to the latter centuries of that history, to the immediate past and present, and to such hopes and fears for the future as the record might suggest.

III

In the plain of Latium the city-state of Rome on the Tiber, a Latin-speaking community of farmers, first ruled by kings including some Etruscans, became a republic at the end of the sixth century B.C. The assembled people entrusted the *imperium* or high command to two annually elected consuls and maintained a senate or council of elders. Roman history for three centuries thereafter consisted of an internal struggle between the classes, patricians and plebeians, and of wars by which Roman authority bit by bit took over central Italy from Sabines, Etruscans, Volscians, Oscans, Umbrians, and other tribes; then southern Italy from Samnites and Lucanians. The Romans built roads and founded colonies, incorporated the conquered as citizens or allies, attracted neighboring peoples to Latin culture and the ceremonious Roman law. By the middle of the third century B.C. all Italy was in effect Roman and a world power with trading interests east and west in the Mediterranean.

By that time Romans had begun learning Greek from the Greek colonies in South Italy, at Cumae, Naples, Tarentum, and elsewhere. Romans crossed the Adriatic on errands of peace and war. In due course they conquered the Greeks and were conquered in their turn by Greek literature, philosophy, and art. And they grew fond, no one quite knows why, of tracing their origin to the emigration of surviving Trojans under Aeneas. Certainly the Aeneas legend had been Italian property for a long time; Etruscan craftsmen in the sixth century liked the image of Anchises riding on Aeneas' shoulders. If the first Etruscans had emigrated to Italy, as Herodotus believed, from Lydia or Maeonia, a region south of the Troad, who should say that the Trojans had not made a similar trek to Hesperia, the western land? What, after all, had become of the Trojans? The Roman clan of the Julii went so far as to claim as ancestors Aeneas and his divine mother.

A hundred sea-miles southwest of Sicily a harbor-site on a projecting spur of North Africa, long since colonized by Phoenicians from Tyre, had become the seagoing power of Carthage, dominant in the western sea, in Sicily, Sardinia, Corsica, and Spain. Now for a century and more the first and second Punic Wars between Rome and Carthage tested Roman stamina and strategy to the utmost. The Romans had to build ships, learn to handle them, and do battle with Carthaginian fleets. They won an early victory at Mylae but endured great reverses and wrecks at sea before driving the enemy from Sicily, which they made the first Roman province outside Italy.

In the second war the Carthaginian general Hannibal, marching from Spain, crossed with his African elephants the western Alps and invaded Italy. He crushed Roman armies in great battles, but though he remained to devastate Italy with his army for fifteen years he could not conquer Rome. Her leaders met the challenge. The consul Fabius Cunctator wore Hannibal down by harassment and delay, avoiding a pitched battle, and Scipio Africanus, a gifted general, finally defeated him at Zama in Africa. In the following years the testy Roman statesman Cato made *Carthago delenda est,* "Carthage must be destroyed," his refrain in the Senate, acted upon in the end when another Scipio in a third Punic War besieged, fired, and razed Carthage in 146 B.C.

All of this, and a great deal more, came to the mind of the Roman reader or listener as Virgil in his exordium told of the Tyrian settlement dear to Juno, implacable enemy of the Trojans, just as Carthage in days to come would be, year after year for many, the most dangerous enemy of Rome. The adventure of Aeneas and his people as guests of the Carthaginian queen would seem to the Roman reader as narrow an escape as that of Rome when beset by Carthage. Dido indeed in her final curse called for future strife without quarter between her descendants and those of Aeneas and prayed for one Carthaginian in particular, *aliquis ultor,* "someone to avenge me." At this the Roman reader murmured "Hannibal."

So far as we can see, there are no comparable historical resonances in the Homeric poems; this dimension of meaning is entirely Virgilian. And it is enriched by literary echoes that no educated Roman ear could miss. Concentrated in the role of Dido, for example, are those feminine distractions of Odysseus, Calypso, Circe, and the princess of Phaeacia. Virgil's simile introducing Dido is almost identical with Homer's simile introducing Nausicaa. Dido then takes the part of Nausicaa's father in welcoming and feasting the stranger and inviting him to tell his tale.

IV

Homer's greatest display of virtuosity, it may well be, lay in handing over to his hero his own job, his art as *aoidos* or singer of tales, for 2,232 lines, a good sixth of *The Odyssey,* Books IX through XII of his twenty-four. Virgil followed suit, giving to Aeneas' tale about the same proportionate length but placing it earlier, in Books II and III of his twelve. As a hero, Aeneas has not always had a good press in modern times, but it would be hard to deny the power lent him by Virgil as a narrator of Troy's fall. In *The Confessions,* Saint Augustine reproached himself for overlooking his own *errores* when young in favor of the romantic but fictive wanderings of Aeneas, *Aeneae nescio cuius,* "some Aeneas or other." Reading this in Augustine's passionate Latin when I was seven years out of college, I exhumed my Virgil, read Aeneas' tale, and perceived for the first time that those pages down which I had clambered from construction to construction as a toiling schoolboy were in fact a masterpiece of narrative art.

Beginning with Aeneas' first lines in Book II, like long and shuddering bell-notes on the gay banquet scene, the story moves from memory to memory in a steady progression of effect. Aeneas' account of Sinon's performance has the qualities of a big scene in a play—a Greek play, complete with at least one daring touch of dramatic irony. And the attitude of the narrator is that of an honest Roman before his time: grim wonderment at Greek trickery, with a sense that the Greeks are too clever by half, too brazenly good at histrionics and dissimulation.

But here Aeneas' tale itself is dramatic and could hardly be more so: first the parley, touch and go, of the Trojans; the misread omen of the sea serpents and Laöcoön; the clang of arms inside the wooden horse, four times jarred to a halt on the city threshold; the festal celebration and repose of the Trojans; the tremendous night through which the Greek fleet glides . . . ; Aeneas' dream of the ravaged Hector; the glare and seething of the fires; the tumult and fighting in the streets; the giant glittering figure of Achilles' son, Neoptolemus or Pyrrhus, breaking through into the palace where terrified women wail and cling . . .

It has been said that in the rhythm of Virgil's composition scenes of intensity or violence are succeeded and relieved by quieter scenes. That is to take the matter hind-side before. Time and again throughout *The Aeneid* we see a repetition of the very first pattern in Book I, when a sunlit scene, a squadron happily under sail, provokes Juno to send, through Aeolus, her wild hurricane. Refuge and welcome at Carthage bring on Dido's deathly passion and Aeneas' reenactment of Troy's ruin. In Book III a promise of settlement in Thrace turns to horror at Polydorus; fresh Creteward sailing, in hope stirred by the oracle at Delos, brings the Trojans to famine and plague; the windfall of beef and goat-flesh in the Strophades is befouled by the Harpies . . . In Book V, successful games, peaceful hilarities, trained horsemanship proudly on display—all this has its climax in disaster when the Trojan women fire the ships. This is the rhythm of composition in *The Aeneid,* and in the second half of the poem episodes that are literally hellish make it bitter indeed.

v

The composer of *The Aeneid,* following his Homeric models, surely planned no falling off but rather a progressive heightening of interest from middle to end of his poem. He says as much himself at the opening of Book VII:

> A greater history opens before my eyes,
> A greater task awaits me . .

Among other misfortunes, *The Aeneid* has had to suffer from a relative neglect in the schoolroom and elsewhere of Books VII through XII in favor of I through VI, with special attention to II and IV—the two books, for example, chosen by the Earl of Surrey in the sixteenth century for translation into the first English blank verse. It could be said, and has been, that this is faulty composition. It might seem less so if we could, even for an instant, put ourselves in Virgil's phantom shoes. In this half of *The Aeneid*—and it really begins with Anchises' review of Roman souls in Book VI—the poet was on home ground, his action at last ranging along the river and in the countrysides that he cared for, north, east, and south, among places named and folklore handed down by the fabulists and annalists of Rome. But during his century this land of Italy, this vital culture, defended and built up by the fortitude and political enterprise of generations, had been torn by civil wars between big armies, conducted not only on the peninsula but from Spain to Thessaly over the breadth of the Roman world.

The very success of the Romans in holding and unifying Italy, creating in effect a nation out of a city-state, had brought expanded Roman power too quickly to the conquest of the whole Mediterranean basin. Provinces—and magistracies—were organized in one conquered territory after another, Sicily, Spain, Africa, Macedonia, Asia, Narbonese Gaul, Cilicia, Bithynia, Cyrene, Crete, Syria, Cyprus, finally Gaul, and in too many cases Roman officers and tax gatherers plundered these countries for the enrichment of the capital and themselves. At the same time, sophistication, intrigue, and venality weakened the old Roman virtues of patriotism and probity, on which, at least in the later Roman view, the old institutions of the Republic depended. Those institutions, overburdened in any case, more and more often refused to work.

Powerful men, inflamed by ambition and arrogance, manipulated parties in assemblies and Senate for consulships and military commands. Gaius Marius broke the invading hordes of Cimbri and Teutones in North Italy, but under him a citizens' army in which it had been a privilege to serve the state became a professional army loyal to its general. Lucius Cornelius Sulla led such an army for the first time into Rome itself to claim a command that had been denied him. Later after two years of civil war he became dictator and resorted to proscription, setting up lists of enemies in the thousands whom it was then lawful to kill without trial. Murderers and informers flourished. Romans had endured this much before Virgil was born in 70 B.C. There would be more.

Statesmanship and generalship were now too often the same thing; if you could not command troops, it almost seems, you stayed out of politics. After Marius and Sulla came greater examples: Gnaeus Pompeius, Marcus Licinius Crassus, and Gaius Julius Caesar, who in 60 B.C. formed the first triumvirate to share consular and military power. Crassus had defeated the big slave insurrection led by Spartacus, Pompey had swept the Mediterranean of pirates and triumphed in the East. By their consent Caesar as proconsul for ten years carried out the campaigns that subdued the Gauls in France and Belgium and made Rome's presence felt in Britain and beyond the Rhine. But Crassus lost his life when defeated by the Parthians, and Pompey, estranged after the death of his wife, Caesar's daughter Julia, joined Caesar's enemies at Rome. Caesar chose to lead his formidable legions from Gaul into Italy at the river Rubicon in 49 B.C. and thus to initiate the Civil War. In Book VI of *The Aeneid* Anchises beholds these two among the shades:

> What war, what grief, will they provoke between them—
> Battle lines and bloodshed—as the father
> Marches from the Alpine ramparts, down
> From Monaco's walled height, and the son-in-law,
> Drawn up with armies of the East, awaits him.
> Sons, refrain!

The next year Caesar brought Pompey to battle and routed him at Pharsalus in Thessaly, proceeding to Egypt, where he had Cleopatra as mistress; then he moved with his usual velocity to other victories in Syria, North Africa, and Spain. As dictator this versatile genius ruled and reorganized the Roman world, but barely for four years before Brutus and Cassius on behalf of the old republican order killed him in the Senate house. Plutarch and Shakespeare, each in his day, would tell or stage the story

The old order and republican rule could stave off only briefly the next round between the party of the tyrannicides and the Caesarians, followers and emulators of Julius: his lieutenants, Marcus Antonius and Marcus Aemilius Lepidus, good soldiers both, and his twenty-year-old grandnephew and adopted son and heir, Gaius Julius Caesar Octavianus. In 43 these three contrived official appointment as a second triumvirate. The tyrannicides were outlawed. The *triumviri* proscribed their enemies as Sulla had done. In 42 Julius was formally deified. In the same year Brutus and Cassius, defeated by Antony at Philippi, took their own lives. The victor, married to Octavian's sister Octavia and allotted the East, took Cleopatra as mistress and year by year made himself more openly monarch of Egypt. Meanwhile Octavian outmaneuvered Lepidus and forced him to retire, thus gaining sole power in the West. Antony finally divorced Octavia and declared Cleopatra's son by Caesar the future ruler of the Roman provinces in the East. At Rome this at long last brought a declaration of war against Cleopatra. She and Antony, with her Egyptian fleet and his Roman and Hellenistic army, met Octavian's host by sea at Actium on the eastern shore of the Adriatic and were decisively defeated in 31 B.C. Within a year Antony committed suicide and Octavian entered Alexandria. At thirty-three he held the reins of power over Rome and her dominions.

Octavian had many gifts, including one perhaps denied his great foster father: along with a sense of what the time demanded, a keen sense of how far, and at what pace, he could go. He appears to have been cool, immensely capable, assiduous, and farsighted. As head of state, he had what we call vision, and to his taste and patronage in literature we owe some of the best poetry ever written. He is beyond doubt one of the principal shapers of the world we still inhabit. Making use of inherited political and legal forms that had in fact grown corrupt and undependable, he called himself *princeps*, roughly "first citizen," to placate the old Roman sentiment against kings. His triumph did not obscure for him the poor condition of Italy, her people in city and countryside worn out by a century of fear, discord, and conflict, by the marches and quarterings of armies. Regions of once productive farmland were deserted or handed over to discharged veterans ill-suited to work them. Impoverished countrymen had joined a proletariat housed in tenements in the cities. Long before Actium, Octavian may well have put his mind on the establishment of peace and the reform of Roman life. Like the strong men before him, he had an assisting circle or entourage, in this case a credit to his judgment of men. One member of it was the poet Virgil

VI

Publius was his given name, Vergilius that of his clan, Maro that of his family, and he was a Northerner, perhaps as much Celtic as Italian or Etruscan, born in a rural small town near Mantua. His father owned a farm. Men of this region did not acquire Roman citizenship until Julius Caesar accorded it, in 49 B.C., when the poet was in his twenty-first year. By that time Virgil had studied at provincial private schools in Cremona and Mediolanum (Milan) and finally at Rome. His schooling trained him in Greek and Latin. The pupil with a stylus made his letters on a wax tablet which could then be smoothed. He listened to the teacher's lesson and read or recited his exercise aloud. He wore the Roman *tunica*, a sleeved shirt reaching the knees, and after his fifteenth year the Roman *toga*, a white woolen full-length robe, passed over the left shoulder, brought from behind under the right arm, and then thrown again over the left shoulder. Trousers were Gaulish, therefore outlandish, and were worn only by legionaries in wintry regions. One could wear a hood, or cover one's head with a fold of robe.

At Rome Virgil studied rhetoric, the construction and delivery of speeches, a part of the education of young Romans for public affairs. When Drances and Turnus debate before the Laurentine Senate, when Venus and Juno debate before Jupiter, their creator is drawing upon such rhetoric, though no doubt these and all the speeches in *The Aeneid* owe more to the poetic precedents in Greek theater. At Rome, also, Virgil became a friend of Gaius Asinius Pollio, an honorable politician and a gifted literary man who had known Catullus and shared with him—as now with Virgil—an admiration for the polished Alexandrian Greek poets, whose famous dictum that a big book is a big headache their Mantuan admirer had it in him eventually to flout. Tall and dark-haired, with a dark complexion, Virgil retained in Rome a shy and countryfied air. He had a fine reading voice. He was not robust.

During the Civil War, Virgil retired from the fever of the capital to Naples and the study of philosophy with an Epicurean, Siro. After the *triumviri* triumphed at Philippi, among Italian lands confiscated and given to veterans by Octavian was the poet's patrimony near Mantua. Octavian, to whom his trusted friend Maecenas introduced Virgil, may later have restored this land, as Virgil's *Eclogue I* suggests.

The works by which Virgil's art first became known to others besides his immediate friends were the ten brief *Eclogues*, "Selections," on which he probably worked from 45 to 37 B.C. Imitating the Greek Theocritus often but almost as often no one at all, these pastoral inventions charmed Roman ears. Maecenas encouraged him to a larger enterprise, that of the *Georgics* in four books on the labors and beauties of husbandry, composed between 36 and 29 B.C. and read to Octavian in the latter year on his return to Italy from Egypt. Octavian heard among others the following lines:

> Let not this young man fail to rescue us,
> To rescue the torn world! . . . So many wars,
> So many kinds of wickedness! No honor
> Rendered the plow, but the fields gone to ruin,
> Countryfolk made homeless, and their scythes
> Beaten to straight swords on the blowing forge!
> War from the Euphrates to Germany,
> Ruptured engagements, violence of nations,
> Impious Mars raging the whole world over . . .

For so, no doubt, it still seemed before the finality of Actium and the difference between Octavian and the dictators who preceded him had been fully realized. Virgil had already, however, meditated a poem on Octavian, either an annalistic poem or one curiously figured in Book III of the *Georgics* as an elaborate temple wherein the conqueror would be enshrined among pictured triumphs. This plan underwent a true metamorphosis. Soon after Octavian accepted from the Senate the title of "Augustus" (we might say "The Blest") in 27 B.C. Virgil had freed his imagination for his mythical story of Aeneas, not precisely—and certainly not overtly—a poem on Octavian, but one that dramatized, on an ancient stage, toils and choices as difficult as his and sometimes analogous.

Achilles and Odysseus in Homer were not without communities. The cause of the Achaeans engaged Achilles when it suited him, Odysseus tried to bring his shipmates home and, once there, surgically removed a threat to his island folk and family. But Virgil's hero, Aeneas, had to bring the surviving people of Troy by sea to the unknown land of Italy and to settle them there, united with an indigenous race, to undertake what would be the world-governing task of Rome. The man whom Virgil imagined had to orient himself, as we say, and to go through tests and temperings. His heroism was by no means flawless. *Il débute par un évanouissement*, as Sainte-Beuve put it, when the storm at sea makes him shake and despair. We are embarrassed for him when he shirks his interview with Dido and tries to deny to her the obvious truth. But his *pietas*, responsible care for his father and son and his people, with their household gods and greater gods, distinguishes him in the mind of his creator from the start.

Aeneas is the son of a goddess and gets a great deal of supernatural attention, good and bad. On the last night of Troy the shades of Hector and Creusa appear to him with their strange admonitions. His divine mother in majesty recalls him to his duty. Promissory tongues of divine fire lave the brow of his young son. When he literally does not know where to go at sea, the oracle at Delos tells him; then the Larës and Penatës, Troy's figurine gods of Hearth and Larder, tell him more precisely. Helenus, the old Trojan warrior and seer at Buthrotum, gives him sailing directions and advice on consulting the Sibyl. At Carthage, Mercury makes two eerie appearances with commands from Jove. In Sicily the shade of Anchises urges him onward. His greatest privilege, shared with godlike heroes of the past, is to pluck the golden bough and visit in trance the world of the dead and the still unborn, where his father's shade passes in review for him the souls of Roman worthies in centuries to come. His confidence, his grasp of his mission, cannot fail to be confirmed by all this portentous experience.

Now see him in Book VII leaving behind the nocturnal magic of the Old World for the virgin forests of the New, sailing past Circe's island by night to head in for Tiber mouth in the morning, like our first explorers at the mouth of the Hudson or the James. All seems auspicious here at first in a land at peace recalling the Saturnian peace of old, and the king, Latinus, is disposed by local portent and oracle to welcome the newcomers. Here are the new Latin traditions, effigies, and names: Italus, Sabinus, Janus, Picus, semi-divine figures of woodland and vineyard. The elated Trojans break ground for the walls of a settlement. Only look upward, though.

Often it must have occurred to men that the forces ruling their affairs from above—or below—are not merely punitive or angry but malevolent on a grand scale. It has occurred to us amid the exterminations and abysses of our century. It must have occurred to the Romans during the terrors and massacres of the first century B.C. Juno in *The Aeneid* answers to this nauseating sense of things. The storm at sea in Book I was nothing compared with what she now engineers in Book VII, calling up from hell her hideous Fury to madden Queen Amata and Prince Turnus and to provoke a fray between Italians and Trojans. In a ritual well known to Romans of Virgil's day, the goddess herself pushes open the closed gates of war. Now the Homeric Muses are invoked and there is a big Iliadic passage as the detachments of the home army from their differing regions pass in review, concluding with the splendid figures of Turnus, commander of Rutulians, and Camilla, the Volscian amazon.

Book VIII opens with one of Virgil's tender natural scenes, another hopeful time, as Father Tiber, hoary and magical in a dream vision, comes to Aeneas with reassurances, and selected ships go upstream under oars to the Arcadian realm of Pallanteum. Where one day the imperial city will stand, Aeneas finds hospitality among the penurious and humble huts of origin. His diplomatic mission has good fortune. Not only will King Evander entrust his horsemen and his only son to Aeneas' cause, but he will also mount a troop of Trojans to ride with them into Etruria for alliance with Tarchon's

Etruscans, already under arms. Thunder and flashing armor amid the clouds announce to Aeneas his mother's intervention. The book ends with a description of the divine armor that Vulcan has made for him at her request, especially the shield with scenes from Roman history, and the centerpiece picturing the vast sea-fight at Actium. But now with Book IX war as martial magnificence gives way to essential war, war as combat and slaughter.

I first read through all twelve books of *The Aeneid* in my Oxford Classical Text in the spring, summer, and early fall of 1945, the closing months of the Second Great War, when I was stationed on an island in the western Pacific. Living and working in commodious Quonset huts on neat coral driveways amid palms regularly treated by DDT sprayed from a slow biplane, staff officers had little to suffer but boredom off duty, and Virgil remedied that for me. Our navy's Actium had been fought long before at Midway. But the last island fighting continued, first at Iwo, then on Okinawa, where kamikaze season got into full swing. There we were on our island in our fresh khakis, laundered and pressed, the little bars gleaming on our collars and caps, saluting the old admiral with his snowy Roman head and the urbane operations officer who held in his crystal mind the location, course, destination, and speed of every least landing craft over thousands of miles. The scene could not have been more imperial or more civilized. APO mail from the States came fast. We played tennis, skipped rope, and worked out on the heavy bag. At night at my neat desk in the B.O.Q. I read Virgil by the light of a good lamp. I heard young submarine skippers, the finest Annapolis products, give their lighthearted accounts of shelling poor junks to smithereens in the China Sea. Meanwhile, offshore of the big Japanese island to the north, picket ships were having their prows or upperworks and the men who manned them smashed into flaming junk by Japanese fighters aflame; ashore, men with flamethrowers were doing what I had heard a briefing officer in San Francisco, with an insane giggle, refer to as "popping Japs"; and a good many young and brave of both sides were tasting the agony and abomination that the whole show came down to, in fact existed for. The next landings would be on Honshu, and I would be there. More than literary interest, I think, kept me reading Virgil's descriptions of desperate battle, funeral pyres, failed hopes of truce or peace.

More than literary interest surely moved the first Roman readers of these books of *The Aeneid,* for war, the Roman specialty, had within their memories gone fratricidal and got out of hand. If Virgil intended, as he almost certainly did, an analogy between the task of Aeneas and that of Augustus, the hardest and hugest part for both was waging war to end war, to work out settlements so magnanimous as to challenge no more strife but to promote *concordia* and the arts of peace. This is the meaning of Aeneas' promis in Book XII:

> I shall not make Italians underlings
> To Trojans. For myself I ask no kingdom . . .

—just as Augustus, after defeating his flamboyant Turnus, Antony, had asked for himself no kingship or dictatorship, and (possibly bearing *The Aeneid* in mind) he never did.

One thing is poised against another, however. Take the matter of mercy, *clementia.* Augustus prided himself on showing it as *princeps,* but in his early days he had been capable of great cruelty. Aeneas is eloquent in his expression of *clementia* to the Latin emissaries in Book XI, but at the very end of the poem he cannot help his murderous anger and, though appealed to in the name of his father, kills the suppliant Turnus.

Take the matter of cities. City founding, city building, completed or aborted, and the siege, defense, and destruction of cities: these are recurrent themes in *The Aeneid.* Now and then Trojan enemies recall the dishonesty of Priam's father, Laömedon, who had cheated Apollo and Neptune of their fee for building the massive walls of Troy. Thereupon a sea-monster sent by Neptune plagued the city until the superman, Hercules, killed it on the promise of being given Laömedon's prize horses. Defrauded in his turn, he captured Troy and sacked but did not destroy it, an event remembered by Anchises in Book II as the Greeks and the dread immortals carry out their fiery, and final, destruction. We notice that this conflagration, so fully realized that we can feel the scorching breath of it on our skin, is echoed in Book IV, when the wave of lamentation in Carthage after Dido's fatal stroke is likened to billowing fire—as though in forecast of the fire that conquering Romans centuries later will set to burn the Libyan city to the ground. And *The Aeneid* will not end until the flames of Troy and the imagined flames of Carthage are echoed again in the flames that Aeneas' torches light to enwrap the city of Laurentum. The fire's victim at Troy becomes the incendiary now.

Take, finally, the matter of Fate and those spinners thereof known to the Romans as the *Parcae.* Jupiter, father of gods and men, is privy to the fated future. Venus is not, until he discloses the drift of it to her in Book I. Juno knows it but also apparently knows that the drift of it does not exclude her own ability to twist and retard it. Vulcan remarks that though the fate of Troy was fixed, the city might have held out for another ten years. Jupiter permits Juno to prolong Turnus' life, though briefly. There is a certain amount of play in the inevitable. The free choices of the mortal and immortal actors count for something. Aeneas is free to neglect his mission or to live up to it, though he cannot change it in the long run.

VII

What was a *liber*, a book, at Rome? A roll of papyrus on which the text was inscribed in ink with a reed pen. Publication consisted of the preparation and sale—or presentation as gifts—of copies made by hand. A wealthy man would have copyists on his household staff. There were bookshops, and Augustus founded a public library on the Palatine. Books were valuable, not owned by everybody, and by our standards hard to handle and to read. Words were not set off from one another by spaces but appeared in an unbroken line. You held the scroll in your right hand and unrolled it with your left. This is what Jupiter does metaphorically for Venus in Book I, unrolling the scroll of fate, and in Book IX, line 528, the poet calls on the Muse of Epic to unroll with him, as though on a scroll, the mighty scenes of war. In the first case the text is the future; in the second it is the past.

Virgil had a prose outline and worked at pleasure on one part or another, not necessarily in sequence. He would compose and dictate lines in the morning and later revise and eliminate In early years he seems to have tried various forms, but in his prime he stuck to the hexameters of which he was a master. Many passages of this could be called, in Yeats' phrase, "ingenious, lovely things," and they are not more lovely than they are ingenious. Dryden observed, and one does, that they could embody or enact what they described or narrated. Here is one:

Intonuere poli, et crebris micat ignibus aether.

(Book I, line 90.) Thunder rolls in the first half of the line, and an electric storm crackles in the second. Here is another:

Vertitur interea caelum et ruit Oceano nox,
involvens umbra magna terramque polumque
Myrmidonumque dolos . .

(Book II, lines 250 sqq.) The density of echoing sounds conveys the density of this darkness, especially in the nine successive long vowels of the second line. The poet worked his language to make it appropriate and memorable, whether or not he did so in terms of an analysis like mine.

On his deathbed Virgil asked that his unfinished poem be destroyed. Augustus overruled this and had it "published"—i.e., edited and copied—with no improvements or additions. Incomplete lines appear here and there, and there are other lines that though complete are clearly provisional. There are also inconsistencies in the story, such as Aeneas' attribution to Anchises in Book VII of Celaeno's prophecy in Book III that famine will one day reduce the Trojans to gnawing their tables. One Trojan ship goes down in the storm in Book I, four are destroyed by fire in Book V, and at least two vanish, for the ships that ascend the Tiber to Pallanteum in Book VIII and are then dispatched downstream again to "bring Ascanius news" never do so, never reappear. On these occasions we hear nothing of the anxiety that Cybelë, the great Phrygian mother goddess, is said in Book IX to feel for the ships built of her sacred timber. It is only in IX, when Turnus threatens the remainder, that Jupiter carries out his promise to change them into sea nymphs. The size of the nymphs, incidentally, if it corresponds to the size of ships, may strike us as a bit Brobdingnagian. Finally, Turnus' lieutenant, Messapus, is named with Trojan company—Mnestheus and Asilas—in Book XII, as though the poet had momentarily forgotten in which army he belonged.

Even at our distance in time, it is easy for us to understand the poet's bitterness at not having been able to perfect his work. But we can join many past generations in gratitude to Augustus for giving us this poem. It is a unique story, freshly imagined and often masterfully told. At the core of it is respect for the human effort to build, to sustain a generous polity—against heavy odds. Mordantly and sadly it suggests what the effort may cost, how the effort may fail. But as a poem it is carried onward victoriously by its own music.

—ROBERT FITZGERALD

BRIEF GLOSSARY

ABAS (1) a Trojan leader; (2) a Greek; (3) an Etruscan

ACAMAS a Greek

ACARNANIAN of Acarnania, an area of Greece north of the Peloponnese

ACCA a companion of Camilla

ACESTA a city of western Sicily

ACESTES king of Sicily, friend of the Trojans

ACHAEANS a name for the Greeks, derived from Achaea, a region of the
   northern Peloponnese

ACHAEMENIDES a Greek rescued by Trojans from the land of Cyclops

ACHATES a Trojan, faithful friend and companion of Aeneas

ACHERON a river of the underworld

ACHILLES a Greek hero, son of Peleus and Thetis; enemy of the Trojans,
   slayer of Hector

ACOETES an Arcadian, companion of Pallas, former armor-bearer of
   Evander

ACRAGAS a city on the coast of southwest Sicily

ACRISIUS father of Danaë

ACRON a Greek exile, slain by Mezentius

ACTIUM a promontory in western Greece; site of a famous victory at sea by
   Octavian over Antony and Cleopatra (31 B.C); site of temple to
   Apollo

ACTOR (1) a Trojan; (2) an Auruncan

ADIGE a river north of the Po

ADRASTUS king of Argos, one of the seven kings who fought against
   Thebes

ADRIATIC sea on Italy's east coast

AEACIDES Greek patronymic (descendant of Aeacus father of Peleus), a
   name for (1) Achilles (2) Pyrrhus

AEAEAN of Aeaea, the island of Circe

AEGAEON a name of Briareus

AEGEAN sea on south and east coast of Greece

AENEAS son of Anchises and Venus, leader of the Trojans after the destruction of Troy

AEOLIA realm of Aeolus, home of the winds; identified by Virgil with Lipari, an island north of Sicily

AEOLUS (1) ruler of the winds; (2) name of various Trojans and Greeks, one of whom is an ancestor of Ulysses

AETNA a volcano in Sicily

AETOLIAN of Aetolia, an area of northern Greece, birthplace of Diomedes; an epithet applied to Diomedes and to Arpi, a city founded by him

AFRI a people of Africa

AGAMEMNON leader of the Greek expedition against Troy, king of Mycenae

AGATHYRSANS inhabitants of Scythia, attendants at Apollo's festival on Delos

AGENOR ancient ruler in Tyre, ancestor of Dido

AGRIPPA Marcus Vipsanius Agrippa, important friend, general and son-in-law of Augustus

AGYLLA, AGYLLINA a name of Caerë

AJAX (1) "the lesser" Ajax, son of Oïleus and a character in the *Iliad;* he raped Cassandra and was killed by Minerva, in whose temple Cassandra had sought refuge; (2) "the greater" Ajax, son of Telamon

ALBA LONGA second settlement of the Trojans in Italy, their home for three hundred years

ALBULA ancient name of the Tiber

ALBUNEA name of a grove and fountain near Lavinium

ALCANOR (1) a Trojan, father of Pandarus and Bitias; (2) a Latin, son of Phorcus

ALCIDES Greek patronymic (descendant of Alcaeus), a name for Hercules, grandson of Alcaeus

ALETES a Trojan

ALLECTO one of the Furies

ALLIA a river in Latium near the Tiber, site of a major Roman defeat by the Gauls in 390 B.C.

ALMO oldest son of Tyrrhus, brother of Silvia

ALOEUS father of the Titans Otus and Ephialtes, who waged war against Jupiter

ALPHEUS a river of the Peloponnese; in myth it is personified and pursues the nymph Arethusa underground to Sicily

ALTARS, THE reefs in the sea between Sicily and Italy

AMASENUS a river southeast of Rome

AMATA wife of Latinus, queen of Laurentum

AMATHUS a city of southern Cyprus, site of a temple to Venus

AMAZONS a race of women warriors, allies of Troy

AMOR god of love

AMPHITRYON mortal father of Hercules

AMPHRYSIAN epithet of Apollo derived from river in Thessaly near which he tended sheep for Admetus

AMSANCTUS a valley containing a sulphurous lake, near the center of Italy

AMYCLAE a city south of Rome, in Campania; traditionally referred to as "silent"

AMYCUS (1) name of several Trojans; (2) king of the Bebrycii (a people in Asia Minor); a famous boxer

ANAGNIA a city of the Hernici, southeast of Rome

ANCHEMOLUS a Latin, descendant of Rhoetus

ANCHISES father of Aeneas by Venus, son of Capys; crippled by a flash of lightning by Jupiter because he boasted of Venus' love

ANCUS Ancus Martius, fourth king of Rome

ANDROGEOS (1) a Greek slain at Troy; (2) son of Minos, killed at Athens

ANDROMACHE wife of Hector

ANGITIA a forest near Lake Fucinus

ANIO a tributary of the Tiber

ANIUS priest of Apollo, king of Delos

ANNA sister of Dido

ANTANDER a town on the opposite side of Mount Ida from Troy

ANTENOR a Trojan, founder of Patavium (modern Padua)

ANTHEUS a Trojan leader

ANTIPHATES illegitimate son of Sarpedon, ally of the Trojans

ANTONIUS Marc Antony, rival of Octavian, defeated at Actium in 31 B.C.

APOLLO son of Jupiter, brother of Diana, god of music and the lyre

APPENNINE (FATHER) personification of the Appennines, a mountain range of central Italy

APULIA a region of southeastern Italy

ARAXES a river of Armenia

ARCADIA an area of the central Peloponnese, noted for its simplicity

ARCTURUS brightest star of the constellation Boötes; its rising and setting were associated with bad weather

ARDEA city of Latium, capital of the Rutulians, home of Turnus

ARETHUSA a fountain in Sicily, into which the nymph Arethusa was changed after her pursuit by the river Alpheus

ARGOS a place name with varied referents, often used to refer to a town and region of the Peloponnese especially dear to Juno; also, a generalized name for Greece

ARGUS (1) hundred-eyed guard set over Io by Juno; (2) a guest of Evander
ARGYRIPA a name of Arpi
ARICIA (1) mother of Virbius; (2) a sacred grove in Latium
ARISBA a city in the Troad
ARPI a city of southern Italy, settled by Diomedes
ARRUNS an Etruscan, kills Camilla
ASCANIUS son of Aeneas and Creusa
ASCLEPIUS god of medicine
ASILAS (1) a Rutulian; (2) an Etruscan leader and prophet
ASSARACI two soldiers of Aeneas
ASSARACUS son of Tros, great-grandfather of Aeneas
ASTYANAX son of Hector and Andromache
ASTYR an Etruscan leader
ATHOS a mountain in northern Greece
ATINAS a Rutulian
ATLAS a Titan, son of Iapetus, father of Electra and Maia; a mountain in
    North Africa
ATRIDAE the sons of Atreus, Agamemnon and Menelaus
ATYS a young Trojan
AUFIDUS a violent river in Apulia
AUGUSTUS see Caesar
AULESTES an Etruscan leader
AULIS a seaport in Greece where the Greek fleet gathered before the Trojan
    War
AURORA the Dawn
AURUNCANS a name for the original inhabitants of Italy in Campania
AUSONIA a generalized term for Italy
AUTOMEDON a Greek, armor-bearer for Pyrrhus
AVENTINE one of the seven hills of Rome
AVENTINUS son of Hercules
AVERNUS a lake near Cumae associated with the underworld

BACCHUS god of wine (Greek Dionysus, Latin Liber)
BACTRA the capital of Bactria in Asia
BAIAE a city and resort area south of Rome near Naples; founded by
    Euboean settlers
BARCA a city and people of North Africa; Barca was the name of the family
    to which Hannibal belonged
BARCE nurse of Sychaeus
BEBRYCIAN of Bebrycia, a part of Bithnyia, a district in Asia Minor
BELLONA goddess of war and bloodshed
BELUS father of Dido, ruler of Tyre

BERECYNTHUS a mountain in Phrygia associated with the worship of Cybele

BEROE a Trojan, wife of Doryclus

BITIAS (1) a Phoenician in Dido's court; (2) a Trojan, brother of Pandarus

BOREAS the North Wind

BRIAREUS a hundred-armed giant

BRUTUS Lucius Junius Brutus, leader of the expulsion of the Tarquin kings from Rome

BUTES (1) a famous boxer slain by Dares; (2) aide to Ascanius, former armor-bearer to Anchises; (3) a Trojan warrior

BUTHROTUM a town of Chaonia

CACUS a monster, son of Vulcan, defeated by Hercules

CAECULUS ("the little blind one") an Italian leader, founder of Praeneste, eponymous founder of the Caecilian clan

CAEDICUS (1) a rich man who sent a golden belt to Remulus; (2) an Etruscan

CAENEUS (1) the maiden Caenis, changed by Neptune into a male, then changed back again at death to a female; (2) a Trojan, slain by Turnus

CAERE a city in Etruria

CAESAR (1) Gaius Julius Caesar, famous Roman statesman, general and dictator, slain in 44 B.C.; (2) Gaius Julius Caesar Octavianus Augustus, grandnephew and adopted son of Julius; first Roman emperor (27 B.C. to 14 A.D.); assumed the title Augustus in 27 B.C.

CAICUS a Trojan

CAIETA nurse of Aeneas

CALCHAS chief priest and augur of the Greek fleet at Troy

CALLIOPE Muse of epic, chief of the Muses

CALYBE an old priestess of Juno

CALYDON an ancient city in Greece ravaged by a boar sent by Diana

CAMERINA a city in southern Sicily

CAMERS a Rutulian

CAMILLA leader of the Volscians, daughter of Metabus, slain by Arruns

CAMILLUS Marcus Furius Camillus, recovered Rome from the Gauls after they had taken it in 390 B.C.

CAMPANIA an area of southern Italy on the Tyrrhenian Sea

CAPITOL the top of the Capitoline hill, site of temple to Jupiter Optimus Maximus; also, the name of the temple

CAPITOLINE one of the seven hills of Rome

CAPYS (1) a Trojan leader; (2) a king of Alba Longa

CARIANS a people from western Asia Minor

CARINAE a fashionable residential area of Rome in Virgil's time

CARMENTIS a nymph and prophetess, mother of Evander

CARPATHIAN of Carpathus, an island in the Aegean

CARTHAGE a city of North Africa, founded by Dido and the Tyrian exiles; traditional enemy of Rome

CASPIA the territory surrounding the Caspian Sea

CASSANDRA daughter of Priam; she was beloved of Apollo and endowed with prophetic skill by him, but when she failed to keep her promises to him she was punished in that no one would ever believe her prophecies

CATILINE Lucius Sergius Catilina, conspirator, defeated by Cicero in 63 B.C.

CATILLUS a Latin, founder of Tibur

CATO (1) Marcus Porcius Cato (the Elder), censor, implacably hostile to Carthage; (2) Marcus Porcius Cato Uticensis (the Younger), staunch republican, representative of old-fashioned virtue and justice

CAUCASIAN of the Caucasus, a mountain range in Asia

CAULON a city of southern Italy

CECROPS the first king of Athens

CELAENO leader of the Harpies (the name is associated with dark)

CENTAUR (1) a creature half man, half horse; (2) name of a Trojan ship

CERAUNIA a mountain chain in Epirus (Greek plural name meaning "thunder headlands")

CERBERUS a monstrous three-headed dog guarding the entrance to hell; it was one of Hercules' labors to bring this dog to the upper world

CERES goddess of grain and agriculture (Greek Demeter)

CHALCIDIANS inhabitants of Chalcis, the major city of Euboea

CHALYBIAN of the Chalybes, a people of Pontus in Asia Minor, famous for their work in iron

CHAONIA a part of Epirus

CHARON the boatman of the underworld

CHARYBDIS a monstrous whirlpool, associated with Scylla

CHIMAERA (1) a mythical monster with the head of a lion, the body of a goat, and the tail of a serpent; (2) a Trojan ship

CHLOREUS a Trojan, priest of Cybele

CIRCE a sorceress, daughter of the Sun, a figure in the *Odyssey*

CISSEUS (1) king of Thrace, father of Hecuba; (2) son of Melampus, slain by Aeneas

CITHAERON a mountain in Greece near Thebes, sacred to Bacchus

CLAUSUS a Sabine leader from Curës, eponymous ancestor of the Claudian tribe

CLOANTHUS a Trojan leader

CLOELIA a captive in the Roman war with Porsenna, escaped by swimming the Tiber

CLONIUS name of two different Trojans

CLONUS son of Eurytius, worker in metals, made the swordbelt of Pallas

CLUSIUM a famous Etruscan city

CLYTIUS (1) a Trojan, son of Aeolus; (2) of Lyrnesus, father of Acmon and Mnestheus; (3) a Rutulian, beloved of Cydon, slain by Aeneas; (4) a Trojan, father of Eunaeus

CNOSSUS ancient capital of Minos in Crete

COCLES Horatius Cocles, bridge-defending hero in the Roman war with Porsenna

COCYTUS a river of the underworld

COEUS a Titan, father of Latona

CORAS a Latin, founder of Tibur, twin brother of Catillus and brother of Tiburtus

CORINTH a city of Greece, sacked by the Romans in 146 B.C.

COROEBUS son of Mygdon, King of Phrygia, in love with Cassandra

CORYBANTES worshipers of the Great Mother goddess (Cybele); loud music and excited dances were characteristic of their worship

CORYNAEUS a name of two different Trojans

CORYTHUS (1) son of Jupiter, husband of Electra; (2) a town in Etruria founded by Corythus

COSA a famous Etruscan city

COSSUS Aulus Cornelius Cossus, one of three Romans ever to win the *spolia opima* (awarded for killing an enemy general in personal combat)

CRETE a large island in the Mediterranean south of Greece

CRETHEUS (1) a Trojan warrior and musician; (2) a Greek

CREUSA the wife of Aeneas at Troy

CRINISUS (1) father of Acestes; (2) a river in Sicily

CUMAE the abode of the Sibyl; later the first Greek colony in Italy, established by settlers from Chalcis in Euboea circa 750 B.C.

CUNERUS a Ligurian leader

CUPAVO a Ligurian, son of Cycnus

CUPENCUS a Rutulian priest

CURES capital of the Sabines

CURETES worshipers of Rhea and Jupiter, the earliest inhabitants of Crete, said to have protected the infant Jupiter (who had been hidden from Saturn on Crete) by drowning out his cries with their music

CYBELE Great Mother goddess of Phrygia, associated with Rhea in Crete

CYBELUS mountain in Crete or Phrygia, associated with Cybele

CYCLADES a group of islands in the Aegean

CYCLOPS (1) a race of one-eyed giants dwelling in Sicily; (2) name given to Vulcan's workers

CYCNUS father of Cupavo, changed into a swan while mourning his friend Phaethon

CYDON a Rutulian, son of Phorcus, lover of Clytius, saved from the wrath of Aeneas by his seven brothers

CYLLENE highest mountain in the Peloponnese, birthplace of Mercury

CYMODOCE a sea nymph

CYMOTHOE a sea nymph

CYNTHUS a ridge in Delos (island birthplace of Apollo and Diana)

CYPRUS a large island in the Mediterranean

CYTHERA an island off the south of Greece, near which Venus was born

CYTHEREA a name of Venus, from her place of worship in Cythera

DAEDALUS master craftsman, father of Icarus; he built a labyrinth for Minos of Crete; after helping Ariadne and Theseus to solve the maze, he escaped to Cumae

DAHAE a nomadic people of Scythia

DANAE daughter of Acrisius of Argos; locked in a chest and thrown into the sea by her father; she founded Ardea (home of Turnus)

DANAANS a common name for the Greeks, from Danaus

DANAUS a legendary king of Argos, who incited his fifty daughters to murder their husbands (the fifty sons of Aegyptus); all except Hypermnestra obeyed

DARDANIA (1) generalized name for Troy or the area around Troy; (2) name of a city on the Hellespont founded by Dardanus

DARDANUS son of Jupiter and Electra, son-in-law of Teucer, ancestor of the house of Priam, founder of Troy (or, in some versions of the story, the city of Dardania)

DARES a Trojan boxer, defeated by Entellus

DAUNIANS (1) inhabitants of Daunia, an area of Apulia in southern Italy; (2) the people of Daunus and Turnus; Rutulians

DAUNUS son of Pilumnus and Danaë, father of Turnus, king of Apulia

DECII an important family in Roman history

DEIOPEA a sea nymph, promised in marriage to Aeolus by Juno

DEIPHOBE name of the Sibyl

DEIPHOBUS a Trojan who married Helen after the death of Paris

DELOS an island of the Aegean, birthplace of Apollo and Diana

DEMOLEOS a Greek

DERCENNUS an ancient king of Laurentum

DIANA daughter of Jupiter, twin sister of Apollo, goddess of the moon and hunting (Greek Artemis)

DICTE mountain in Crete where Jupiter was born

DIDO queen and founder of Carthage, daughter of Belus King of Tyre, wife of Sychaeus

DIDYMAON a skilled worker in metals

DINDYMA, DINDYMUS a mountain in Phrygia close to Mount Ida, sacred to
    Cybele

DIONE mother of Venus, daughter of Ocean and Tethys

DIORES (1) a Trojan, descendant of Priam; (2) a Trojan, brother of
    Amycus (perhaps identical with 1)

DIRAE ("the dread ones") when employed by Jupiter—Allecto and
    Tisiphone, Furies, the sisters of Megaera

DIS the god of the underworld (Hades, Pluto)

DODONA a famous shrine of Jupiter near Buthrotum

DOLON a Trojan, father of Eumedes; a character in the *Iliad*, promised the
    horses of Achilles if he spied on the Greek camp, slain by Diomedes
    and Ulysses

DOLOPIANS A people of Thessaly, allies of the Greeks in the Trojan War

DONYSA an island of the Cyclades, near Delos

DOTO a Nereid

DORIANS a name for the Greeks

DRANCES a Latin leader hostile to Turnus

DREPANUM a city in northwestern Sicily

DRUSI an important family in Roman history

DRYOPES a people from northern Greece

DULICHIUM an island near Ithaca

DYMAS a Trojan

EGERIA a nymph, who instructed Numa (second king of Rome) in
    religious and ritual practices

ELBA an island in the Mediterranean between Corsica and Italy

ELEAN of Elis, an area of Greece in the northwestern Peloponnese; also,
    the name of a city

ELECTRA daughter of Atlas, sister of Maia, mother by Jupiter of Dardanus
    and Iasius

ELISSA a name of Dido

ELYSIUM a region of happiness in the underworld, to which the souls of
    the good are sent

ENCELADUS a Titan who fought against Jupiter

ENTELLUS a Sicilian boxer, defeats Dares

EPEOS a Greek, designed the wooden horse

EPIRUS a region of northern Greece on the Adriatic Sea

EPYTIDES a Trojan, bodyguard and companion of Ascanius

EPYTUS a Trojan

ERATO the Muse of love

EREBUS the underworld

ERIPHYLE wife of Amphiaraus; bribed by a necklace, she persuaded her husband to join the war against Thebes in which he was killed; she in turn was slain by her son Alcmaeon

ERULUS king of Praeneste

ERYMANTHUS a mountain in Arcadia where Hercules killed the boar which was devastating Calydon

ERYX a half-brother of Aeneas and a great boxer; after him are named a mountain and a city in northwestern Sicily

ETRURIA a region of Italy north of Latium

ETRUSCANS the people of Etruria

EUBOEAN of Euboea (Euboia), a large island off the eastern coast of Greece

EUMEDES a Trojan, son of Dolon

EUMELUS a Trojan

EUMENIDES the Furies (a Greek name, meaning literally "the kindly-minded ones," euphemistically given to the Furies to propitiate them)

EUROTAS the river on which Sparta was located

EURYALUS a Trojan, son of Opheltes, beloved of Nisus

EURYPYLUS a Greek

EURYSTHEUS king of Mycenae for whom Hercules was forced to perform twelve labors by Juno

EURYTION a Lycian ally of the Trojans, a famous archer

EVADNE wife of Capaneus (one of the seven kings who fought against Thebes); she threw herself on her husband's funeral pyre

EVANDER king of Pallanteum, father of Pallas, ally of Aeneas

FABII an important family in Roman history

FABIUS MAXIMUS Quintus Fabius Maximus Cunctator, Roman general, saved the city from Hannibal

FABRICIUS Gaius Fabricius Luscinus, a Roman general famous for his integrity

FAUNUS an Italian woodland god, son of Pilumnus, father of Latinus

FERONIA (1) a grove on the coast of Italy, south of Rome; (2) an ancient Italian goddess, mother of Erulus

FIDENAE an ancient town near Rome

FIDES Roman goddess of faith and loyalty

FUCINUS a lake east of Rome in the territory of the Marsi

FURIES avengers of bloodshed, powers of Hell, Allecto, Tisiphone, and Megaera

GABII an ancient town near Rome, site of Juno's worship

GAETULANS a people to the south of Carthage

GALAESUS the "fairest-minded" of the Latins, slain at the beginning of the war

GALATEA a Nereid

GANYMEDE a son of Tros; snatched away by Jupiter's eagle, he became Jupiter's favorite and cupbearer

GARDA lake from which the Mincius River flows

GARGANUS a mountain of southeastern Italy

GARAMANTES a people in Africa, south of the Gaetulans

GAUL modern France

GELA a city and river in southern Sicily

GELONIANS a people of Scythia

GERYON a three-bodied monster, defeated by Hercules in one of his twelve labors

GETAE a people of Thrace, living near the Danube

GLAUCUS (1) a sea god; (2) father of the Sibyl, perhaps the same as 1; (3) a Trojan, son of Antenor; (4) a Trojan, son of Imbrasus

GORGON one of three monstrous sisters, daughters of Phorcus; the most famous was Medusa

GRACCHI a famous Roman family

GRADIVUS an epithet of Mars

GYARUS an island adjacent to Delos

GYAS (1) a Trojan leader; (2) son of Melampus, slain by Aeneas

GYLIPPUS an Arcadian, father of nine sons

HAEMON (1) a Rutulian; (2) a Latin

HAEMONIDES a Latin, priest of Apollo and Diana, slain by Aeneas

HALAESUS a Latin king

HARPALYCE a nymph

HARPIES monstrous creatures: birds with the faces of women; associated with the Furies

HEBRUS (1) a river of Thrace; (2) a Trojan

HECATE goddess associated with underworld, witchcraft and the moon; also, goddess of the crossroads and called Trivia ("three ways"), identified with Diana of the Crossroads

HECTOR son of Priam, leader of the Trojan forces in the *Iliad*, killed by Achilles

HECUBA daughter of Cisseus, wife of Priam, mother of Hector

HELEN daughter of Leda by Jupiter (her mortal father was Tyndareus), wife of Menelaus, abducted by Paris and the cause of the Trojan War

HELENOR son of Licymnia, a Maeonian ally of the Trojans

HELENUS prophet, son of Priam, husband of Andromache in "Little Troy" after the death of Pyrrhus

HELICON a mountain in Greece, home of the Muses

HELORUS a river of eastern Sicily

HELYMUS (1) a Trojan; (2) a Sicilian, in foot-race

HERCULES famous Greek hero, son of Jupiter and Alcmena; he performed twelve great labors

HERMIONE daughter of Helen and Menelaus

HERMUS a river in Lydia

HESIONE sister of Priam, wife of Telamon king of Salamis

HESPERIA the "Western Land," a name for Italy

HESPERIDES (the daughters of Hesperus) "the Western maidens," keepers of a garden of golden apples guarded by a dragon in the distant west

HIPPOCOON a Trojan, son of Hyrtacus, in the archery contest

HIPPOLYTA a queen of the Amazons who fell in love with Theseus

HIPPOLYTUS son of Theseus and Hippolyta; his stepmother, Phaedra, after being spurned by him, told Theseus that Hippolytus had tried to sleep with her; Theseus prayed to Neptune and Hippolytus was slain; transported to Italy, he was brought back to life by Asclepius

HOMOLE a mountain in Thessaly, home of the Centaurs

HYDRA a many-headed monster, figure of fright in the underworld (*see also* Lerna)

HYLAEUS a Centaur, killed in battle with Lapiths

HYPANIS a Trojan

HYRCANIAN of Hyrcania, a savage land near the Caspian Sea

HYRTACUS (1) a Trojan, father of Hippocoön; (2) a Trojan, father of Nisus

IAPYX (1) an area of Apulia in southeastern Italy; (2) a Trojan, physician of Aeneas, son of Iasus

IARBAS an African king, son of Jupiter Hammon, suitor of Dido

IASIUS son of Jupiter and Electra, brother of Dardanus with whom he migrated from Italy to Asia Minor

ICARUS the son of Daedalus, who escaped with his father from Minos on wings attached with wax; when he flew too close to the sun, the wax melted and he fell into the sea

IDA (1) a mountain of Phrygia, near Troy; (2) a mountain in Crete; (3) the mother of Nisus

IDAEUS (1) a Trojan, seen by Aeneas in the underworld; (2) a Trojan

IDALIA, IDALIUM site of Venus' worship in Cyprus

IDAS (1) a Trojan, slain by Turnus; (2) a Thracian

IDOMENEUS a Greek leader in the Trojan War, king of Crete

ILIA a name of Rhea Silvia

ILIONE oldest daughter of Priam

ILIONEUS a Trojan leader

ILIUM a common name of Troy

ILLYRIUM of Illyria, a region on the coast of the Adriatic

ILUS (1) a name of Ascanius; (2) son of Tros, founder of Troy (Ilium); (3) a Rutulian

INACHUS legendary first king of Argos, father of Io

IO daughter of Inachus, persecuted by Juno because of her affair with Jupiter

IONIAN SEA sea between Greece (the Peloponnese) and the tip of southern Italy

IOPAS singer and poet of Dido's court

IPHITUS a Trojan

IRIS goddess of the rainbow, messenger of Juno

ISCHIA an island near Baiae

ISMARUS (1) a Lydian; (2) a mountain in Thrace

ITALUS legendary eponymous ancestor of the Italians

ITHACA island homeland of Ulysses in western Greece

IULUS a name of Ascanius

IXION king of the Lapiths, father of Pirithous, punished by Jupiter for attempted rape of Juno

JANICULUM ancient town founded by Janus

JANUS two-headed god of beginnings and entrances

JOVE common name of Jupiter

JULIUS see Caesar

JUNO sister and wife of Jupiter, fiercely hostile to the Trojans (Greek Hera)

JUPITER son of Saturn, husband of Juno, the supreme god (Greek Zeus)

JUTURNA a nymph, sister of Turnus

LACEDAEMON a name of Sparta

LACINIAN epithet of Juno, from Lacinium, a promontory in southern Italy, site of a famous temple to Juno

LACONIAN of Laconia, region of the southeastern Peloponnese in which Sparta was located

LAERTES father of Ulysses

LAMUS a Rutulian

LAMYRUS a Rutulian

LAOCOON a priest of Neptune at Troy

LAODAMIA wife of Protesilaus, the first Greek killed at Troy; she killed herself to join her dead husband

LAOMEDON king of Troy, son of Ilus; cheated Neptune and Apollo of promised reward for building walls of Troy

LAPITHS a people of Thessaly who fought a famous battle with Centaurs

LAR a household god, the god of a place, the protecting deity

LARIDES a Rutulian

LARINA a companion of Camilla

LARISSA a town in Thessaly near Phthia; sometimes given as the home of Achilles

LATINS the inhabitants of Latium

LATINUS son of Faunus and Marcia; king of Laurentum in Latium

LATIUM a low-lying region of central Italy

LATONA mother of Apollo and Diana (Greek Leto)

LAURENTUM a town or region of Latium, over which Latinus is king

LAUSUS son of Mezentius, killed by Aeneas

LAVINIA daughter of Latinus and Amata, destined wife of Aeneas

LAVINIUM the first Trojan settlement in Italy

LEDA mother of Helen by Jupiter, wife of Tyndareus

LELEGES a people of Asia Minor

LEMNOS an Aegean island on which Vulcan fell when he was hurled out of heaven by Jupiter

LERNA a swamp near Argos, home of the famous hydra, a nine-headed monster slain by Hercules

LETHE a river in the underworld; those who drink from it forget the past

LEUCATA dangerous promontory on the southern tip of the island of Leucas, near which the battle of Actium took place; site of a temple to Apollo

LIBURNIANS a people living in Illyria, on the Adriatic

LIBYA a country of North Africa in which Carthage was founded

LIGER an Etruscan, brother of Lucagus, slain by Aeneas

LIGURIAN of Liguria, a region north of Etruria

LILYBAEUM a promontory in western Sicily

LIPARI an island north of Sicily, apparently identified by Virgil as home of Aeolus

LOCRIANS a people of northern Greece, colonizers of extreme southern Italy

LUCAGUS an Etruscan, brother of Liger, slain by Aeneas

LUPERCAL the grotto of Faunus (also known as Lupercus) at the foot of the Palatine hill; home of the wolf who nursed Romulus and Remus

LUPERCI priests of Faunus (Lupercus), they led the Lupercalia, one of the chief festivals of ancient Rome (held in February)

LYAEUS ("the looser") a name of Bacchus

LYCAEAN an epithet of Pan (from Greek word for "wolf")

LYCAON (1) a sword-maker and artist of Cnossus; (2) a Trojan, father of Ericetes

LYCIA a region of Asia Minor allied to Troy

LYCTUS a town of eastern Crete

LYCURGUS an ancient ruler of Thrace

LYCUS a Trojan leader

LYDIA a region of Asia Minor, original home of the Etruscans

LYRNESUS a city in the Troad

MACHAON a Greek warrior and physician

MAEON a Rutulian, one of the sons of Phorcus, brother of Cydon

MAEONIAN (1) of Maeonia, a region of Lydia; (2) Trojan, a generalized term

MAEOTIA an area of Scythia north of the Black Sea

MAGUS a Latin slain by Aeneas

MAIA daughter of Atlas, sister of Electra, mother of Hermes

MALEA a promontory in southeastern Greece, dangerous to navigation

MANLIUS Marcus Manlius Torquatus, saved the citadel of Rome from the Gauls

MANTO a prophetess, mother of Ocnus

MANTUA a city north of the Po, near which Virgil was born

MARCELLUS Marcus Claudius Marcellus: (1) a Roman general in the Second Punic War; (2) the younger Marcellus, nephew, son-in-law and destined heir of Augustus, died in 23 B.C.

MARPESIAN of Marpesus, a mountain in Paros containing famous marble quarries

MARRUVIUM a town on Lake Fucinus

MARS god of war, son of Jupiter and Juno (Greek Ares)

MARSIAN of the Marsi, a people living to the east of Rome around Lake Fucinus

MASSICUS (1) a mountain in Campania famous for wine; (2) an Etruscan

MASSYLIANS a people living to the west of Carthage

MEGAERA one of the Furies

MEGARA BAY a bay on the eastern coast of Sicily

MELAMPUS a companion of Hercules, father of Gyas and Cisseus

MELIBOEA a city of Thessaly, home of Philoctetes

MEMNON king of the Ethiopians, a Trojan ally

MENELAUS king of Sparta, brother of Agamemnon, husband of Helen

MENOETES (1) a Trojan, helmsman of Gyas; (2) an Arcadian, "hater of war," slain by Turnus

MERCURY son of Jupiter and Maia, messenger of Jupiter (Greek Hermes)

MESSAPUS a Latin leader

METABUS father of Camilla, exiled king of Privernum

METISCUS a Rutulian, charioteer of Turnus

METTUS Mettus Fufetius of Alba Longa, reneged on promise to aid Rome in war against Fidenae, torn to pieces as punishment

MEZENTIUS exiled Etruscan king, father of Lausus

MIMAS a Trojan, companion of Paris, son of Theano and Amycus, born on the same night as Paris

MINCIUS a tributary of the Po

MINERVA warrior goddess of wisdom and the crafts, daughter of Jupiter (Greek Athena or Pallas Athena)

MINOS ancient king of Crete, after his death a judge of the underworld

MINOTAUR a monstrous creature born by Pasiphaë (wife of Minos) after she mated with a bull; it was confined in a labyrinth built by Daedalus; slain by Theseus

MISENUS trumpeter of the Trojans

MNESTHEUS a Trojan leader

MORINI a people from northern Gaul

MULCIBER a name of Vulcan

MUMMIUS Lucius Mummius Achaicus, a Roman general who captured Corinth in 146 B.C

MURRANUS a Latin

MUSAEUS a mythical singer and poet

MYCENAE a city of the Greeks, Agamemnon's capital

MYCONOS an island adjacent to Delos

MYRMIDONS followers of Achilles

NAR a tributary of the Tiber

NAUTES a Trojan

NAXOS an island of the Cyclades, near Delos, associated with Bacchus

NEMEA a city of Greece, site of the first labor of Hercules: to kill the Nemean lion; the lion skin was associated with Hercules

NEOPTOLEMUS a name for Pyrrhus ("new warrior")

NEPTUNE brother of Jupiter, god of the sea; with Apollo he built the walls of Troy for Laömedon (Greek Poseidon)

NEREIDS Greek patronymic (daughters of Nereus), sea nymphs

NEREUS a sea god, son of Ocean

NERITOS an island near Ithaca

NISUS a Trojan, son of Hyrtacus, lover of Euryalus

NOMENTUM a town of the Sabines

NUMA (1) Numa Pompilius, second king of Rome; (2) a Rutulian, slain by Nisus and Euryalus; (3) a Rutulian, slain by Aeneas

NUMANUS a Rutulian, brother-in-law of Turnus

NUMICIUS a river of Latium

NUMIDIAN of Numidia, a region of northwestern Africa west of Carthage

NUMITOR (1) king of Alba Longa, father of Ilia; (2) a Rutulian

NYSA the mountain and city of India in which the young Bacchus was raised

OCEAN personification of the river supposedly surrounding the inhabited earth

OCNUS son of Manto, founder of Mantua

OEBALUS son of Sebethis and Telon, a Campanian, leader of a contingent opposing Aeneas

OECHALIA a city in Euboea, destroyed by Hercules when its king refused him his daughter after she had been promised to him

OENOTRIA (1) southern Italy; (2) generalized term for all of Italy

OLEARUS an island of the Cyclades, near Delos

OLYMPUS dwelling of the gods, a mountain in Thessaly

OPIS a huntress, attendant of Diana

ORCUS the underworld

ORESTES the son of Agamemnon and Clytemnestra; he killed Clytemnestra to avenge her murder of Agamemnon

ORICIAN of Oricium, a town in northern Greece

ORION a great hunter of mythology, after his death transformed into a constellation whose setting in autumn heralded the stormy season

ORITHYIA wife of Boreas (the North Wind)

ORODES a Trojan, slain by Mezentius

ORONTES a Lycian leader

ORPHEUS legendary poet and singer; tried to rescue his wife, Eurydice, from the underworld; killed by Maenads

ORSILOCHUS a Trojan

ORTYGIA (1) another name of Delos; (2) island in harbor of Syracuse in Sicily

OSINIUS an Etruscan, king of Clusium

OTHRYS a mountain in Thessaly, home of the Centaurs

PACHYNUS a promontory of southeastern Sicily

PACTOLUS a river of Lydia, famous for gold

PADUA a city near Venice founded by Agenor

PAEONIAN from Paeon (or Paean), an epithet of Apollo; as an adjective it means "like a doctor"

PALAEMON a sea god, son of Ino

PALAMEDES a Greek famed for his widsom; slain by the Greek army through the treachery of Ulysses; cited by Sinon as a kinsman

PALATINE one of the seven hills of Rome

PALICUS a Sicilian deity, worshiped near the Symaethus River

PALINURUS a Trojan, chief helmsman of the Trojan fleet

PALLADIUM a sacred image of Pallas Athena on which the safety of Troy depended; stolen by Ulysses and Diomedes

PALLAS (1) another name for Minerva; (2) ancient king of Arcadia, ancestor of Evander; (3) son of Evander

PALLANTEUM (1) the city of Evander, on the site of future Rome; (2) a city in Arcadia

PAN Greek rustic god; identified with Latin Faunus

PANDARUS (1) a Lycian ally of the Trojans, famous as an archer; (2) a Trojan, brother of Bitias, son of Alcanor and Iaera

PANOPEA a sea nymph

PANOPES a Sicilian, in the foot-race

PANTAGIA a river of eastern Sicily

PANTHUS a Trojan, priest of Apollo

PAPHOS seat of Venus' worship in Cyprus

PARCAE the Fates; Italian goddesses presiding over birth and death, identified with the three Greek Fates: Clotho (who spins the thread of life), Lachesis (who allots the portion of thread to each individual), and Atropos (who cuts the thread of life)

PARIS son of Priam and Hecuba, brother of Hector; his abduction of Helen caused the Trojan War

PAROS an island famous for marble

PARTHENOPAEUS one of the seven against Thebes

PARTHIAN of Parthia, a land of central Asia hostile to Rome

PASIPHAE wife of Minos, mother of Phaedra; she mated with a bull and gave birth to the Minotaur

PATRON an Arcadian, in the foot-race

PAULUS Aemilius Paulus, a Roman general who defeated King Perseus of Macedon in 168 B.C.

PELASGIANS the earliest inhabitants of Greece

PELEUS father of Achilles, son of Aeacus

PELIAS a Trojan

PELIDES Greek patronymic (descendant of Peleus), a name for Achilles

PELOPONNESE a peninsula forming the southern part of the Greek mainland

PELOPS an early king of Mycenae, of Lydian (?) origin, ancestor of Agamemnon and Menelaus; he gave his name to the Peloponnese

PELORUS a promontory of northeastern Sicily

PENATES household gods of the Trojans, transferred to Rome

PENELEUS a Greek

PENTHESILEA queen of the Amazons, slain by Achilles according to a tradition that Virgil ignores

PENTHEUS king of Thebes, slain by Maenad followers of Bacchus (among them his mother and aunts)

PERGAMA, PERGAMUM (1) name of the citadel of Troy; (2) another name for Troy; (3) settlement of the Trojans under Aeneas on Crete

PERIPHAS a Greek

PETELIA a city in southern Italy founded by Philoctetes

PHAEACIA land ruled by Alcinous, visited by Odysseus in the *Odyssey*

PHAEDRA daughter of Minos, wife of Theseus, fell in love with her stepson, Hippolytus; after he rebuffed her, she caused his death, whereupon she committed suicide

PHAETHON son of the Sun-god, tried to drive his father's chariot through the sky, slain by Jupiter when he lost control of the chariot and started to scorch the earth

PHEGEUS (1) a servant of Aeneas; (2) a Trojan, slain by Turnus

PHENEUS a city near Mount Cyllene and Lake Stymphalus, site of worship of Mercury

PHILOCTETES famous Greek warrior, bowman hero of the Trojan War

PHINEUS punished by Zeus: the Harpies snatched his food from him and polluted what remained

PHLEGYAS king of the Lapiths, father of Ixion; set fire to a temple of Apollo because the god had made love to his daughter

PHOEBUS a name for Apollo

PHOENICIANS a name for the Tyrians, the inhabitants of the kingdom of Tyre on the east coast of the Mediterranean

PHOENIX a Greek, tutor of the young Achilles

PHOLOE a Cretan slave of the Trojans, given as a prize in the ship race

PHOLUS (1) a Centaur, killed in battle with Lapiths; (2) a Trojan

PHORBAS a Trojan

PHRYGIA a region of Asia Minor allied to Troy; Trojans are sometimes referred to as Phrygians

PHTHIA a region of southern Thessaly, home of Achilles

PICUS an Italian woodland god, father of Faunus, son of Saturn

PILUMNUS an Italian woodland god, ancestor of Turnus

PINARII a clan associated with the worship of Hercules

PIRITHOUS son of Ixion; at his marriage to Hippodameia there occurred a battle between his people (the Lapiths) and the Centaurs; with Theseus he at a later time tried to carry off Proserpina from hell

PISA a city in Etruria; founded by settlers from a city of the same name in Elis (Greece) on the banks of the Alpheus River

PLEMYRIUM a promontory in Sicily near Syracuse

PLUTO god of the underworld, brother of Jupiter (Dis, Hades, Orcus)

PO a river of northern Italy

POLITES a Trojan, son of Priam, slain by Pyrrhus

POLLUX famous as a boxer, son of Jupiter and Leda, immortal brother or half-brother of Castor, who was mortal; when Castor died, Pollux arranged with Jupiter that they each would spend in turn one day in the upper world and then one day in the underworld; the brothers were known as the Dioscuri

POLYBOETES a Trojan, priest of Ceres

POLYDORUS youngest son of Priam, treacherously slain by Thracians

POLYPHEMUS one of the Cyclops, blinded by Ulysses

POPULONIAN of Populonium, a city on the western coast of Italy opposite Elba

PORSENNA Lars Porsenna, an Etruscan king who attacked Rome in order to force restoration of the exiled Tarquin

PORTUNUS god of harbors

POTITIUS an Arcadian, traditionally associated with the worship of Hercules

PRAENESTE a famous city of Latium

PRIAM king of Troy, father of Hector, killed by Pyrrhus

PRIVERNUM a city of the Volscians

PROCAS a king of Alba Longa

PROCRIS wife of Cephalus, accidentally shot by her husband when jealously following him

PRODICA an island near Baiae

PROSERPINA daughter of Ceres, wife of Pluto, queen of the underworld (Greek Persephone)

PYGMALION brother of Dido; he murdered Sychaeus

PYRGO a Trojan woman, nurse of Priam's children

PYRRHUS a famous Greek warrior, son of Achilles and Deidamia

QUIRINUS another name for Romulus

QUIRITES (1) inhabitants of Curës, the Sabine capital; (2) a name for Roman citizens

REMULUS (1) from Tibur, received a golden belt (which Euryalus plundered from Rhamnes) as gift from Caedicus; (2) a name for Numanus; (3) a Rutulian

REMUS (1) brother of Romulus, slain by him; they were sons of Ilia and, in legend, nursed by a she-wolf; (2) a Rutulian

RHADAMANTHUS brother of Minos, one of the judges of the underworld

RHAEBUS the horse of Mezentius

RHAMNES a Rutulian leader, slain by Nisus

RHEA SILVIA mother by Mars of Romulus and Remus

RHOETEUM a promontory near Troy

RHOETUS (1) a Rutulian; (2) ancestor of Anchemolus

RIPHEUS a Trojan noted for his justice

ROMULUS descendant of Aeneas, son of Rhea Silvia, twin brother of Remus, founder of the city of Rome

RUTULIANS a people of Latium ruled by Turnus

SABEANS Arabians, from Sheba

SABINES a rustic, mountain-dwelling tribe of central Italy

SABINUS legendary eponymous ancestor of the Sabines

SACES a Rutulian

SAGARIS a Trojan, servant of Aeneas

SALAMIS an island south of Athens, ruled by Telamon

SALII ("leaping ones") dancing priests associated with Mars

SALIUS (1) an Acarnanian, companion of the Trojans; (2) a Rutulian

SALLENTINE a plain in Calabria

SALMONEUS a son of Aeolus; he tried to imitate the lightning bolt of Jupiter

SAME an island near Ithaca

SAMOS an Aegean island, site of the worship of Juno and a famous temple dedicated to her

SAMOTHRACE an Aegean island south of Thrace

SARNUS a river in Campania

SARPEDON a Trojan ally, leader of the Lycians, son of Zeus, killed by Patroclus

SARRASTIANS dwellers near the river Sarnus in Campania

SATURN father of Jupiter, Juno, and the other Olympian gods (Greek Cronos)

SATURNIA (1) epithet of Juno as the daughter of Saturn; (2) an ancient city founded by Saturn

SCAEAN the main gates of Troy on which the city's safety depended

SCIPIOS members of an important family in Roman history

SCYLACEUM a coastal city of southern Italy

SCYLLA (1) a monster with six heads, dangerous to seafarers, associated with Charybdis; (2) name of a Trojan ship; (3) type of monster at the entrance to hell

SCYROS the island where Pyrrhus was born

SCYTHIA regions of Europe and Asia north of the Black Sea

SELINUS a city of southern Italy (the name means "palmy")

SERESTUS a Trojan leader

SERGESTUS a Trojan leader

SERRANUS (1) Gaius Atilius Regulus, famous Roman consul; (2) a Rutulian

SIBYL the priestess of Apollo at Cumae

SICANIANS an ancient people of Italy

SICILY a large island at the southern tip of Italy

SIDON an extremely old city of Phoenicia, from which Tyre was founded

SIGEUM a promontory near Troy

SILA a mountain in Bruttium in southern Italy

SILVANUS Roman god of woods

SILVIA daughter of Tyrrhus

SILVIUS son of Aeneas by Lavinia

SILVIUS AENEAS later king of Alba Longa

SIMOIS a river of Troy

SINON a Greek who works the stratagem of the wooden horse

SIRIUS the Dog Star, associated with heat and fever

SOMNUS personification of sleep

SORACTE a mountain in Etruria

SPARTA a city of the Peloponnese, home of Helen and Menelaus

STHENELUS (1) a Greek; (2) a Trojan

STROPHADES group of small islands west of the Peloponnese

STRYMON a river in Thrace

STYX a river of the underworld

SULMO a Rutulian, four of whose sons are sacrificed by Aeneas

SYCHAEUS husband of Dido, murdered by her brother Pygmalion

SYRTES (1) an area of quicksand to the southeast of Carthage; (2) two
     shallow bays with sand bars on the northern coast of Africa, dangerous
     to navigation

TABURNUS a mountain in the territory of the Sabines

TARCHON a leader of the Etruscans, ally of Aeneas

TARENTUM a city and gulf in southern Italy

TARPEIA a companion of Camilla

TARPEIAN epithet of a cliff on Capitoline hill, named after one Tarpeia,
     who betrayed Rome in the time of Romulus; at times an epithet of the
     hill itself

TARQUIN name of the fifth and seventh kings of Rome; the seventh king,
     Tarquin the Proud, was expelled in 509 B.C.

TARQUITUS a Rutulian, son of Dryope and Faunus, slain by Aeneas

TARTARUS (1) a part of the underworld in which the wicked are punished;
     (2) a generalized term for hell

TATIUS Titus Tatius, a king of the Sabines

TEGEAN of Tegea, a town in Arcadia

TENEDOS an island off the coast of Troy

TEUCER (1) original king of Troy from Crete, father-in-law of Dardanus;
     (2) a Greek, son of Telamon, brother of the "greater" Ajax, founded
     Salamis in Cyprus

THAPSUS a city and peninsula in eastern Sicily

THAUMAS father of Iris

THERMODON a river near the Black Sea

THERSILOCHUS (1) a Trojan, in the underworld; (2) a Trojan killed by Turnus

THESEUS king of Athens, son of Aegeus; slew the Minotaur; aided Pirithous in his attempt to carry off Proserpina

THESSALY a region of eastern Greece

THESSANDRUS a Greek

THETIS most famous of the Nereids, mother of Achilles

THOAS (1) a Greek; (2) a Trojan slain by Halaesus

THRACE a territory to the north of Macedonia

THYBRIS a king of the ancient Italians from whom the Tiber was named

THYMBER a Rutulian, identical twin of Larides

THYMBRA a city of the Troad, site of a famous temple to Apollo

THYMOETES a name of two different Trojans

TIBER the river of Italy on which Rome is located

TIBERINUS the river-god of the Tiber

TIBUR a city of Latium (modern Tivoli)

TIBURTUS a Latin from Tibur, which was named after him

TIMAVUS a river of northeastern Italy, flows into the Adriatic

TIRYNS a city of Greece, birthplace of Hercules

TISIPHONE one of the Furies

TITANS giant children of Earth; they waged war against Jupiter, were defeated and punished

TITHONUS son of Laömedon, father of Memnon; beloved by the goddess Aurora, who asked Jupiter that he might live forever, but forgot to ask that he also remain young

TITYOS a Titan who tried to rape Latona, slain by Apollo and Diana

TMARIAN of Tmarus, a mountain in Epirus

TMARUS (1) see Tmarian; (2) a Rutulian

TOLUMNIUS a Latin augur

TORQUATUS Titus Manlius Torquatus, famous Roman consul and general

TRINACRIA a name for Sicily, perhaps derived from Greek words meaning "three headlands" (referring to the island's triangular shape)

TRITON a sea-god, son of Neptune

TRITONIA a name of Minerva from Lake Tritonis in North Africa, near which she was born

TRIVIA (1) a name ("three ways") of Diana as goddess of the crossroads; (2) a name of Hecate; (3) a lake in Aricia

TROAD the region around Troy

TROILUS a son of Priam killed by Achilles

TROS grandson of Dardanus; father of Ilus, Assaracus and Ganymede

TROY a city in Asia Minor, home of the Trojans; also referred to as Ilium

TULLA a companion of Camilla

TULLUS Tullus Hostilius, third king of Rome

TURNUS son of Daunus and Venilia, king of the Rutulians, leads the Italian forces against Aeneas

TUSCANS another name for the inhabitants of Etruria, the Etruscans

TYDEUS father of Diomedes, one of the seven against Thebes

TYNDAREUS husband of Leda, "mortal" father of Helen

TYPHOES a Titan who fought against Jupiter

TYRE homeland of Dido, capital of ancient Phoenicia in the eastern Mediterranean

TYRRHENE sea on the western coast of Italy

TYRRHUS chief herdsman of Latinus

UCALEGON a Trojan

UFENS (1) a Latin, leader of a contingent opposing Aeneas; (2) a river in Latium

ULYSSES a Greek warrior, major figure in the *Iliad* and *Odyssey,* particularly hateful to the Trojans (Greek Odysseus)

UMBRIAN of Umbria, an area to the north of Rome, east of Etruria, noted for its fine hounds

UMBRO a Marsian, leader of a contingent opposing Aeneas

VELIA a town on the coast of southern Italy

VELINUS a lake in the land of the Sabines

VENILIA a nymph, mother of Turnus

VENULUS a Latin leader, sent to ask help from Diomedes

VENUS goddess of love, daughter of Jupiter, mother of Aeneas by Anchises (Greek Aphrodite)

VESTA Roman goddess of the hearth

VESULUS a mountain of Liguria, near the source of the Po

VIRBIUS (1) son of Hippolytus and Aricia; (2) a name given to Hippolytus after he was brought back to life by Asclepius

VOLCENS a Latin cavalry leader

VOLSCIANS a tribe of southern Italy, led by Camilla

VULCAN (1) god of fire and the forge, husband of Venus, son of Hera (Greek Hephaestus); (2) a term for fire

XANTHUS a name of the Scamander River

ZACYNTHOS an island near Ithaca

ZEPHYR the west wind

NOTE

Such fidelity as has been achieved in this version owes a great deal
to the kindness of two Harvard colleagues. Mason Hammond read
and annotated the first draft of each Book, holding good sense and
Latinity patiently before the translator. Wendell V. Clausen gave
the whole poem in final draft a Virgilian scholar's generous and
sensitive reading. Neither is to blame for inveterate faults
or unamended ones.

For aid and encouragement in various forms the translator is
grateful to Gerald A. Berlin, Christine Froula, Colin G. Hardie,
Anthony Hecht, John Hollander, Rachel Jacoff, Pyke Johnson, Jr.,
Charles Johnston, Cathleen Jordan, Constance Kolker, Robert
Lescher, William Maxwell, Emily Maxwell, Edward Mendelson,
Frank Nisetich, Brewster Perkins, Judith Perkins, John L. Sweeney,
and Samuel S. Vaughan. Throughout his labor he rejoiced
in the interest shown by his children.

The writing and the writer were beneficiaries of Anne Freed-
good's care and taste as editor. And Penelope Laurans Fitzgerald,
best companion and critic, tried every line of the work
on her excellent ear.

ABOUT THE TRANSLATOR

Until his death in 1985, ROBERT FITZGERALD was Boylston Professor of Rhetoric and Oratory Emeritus at Harvard University, a member of the National Academy of Arts and Sciences and a Chancellor of the Academy of American Poets. He published four volumes of his own poetry and translations, with Dudley Fitts, of *Alcestis*, *Antigone* and *Oedipus Rex* in addition to his *Iliad* and *Odyssey*.